A Communion of Shadows

A COMMUNION OF SHADOWS

RELIGION AND PHOTOGRAPHY IN NINETEENTH-CENTURY AMERICA

RACHEL MCBRIDE LINDSEY

THE UNIVERSITY OF NORTH CAROLINA PRESS

Chapel Hill

Publication of this book was supported by grants from the Grace May Tilton Fund in the Program in American Studies of Princeton University and the John C. Danforth Center on Religion and Politics at Washington University in St. Louis.

© 2017 The University of North Carolina Press

Manufactured in the United States of America

Designed by Jamison Cockerham
Set in Arno and Church in the Wildwood
by Tseng Information Systems, Inc.
Cover photograph: [Unidentified woman with male "spirit" pointing upward, 1862–75], William H. Mumler (American, 1832–84), albumen silver print, 9.9 × 5.7 cm (3⅞ × 2¼ in.). The J. Paul Getty Museum, Los Angeles. Digital image courtesy of the Getty's Open Content Program.

The University of North Carolina Press has been a member of the Green Press Initiative since 2003.

LIBRARY OF CONGRESS CATALOGING-IN-PUBLICATION DATA
Names: Lindsey, Rachel McBride, author.
Title: A communion of shadows : religion and photography in nineteenth-century America / Rachel McBride Lindsey.
Description: Chapel Hill : University of North Carolina Press, [2017] | Includes bibliographical references and index.
Identifiers: LCCN 2017003594| ISBN 9781469636481 (cloth : alk. paper) | ISBN 9781469633725 (pbk : alk. paper) | ISBN 9781469633732 (ebook)
Subjects: LCSH: United States—Religious life and customs—19th century. | Photography—United States—History—19th century.
Classification: LCC BL2525 .L553 2017 | DDC 204/.4—dc23
LC record available at https://lccn.loc.gov/2017003594

Portions of chapters 4 and 5 appeared earlier in somewhat different form in Rachel McBride Lindsey, "Haunting the Streets of Cairo: Visual Habits of the Biblical Imaginary in Nineteenth-Century Holy Land Photography," Bulletin for the Study of Religion 43, no. 2 (April 2014): 4–11.

For ZOË and WILLOW

who encompass my communion of shadows

and in memory of CHARLOTTE

who taught me to behold

Contents

FIGURES

ACKNOWLEDGMENTS

When I was a girl, my mother took pictures, my grandmother saved pictures, and I beheld pictures. Some of my fondest childhood memories are of family nights nestled around the Kodak carousel, transfixed by its metrical click and the earlier versions of my mother's family festooned in tropical shirts, too-tight athletic uniforms, and goofy grins as they splashed across the screen. My grandmother's house was filled with pictures. Her parent's wedding certificate, with vignette portraits of a dapper young couple, hung on the wall in the upstairs hallway. A copper bowl of stereographs that had once belonged to her grandmother sat on the built-in chest at the bottom of the stairs. Large portraits of ancestors — unknown to me — loomed over the dining room in gilt frames. Albums assembled by great-grandmothers and great-grandfathers, with crumbling paper covers or richly textured leather binding, were packed away in drawers and cabinets. Small square snapshots from generations past were displayed alongside glossy color prints of my own childhood in nearly every room. Shoeboxes filled with negatives spanning decades were tucked into closets and set upon shelves. She even had an enlarger — the contraption used to make photographic prints from film negatives — that I used in my own darkroom in high school. Here, in the glowing red light, I would bring the faces of the past back into my present. A print from a deteriorating negative, taken of my grandmother as a little girl, now hangs outside my own daughters' bedroom. In my grandmother's house, pictures collapsed time and bridged the living with those who had gone before. Before I could name it, or even wonder about it, my grandmother had introduced me to a communion of shadows.

A Communion of Shadows is not my family's story, but writing it has helped me know my world a little more and see it more clearly. The communion of shadows that my grandmother revealed to me began in the earliest years of photography; it had a history that was inseparable from habits of beholding that were themselves shaped by broader currents in American culture, politics, and religion. This book works to bring that history to the surface. My grandmother, Charlotte, passed as this book was coming into completion. In life, she was my favorite historian, the wellspring of my intellectual curiosity and historical imagination. This book would never have been written without her example, counsel, humor, and, of course, pictures.

My gratitude extends to the networks of colleagues, students, mentors, librarians, archivists, and others who have carried this book through to completion. I have had the tremendously good fortune to develop, research, and draft this book at Princeton University and Florida State University and to bring it through to completion at Washington University in St. Louis. My new colleagues at Saint Louis University proved themselves to be superlative cheerleaders in the final critical weeks of revision. The research in this book was supported by the American Counsel of Learned Societies, the Center for the Study of Religion at Princeton, and the John C. Danforth Center on Religion and Politics at Washington University in St. Louis. A Grace May Tilton Award from the Program in American Studies at Princeton made it possible to include more than forty reproductions of vernacular photographs in this book.

Beyond this institutional support, there are many people I want to thank in print for their role in nurturing this book from an incipient curiosity — "What about photographs?" — into a sustainable research project and, finally, the book you hold in your hands. Judith Weisenfeld is at the top of such list. Without her patient guidance and critical support, this book would never have seen the light of day. My gratitude extends also to Martha Finch, my undergraduate mentor at Missouri State, who continued to support my research and teaching through graduate school and beyond, all the while gracefully transitioning into a dear friend. Marie Griffith is to blame for this entire affair, for without her mentorship and encouragement as a summer program mentee I would never have taken the brazen first step of applying for graduate school. The opportunity to work with her at Washington University was a highlight of my professional life, and her guidance through life's twists and turns has been a steadfast anchor across seasons of change. Mika Ahuvia, April Armstrong, Wallace Best, Annie Blazer, Joel Blecher, Jessica Delgado, Sarit Kattan Gribetz, Ryan Harper, Katie Holscher, Eduard Iricinschi, Lance Jennot, Jenny Wiley Legath, Kathryn Gin Lum, Emily Mace, Caleb

Maskell, Levi McLaughlin, Samira Mehta, Anthony Petro, Amy Sitar, Jeffrey Stout, and Mairaj Syed were always ready with varying historical and cultural perspective, insightful conversation, and moral support through the earliest drafts. Cara Burnidge, Emily Clark, Mike Graziano, Martin Kavka, Charlie McCrary, Adam Park, Amanda Porterfield, and Jeffrey Wheatley read early drafts and remain cherished colleagues. At Washington University I benefited tremendously from the rigorous intellectual support of Iver Bernstein, Anne Blankenship, Darren Dochuk, Stephanie Gaskill, Sarah Barringer Gordon, Emily Johnson, Mark Jordan, Maryam Kashani, Heidi Kolk, Scott Libson, Laurie Maffly-Kipp, Lerone Martin, Kate Moran, Leigh Schmidt, Ronit Stahl, Lauren Turek, Mark Valeri, Stephanie Wolfe, the dozens of visiting scholars, and most especially Martha Sandweiss, who lent me an ear to suss out a question about visuality, politics, or materiality in the study of religion. Rachel Gross and Nicole Kirk have been anchors throughout the entire project, guiding junky drafts and proposals into matured chapters. There are many more whose fingerprints cover the pages of this book and whose commitments as scholars and educators model the best of what this profession offers to the world. And without a doubt this project is what it has become through the tireless editorial work of Elaine Maisner and the brilliant team at UNC Press. But the burden of my debt and my boundless gratitude go to Zoë and Willow. You have taught me how to see with new eyes and to love fully and completely. You make me a better teacher, writer, and person. Now, let me show you some pictures. . . .

A Note on the Images

In 1855, the *Spiritual Telegraph* ran a story about a man in Indiana who wanted to explain the "wonderful and incontrovertible manifestation of spiritual phenomena" that had recently appeared in a daguerreotype portrait. Daguerreotypes were the first commercial photographs in the United States and had quickly become the nation's favored form of portraiture in the years since 1840. This portrait of an infant and his grandmother likely started as any other. Perhaps the woman had read the famous Boston artist Albert Sands Southworth's "Suggestions to Ladies Who Sit for Dageurreotypes [*sic*]," published the year before. "Expression is everything in a daguerreotype," he had insisted. "All else,—the hair—jewelry—lace-work—drapery or dress, and attitude, are only aids to expression. It must at least be comfortable, and ought to be amiable. It ought also to be sensible, spirited and dignified, and usually with care and patience may be so." Southworth had also coached ladies whose "figure is not well proportioned" to select a dress that would "make it appear so as nearly as possible." "It is ridiculously absurd for all females to adopt the same fashion," he continued, "and whatever the fabric selected, avoid large figures or broad stripes." The famed photographer then advised his ladies on how to select the appropriate frock for infants and how to arrange the child so as to "show parts of the bottom of the skirt, and the feet and ankles, and all be in good keeping and taste."[1] Even if she had not read Southworth's meticulous instructions, the grandmother in this daguerreotype would have approached the occasion with careful preparation. One's likeness was precious and the occasion momentous.

As had the sitter, the photographer would also have made careful preparations. He, or perhaps she, would have sensitized the silver-plated sheets of copper on which the likeness was captured and calculated the duration of exposure according to the time of day, whether the skies were clear or overcast, and whether the air was dry or humid. The operator would have had to position the woman's head in a device to keep it stable for the long exposure (contraptions were endlessly being patented for this purpose) and to wait for the babe to sleep or to settle into his grandmother's arms to ensure the likeness was clear. After making the exposure, the operator or perhaps an associate would have taken the exposed plate out of the sunbathed skylight room and into the fetid darkness of the developing room, where another alchemy of chemical solutions was used to bring out the likeness and, because the daguerreotype produced such a fragile image, to encase it according to the patron's wishes. The entire process was, still in 1855, rather wondrous. But this particular likeness was especially so. When the plate was developed, "a bright ray of light [was] streaming from the top of the picture, in a slanting direction to the child's shoulder," that was explained by initial beholders "as a spiritual manifestation of the guardian angel of that peculiarly favored infant." Not everyone was convinced. The Indiana reader reported in the *Spiritual Telegraph* disagreed with the "incontrovertible manifestation" and reasoned that the light was "caused, probably, by one of the old lady's hoary hairs, which had strayed from under her cap."[2]

In these early years of photography, the cumbersome practice of picture making was at once the product of an empirical tradition of scientific discovery and, for many, a vehicle of divine revelation in the modern world. The daguerreotype of the unnamed grandmother, the *Spiritual Telegraph* insisted, was a matter of faith, not science, another instance of truth revealed in this new dispensation of religious awakening. The portrait and the disagreements surrounding its disclosures—Was it a stray hair or a guardian angel?—encapsulate the uncertainties of the new technology in nineteenth-century America. Though the spirits may have been willing in 1855, American beholders were still working out their confidence in the power of the photograph to reveal truths beyond their mortal frame. Between the fall of 1839, when detailed instructions for producing daguerreotypes first arrived in the United States, and the spring of 1900, when George Eastman introduced a low-cost camera to American consumers, photography changed the way Americans saw, felt, and imagined the world, from the contours of their own bodies to the dramas of enslavement, reform, and conquest. Nineteenth-century Americans were born into a newly mirrored world.

For anyone born before the autumn of 1839, the change was momentous. Along with steam and electricity, humanity had tapped the power of the sun. The tectonic shifts are easier to identify from hindsight, though the tremors were certainly felt across the country, at different times and in different intensities, as the daguerreotype and successive photographic techniques spread from Philadelphia, Boston, and New York throughout the states and into homes, lives, memories, and imaginations. Estimates of how many photographs were produced are difficult to ascertain, especially from the 1850s and later when wet-plate and, later, dry-plate and film techniques were popularized, producing negatives from which seemingly endless numbers of prints could be made. Estimates of how many photographs were beheld are unquantifiable. Still, conservatively, between September 1839 and the turn of the twentieth century, several million photographs were taken, developed, and beheld. These images traversed American culture, from geology to statecraft to social reform to fine art to, as I argue in this book, religion.

And yet just as it requires effort to put ourselves in the daguerreotypist's studio, it is also difficult for us to see as the people discussed in this book saw, to behold as they beheld. Our world is so saturated by photographs that it is an exercise of hermeneutic suspension to imagine a world in which they were new or, by later in the century, commonplace but still precious. It is estimated that around 95 million photographs and videos are uploaded to Instagram each day. Facebook announced in a 2013 white paper that it had surpassed 250 billion photographs on its site and that its users were uploading around 300 million each day. In 2015, Snapchat's users uploaded 8,800 photos every second. Even allowing for overlap between social media sites, the most conservative estimates suggest that we now *share* more pictures each day than were *taken* in the entire nineteenth century. Another point of reference: The most photographed American before 1900 was Frederick Douglass, the former slave and renowned statesman. Between 1840 and his death in 1895, Douglass sat for the camera at least 160 times. I began researching this book shortly after the birth of my daughter. Before I drafted a proposal later that year, my spouse and I had taken more than a thousand pictures of her. My experience is, of course, anecdotal. But even if there are variations in access to photographic technology in the twenty-first century that betray deeper social inequalities—and there are—we can also speak with some confidence about those seismic cultural shifts that separate us all from the world described in this book.

Indeed, between the point where this book ends in the early twentieth century and where we sit now in the twenty-first century, Americans have, in the words of Susan Sontag, come to "look at the world as a set of potential photographs."[3] Sitting in a public library in St. Louis, I look up to shelf upon shelf of magazine covers splashed with photographs of men and women, from *Humanist* to *GQ* to *Runner's World*. I reach into my wallet and find my own likeness on no fewer than four forms of identification. Sporting events, presidential campaigns, graduation, the birth of children, and breakfast are all photographs before we click the shutter. Sontag was writing in 1977, before digital photography and the Internet revolutionized photography yet again. But her point remains. It is not simply that there are more photographs today than there were in 1840 or in 1910. The point is that we now, more than any generation before, think through photographs. They have become a primary lens through which we know others and ourselves.

This was not always the case. Until the early twentieth century most Americans experienced photography from in front of the lens or through photographic objects. As such, this book displaces emphasis from producers to consumers and, most especially, beholders. It argues that nineteenth-century Americans experienced religion, to a previously unexplored degree, through photographs. And it posits that the very category of religion was created through circumstances of beholding. You will probably find some of the pictures in this book boring. Many of them were never meant for your eyes to see, for any eyes but those of a beloved. Others were on a great commission, intended for the world to see and to behold the glories that their surfaces limned. Even in these instances, however, we must remind ourselves that these images are shadows of a world that we do not know and that we must work to see.

Finally, the last chapter in this book explores a particularly involved method of photography. More than other images in this book, stereographs were never meant to be viewed in a book or on a screen. They were designed to fit into devices of varying size that, when beheld through a prismatic lens, thrust the image into seemingly three-dimensional relief. You can find inexpensive viewers through many online retail outlets. Alas, Oliver Wendell Holmes's vision for a vast stereographic library never materialized, but many local and university libraries have stereographic collections available to patrons. To a world where "virtual reality" infrastructures and gadgets are rapidly becoming available to the masses, the clunky stereoscope of yore reminds us of a similar moment in time when the newest technologies promised to reveal great new truths. In the pages that follow, I invite you not only to see and to reflect on photographs from the past but also to behold the communion of shadows.

A New Testament

Walter Jones was twenty-two years old when he enlisted in Company C of the 8th New York Calvary in the sizzle of late August 1862. As he put his affairs in order and packed the few belongings that he would take with him—a book or two, perhaps, some writing paper, and maybe a small likeness of his wife, Lola—his stepmother, Lucy, gave him a small New Testament to carry with him throughout his service. And like thousands of other recruits, wealthy and poor, black and white, North and South, the young farmer with piercing blue eyes also sat for a photographer. In his enlistment portrait, Private Jones sits in front of a painted background of the Union standard waving above his left shoulder, legs crossed, clasping his left fist around the hilt of his saber and resting his right hand on his right knee (fig. 1). Although he could not have known it at the time, the Testament and the portrait would together become relics in an unfolding narrative of providence.[1]

In the early summer of 1840, Walter Godfrey Jones had been born into a newly mirrored world. The previous September, news from Europe had arrived in American harbors detailing a newly successful technique for securing "images from life." Although the eponymous technique attributed to the French painter Louis J. M. Daguerre was not the only method of securing such images at the time, it quickly became the most commercially viable in the United States. Daguerre's method utilized a careful alchemy of chemical solutions to fix single-exposure, inverted images on polished plates of silvered copper and resulted in highly reflective images that were so sensitive to touch that they had to be preserved in a protective casing. By the time war broke out in 1861, the daguerreotype had been succeeded by other photographic techniques in the United States, including ambrotypes (images on

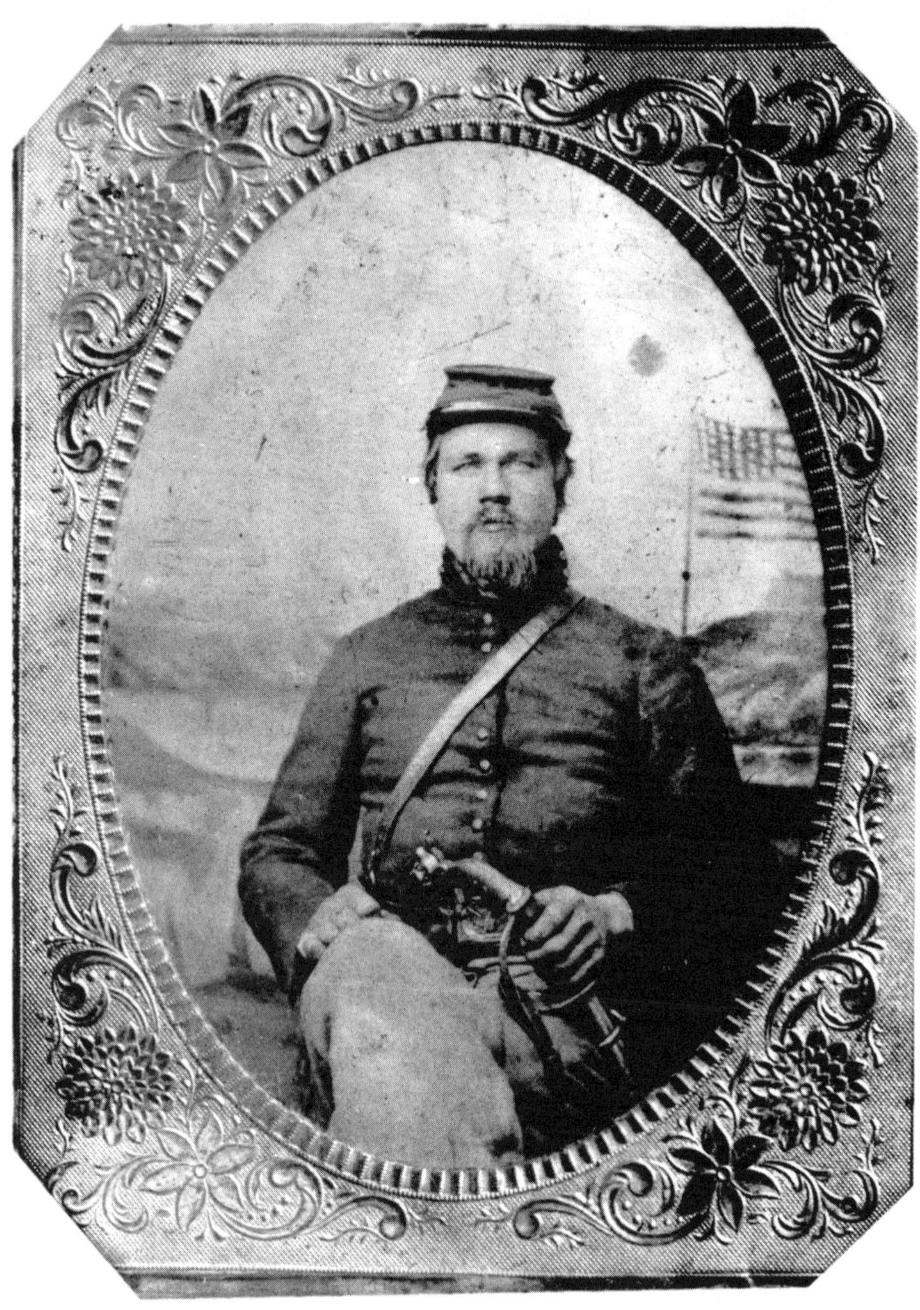

Figure 1. Detail of "Photograph of Walter G. Jones, Pvt., 8th New York Cavalry, Co. C., U.S.A." Library of Congress, Prints and Photographs Division.

glass), tintypes (images on thin sheets of iron), and albumen prints (positive exposures on paper). In many respects, Jones's enlistment portrait was not unlike thousands of others of Union and Confederate soldiers in the early years of the American Civil War. We can imagine that it sat on an intimate table during his years of absence or perhaps proudly on a mantle. The small portrait, about the size of a calling card, could also have been tucked into Lola's hand when pangs of fear or separation trembled in her breast and cradled by his toddling son, Eddie, during bedtime prayers. The likeness was ordinary, familiar, common. But in September 1899, thirty-five years after he was mustered out of the Union army, Jones secured a copyright of his likeness, now an albumen print of the original, and titled "A Testament."[2]

What was the testimony of this commonplace likeness? What lifted it from an object of familial intimacy into an artifact for public posterity and scrutiny? Although it was a common enough practice to take photographs of photographs, the surviving print is not a reproduction of the original portrait but rather a composition in which Jones's uniformed likeness is surrounded by a tattered New Testament and two discharged bullets. In 1899 Jones was still living, and his decision to include the enlistment portrait instead of a more recent likeness hints at how the likeness was beheld. More than a message to be deciphered, more than a record of his participation in the Civil War, Jones's print was itself a material object that brokered an immaterial past with the perceptible present. Like the Bible and the bullets, the photograph was a relic. The caption to "A Testament" printed below the assembled artifacts, told of how Jones "carried this little Testament in my blouse pocket" during the war and how "in two battles" it "saved my life from bullets," once at Cedar Creek, Virginia, in 1864, the other at Appomattox in 1865 (fig. 2). The son of a Baptist minister, Jones loved to tell the story of the Testament, and there is little doubt that the title of the composition referred, in Jones's mind, to the tattered scriptures. But in the print, the Bible was not a text to be read. In "A Testament," Jones's portrait, the disfigured scriptures, and the mangled bullets were each material objects that together worked to reveal the soldier's narrative of divine intervention through the marvel of print photography. In short, the photograph had become Jones's new testament.

This is a book about photographs and religion in nineteenth-century America. Rather than a history of "photography" as an abstracted, totalizing system, it turns to the grain and heft of specific objects to cast light on a communion of shadows that drew nineteenth-century Americans into physical association with each other, their beloved in glory, and the biblical

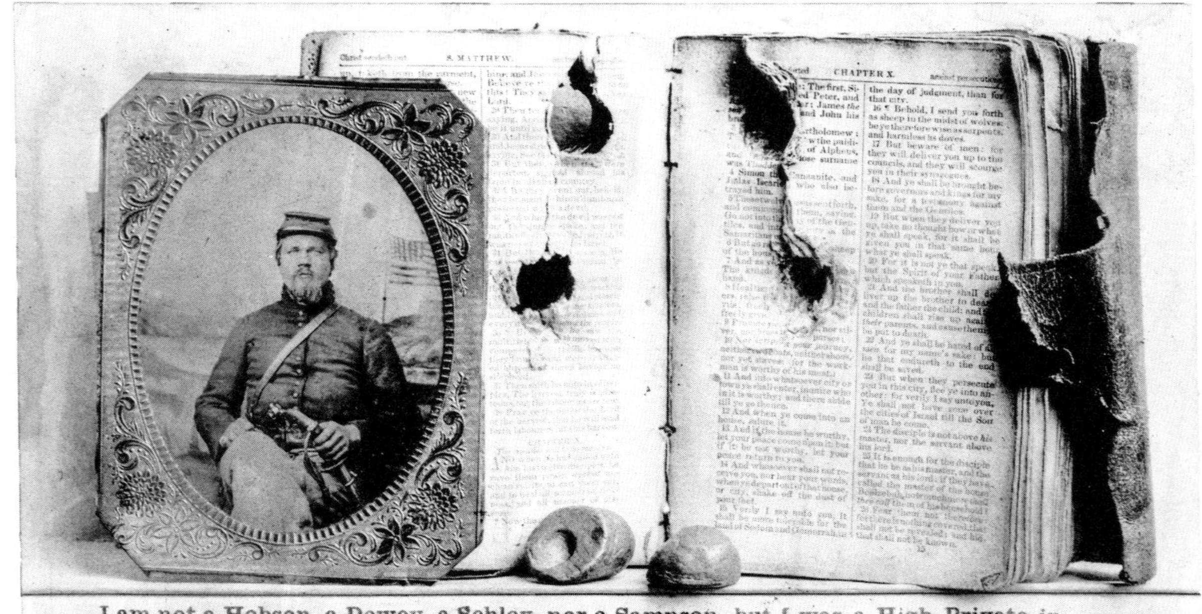

Figure 2. "Photograph of Walter G. Jones, Pvt., 8th New York Cavalry, Co. C., U.S.A." Library of Congress, Prints and Photographs Division.

past through commonplace photographs. Throughout the nineteenth century, drawing on the ritual practice and sacred symbolism of the communion table, American divines bespoke a "communion of saints" that bound the faithful on earth and in glory.[3] The language was, of course, ancient, woven into creeds Catholic and Protestant, but the revivalism of the early nineteenth century and the palpable threat of secession in the antebellum period imbued the sacred notion with urgent cause. "Around the throne of grace, the friends of Christ have rallied with mutual love and strong desires for the salvation of sinners, and the advancement of the Redeemer's kingdom," opined the *New York Observer and Chronicle* in an 1858 defense of open communion, before surmising that "strange, indeed, it would be if they could turn away from such scenes of common interest and sacred intercourse, and have no desire to sit together in the banqueting chamber of the King, under his banner of love."[4] Not unlike the communion of saints, the communion of shadows was a "traffic in objects" that at once bound communities into proximity with one another and generated boundaries of exclusion.[5] Put bluntly, the conviction behind this book is that we do not fully know nineteenth-century American religion apart from this communion of shadows, apart from the objects themselves and the habits of beholding they conditioned. "Hand in hand," intoned the revered African American statesman and former slave Frederick Douglass in an 1865 lecture on photography, "this picture-making power accompanies religion, supplying man with his God, peopling the silent continents of eternity with saints, angels, and fallen spirits, the blest and the blasted, making manifest the invisible, and giving form and body to all that the soul can hope and fear in life and in death."[6] This book blows the dust off of that great album of saints and angels, known to Douglass but lost to us, so that we, too, may behold nineteenth-century Americans in their work of peopling the silent continents of eternity through the new marvel of the camera.

With the invention of photography in 1839, Americans inherited a new repertoire of material practice that transformed habits of perception, recognition, and representation by freighting discourses of scientific objectivity alongside artistic innovation and spiritual revelation. If *religion* emerged in the nineteenth century as a subject in trade catalogues, defined by compositional emphases on Bibles, buildings, exotic bodies, foreign vistas, and forms of attire, it was also something that was conditioned through exchanges between photographic artifacts and their beholders. Photographic technologies generated rich material archives—cameras, plates, albums, prints, viewing apparatuses, studio furnishings—that structured new religious subjectivities by mediating exchanges between these artifacts and the bodies of beholders. As such, nineteenth-century photographs provide not only a visual iconography of American religion but also a body of relics that, in the imaginaries of beholders, disclosed an otherwise inaccessible past into their sensorial present. To the extent that historians, too, encounter this traffic in objects—in museums, archives, attics—this book is also an exercise in disciplining historically conditioned sensorial economies to avert misapprehension of artifacts encountered in attics and archives. *A Communion of Shadows* registers methodological debates in the study of material culture and visual studies but strives to keep material and imaginative encounters between photographic objects and their historical beholders in focus. To that end, the chapters that follow start with the gritty, sometimes decaying, as well as the polished, carefully cherished, material traces of a world we can never fully know but that continues to shape the world in which we live.

My immodest goal in this book is to make a strong case for anyone who studies or otherwise encounters American religion—it's a big tent—to see not only how photography was (and is) part of visual and material landscapes but also how this newly mirrored world actively shaped imaginative, intellectual, political, and theological worlds.[7] More than documents of religious practices, figures, or events, commonplace photographs brokered the religious worlds their beholders inhabited. My hope is to provide a model within the study of religion that neither silos photographs as "visual culture" somehow distinct or extractable from "religion" nor, relatedly, utilizes images solely for illustration of conclusions drawn from textual sources. Photographs were generative cultural artifacts, doing as much to shape religious sensibilities and political imaginations as to represent religion in a visual grammar. Beholding was a cultural and a political act that had everything to do with American religion between 1839 and 1900. If nothing else, this is what the book aims to show.

In support of this goal, I weave three interpretive threads throughout *A Communion of Shadows*. First, in the rapidly expanding universe of photographic material, I position commonplace, or "vernacular," photographs at the center of a story of American religion and culture in the first several decades of the medium. Vernacular photographs were, like Private Jones's enlistment portrait, the kinds of photographs that Americans were most likely to encounter in the course of their daily lives and that, through this familiarity, provide a surface upon which to explore habits of perception and recognition. Specifically, *A Communion of Shadows* examines five kinds of these commonplace photographs through stories of people who sat for, made, circulated, and beheld them. Studio portraits, death and mourning pictures, spirit photographs, halftone reproductions in books and periodicals, and stereographs were not the only inventories of commonplace photographs, but they gesture to the expansive breadth of photography and American religion as well as to the multiple habits of beholding that limned the communion of shadows. Indeed, the ubiquity of commonplace photographs sits oddly with their absence from historical narratives, and one of the central projects of this book is to chart a course for incorporating this vast archive of American culture into analyses of religion.

Second, turning to vernacular photographs shifts attention from how religion was represented in photographs toward how religion was defined through the camera and the practices of beholding that photographs facilitated. The story I tell is less a history of photographic representation than a study of beholding. *A Communion of Shadows* draws on the insights of a number of historians who have turned to photographs, mostly as official state, religious, or artistic projects, as generative historical sources in the study of religion in America.[8] From nineteenth-century landscapes to government-commissioned documentary photographs to Polaroids of a Marian apparition site, the existing field of religion and photography is wide. *A Communion of Shadows* lingers on select artifacts to tell a thicker story about the first century of photographs in the United States. Put differently, this story is not only one of photographic production but also a history of the indices of power that masquerade under the seemingly natural act of seeing. Throughout the book, we see how beholding — my shorthand for the fuzzy mechanics of perception, recognition, and imagination — was (and remains) a cultural and political as well as a religious act. Somewhat distinct from the biological processes of sight, then, I approach beholding as a historically situated act. In this regard, the work of anthropologists and visual theorists who have brought critical attention to the visual regimes of power in nineteenth-century visual culture help me see more shadows in these images.[9]

This point is worth lingering on for just a moment longer. In the first several decades of photography in U.S. trade catalogues, religious leaders, art critics, and others were quick to define "religious" subjects almost always in relation to the image that was conveyed — forms of dress, religious authorities, architecture, landscapes. For instance, a page from one catalogue of stereoviews classified selections as "Bible lands," "Bible themes," and "illustrated hymns." This is one way to define religion and photography in America, and for better or worse, it has been the most common. In a word, we have tended to approach photographs as evidence of religion, or as windows into a religious past that existed outside the frame, instead of as generative sources of religious meaning, experience, and practice — so long consumed by what photographs depict that we have missed what they are. This distinction is important for a number of reasons but primarily because religion itself resisted clear definition within the broader compass of American culture. The stillness, the clarity of a photograph, betrays the pulsating incertitude of life beyond and within the frame. Thus instead of parceling "religious" artifacts or images in a separate inventory, in which this frontloaded categorization influences subsequent analysis, I frame commonplace photographs as generative cultural sources that traversed, undercut, and intersected numerous fields of knowledge, reflection, and practice.[10] Unlike other areas where religion and media intersect, then, *A Communion of Shadows* is not a story of "photograph religion" in which we can use the modifier "religion" to wring exceptional meaning from concomitant and entangled measures of beholding.[11] The story of religion and photography must cast a wide interpretive net; it must look beyond catalogue series and even the compositional field of photographs themselves. The question of what people beheld is a very different question from what the camera recorded. This book charts a course for approaching habits of perception and recognition that did not always map neatly onto the recorded image and in the process considers not only where but also *how* we look for religion in nineteenth-century America.

Lastly, my third underlying claim in this book is that focusing on vernacular photographs and practices of beholding invites us to recognize the materiality of photographs. Among nineteenth-century Americans, photographs were beheld as relics as well as icons. Bearing messages that exceeded their compositional referent, they were also, and just as importantly, tactile artifacts embedded in systems of production, circulation, display, and beholding. They were more than visual fields to be deciphered. Like the medieval devotional objects that Carolyn Walker Bynum researches, there was a "power in the matter of the object" that was not reducible to "an iconography to be decoded." Although there are historical differences between the two studies, what was true in the case of devotional objects created of vellum and ink, wood and paint, was also true for objects created from glass and iron, paper and albumen, thermoplastic casings and leather bindings. By recognizing that photographic objects "disclose, not merely signify, a power that lies beyond," we are better equipped to understand why studio portraits were placed in family Bibles, how pictures of dead babies could become testaments of their eternal life in glory, and the ability of stereographs to reproduce the Holy Land for those who had eyes to see.[12] Such commonplace

          Introduction

artifacts both *meant* something to their beholders and comported a presence that *did* something.

In the digital world of the early twentieth century, this point is worth emphasizing. Daguerreotypes were quite literally chemically sensitized sheets of metal, encased in thermoplastic and often padded with velvet or other soft material. Later techniques, such as tintypes and ambrotypes, exposures on iron and glass, respectively, were also intensely material. Even paper prints, which became common in various forms beginning in the late 1850s, were objects that were seen but also cradled, worn, displayed, and discarded. Americans throughout the century associated their likenesses with other material objects as well, from thick albums to heavy Bibles to viewing apparatuses to the hair of their beloved. Photographs, in short, constituted a vast material archive that invites consideration as objects of inquiry. What did people see, yes, but also, what were the material conditions in which beholding transpired? Recognizing photographs as material objects invites us, as distant spectators, to position them within broader material inventories and in particular to the ways in which photographs were beheld as relics, as material fragments that disclosed, among other things, spiritual and religious truth into the present. For much of the nineteenth century, the term "relic" was used synonymously with "remains" and carried a connotation that would only later be consumed, in common parlance, by sacred meaning. From the beginning, Americans understood photographs as extensions of their physical beings, as material remains that could be, and should be, passed down through the generations. Quite literally, within the communion of shadows, photographs became fragments of the body. Thus throughout the nineteenth century, photographs were at once icons and relics, images that underscored their materiality and worked to disclose discarnate pasts, however proximate, into the sensorial present.[13]

A Communion of Shadows is a book of cultural history, but it is grounded in methodological approaches to the study of religion and materiality that warrant a brief surfacing. In particular, a question that has haunted this project from the beginning asks, what does it mean to approach material artifacts as touchstones to cultural experiences of generations removed? In other words, recognizing that objects matter, that they can be productively enlisted in the study of religion and culture, what are the interpretive conditions of this approach? Birgit Meyer has succinctly summarized the interpretive bias against material objects in the study of religion, a bias that has been poured into the epistemological foundation of the discipline. This bias now shows signs of fracture, but in these cracks the edifice itself may be in peril.

Does the academic study of religion exist apart from the intellectual genealogy of bibliocentricism? *A Communion of Shadows* does not make any sweeping indictments or defenses of the state of the field, but it does echo cries for a thorough accounting of an interpretive past that subordinated, maligned, or otherwise dismissed the material world in pursuit of the mind and soul, long figured to be best approximated through kindred introspection of the word. In this book, Protestants lived in an abundant world, where objects mediated past and present, heaven and earth, individual souls and the pageantry of salvation. Indeed, the Word became flesh through the transfiguring power of the camera.

In the same breath, this book challenges latent suppositions of material autonomy, the idea that ethnographic or historical fragments are reliable indices of practice, belief, or imagination. The shadows in this book are made, not found. "Objects become ethnographic," writes Barbara Kirshenblatt-Gimblett, when they are "defined, segmented, detached, and carried away by ethnographers." So too with historians: "Disciplines make their objects."[14] Not unlike Walter Jones transforming his likeness into a relic through the mechanics of display, there is a politics of representation at work here that implicates the historian in the communion of shadows. These hauntings are amplified when commonplace or quotidian objects are placed at the center of analysis. As such, at the outset it is instructive to move away from any specific artifact to consider what attention to such relics yields to historical inquiry. What, in short, do the contents of attics — the often forgotten and decaying remnants of daily lives, and the class of objects most closely attended to in this book — contribute to the study of religion? To the study of history? What interpretive value do we assign to them? And what do these assignments reveal about the role of material culture in these disciplines? *A Communion of Shadows* does not settle these questions, but I do recognize within them a tension between a responsibility, a professional ethics, to see as our subjects saw and, through the looking glass, to articulate a more rigorous analytics of historical materiality.

Attics and Archives

Like so many shadows in this book, "A Testament" is a historical fragment. Such shadows survive in attics, shoeboxes, flea markets, and crumbling albums more than professional archives available to researchers. We find them by accident, if they have survived at all. Walter Jones was confident enough in the testimony of his experience that he wrote a book that recorded his story, aptly titled *History of the Testament*. In addition to the book, prints of "A Testament" were displayed in patriotic venues, including conventions of the Grand Army of the Republic, and featured in press reports of local curiosities. In September 1899—the same month Jones submitted copies of the print for copyright—the *North American* ran a story on "Comrade Jones" and the "little Testament in which two rebel bullets are deeply imbedded." Three years later, on Memorial Day weekend 1902, the *Westfield (N.Y.) Republican* described a "unique photograph . . . of Walter E. Jones . . . and the Testament that saved his life in two battles" that Mr. Philander W. Bemis, himself a veteran of the Civil War, had shown the paper's editors.[15] Jones's *History of the Testament* was swallowed and purged by the Library of Congress in the early twentieth century, and the Testament gifted by his stepmother was destroyed by fire in the 1960s. All that remains is the photograph. But even if all these objects relating to the photograph had survived, it would still be a fragment by virtue of its detachment. "We make fragments," Kirshenblatt-Gimblett asserts, and in the process, we confront the process of "rendering the quotidian spectacular."[16]

Such a process of rendering the quotidian spectacular, of asking commonplace objects to bear the weight of history, gestures to a broader analytic field of the familiar in studies of religion and American history. The association of material culture with quotidian experience has lent confidence in the power of the object to disclose a more authentic account of human experience, particularly among demographics less likely to have left textual records. Forensic analysis reveals much about an artifact's history—how it was made and used, who used it in what ways, trade habits and technologies, fields of exchange and modes of accessibility. But do objects in fact bring us closer to the people we study? More than a descriptive and interpretive arena, the category of the quotidian and its analogues—everyday, commonplace, vernacular—are recognized in this book as constructed theoretical spaces for investigating the social processes, including seemingly natural processes of perception and recognition, that mediate individual and collective identities. If the communion of shadows was a traffic in objects—as I argue it was— then the question lingering just beneath this statement is, quite simply, what does this analytic approach assume about the association between material culture, quotidian practices, and religious experiences? How, in other words, do we move between historical fragments and human experiences?[17]

On the heels of the social and cultural turns of the late twentieth century, histories of both religion and photography advanced a turn to "the vernacular." In studies of religion, Leonard Primiano proposed "vernacular religion" as an alternative to the tired and overburdened category of "folk religion." Along with its more popular cousin "lived religion," for Primiano the concept of vernacular religion provided new ways of imagining the hegemony of official institutional religion in the lives of individual believers and the communities in which they were ensconced.[18] Shortly after Primiano advocated for the adoption of vernacular religion in the fields of folklore and religious studies, the art historian Geoffrey Batchen began advancing the nomenclature of "vernacular photography" as a turn to the "popular face of photography" that had been "largely ignored by the critical gaze of respectable history."[19] Neither Primiano nor Batchen were the first to recognize the social life of their subjects.[20] But a social history is not the same as a critical orientation that places vernaculars, in Batchen's terms, as "the organizing principle" of inquiry.[21] Still, in these early studies, *vernacular* operates more consistently as analytic shorthand rather than a critical term attentive to its own history and implication. For both, it invokes the familiar and, especially, the domestic without reflecting on the systemic political implications of such a designation. Does the turn to vernaculars in the study of religion and photography offer new insights into regimes of power, or does it gesture to isolated acts of resistance or creativity within inescapable conditions and circumstances? Beyond identifying new troves of inquiry and analysis within an existing system of interpretation, what do commonplace objects teach us about religion in nineteenth-century America?

The field of vernaculars positions critical reflection on the interconnectedness of commonplace artifacts, metrics of identity, and regimes of power. In studies of vernacular religion, these connections have for the most part been overshadowed by privileging individual actors within a system defined by belief.[22] Underlying analytic interests in bringing attention to individual actors as active participants in and creators of religion is a tremendous contribution to the field at large, bringing the critical apparatus of folklore studies to religious studies and strengthening the field in the process. And yet two problems persist in this approach. First, by prioritizing individual agency through analytics of belief, existing literature on vernacular religion has the effect of deemphasizing social politics shaping actions and belief in myriad direct and oblique ways. Regimes of power — religious, political, social — and

Introduction

operating metrics of identity, so long embedded in the very category of the vernacular, are conspicuously absent from the narrowly cropped vignette of the individual actor and, I would add, object. Second, whereas we might expect the study of material culture, trained as it has been to the domain of the quotidian, to open up new ways of beholding, conceptualizing, and analyzing the category of religion, to put the matter bluntly, definitions of the vernacular to date have instead continued to reinscribe the very categories generated and sustained by textual traditions historically indifferent — if not at times hostile — to physical objects. In this way, vernacular religion comes across as the analytic inheritance of a liberal political legacy — privileging autonomous actors operating from a state of deliberative volition — and it is no wonder that belief, as an interiorized state that is expressed through various media even as it remains a fundamentally different ontological order, can remain largely unproblematized within an otherwise sweeping critique of the study of religion. The assertion of anthropologist Webb Keane that materiality "can never be reduced only to the status of evidence for something else, such as beliefs or other cognitive phenomena," has not found traction in definitions of vernacular religion.[23] To the contrary, vernacular religion has positioned material culture as a back door to belief.

Belief is, of course, central to the lives of many people we study. But we should also be attentive to the interpretive undertow of the disciplinary anchor of *belief* in the study of material objects, vernacular or otherwise. In its current formulation, the category of the vernacular remains addled by inherited suppositions about what such objects can yield to the study of religion. All is not lost. Existing limitations in the analytics of "vernacular religion" — the potentially illusory interpretive potential of individual actors and the troubled relation with material objects — extend from attempts to define the vernacular as a modifier rather than a category of analysis. In an attempt to penetrate the tangle of material culture, religious experience, and quotidian practice raised by this study of commonplace photographs as historical fragments, I dispense with the notion of "vernacular religion" in order to find a more nimble field of inquiry that lingers on specific objects in relation to authorizing discourses without positing fixed arenas of action or conviction. By turning to the communion of shadows, we see, we behold, how the traffic between the visual and what is marked as sacred is continuous, even within a tradition (the study of religion) attempting to overcome the conditions of its own materiality.[24]

A New Testament

One might say that, like Private Jones's staging of his youthful likeness along-side battlefield remains, commonplace photographs hearken a new testament in the study of religion. Even as the intellectual elite of the nineteenth century mounted assaults against dull materiality in their exaltations of spirituality—in fields from theology to politics to aesthetics—the very contours of American aspirations were profiles limned by a material landscape. Relics, souvenirs, and mementos were not only sentimental tokens—though that they often were—but also instruments of nationalism and biblical promise, remains that were revealed as agents of a new dispensation. The gospel of the photograph is simple: the word is not the only measure of history. Texts are a vital part of the historical record, but objects offer something new, something else, something potentially transformative to historical inquiry when we see them as more than an encrypted textual record.

Like other gospel narratives, this new testament is a mode of remembering that suggests the values and aspirations of the beholder as much as, if not more than, it discloses the transpiring of actual events. Commonplace photographs are relics, but historians of religion ask questions of them different from those of their original beholders. Lola Jones cradled the likeness of her beloved to bridge the distance between them while Walter fought on distant battlefields. Mothers of young children had daguerreotypes made of their lifeless babes and tucked pieces of hair into the elaborate cases, signaling a bond between the shadow of their likeness and their earthly frame, which now remained accessible to the caress of the bereaved. These shadows—the daguerreotypes—were not beheld as commemorations of a mortal coil but rather as clouded reflections of celestial glory and the abiding promise of heavenly reunion. Over the course of the century, others applied this association to photographs of spirits among the living, many of which in the earliest days were commissioned by persons in mourning who longed for reassurance of the soul's survival in death. With halftone prints of the Holy Land, Americans beheld relics of the land where Mary prayed and Jesus wept, and with stereographs Americans themselves entered the biblical past. Among these earliest communities of photographic beholding, the materiality of the image was inescapable. For historians who find these remains, who approach them as interpretive sources, however, this lure of the relic is also the seed of its demise.

Connections between religious experience and quotidian objects are ingrained in disciplinary habits of beholding. Something in this connection merits exploring, and commonplace photographs introduce a rich archive for such investigations. One common photographic practice, having little to do with religion, is particularly helpful for surfacing the exchanges between photographic subjects, objects, and beholders, on the one hand, and interpretive expectations in object studies, on the other. Exposure speeds improved rapidly over the first generations of photography, and processes that once required several minutes in the earliest days had been reduced to mere seconds by the 1860s. Still, when taking studio portraits during these early decades of photography, contraptions were devised to still heads and torsos to ensure a sharp image. When it came to the youngest crowd, instead of mechanical aids, it was common for mothers (or surrogates) to hold their children to keep them still for the duration of the exposure. It was also common to cover these women with blankets. As figure 3a, a full-plate tintype, demonstrates, however, the woman's form was often still quite evident in the resulting image. Other techniques for disguising these maternal restraints included not developing the mother's face and the far more invasive practice of scratching her likeness off of the developed image.[25] At least as common was the practice of merely obscuring mothers from view in display mounts. Figure 3b, a ninth-plate tintype — about two inches wide by two and one-half inches tall — clearly depicts the residue from decades of strategic revision of the camera's field of vision. In its mount, the unknown mother's upper right sleeve would still have been visible, as would part of her veil. Perceptive beholders would have known that someone else's likeness, however fragmented, was on the plate.

In addition to offering insight into a curious practice with profound social implications — consider, for example, the difference between hiding mothers and displaying slaves in domestic portraiture — hidden mothers also teach us something about the study of historical fragments. On the one hand is the counsel of cultural historian Lawrence Levine, who wrote that "we must . . . prepare ourselves for the possibility that these people whose lives we are sharing for the moment are not necessarily earlier versions of ourselves whom we can know just by knowing ourselves."[26] Twentieth- and twenty-first-century visual campaigns have taught beholders to identify with the likeness in the photograph, to discern a universal humanity in banality and horror alike. But this approach betrays both the privileged gaze of a certain idealized beholder — white, male, Western — and also the visual politics of appropriation and representation.[27] Relics, conceived as remains, as historical fragments, constantly call attention to their materiality and their historical legacies, including an imagined relation to the bodies of those who have

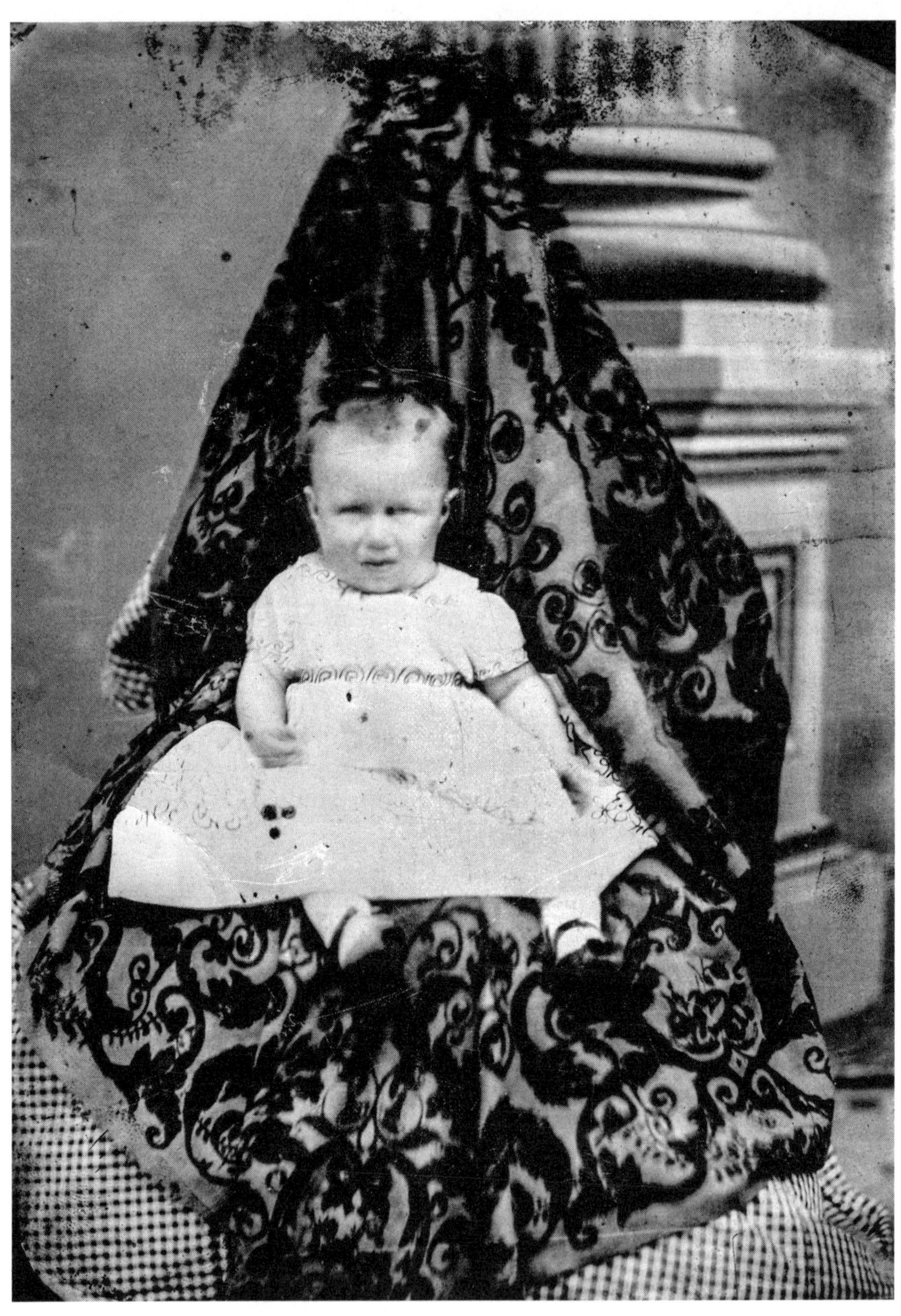

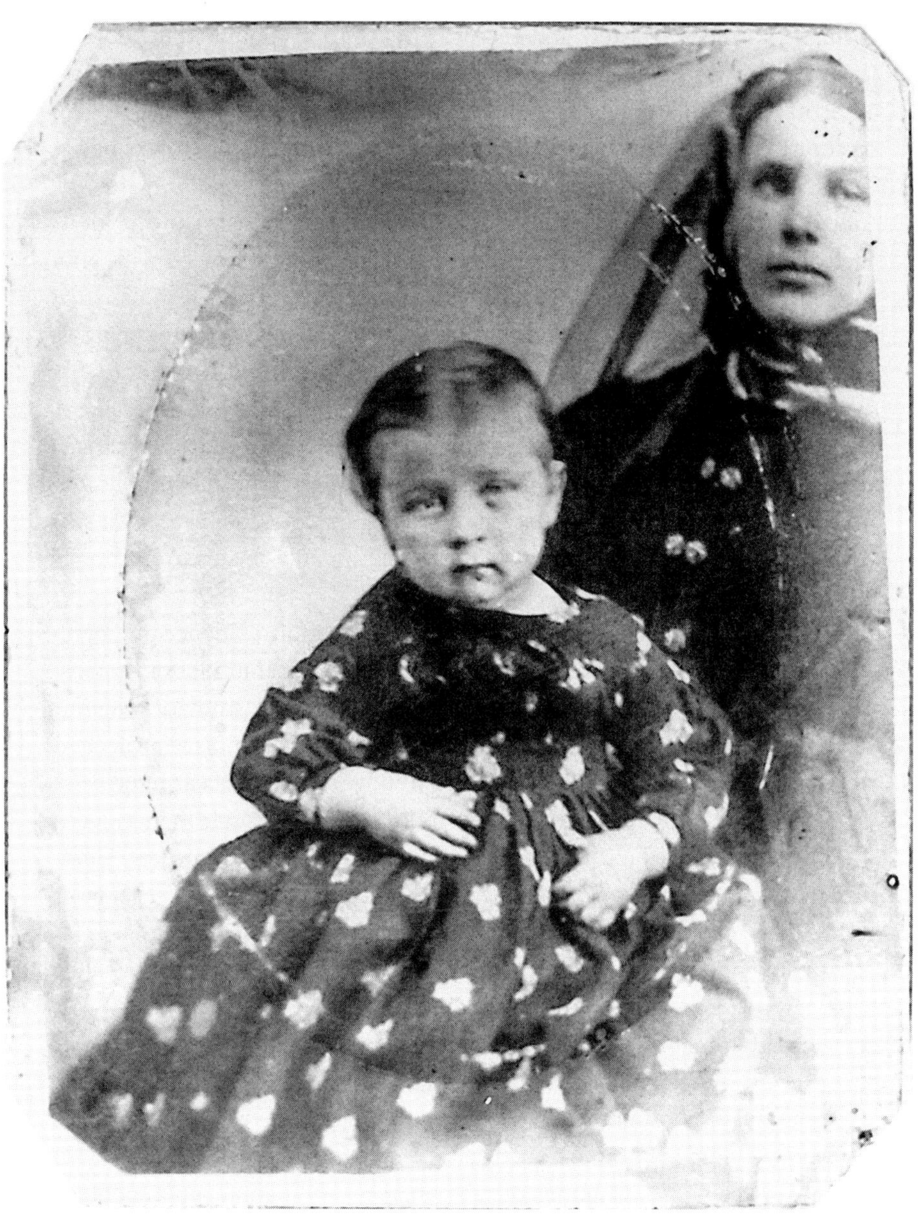

Figures 3a and 3b. Full-plate (8½ by 6½ inches) (*opposite*) and ninth-plate (2 by 2½ inches) tintypes, ca. 1865. From the collection of Merry Gordon. Used with permission.

held, seen, smelled, tasted, and heard them at various points in the object's history. And yet Levine's advice cautions against presuming the autonomy of artifacts as well as texts. Despite the preservation of an object across generations, by intent or by accident, and thus our ability to touch it, to smell it, in short, to behold it, we must prepare ourselves for the possibility that the object does not bring us closer to the people of generations past who felt its heft, whose fingers moved along its grain, whose hearts swelled with grief upon its sight. The convention, embedded in analytics of the quotidian, that material culture somehow brings us closer to "religion" by introducing us to a still-tactile legacy of generations past is powerful. But it also warrants a closer interrogation of the relationship between objects and experiences, tactility and belief, both among contemporary beholders and among scholars who happen across these fragments. Surely our own bodies are implicated in the historical process. In the communion of shadows, our senses are just as mediated as our imaginations. Material culture only gets us to the tips of our fingers.

If material artifacts are not, in Keane's formulation, evidence of "cognitive phenomena" — or expressions of belief, in current definitions of vernacular religion — what are they? What do they bring to the study of religion? Perhaps the greatest contribution of the study of commonplace artifacts is to open new ways of defining religion, to render such objects as remains of something that we are resigned never to know in full, rather than as icons that offer access to the spiritual lives of individuals past and present. Commonplace photographs are not synecdoche of an intact historical legacy any more than they are interchangeable with other historical remains. For its own part, this particular body of artifacts reveals a world of visual habits that traversed the ostensibly distinct cultural arenas of religion, law, history, entertainment, and science, a world in which the heuristic advantage of singling out "religion" as a distinct mode of beholding loses analytic traction. Commonplace photographs, in short, did not represent religion so much as constitute a mode of production, display, and beholding that facilitated conditions whereby the categories of religion, race, and nation, among others, could be articulated. Such a claim exposes a seam joining two sides of the vernacular interpretive approach: empathy toward nineteenth-century beholders who recognized "something else" in their photographs and the analytic conviction that the study of material artifacts should not be reduced to ciphers of belief — that materiality is fraught, but culturally and analytically generative all the same. Rather than hide this suture, the study of commonplace photographs asks us to leave it be, not as an unsightly scar but as a visual marker of the historian's craft—we should remain in the picture, even if at times we hide under a blanket.

A Communion of Shadows

"A book is not an exhibit," historian Laurel Thatcher Ulrich reminds us. These pages display neither texture nor heft, nor do they replace the embodied technics of beholding. Even still, a book about objects might bring us "into that dimly seen and never fully realized space we call history, giving us blood and greed as well as beauty, exhibiting things that did not get saved."[28] In the chapters that follow, I attempt to give bones to the communion of shadows by walking readers through a gallery of ghosts. Chapter 1 examines family Bible portrait galleries within the context of studio portraiture and nineteenth-century notions of "likeness." Portrait galleries for small, card-size "carte de visite" studio portraits became popular additions to family Bibles in the 1860s and remained so through the end of the century. This chapter positions these galleries against stand-alone photograph albums and other forms of memory work within family Bibles to consider what genealogies these silent likenesses created for their beholders. As a point of entry into the communion of shadows, this chapter argues that family Bible portrait galleries were sites where knotted threads of race and nation were smuggled into sacred history—unwittingly, perhaps—under the guise of family pictures.

Chapter 2 turns to death and mourning pictures to explore a shifting memorial culture that was rooted in historical modes of representation and theologies of redemption. Over the course of the nineteenth century, photographic portraiture emerged within this memorial culture as both the preferred iconography of mourning in nineteenth-century America and, significantly, as a relic of the departed that disclosed future glory to the bereaved. In this chapter, I explore the role of photographs as relics that illuminated the communion of shadows by mediating the body of the deceased with the grieving body of the bereaved. Here, photographs were devised as tokens not of the moldering body of the deceased but of promise of celestial reunion in glory. As memorial portraiture focused attention on the body of the deceased, another facet within the communion of shadows purported to provide evidence of the soul's survival after death. Intense debates around spirit photography started immediately upon its discovery in late 1862. Chapter 3 frames these debates around the career, trial, and demise of America's first and most notorious spirit photographer, William Howard Mumler. Spirit photographs emerge within the communion of shadows as a hinge between corporeal referents in studio portraiture, on the one hand, and practices of biblical beholding, on the other, that asked beholders to see what was really there.

Chapter 4 spirals out from one commissioned photographic tour of Palestine in 1894 to consider the broader framework of halftone photography as a mechanism of ethnographic display and imperial regimes. The chapter follows a set of negatives made by the St. Louis photographer Robert Edward Mather Bain in 1894 from their original publication as part of a commercialized art folio into the pages of the Bible. Here, the communion of shadows cast living inhabitants of Palestine — Bain's photographic contemporaries — as relics of a biblical imaginary that affirmed American beholders' confidence in the power of the camera to capture on glass the Holy Land of the Bible. Chapter 5 brings the communion of shadows into the twentieth century through the optical marvel of the stereoscope. Like halftone tours and biblical photographs, stereographs of the Holy Land invited beholders to dismiss the photographic contemporary in their sights on a biblical imaginary. But through the stereoscope, beholders envisioned themselves entering the biblical past in a way previous photographic technologies had not enabled. The epilogue marks the sea change in vernacular photography that resulted from the popularization of inexpensive handheld cameras in the early twentieth century. For the first time, middle-class Americans were producers of the shadows they had so long been in communion with.

Practices of beholding that approached commonplace photographs as both icons and relics surface throughout the book, as do visual habits that instructed beholders to see through what the camera recorded to what was really there, be it celestial glory or biblical tableaux. Each of the chapters highlights particular dimensions within the communion of shadows and, at times, reaches across time or space to draw connections between the varieties of commonplace photographs that populated nineteenth-century American homes and imaginations. But these artifacts tell many stories. *A Communion of Shadows* bounds a space for us to encounter and behold, but it is neither an exhibit nor an album nor a window into a stable past. To paraphrase Ezra Pound, through the voice of Confucius in his Cantos XIII, we ought well to remember that there was a time when historians left blanks in their writings. There is much to behold in the communion of shadows, and there are many blanks in these pages for what we cannot know.

Nineteenth-century visual technologies changed the way Americans saw themselves, represented one another, and imagined the cosmos. Approaching photographs qua photographs—as material sites of cultural exchange, reaching beyond the surface image to practices of beholding—helps us survey, investigate, and interpret the nineteenth century in ways that texts alone can never quite facilitate. Photographs were objects that were seen but also worn, displayed, and left in the dusty corners of history. They were "vernacular" not by their content but by their accessibility and familiarity and by the way they trafficked between quotidian practice and regimes of power operating through new technologies and attending practices of representation. In a word, the visual habits of photographic beholding, steeped in a material landscape that conditioned encounters between artifacts and their beholders, constituted a lingua franca that has been critically absent from the interpretive lexicon of the American religious past. This is not merely the stuff of history. The legacy of the photographic regime created in the decades following 1840 has cast a long shadow, shaping categories and classifications of identity, policies of belonging and exclusion, and procedures of accessibility and surveillance that continue to define modern life into the twenty-first century. Religion has not been incidental to these developments; indeed, the visual habits of photographic beholding in the decades surrounding the American Civil War were sites where inherited convictions were negotiated with emerging aspirations, both of which blurred boundaries between religion, culture, and nation. As more than records of the imperceptible, commonplace photographs worked to constitute the subjectivities necessary for the formation and recognition of ideas and beliefs.[29] Their contribution to the study of religion is not in the accident of their existence but in their cloudy reflection of the beholder.

ONE

When I Awake with Thy Likeness

Sometime after James Nash and Mary Sheldon were married at Minersville, Pennsylvania, on July 4, 1868, they purchased a full-gilt *New Illustrated Devotional and Practical Polyglot Family Bible* in luxurious Turkey morocco binding. By the time they bought their Bible, most likely from a canvassing book agent who would have assured them that the binding was the only option for "persons who want a magnificent Bible," the Nashes had moved seventy miles north from Schuylkill County to Lackawanna Township and had welcomed the birth of their first daughter, Annie. Like most other men in the largely immigrant neighborhood, James was working in the coal mines while Mary was at home with Annie, likely already expecting the arrival of their second child, Elizabeth, who was born in February 1872. Whatever the precise date of purchase, the event marked not only an investment in a sacred text but also a material declaration of the Nash family—the Bible, in other words, was intended not only as scripture but as a lasting testament of James and Mary's legacy.[1]

For a family of three or more on a miner's paycheck, the Bible's purchase price of between $9 and $13 well exceeded the cost of other options—for instance, the similarly sized (10½ by 13 inches) roan-bound "Pica Bible," with references, published by the American Bible Society and sold for $3—and thus established the investment as a desire for something more than a copy of the scriptures.[2] In addition to whatever value the Nashes attached to the sacred text concealed beneath the heavy raised panels of the leather binding, the Bible was a cultural space that not only signified devotional practice but also established through specific gestures—purchase, display, transcription, accumulation—historical presence, a presence that was signaled before one even opened the cover of the enormous leather-bound compendium of sacred knowledge, elegantly embossed with gilt decorative work and James's initials and that lasted long after the family's corporeal demise. This family was here, it declared. And here is their story.

Signaling historical fortitude and inviting those who would finger the enormous volume to reflect not only on its scriptural content but also on the family whose story it told, the Nashes' Bible was not unlike other family Bibles popularized after the American Civil War. In addition to the biblical text, for instance, its contents featured "A history of the religious denominations of the world," many "valuable treatises," including a "History of the Translation of the Bible," and a host of "Chronological and Other Useful Tables, Designed to Promote and Facilitate the study of the Sacred Scriptures." Among the latter was "A Table of Kindred and Affinity: Forbidden to Marry Together," buried in the back pages and evidently included to clarify appropriate nineteenth-century familial relations.[3] Along with the written material, moreover, the Bible included a number of maps of the Holy Land and was "Embellished with Over 200 Fine Scripture Illustrations." In pages strategically positioned between the Old and New Testaments and continuing the practice of generations of Americans before them, moreover, the Nashes dutifully recorded their matrimony and the births of their ten children over the next two decades (as well as the deaths of four) in the printed registries provided by the publisher, thus positioning their own family history within a biblical chronology.[4] Unlike previous generations of recording practices, however, the Nashes' Bible also included a "Photographic Album for Sixteen Portraits" (fig. 4).

Introduced in the early 1860s, when card-size carte de visite prints became an immensely popular social currency, family photograph albums within family Bibles typically consisted of two leaves with four apertures on each facing page.[5] Among the family portraits preserved in the Nashes' sanctified album were twelve such mounted calling card–size prints, as well as four tintypes taken by "J. Y. Barry, Artist." Although placed at the end of the volume rather than between the Testaments, these visual genealogies shared with their textual counterparts the simultaneous effect of recording the ordinary course of the Nash family's lives and positioning their lineage within a sacred chronology that was guided less by the accidents of history than by the masterful plan of the album's Creator. Throughout the latter half of the nineteenth century, family Bible portrait galleries brought communities of saints past, present, and future into a communion of shadows.

Few Americans committed their encounters with family Bibles to writ-

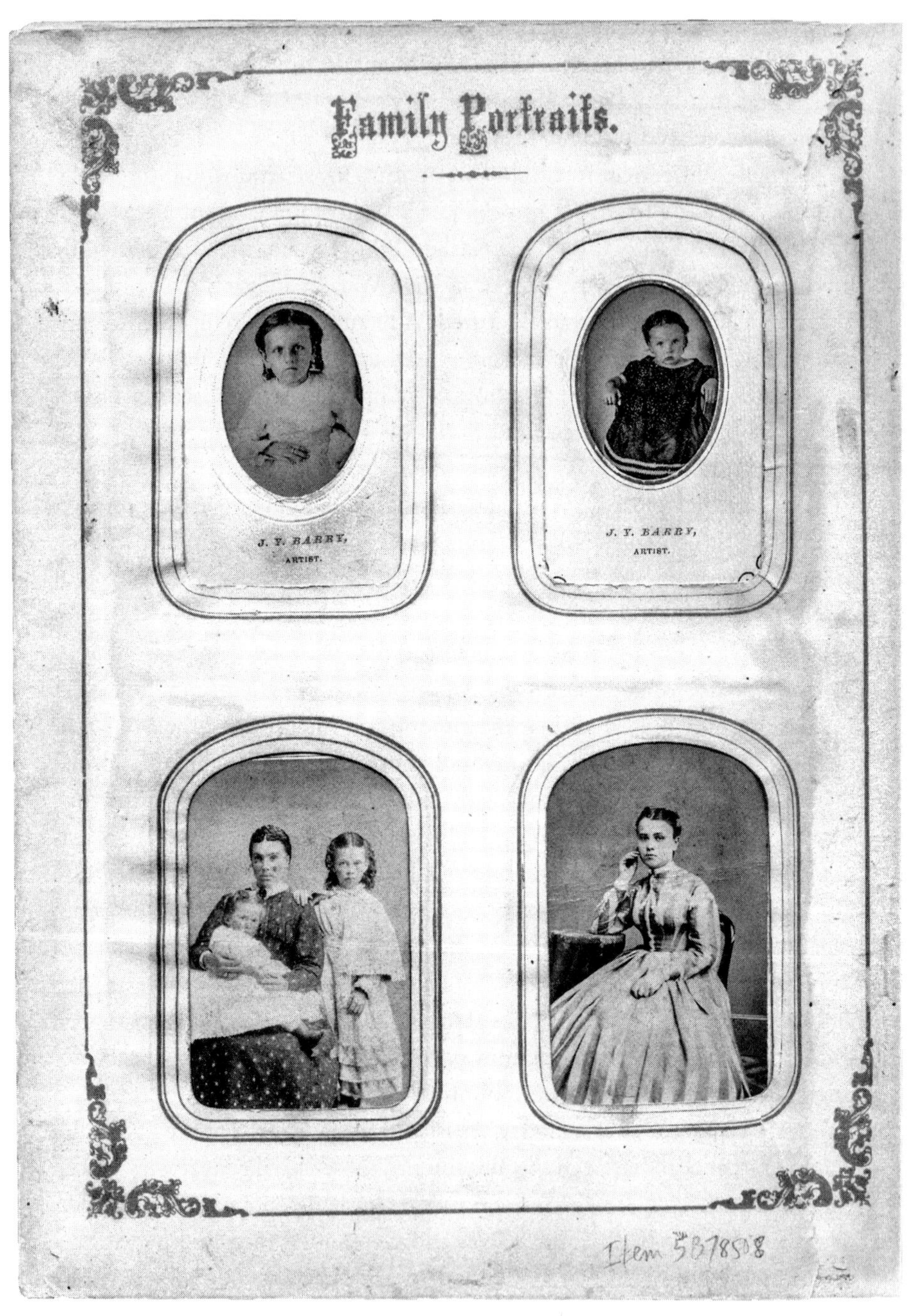

Figure 4. Nash Bible "Family Portraits" album page, New Illustrated Devotional and Practical Polyglot Family Bible (Philadelphia, 1870). Princeton University Library. Used with permission.

ing. In her 1929 memoir, Anne Ellis was an exception. The "ordinary woman" recalled that her childhood "big family Bible . . . had designs all around the leaves, places for photographs, also places for births, deaths and marriages." "It must have been made to sell, certainly not . . . to be read," Ellis conjectured, but she remembers specific episodes in her girlhood associated with the massive book—her Mama and the biblical Rachel "weeping for [their] children," her brother Frank hiding a nickel between the leaves and then cutting them out with a knife in his effort to rescue the coin, finding flowers from "Mama's old home" and "from a dead baby's coffin" tucked between its leaves, the latter twined with a lock of hair. But in contrast to these vivid memories of the Bible, Ellis is silent on whether or how her mother placed photographs in the designated pages. Much like Ellis, cultural memory has forgotten about the photographs.[6] Throughout the latter half of the nineteenth century, Bibles and photographic portraiture were commonly associated in material form and in display practices that linked individual likenesses with broader narratives of family, race, and sacred history. When placed within the pages of the Bible, I argue, photographic portraiture's long-acknowledged contribution to constructions of race and nation were accompanied by an equally significant visual reckoning of the soul.

When asked by his precocious nephew, Tom, about the origins of "the art of photography" in 1879, an essayist in the British youth magazine *Little Gleaner* responded with a tidy history of the medium's nineteenth-century "discovery" and development. When he concluded that its success was evident in the fact that "there is scarcely a house in the kingdom, from the royal palace to the humblest cottage, but possesses some specimen of photography," Tom mused in wonderment at the possibility of gathering "all those photographs together": "what a monstrous album would be required for them!" Evidently an eager pedagogue, Tom's uncle responded with the observation that "it occurs to me I have seen such an [*sic*] one as you suggest." To his nephew's mirthful skepticism, the essayist continued: "Nay, lad, I am serious. Do you not think most people possess a Bible? and is it not comparable to an album? for it contains portraits drawn by God, who is essential light; and, as proof of its magnitude, there is not a person in the world but what, if they had the seeing eye, might discover themselves in it." More than a record of ancient lives, the Bible, through God's "essential light," was continuously augmented with the likenesses of the generations: "By carefully looking over the blessed book we have been talking of, discover your portrait, for it abounds with precious likenesses which will shine like jewels in your eyes if you can but get a proper light thrown upon them by the Holy Spirit being your Guide."[7]

If Tom's uncle was using the common portrait album as an allegory for the volume of "precious likenesses" of the ancients, he was nevertheless writing at a time when portrait albums had been part of the physical arrangement of family Bibles for nearly two decades in both Britain and America. Hardly an isolated association, moreover, his lesson echoed a then-familiar mode of identification between albums and Bibles. In his early social history of photography, published in 1938, Robert Taft recounts pioneer reminiscences of a flour barrel, domesticated by a white lace coverlet, "whereupon reposed the family Bible and photograph album." Taft uses this anecdotal evidence to elevate the status of the common enough family album to a level on par with that of the equally ubiquitous family Bible. Decades later, cultural historian Martha Langford observed that "if the album tore a page from the family Bible, it was the 'family record.'" While her observation registers a degree of collaboration between visual and transcribed records, Langford nevertheless positions albums as biblical *replacements* rather than as contemporary counterarchives. But albums and Bibles mirrored each other in a variety of ways, reflecting back on each other both their physical form and ideological legacies, among them the racialized construction of family heritage. Such mirrorings notwithstanding, likenesses within family Bibles further entangled these ideational chords with a biblical narrative that purposefully dismissed the pesky constraints of historical time.[8]

Although historians of photography have made interpretive correlations between albums and Bibles in order to augment albums' cultural authority and historians of religion have recognized the visual history of family Bibles, the study of photographic studio portraiture within family Bibles raises new questions about religion in nineteenth-century American culture. Paul Gutjahr and Colleen McDannell have each noted the existence of these galleries in passing, but within the broader sweep of the communion of shadows we learn something from a longer look.[9] To this end, this chapter builds out from existing scholarship to chart an interpretive history of family Bible portrait albums, a practice that began shortly after 1860 and continued through the end of the century. During this period, at least twenty-five Bible publishers with locations in more than fifteen cities—primarily in New York, Philadelphia, and Boston, long-established hubs of Bible publication in the United States—provided family Bibles that included pages for "family portraits" or "family galleries."[10] Placed almost uniformly at the end of the binding, these galleries appeared in Bibles of both Authorized and Douay-Rheims trans-

 When I Awake with Thy Likeness

lations and, after 1881, in "combination" editions that provided parallel columns of both Authorized and Revised translation.[11] Despite the augmentation of materials included in family Bibles over this period, and in particular the heightened use of chromolithography and "illuminated" engravings of biblical events and figures based on the works of popular contemporaries Gustave Doré and Heinrich Hofmann, moreover, the photographic leaves remained remarkably consistent over the course of four decades. Variations of page ornamentation on photograph leaves occurred, but by and large publishers included space for between thirteen and seventeen portraits in roughly the same format: four rectangular die-cut openings per side of two leaves of heavy stock or, after 1866 when the larger "cabinet card" portrait was introduced, a space for this larger photograph at the beginning of the album section followed by three or four pages of the smaller apertures.[12]

Both their shared physical characteristics with albums and the visual habits informed by portraiture convention conditioned the interpretive possibilities of Bible portraiture. Photographic historians have established a number of conventions for dividing portrait photographs into various classifications that supposedly evoked differing visual strategies. Anna Pegler-Gordon, for instance, has identified one such binary as "the honorific self-presentation of bourgeois subjects" and the "repressive representation of prisoners, patients, and the poor."[13] Shawn Michelle Smith makes a similar distinction between "scientific and criminological mug shots," on the one hand, and "middle-class portraits," on the other.[14] Barbara McCandless has taken a different approach, identifying the two modes in which to categorize early photographic portraiture as the "democratic" appeal of making affordable likenesses of family and friends and the "morally instructive" practice of beholding "images of society's leaders."[15] While helpful to map the visual culture of photographic portraiture, that is, the different ways in which portraits were approached and interpreted, these distinctions also risk obscuring the ways in which affordable likenesses of family and friends, made according to established conventions of representation, could be at the same time morally instructive, racially informed, and ideologically charged in ways that did not necessarily map onto the intentions of photographers, scientists, or state officials. In other words, such interpretive compartmentalizations of photographic portraiture privilege the intent of an authorized gaze according to aesthetic convention rather than the tangle of visual habits that could prompt any number of interpretations of a particular likeness.

Moreover, these existing classifications typically assume that photographic portraits were always made to document the present. As historian

Martha Sandweiss advances in her study of photography in the American West, however, from an early period, photographs "were invested with the power of myth and cloaked in the gauzy haze of nostalgia; they evoked a longing for the past rather than an understanding of the present."[16] Sandweiss is here considering the ironic use of staged cowboy photographs as "straightforward reportage" in subsequent histories of the American West, but her attention to the ambiguous temporal positioning of photographic portraiture speaks to the unstable—indeed, the mischievous—operation of time in photograph albums as well. More than a document of a particular moment, photographic portraits brokered an imagined past with an anticipated future through a selective present. It was in this unstable encounter between beholder and likeness, between an embodied present, an imagined past, and an anticipated future, that Bible portrait galleries were firmly positioned within the charged chronography of sacred time.

Photograph albums were ordinary objects where beholders were instructed and inspired by the likenesses of friends and family no less than those of greater fame. Even outside of the charged archival context of the family Bible, the physical arrangement of albums was believed to inspire personal reform in anticipation of celestial reunion, as demonstrated in a placard inserted into an early album of card portraits that waxed in verse how communion with these familiar shadows prompted beholders toward "the home . . . beyond the sky":

> This book contains much choicer gems
> Than any casket on the earth,
> It holds the Portraits of our friends,—
> Some who have known us from our birth;
>
> . . . .
>
> Memory of such we'd always have,
> But, haply, some who're here portrayed,
> Have left the changing scenes of time,
> To dwell among a holier throng,
> To labor in a happier clime.
> *The thoughts of those thus brought to mind*
> *Shall raise our aspirations high,—*
> *Shall help us on to seek the home,*
> *That they have found beyond the sky.*[17]

The relationship among visual habits of the present, memories of the past, and aspirations toward the future the poem articulates can be mapped

When I Awake with Thy Likeness

onto contemporary photographic discourse in a way that emphasizes the ideological and indeed theological roles of photographic portraiture without assuming a causal relationship between aesthetic convention and a photograph's meaning for its beholders. And whether the card was tucked into a photograph album or a Bible gallery, its sentiment underlined a viewing habit common to both archives, namely, that beholding the likenesses of friends and family carried the aspirational potential that parallels the shadows of more famous folk. In short, in these verses we behold a silhouette of a much deeper communion of shadows.

Using family Bible portrait galleries as a point of entry into the communion of shadows, in this chapter I unravel the aesthetic, scientific, and theological idioms of "likeness" at work in the first several decades of photographic portraiture. In most cases these differing idioms agreed on a fundamental correspondence between interior states—whether figured as one's character or one's soul or one's natural dispositions—and externalized counterparts available to sensory perception. Despite this accord, however, the aim of the chapter is not a plucky narrative of discursive synchrony. Rather, by training our gaze on the constellation of visual and discursive contexts that informed the manufacture of Bible albums in the latter half of the nineteenth century, it is a story of how the knotted threads of race and nation were smuggled into sacred history—unwittingly, perhaps—under the guise of family pictures.

"What an Array There Is of Heads!": Portraiture, Bibles, and Habits of Beholding

Soon after news of Louis-Mandé-Jacques Daguerre's method for securing images from life arrived on the *British Queen* in September 1839, Americans rushed to purchase the necessary furnishings—chemicals and plates—and to jury-rig their cameras from household objects. Joseph Saxton of Philadelphia made his contraption from a magnifying glass and cigar box, exemplifying the eagerness and resourcefulness of the first generation of American photographers.[18] By the end of the week, Samuel F. B. Morse, who had met with Daguerre earlier in the year while touting his Electro-Magnetic Telegraph in Paris, boasted a view of the Unitarian Church taken from the third-story staircase of the gothic revival University of the City of New York on Washington Square, where he was currently installed as professor of literature of the arts of design.[19] Although these earliest experiments were in keeping with Daguerre's own preference for inanimate subjects—"rural scenery, buildings, &c."—Morse, a portrait painter by training, and his fellow compatriots were eager to capture not only their environments on silver but also their own reflections. In fact, Daguerre's skepticism "in regard to the practicability of taking portraits of *living persons*" did little to deter Morse and others from just such pursuits, the lengthy exposure times—"fifteen to twenty minutes" in strong outdoor light in those earliest days—notwithstanding. Within a month Morse claimed to have taken full-length portraits of his daughter and her friends, "out-of-doors, on the roof of a building, in the full sun-light," and, given the exposure time of "ten to twenty minutes," with "the eyes closed." To the great fortune of these early experimenters, by the following spring, having adjusted the lens and focal length of the camera and "dusted the sitter's face with flour," Morse's colleague at the university, John Draper, was able to reduce the exposure time to just over one minute. No one seems to have commented on the underlying politics of whiteness the flour invoked.[20]

Despite such a rough start, by the following spring John Johnson and Alexander S. Wolcott had opened "the first daguerreotype gallery for portraits" in New York, and Robert Cornelius had established a portrait gallery in Philadelphia. Although daguerreotype portraits had in fact been made in France by the end of 1839—one Parisian satirical magazine instructed in August, for instance, that to make "a portrait of your wife . . . you fit her head in an iron collar to give the required immobility, thus holding the world still for the time being"—Americans were quick to assert the technical improvements and market savvy that made their work stand apart. As one career daguerreotypist later reflected on these early years, "the daguerreotypes made in Europe did not compare with the *Yankee work*."[21]

Driving early studio portraiture was the hermeneutics of civic iconography. In portraits of elite citizens, the guiding principle went, the American public encountered icons of civic virtue that would manifestly influence American society. As early as 1840 the Philadelphia daguerreotypist Robert Cornelius used portraits of his city's elite citizenry to draw clients into his studio, and the same strategy was used by John Plumbe Jr. to promote his franchise in studios across the Northeast.[22] In 1843, Edward Anthony, a mogul of photographic supplies and prints for much of the mid-nineteenth century, along with his partners at the time, Jonas Edwards and J. R. Clark, had assembled the National Daguerreotype Miniature Gallery at the New York address of 247 Broadway. "Consisting entirely of likenesses of distinguished persons," wrote the editor of the *Democratic Review* in 1845, Anthony's gallery was deemed "one of the most valuable and interesting objects connected with art." "What an array there is of heads!" the *Knickerbocker* concurred

When I Awake with Thy Likeness

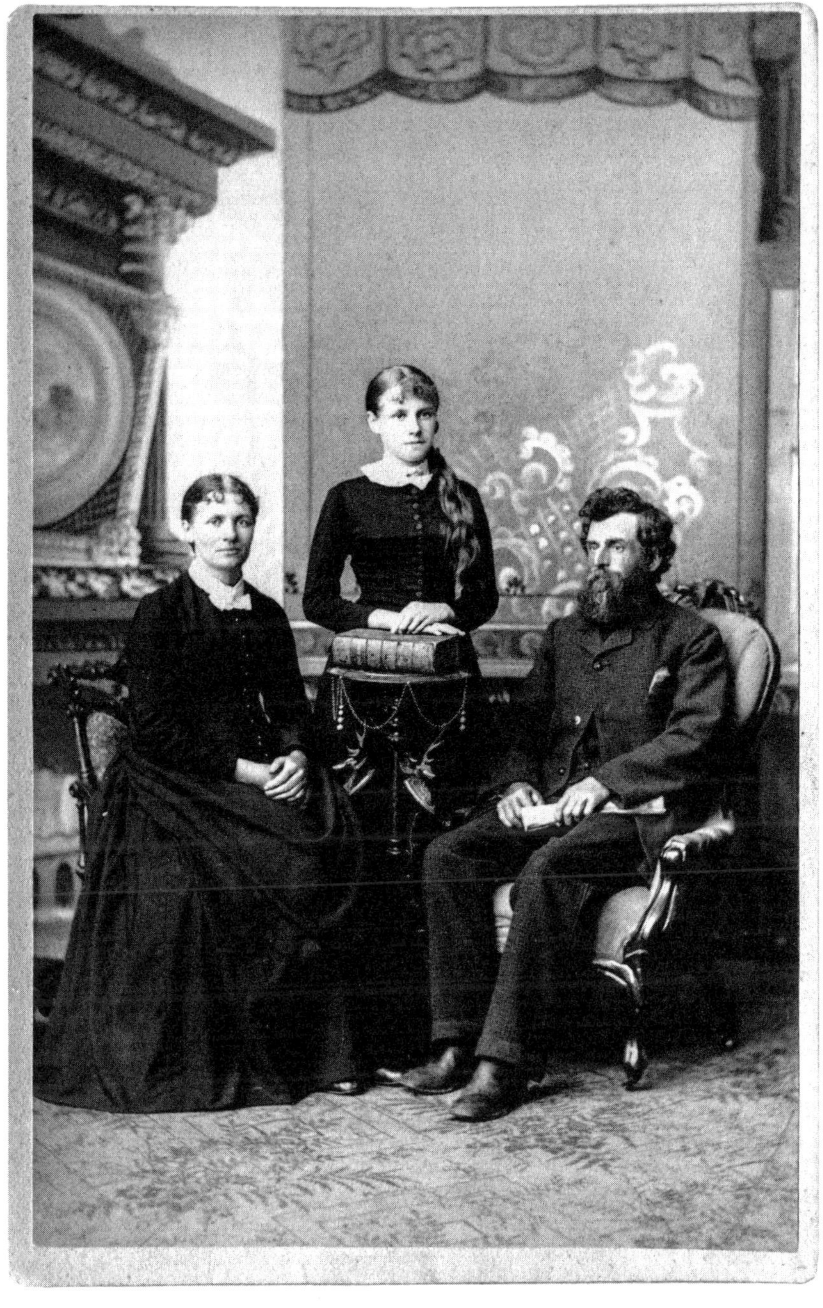

Figure 5. Unidentified family studio portrait, ca. 1880. Cabinet card. Author's collection.

a year later, "poets, painters, statesmen and heroes; the evidence of truth stamped upon each likeness." The collection was especially noted for its "counterfeit presentments" of Congress, which were "regularly transmitted to New York . . . with the autographs of each person" for display. Unlike other studio galleries that were designed to attract passersby not only as beholders but as clients, at Anthony's miniature gallery "for seeing them there is no charge, as the gallery is free to all."[23]

Around forty years later, at his studio in Oconomowoc, Wisconsin, using photographic techniques that produced negatives on plates of glass that could then be used to make countless prints on paper, Douglas Munger peered through his camera at the trio comported and composed in front of him.[24] Whatever other uses the camera had been put to in the decades since the introduction of Daguerre's process—and there were many—the making of likenesses had become the signature operation of photography for most Americans, and this was especially so after the popularization of card photographs in the 1860s. As with civic photography throughout the century, studio portraiture of ordinary citizens also freighted iconographic meaning. In this newly mirrored world, "likeness" was a versatile category—one could say prismatic—that reflected not only the lineaments of one's flesh but the state of one's soul, the integrity of one's lineage, and the virtue of one's character. Frequently the perception of these less apparent qualities was effected through visual cues, and among the most charged props were books, described by the Broadway photographer Abraham Bogardus at the end of his career as "just the thing" to communicate "an attitude of importance."[25] We know nothing of Munger's religious affiliation or that of the family who now sat before him. What we do know is that someone thought it important— whether aesthetically, socially, or piously—to place a large family Bible in the middle of the composition and, notably, that the other people involved in the portrait agreed.

The photograph is presumably a family of three: mother, father, daughter. The two older figures sit in elegant parlor chairs, hands on their laps, shoulders and hips pointing toward the opposite edge of the frame. The woman, sitting on the left side of the composition, looks directly into the camera, the dimple on her right cheek betraying the slightest grin. The man, sporting a full beard, holds a rolled newspaper in his left hand and stares obliquely across the frame. Between these two figures stands a young woman, gazing to the right of the frame, seemingly over the camera's lens, her long light-colored hair draped over her left shoulder and her hands resting on an enormous book whose spine clearly reads "Family Bible." The Bible itself sits on

                                    When I Awake with Thy Likeness

an elegantly carved table adorned with a delicate chain. The entire scene is set before what appears to be an enormous mantle and ornamented wall, but that is in fact a painted backdrop. As with other portraits that feature Bibles, or any prop for that matter, it is ultimately unclear just what the Bible is doing for the composition and how the artifact figures in relationship to the people being photographed. Was this a studio prop or a family treasure? Was it part of their daily lives? How so? Does it mean anything that, within this particular portrait, the Bible is depicted in closest proximity to the girl, rather than her father or mother? Why does the man hold a newspaper and look away from the Bible? Are we, as accidental beholders, to detect a message within the frame?

In her work on American material religion, Colleen McDannell has examined the nineteenth-century Protestant iconography of family Bible reading as evidence of a transition from paternal to maternal instruction, which was itself part of a broader domestication of the Bible among Victorian Protestants. Photography was certainly part of this iconographic tradition, as McDannell indicates in a reproduction of an 1860s stereograph that, in her words, "reflects popular engravings of the time" that were themselves modeled after Jean-Baptiste Greuze's eighteenth-century painting *Père de famille expliquant la Bible à ses enfants* (1755).[26] More common than this genre-style photography, in which the composition was intended to narrate a story, was the practice of posing for a portrait, perhaps with one or two others, while simply holding the Bible on one's lap or, as in Munger's photograph, resting it on a nearby table. Soon after Daguerre's invention was adopted by American photographers, props became a regular feature of daguerreotype portraits, and books were among the most frequently utilized, particularly in portraits of women and children.[27] But whereas books in portraits have frequently been remembered as Bibles, it is often difficult to determine the veracity of such claims. Take, for example, the tintype of "Gr. Grandpa Dikeman" (fig. 6). Is it in fact a Bible, as later generations have remembered it? Does it matter? Despite the challenges of cataloguing or quantifying the prevalence of Bibles in early vernacular portraiture, there is sufficient evidence that the practice was common enough to nurture such assumptions. McDannell's discussion of the cultural significance of Bibles in the late nineteenth century—it was, as she says, a "revered object" no less than a "text telling of salvation"—provides some rationale for later acts of inventive remembrance. But close inspection at times proves such claims to be incorrect, as in the otherwise emblematic real photo postcard of an elderly woman posing in front of a corner cabinet decked with family photographs, holding

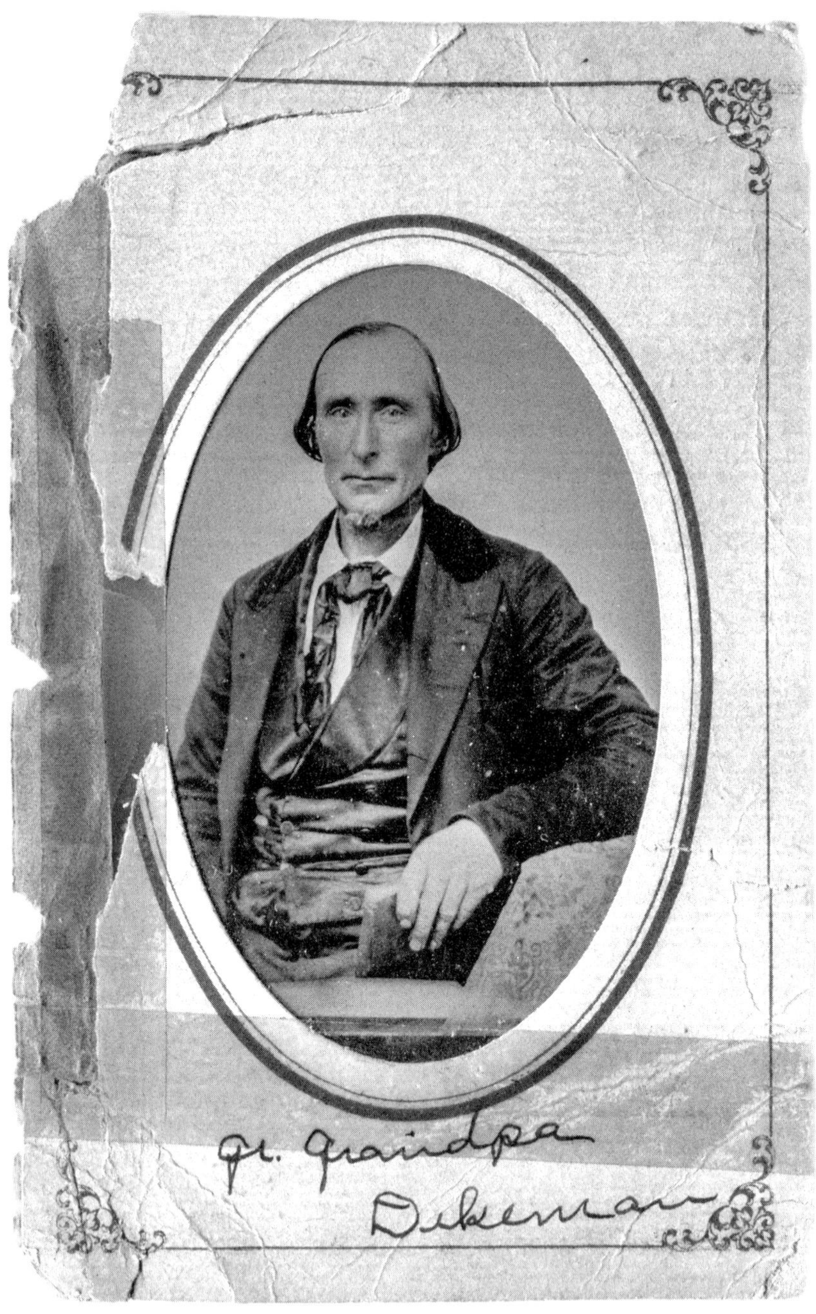

Figure 6. Undated tintype (ca. 1865) of "Gr. Grandpa Dikeman" holding a book that appears to be a Bible. Author's collection.

Scott's *Life of Napoleon*. Regardless of claims to civic or devotional instruction, photographic iconography was a slippery cultural signifier.

Notwithstanding the instructive promise of iconographic analysis of these photographs, then, there are problems with investing too much signifying agency in any particular prop. In 1864 a Broadway photographer instructed the "fraternity" in some "hints" to produce "ease and grace in a portrait": "The hands of a lady may rest easily upon the lap, and should be presented edgewise, neither too high nor too low, which will give them a small, delicate appearance. Or one hand may be laid upon a table, while the other hand may hold a book or some other object, if the sitter so choose. For myself, however, I think a pretty hand is much the prettiest when empty."[28] In an undated carte de visite taken by "Miss R. M. Thorp" of Geneva, Ohio, the aging sitter, one Mrs. Williams, seems to have struck a compromise with these hints, her hands "resting easily" upon a massive family Bible (fig. 7a). Clasping her hands on the edge of the closed volume, the ancient Williams purses her lips and looks intently into the camera. On the back of the card (fig. 7b), someone, at some time, wrote "Lucian Williams / Mother" above the photographer's stamp and "she never weighed 100 pounds" below it.

Interpretive paradigms that define images as iconography, in short, only get us so far. Understanding the place of vernacular photographs in nineteenth-century American religion requires that we move beyond such modes of analysis to map practices of beholding and displaying. Prior to the turn of the century, studio portraits were the variety of photograph most commonly included in family Bibles. Many of the same interpretive problems associated with studio portraits of sitters holding family Bibles carry over into studio portraits tucked into Bible albums. Who were they? What did this visual association with a Bible mean? Who were their anticipated beholders? How have the practices of their descendants shaped later interpretations of their likenesses? Before turning to the Bibles themselves, however, it is first helpful to outline the conceptual coordinates of "likeness" within nineteenth-century religious and photographic discourse. As an idiomatic category, it is important not to overburden the term with definitional precision and yet it is also important to point to nodes of congruence in the term's broad web of signification.

"As Even Thine": The Body and Soul of Likeness

In early December 1841, Mary Van Lennep retreated to her room, a space for "which I have long wished for." The wife of Henry Van Lennep, a missionary

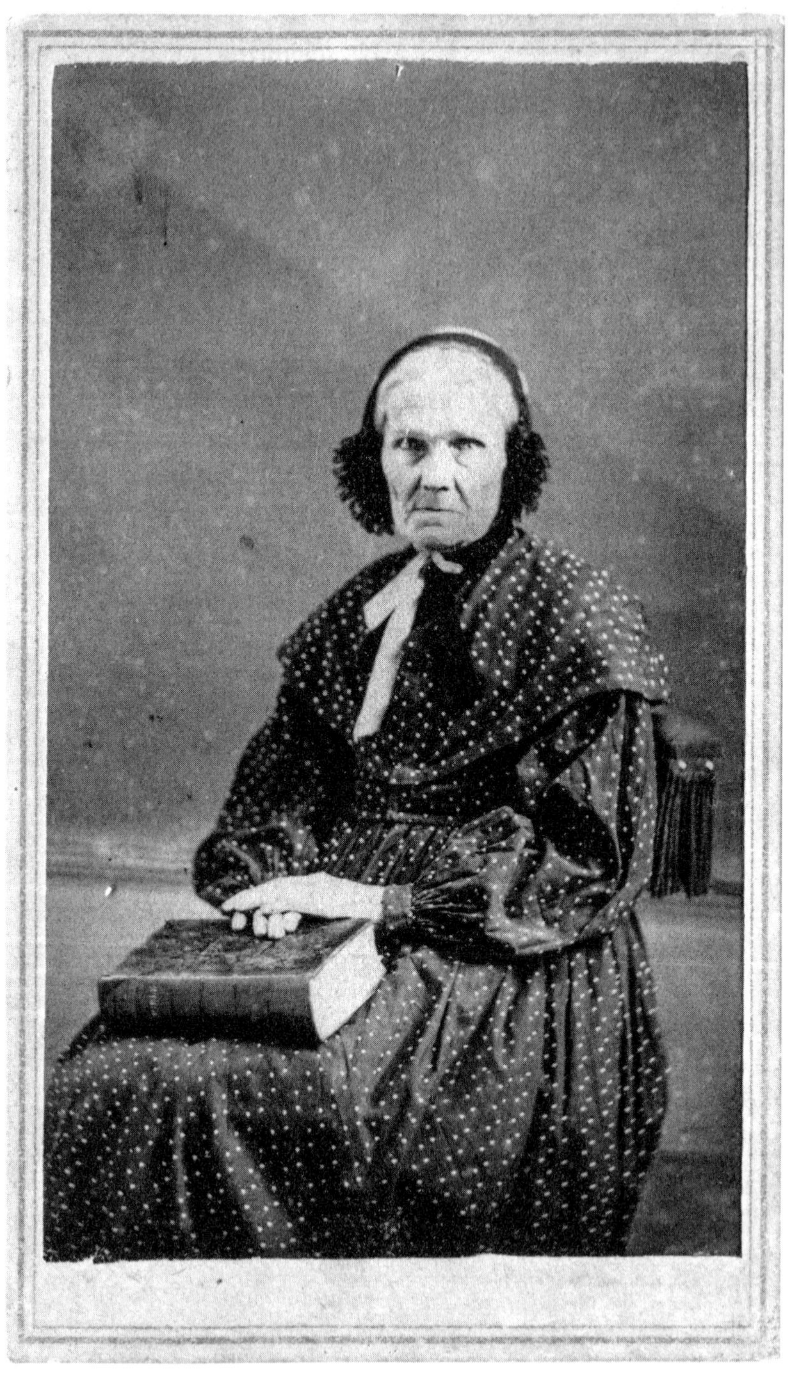

Figures 7a and 7b (*opposite*). Carte de visite (front and back), "Lucian Williams Mother," ca. 1860–70. Author's collection.

Lucian Williams

Mother

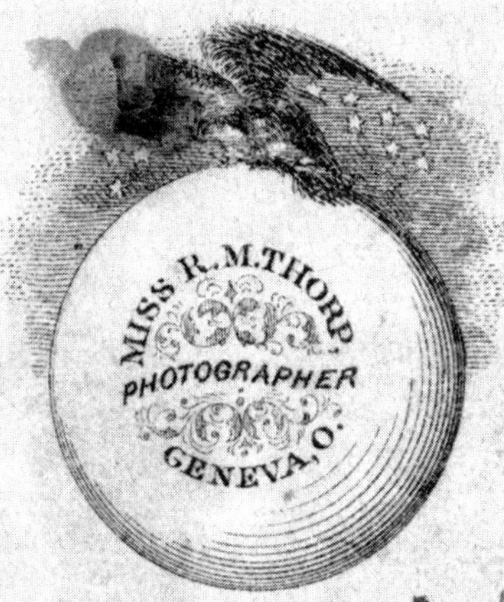

she never weighed
100 pounds

Additional Copies from the plate from which
this picture is taken can be had if desired.

in Turkey, Mary had long waited for "a day in which to look over my future course, and endeavor to adopt those principles upon which I can safely act in after life." Trembling at the weightiness of her meditations, she wrote that "God has placed me in this world to glorify him, by preparing my own soul for his kingdom, and by doing all I can to lead others to do so. He is sparing me in this world, that my character may be formed into a likeness to his own perfect character, that I may continually increase in holiness, and receive those blessings for which the Saviour died."[29] For Mary Van Lennep, to grow in likeness to God was a process of conforming to his character, of preparing her soul for the rewards to come, and, through these actions, of leading others to adopt her course.

The phrase "awake in Thy likeness" is taken from Psalms, but the concept of a likeness to God or to Jesus was one that nineteenth-century Christians found from Genesis through the Gospels. And while ministers and laypersons who invoked the concept in their sermons, diaries, and memoirs certainly did not agree on all points, its consistent invocation certainly suggests its ubiquity as both a devotional and a theological concept that, in turn, we can map onto the visual habits of photography's earliest beholders. William Ellery Channing's 1828 sermon "Likeness to God" at the ordination of Frederick Augustus Farley in Providence, Rhode Island, first published in January 1829 and in print throughout the century, provides one contemporary meditation on "the importance of this assimilation to our Creator" among nineteenth-century Americans.[30] Channing articulates a definitive Unitarian exegesis, pushing further than his "orthodox" contemporaries on the issue of humanity's "kindred nature with God." His sermon, however, was nevertheless an important touchstone in the effort to map the overlapping terrains of theological and photographic conceptions of likeness.

In his sermon, Channing noted that "likeness" did not correspond to God's "figurative resemblance to man" but rather a recognition of "kindred mind, which interprets the universe by itself" and thus sets humans apart from other beasts in God's creation. For Channing, "to grow in the likeness of God, we need not cease to be men. This likeness does not consist in extraordinary or miraculous gifts, in supernatural additions to the soul, or in any thing foreign to our original constitution. . . . I repeat it, to resemble our Maker we need not quarrel with our nature or our lot." Neither beast nor saint nor angel, human beings in their very constitution were made to "resemble [their] Maker." Channing hinges his evidence of such kindred nature with the New Testament notion of God as Father, "and a brighter feature of that book cannot be named." For Channing, then, religion "is not the adora-

   When I Awake with Thy Likeness

tion of a God with whom we have no common properties . . . but of an all-communicating Parent. It recognizes and adores God, as a being . . . who has made man in his own image, who is the perfection of our own spiritual nature, who has sympathies with us as kindred beings, . . . who looks on us with parental interest, and whose great design it is to communicate to us for ever, and in freer and fuller streams, his own power, goodness, and joy." Thus likeness to God was a temporal aspiration for Channing that was to be effected through cultivation of God-given faculties of mind and soul, in whatever lot one was given. It was nevertheless conceptualized as a hereditary nature, passed from parent to child, a paradigm that would become increasingly important in the growing culture of vernacular photographic portraiture.[31]

To whatever degree Channing's theology bristled against the grain of antebellum evangelicalism, as a public figure of great repute there is no doubt. As the only minister to be featured in Mathew Brady's *Gallery of Illustrious Americans* (1850), the first bound volume of lithographs based on daguerreotype portraits of "representative" Americans, moreover, he marks an important intersection in this history of likenesses.[32] Nevertheless, the theological idiom of likeness was hardly limited to the Unitarian pulpit. While serving as rector of St. Peter's Episcopal Church in Westchester, New York—a post that he held from 1848 to 1871—Charles D. Jackson also sermonized on the "Divine Likeness." While for Jackson one's "awakening" was delayed until "the morning of the Resurrection Day," after all had "laid down their precious dust in the sweet repose of death," he nevertheless enjoined his parishioners that "we are not fashioned into this likeness of Christ by a single abrupt act of omnipotent power first exerted at the resurrection, but it is a likeness into which we grow." If for Channing one's likeness to God was inherent to humanity, for Jackson the "immortal beauty of body and soul"—in short, one's likeness to the resurrected Christ—was similarly "but the ultimate development of vital forces now planted and working in our nature,—a life hid with Christ in God."[33]

Echoing Jackson's exegesis of a soul awakened as the site of divine likeness, the Presbyterian missionary William Jessup Armstrong wrote that "the likeness of which the psalmist speaks is a conformity of the soul to God" and that it "will consist in a similarity between the qualities of [persons'] souls and the attributes of the Divine nature . . . when they awake from this dream of life." Despite important theological differences from Channing, the Congregationalist Jackson and the Presbyterian Armstrong nevertheless acknowledged that, however "partial in the present life," traces of this future likeness were perceptible, in Armstrong's words, within the "gross material body."[34] Armstrong, to be sure, was more suspicious of the powers of perception, writing that "enveloped in the mists of sense, and covered with the darkness of sin, we see objects very superficially, and often they do not appear to us as they really are," and his sermon was accordingly a stronger exhortation on "the future likeness of the saints to God" than either Jackson or Channing mounted.[35] Armstrong's suspicions of human perception, however, better reflect the philosophical moorings of the seventeenth and eighteenth centuries than the visual habits of the nineteenth, when confidence was increasingly placed in sciences of observation and measurable correspondences between referents and beholders.[36]

As a ubiquitous if theologically slippery concept, nineteenth-century Protestant notions of divine likeness are also to be found in the records of the saints. On Ash Wednesday in 1850, Susan Allibone pleaded in her diary, "Oh! my Savior, take me to thyself whenever it shall seem good to Thee. I shall be satisfied when I awake with Thy likeness." Whether Allibone's modification of the psalmist's preposition (the scriptural "to" becomes "with") constitutes a deliberate theological move—and one that transforms the penitent from being in the audience of the divine to being in communion with him—we cannot know, but it is clear that the prayer was often on the tip of her pen and, we might imagine, her tongue as well. Even as she was "cut off from the enjoyments of health, and confined to the couch of languishing," wrote Episcopal Bishop Alfred Lee, who first published her diary and letters in 1855 (they were still in print a decade later), "the grace of God which was in her could not be hid." Allibone's utterance of the prayer to "awake with Thy likeness" seems, less like Channing and more like Jackson and Armstrong, to anticipate a future, celestial awakening rather than an earthly aspiration of similitude to a kindred nature with God. And yet, by publishing her memoirs "to present to the disciples of Christ such an exhibition of profound and living piety," Bishop Lee presented Allibone's own life as one to emulate while still enrobed in fleshly garb.[37]

Three weeks before her sixtieth birthday in the "seventh month" of 1857, Sarah Hunt of the Society of Friends reflected on her recent journey to the Genesee Yearly Meeting in Farmington, New York. Although her "exercises were very great," for "the duties of home seemed pressing," her decision to attend the meeting was rewarded by a "Master [who] was good to me, and on various occasions unsealed the spring of Life, that I could speak of His goodness in the great congregations." After describing various meetings and the "blessings showered down," Hunt closed her entry with a prayer for her "companions in life," particularly those "who think life is given for

    When I Awake with Thy Likeness

amusement and to trifle away," for an "abundance of Thy goodness . . . ; and embracing its unfoldings be transformed into Thy likeness, and beautified with salvation."[38] While still operating on a spiritual register rather than one of "figurative resemblance," for Hunt the transformation into a likeness of Christ was one that manifested itself through perceptible traits. Although her memoir was published posthumously in 1892, the frontispiece supports the notion of a link between one's recordable visage and one's spiritual state, particularly through the medium of portraiture. No doubt based on a photograph, below the partial profile engraving of Hunt is what appears to be her manuscript valediction, "as even thine / Sarah Hunt." Whatever meaning these words invited in the context of written communication, their proximity to Hunt's portrait in the journal suggests a constructed correspondence between one's physical likeness and one's likeness to Christ, "beautified with salvation."

While maintaining a conceptual distinction between spiritual and corporeal likeness, theological invocations of the idiom, particularly among the laity, introduce a healthy measure of ambiguity, as when Deborah Cushing Porter prayed in 1839, "Oh, draw the outlines of thy likeness in my heart, and never leave the work, until all its lineaments are filled up, and every feature is fashioned and finished in thy likeness, and made to supplant all the image of the earthly."[39] Though her similitude to Christ was supposedly manifest "in my heart" and not in the flesh, her language, like that of many of her contemporaries, suggests that this primary signification of an inward cultivation was understood to influence one's outward appearances as well. Indeed, as the century progressed, greater confidence was placed in the correspondence between physical and spiritual constitutions, particularly among those Protestant reformers who identified Jesus as a model of physical perfection no less than spiritual aspiration. By shaping the visual habits of religious Americans, portrait photography no doubt played an important role in this theological transition.[40]

At a time when likeness was becoming increasingly associated with physiognomy, on the one hand, and with a calculable correspondence between "form" and the inner workings of one's soul, on the other, these preacherly pronouncements and saintly scribbles echo conversations in other quarters concerning the linkage between present, past, and future in lineages facilitated through perceptible comportment. The ability to discern the state of one's soul through outward registers has been well documented in histories of American religion, but what has not been addressed in this literature is how during the mid-nineteenth-century discourses surrounding the new medium of photographic portraiture also emphasized a mutual correspondence between what the camera recorded and what the beholder perceived beneath, as it were, the surface.[41] Within a decade of photography's invention, writes historian Barbara McCandless, "the standard for a truly accurate likeness had become not merely to reproduce the subject's physical characteristics but to express the inner character as well." She goes on to describe such nineteenth-century sensibilities as a "naïve belief that outer physical features could be clues to inner character," citing as her example a transformation in the period's professional literature from "aesthetic treatises into a series of formulas" designed to produce the right effect in the sitter's likeness.[42] Even if her assessment of these logics of correspondence as "naïve belief" undermines the intellectual, theological, and aesthetic discourses that supported their currency throughout the century, and her reference to shifts in professional literature overlooks the ways in which studio manuals borrowed from aesthetic treatises, McCandless is nevertheless correct to identify an uncertain terrain between similitude and likeness that was navigated, in part, by the compass of "expression."

To counter accusations from established art traditions — primarily portraiture painting and its more popular cousin, miniature portraits — that daguerreotypists were merely "operators" and not "artists," studio proprietors who catered to affluent clients clambered for aesthetic excellence even as they articulated the challenges of securing a "true likeness" in but a moment's time. It was a hard sell. "Thus a portrait is satisfactory in so far as the painter has *sympathy* with his subject," the celebrated American painter Rembrandt Peale quoted one Mrs. Jamieson in 1857. "This may be the reason why a daguerreotype, however beautiful and accurate, is seldom satisfactory or agreeable; and that while we acknowledge its truth as a fact, it always leaves something for the sympathies to desire." While Peale took care to position himself as an expert on the subject, unlike the "amateur" Mrs. Jamieson, he nevertheless agreed that the daguerreotypist's "pictures may be *true*, as regards the proportions of the features; . . . but sometimes they are more true in recording the strong marks of age and some fixed expression, than is agreeable to the person represented." Thus he predicted that portraitists in his medium would now have to make their works "not only *as* true, but expressively *more true* than the daguerreotypes, with which but few, at present, are content."[43]

Peale was writing at what would only later become known as the end of the daguerrean period. Over the next few years, using techniques that had been around since around 1850 but that had not yet become commercially viable in the United States, studio photographers would begin selling more likenesses on paper than on metal, especially after 1860, when the card-size carte de visite came into vogue. And yet the articulated disjuncture between "truth" and "representation"—indeed, the excessive truthfulness of the camera as a representational failing—in photographic portraiture was noted by later photographers as well. In his 1864 historical account of "the heliographic art," Marcus Aurelius Root, who consistently distinguished between "artists" and "mere mechanics," wrote that the aim of photographers was "not *merely* to get an exact outline of his sitter's face" that could then be tinted and colored so that "it shall be true to the original." However "essential to a *perfect* portrait," such accuracies of light and shadow "are insufficient, in the absence of that expression which reveals the soul within,—that *individuality* which distinguishes *this* from all human beings beside." So sure was he that expression trumped "outline" that he declared, "If the artist cannot detect and seize *this*, he makes no portrait." Thus even if Root could identify "verity of likeness" as the "first point of excellence" in a studio portrait, he could with equal gusto proclaim that such a portrait was "worse than worthless if the pictured face does not show the *soul* of the original,—that *individuality* or *self hood* which differentiates *him* from all beings, past, present, or future." Root likened the process to that of the "Supreme Proto-Artist," who, in creating Adam, "formed the man of the dust of the ground"—that is, established his corporeal frame—and only then "breathed into his nostrils the breath of life, and man became a living soul." Writing to an audience of professional photographers, Root explained that to succeed, his readers "must copy, throughout, the process of this Divine Exemplar."[44]

Peale's appeal to the sympathetic eye of the artist as a superlative rubric of likeness and Root's adoption of religious language to explain the heliographer's art suggest common ground between theological and aesthetic understandings of likeness at work in nineteenth-century American culture. What is further important to note, however, is how both portraiture and religion drew upon emerging racial discourses that sought to baptize this correspondence between character and comportment in the cool springs of scientific observation. McCandless notes, for instance, that the contemporary notion that portraits could "express the essence of the subject—the sitter's true moral character" was profoundly influenced by popular understandings of physiognomy and phrenology, although we might also add to this the collaborative sciences of anthropology, craniology, and anatomy. Molly Rogers further considers how these eighteenth-century disciplines "were used to get beyond the awkward surface of race—the color of skin—and attempt to construct racial difference more objectively."[45] Of course, recall that a tactile semiotics of race was instilled in daguerrean portraiture from the beginning, in the form of flour dusted on the sitter's face to make her skin white enough for the "objective" chemical process to transpire. If it is too much conjecture to argue that all beholders of photographic likenesses consciously wove these racialized disciplines into the interpretive moment, which it is, it is not off mark to argue that they nevertheless profoundly influenced viewing habits, particularly as likenesses became increasingly salient registers of hereditary lineage. American Protestants were caught up in the heat of these fiery agnotologies.[46]

In his heliographic essay, Marcus Aurelius Root drew upon the popular sciences of phrenology and, especially, physiognomy to instruct his readers in the art of delimiting not only the sitter's likeness but, more important, her soul: "The human face . . . is the most perfect of all mediums of expression; the medium, too, for expressing that intelligence and affection whereon rests man's claim to be 'made in the image of God.'"[47] Beginning with the premise that "the face is . . . the index of the soul," Root clarifies "that in a considerable degree, the face is an index both to the intellectual and moral character, is beyond dispute. Indeed, we are all physiognomists in practice, if not in theory."[48] Tellingly, daguerreotype portraits were sometimes called "physiognomies," suggesting that long after eighteenth-century Swiss Protestant theologian Johann Caspar Lavater had recognized the infinite complexity of facial expression, and thus the impossibility of securing a stable system of physiognomic classification, the idea remained firmly entrenched in the imagination of many Americans—the same place, not incidentally, where photographs were imbued with meaning through acts of beholding.[49] Physiognomy, in short, was an imaginative exercise that wed Christian theories of divine impression with practices of photographic beholding. Historian of American Christianity R. Marie Griffith finds "notions of corporeal and spiritual equivalence" in nineteenth-century discourses of phrenology that continued to have "a conspicuous impact on American body culture" well into the twentieth century. The physiognomic theologies of Lavater—who, in Griffith's turn of phrase, "believed that the soul carried somatic evidences"—influenced nineteenth-century Protestants, who "seized upon" phrenology as a system through which character, even virtue, was ossified in the anatomy of the skull. Although phrenology was first introduced to the United States in the 1820s, during the 1830s it was popularized among literary elite, in no small part due to Johann Gaspar Spurzheim's ill-fated visit to America in 1832 (Spurzheim was phrenology-founder Franz Joseph

When I Awake with Thy Likeness

Gall's student and died while on his American tour). Even as phrenology came to be at home in popular entertainments no less than halls of science, it nevertheless, in Griffith's estimation, "promised to satisfy Christian hopes for authenticity and transparency, teaching that physical traits . . . perfectly disclosed the inner worlds of their bearers." Here the claims of the photographer and the phrenologist aligned with long-standing Christian theories of the soul's impression on the "outer man."[50]

Even as body sciences such as physiognomy and phrenology located individual character traits in anatomical features, such readings were conscripted into social and cultural registers of meaning. What mattered most was how each individual related to the body politic. Religion was one such register; race was another. In the decades after Daguerre's invention, photographic likenesses were co-opted into narratives of descent that drew upon and conditioned habits of beholding. Family Bibles were one especially generative site where racialized theories of descent, informed by broader cultural concerns with surface and depth, were baptized in sacred histories of Christian glory.

AN "ENTIRELY NEW AND ATTRACTIVE FEATURE":
PORTRAIT GALLERIES IN FAMILY BIBLES

A decade after James and Mary Nash bought their hefty family Bible, their family of three had grown to seven.[51] Eleven-year-old Annie was now at school, and Mary was home with daughters Elizabeth, age eight, and Mary, age three, and her infant son, George. Also living with them in 1880 was Mary's father, George Sheldon, the namesake for the Nashes' only surviving son. As was all too common during the nineteenth century, James and Mary had also suffered loss in the intervening years. In December 1875, their two-year-old daughter, Mary, the name with which her sister was later christened, died the week before Christmas, and a year later they buried their infant son, James.[52]

In addition to tucking studio portraits into the designated pages at the end of the Bible, over the years the family had placed other mementos within its pages. A clump of short, fine, light-colored hair rests in the Gospel of Mark, perhaps snipped from baby James's fevered head or his sister's ailing brow. A news clipping tucked in the Wisdom of Solomon bears witness to the elder Mary Nash's "final tribute." A calling card from Grace Weiser Davis of Jersey City in the fold of Maccabees proclaims, "Under all circumstances, Look to Jesus!" and in the New Testament book of 1 Corinthians, between chapters 14 and 15, there is a stemmed yellow flower. Though the presence of the flower does not alone indicate a deliberate association with the text, it is at least suggestive that 1 Corinthians 15 concludes with the promise of victory over death through Christ: "O death, where is thy sting? O grave, where is thy victory," poignantly symbolized in the flower that has not faded.

The registries, photographs, and mementos preserved in the Nash family Bible all contributed to a form of memory work that was linked, by its material association with the scriptures, to sacred history no less than with the rather inglorious human predicament of birth, procreation, and death. But what is less immediately visible in the Nash Bible is what role the photographs, in particular, played in constructing these narratives. Contemporary amateur genealogical projects that facilitated racialized discourses under the aegis of "ancestry" lend insight into ways in which lineage was plotted on sacred no less than racial or cultural arcs. Photographic technology enabled ethnologists, law enforcement agencies, and ordinary studio photographers to manufacture visual records of belonging—according to classifications of race, criminality, and social standing—that were woven into narratives of destiny and progress under the authorizing discourse of technological empiricism. This use of photography to construct visual archives of descent—whether to the benefit or detriment of those represented—was most visible in the popularity of photograph albums in the 1860s. The prospective implications of genealogical narratives, moreover, was also evident in albums that assembled "portraits of our friends" in order that beholders "raise our aspirations high." Family Bible portrait albums, with their physical proximity to the written family records and to the pearls tucked between the pages, as well as the physical similarities between albums and Bibles, made Bible galleries important archives of these intersecting modes of representation.

As early as 1862, the *Saturday Evening Post* made reference to a family Bible that "has been published in which adjacent to the pages usually bound in the book for the registration of births, deaths, etc., are arranged in sheets any convenient number of card cases, such as contain the ordinary photographic albums, in which may be inserted the photographs of the different members of the family."[53] Although its details are scant—Who published the Bible? Where was it sold? How much did it cost?—this notice already shifts our understanding of the practice of including portrait pages in family Bibles from a post–Civil War phenomenon, as Paul Gutjahr has suggested, to one that was more closely linked with the rise of portrait albums in the United States around 1860, once card-size paper prints had become commercially viable. In December 1864, L. Clark and Company of Baltimore listed among

     When I Awake with Thy Likeness

their "Christmas goods" for the holiday season "a splendid assortment of PHOTOGRAPH BIBLES at very low prices." While the language of this advertisement does not point directly to the types of photographs the Bibles included, a year later the Baltimore publishers and booksellers at Murphy and Company, located two doors down from Clark, described their photograph Bibles as "QUARTO BIBLES arranged to contain in connection with the Family Record Photographic Portraits of the Family." Arranged for sixteen "family portraits," this "entirely new and attractive feature" was to be found in a selection of Bibles "bound in the most beautiful and superb styles" and sold "at *very low prices*."

Although both merchants advertised photograph Bibles, they catered to different clientele, as indicated by accompanying advertised goods. Clark and Company, for instance, noted its "splendid stock" of photograph albums, its plated ware, including tea sets, ice pitchers, coffee urns, wine stands, and butter dishes, among other sundries, as well as watches, jewelry, and a stock of "fancy goods" from "china vases of all kinds" to mahogany writing desks and "a splendid assortment of fine French perfumery."[54] In contrast to the stock at Clark, Murphy and Company specialized in books and religious goods. In addition to its selection of photograph albums and "juvenile books etc.," for instance, the company also supplied prayer and devotional books "in every variety of CARVED IVORY VELVET TURKEY MOROCCO CALF and other superb bindings," a stock of Catholic prayer books "of their own publication," ranging in price from twenty cents to forty dollars per volume, in bindings "upward of ONE HUNDRED different styles," and "a very large stock of FINE ROSARIES . . . SILVER and GOLD MEDALS FINE CRUCIFIXES STATUETTES &c."[55] An advertisement from June 1864 further clarifies what the later print subtly suggests. Under the boldfaced caption "Something New and Appropriate. Photograph Bibles," Murphy and Company invited "such as may want a good Cheap Family Douay Bible . . . to call and examine prices, &c, at the *Cheap Up-Stairs Bookstore*" at its premises at 182 Baltimore Street.[56]

More common than bookstores, however, most households in the nineteenth century were introduced to family Bibles through publishers' agents. Often nameless to posterity or remembered only as unscrupulous catchpennies peddling the Word of God, Bible agents in fact mediated the world of publishers with that of consumers. Armed with specimen copies of the scriptures that were bedecked with three or four binding styles and that dazzled prospective buyers with vibrant chromolithographs and ornamental presentation plates, the agents' impossible task was to mediate a timeless truth with the discriminating taste of middle-class Americans. Seldom are historians invited into this exchange. What was the course of conversation, for instance, that persuaded Andrew Roberts and Mrs. John Muzgy of Saranac, New York, to order the *New Devotional and Practical Pictorial Family Bible* in American Morocco, or W. W. Knight, E. J. Onusbee, and F. E. Prickeauau to buy it in the finer grade of Turkey? How did agents pitch the merits of each feature? How did the domestic context influence the conversation? Were selections determined by the depth of one's pocketbook alone, or were other considerations of equal or greater influence? A number of publishers in the latter decades of the nineteenth century included photograph albums in their canvassing Bibles, including P. W. Ziegler, the Hubbard Brothers, Bradley, Garreston & Co., W. A. Burnham, and Ziegler & McCurdy, in territories that stretched from Philadelphia to Houston to San Francisco. Most of these agents left the album pages blank, perhaps inviting their clients to fill them with their mind's eye. At least one agent, however, decided not to leave such matters to the imagination alone. With no other identifying information in the volume, this enterprising salesman placed nine cartes de visite and one gem tintype portrait in the specimen "family portraits" pages (fig. 8). The canvassing book lacks subscription information in the designated pages and other markers of interaction with subscribers, making it difficult to discern whether including images generated more sales. Even still, the inclusion of portraits in the canvassing book corresponds with uses of studio photography in family Bible galleries. Moreover, that both Protestant and Catholic Bible publishers came to offer photograph galleries in their products, and that these "new and appropriate" options were sold in a variety of commercial venues, suggests that Bible portrait albums were a wider cultural phenomenon than has been previously noted by historians of religion or photography.[57]

Although it has been thought to be a mostly Protestant trend, both Catholic and Protestant publishers both included portrait galleries in their Bibles.[58] John Kelly and John E. Potter of Philadelphia and D. and J. Sadlier of New York, for instance, produced a number of Douay and Rheims editions that designated spaces for family photographs.[59] John and Mary Droney of Brooklyn owned an 1884 Douay and Rheims translation, complete with Haydock's "Notes and References" published by the Lovell Manufacturing Company of Erie, Pennsylvania, and copyrighted by the National Publishing Company. In addition to the section for "Family Portraits," the Bible also included selections from Gustave Doré's *Gallery of Scripture Illustrations*, graphic content that was frequently included in Protestant translations as well.[60] While Catholic and Protestant publishers may have ap-

When I Awake with Thy Likeness

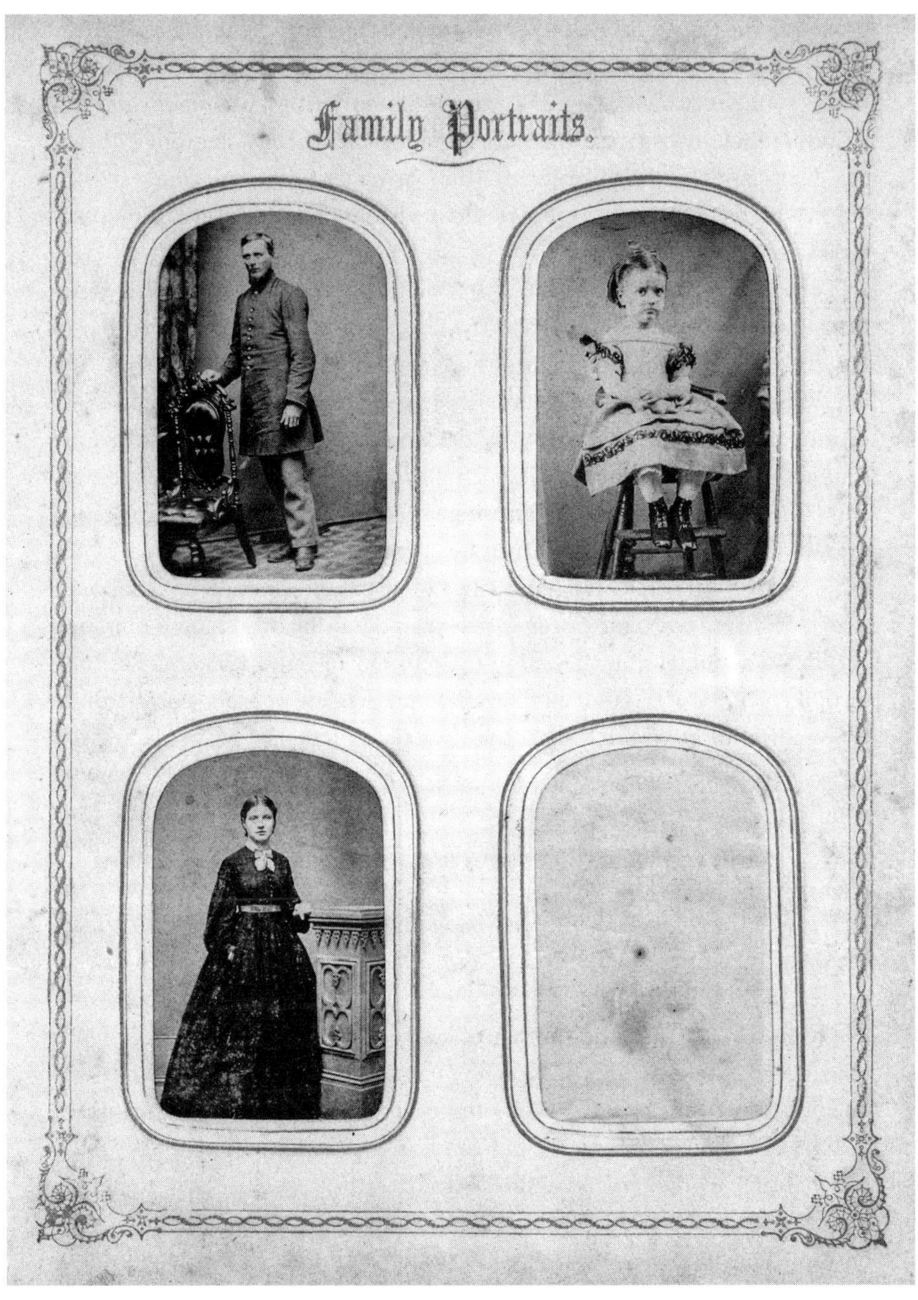

Figure 8. "Family Portraits" page from canvassing Bible. Michael Zinman Collection of Canvassing Books, University of Pennsylvania Rare Book and Manuscript Library Collections. Used with permission.

proached the conventions of portraiture to different effects within family Bibles as a whole—for instance, Catholic publishers included lithographic portrait studies of divine figures and ecclesial authorities, whereas Protestant editions stuck to visualizations of archaeological artifacts, paintings, "biblical" landscapes, and stylized text—the particular usages of family photograph albums nevertheless seem not to have differed significantly along sectarian axes.[61]

The Droneys' Bible, in fact, better demonstrates shared archival practices than theological differences. The enormous Bible was copyrighted in 1884 but bears no records before the Droneys' marriage in July 1892. The family portraits included apertures for two cabinet photographs and eight card photographs. The photographs that were preserved in the Bible include tintypes and paper prints, studio portraits and snapshots, men and women, and photographs of both individuals and groups of two or more. The range of photographic methods demonstrates the passing of time, but that is not the only story they tell. The abundance of visual information is juxtaposed with a dearth of written records. Other than the brilliantly colored marriage certificate documenting the union of John Droney and Mary McKee, the birth records for Mary and her daughter, and the date of Mary's death, there is no indication of whom the photographs picture. In fact, Mary died within three years of their marriage, leaving her husband a twenty-seven-year-old widower with a nearly two-year-old daughter. In June 1900, John and his daughter, who was also named Mary and was now six, were boarding with his in-laws, who had immigrated decades earlier. By 1910 John had married Annie, and the three of them were living on their own in Brooklyn. Despite the presence of photographs taken after Mary's death in 1895, the dates recorded in the Bible are those of her birth, marriage, childbirth, and death. While on the one hand the absence of later written records—such as John's marriage to Annie—might suggest an integrity of descent that the Bible was deemed to preserve, the inclusion of photographs indicates that the images did not merely confirm what had been transcribed in the pages of records but that they worked to create their own narratives. In this case, the photographs charted a visual family history that disregarded the temporal bookends of the written registers. It was a narrative, in short, that defied the finality of death by refusing to subordinate a "living hagiology" to the dictates of recorded time.

Family Bibles were used not only to document but also to construct the family through visual and material narratives. Turn, for a moment, to the Bible belonging to the family of Enoch Look Hemenway and Clara Davis.

                                   When I Awake with Thy Likeness

As war engulfed the nation, Enoch and Clara were married in Framingham, Massachusetts, on April 22, 1863. Less than four years later, Clara had given birth to two sons, Seth Carleton and Harry Windsor. If they had any more children during the next decade, these births were not recorded. In September 1876, more than eleven years after Harry was born, Clara gave birth to her only surviving daughter, Bertha, around which time the Hemenways purchased the "Latest Illustrated Family Bible." Published by Henry S. Goodspeed & Co. of New York and Cincinnati in 1877, and stamped with the Holman device (or, in later parlance, "logo") of 1874, the Hemenways' Bible included "nearly two-thousand illustrative engravings on steel, wood, and in colors"—ten times the number of illustrations in the Nashes' Bible less than a decade earlier. In Family Portraits at the end of the binding, six photographs of Clara, Seth, Harry, and Bertha remain.[62]

In addition to the album photographs, however, other material points to how the Bible was used as an archive of familial descent, that is, a narrative device, not unlike photograph albums, that shaped the ways in which the family's lineage would be remembered by triangulating the relationship between the moment of encounter, the imagined past, and the projected memory. What this Bible demonstrates most clearly are the racialized implications at work in these materialized memories. Alongside other material stuffed inside the front cover, including a landscape photograph of Chester, Massachusetts, with ballpoint markings identifying two ancestral residences, for instance, was a membership certificate certifying Bertha's inclusion in the "Detroit Colony" of the National Society of New England Women and a two-page "Ancestral Chart for Six Generations," recording the lineage of Bertha and her daughter, Doris. Conferred by "virtue of her New England Ancestry," for an "active" membership Bertha would have been pressed to demonstrate to the colony—one of thirteen such bodies in the nation, "prophetic of great results to follow in building up a staunch and imperishable fraternity"—either her own New England nativity or that of her husband or parents.[63]

Although Bertha's membership was not conferred until 1928, the National Society of New England Women had been established in 1895 "when citizens from foreign countries are becoming nationalized in such large numbers," E. Marguerite Lindley explained, that "we of the old New England stock need to band together in a common fraternity . . . in order to preserve those grand old days of which we are so justly proud."[64] With the stated purpose "to perpetuate the memory of our glorious ancestry," the Society of New England Women shared with other hereditary societies formed in the late nineteenth century an interest in genealogical pursuits aimed at securing America's racial "stock" through a careful inventory of ancestral characteristics.[65] In an essay titled "The Value of Genealogy" published in the same volume as Lindley's essay on the Society of New England Women, G. W. Dial identified a "moral value seldom recognized" in genealogical research that was ciphered through the racialized discourse of "miscegenation." Dial argued that "dominating characteristics, noble and generous as well as groveling, may be transmitted not only to immediate offspring but to later generations." He went on to demonstrate his case with the occasional "arrival, in a white family, of a baby with wooly hair, thick lips, and a flat nose" that "reveals a carefully concealed case of miscegenation." "It is then too late," Dial laments, "to regret that the family tree was not traced previous to marriage." By coding race as "morality" in a way that situates visual cues as imperfect signifiers of racial "belonging," Dial's essay underscores the often covert conceptual calculus at work in genealogical projects whose explicit vocabulary of "ancestry" or "descent" or even "family records" freighted racialized ideologies through the "glowing eye" of filial interest. Photographs, and photograph albums especially, were no less a part of this genealogical project than transcribed records, even if, as Dial warned his readers, visual cues alone were not always transparent. As collective archives of family records, photographs, and realia, family Bibles, such as that inherited by Bertha Hemenway, wove the racially charged practice of constructing family lineage into the biblical pageantry of redemption.[66]

Morphological similarities between family Bibles and photograph albums supported their association, with a little nudge from advertisements, in nineteenth-century viewing habits and narrative sensibilities. A number of booksellers in the 1860s and 1870s, for instance, linked Bibles and albums through their placement in advertising, including H. H. Moore of San Francisco, who, in 1870, listed in succession the stock of "Bibles and Prayer Books, in ornamental binding; Photographic Albums, with patent flexible backs, of all sizes, and of the most elegant styles" available at his newly opened store off of Merchant Street.[67] At the end of the specimen book for James P. Boyd's *Wonders of the Heavens, Earth, and Oceans,* copyrighted in 1887, were facing ads for albums, "of matchless elegance and superlative excellence," and Bibles that included "a Family Album holding 2 Cabinet and 8 Card Photographs."[68] Either through circumstances of mercantile display or marketing strategy—and probably some of both—albums and Bibles were commonly juxtaposed in contemporary classifieds and advertisements. Some firms, however, made the association explicit. The earliest evidence of such delib-

    When I Awake with Thy Likeness

erate association comes from none other than D. Appleton & Company of New York, long presumed to be the first American agency to merchandise photograph albums. Advertising its "complete and extensive assortment, including several new styles" of albums "for the Carte de Visite" in December 1861, Appleton noted that the newly popularized albums presented "at once a mild form of hero-worship and an illustrated book of genealogy" and speculated that "it does duty for a living hagiology, and it will supersede the first leaf of the family Bible."[69] Portrait albums did not, in fact, replace the "first leaf of the family Bible," and whereas Bible albums eventually fell out of vogue after the turn of the century, not incidentally once commercially available hand cameras introduced a new era of "albumania," one could still find pages to record life events well into the twentieth century. And yet, while Appleton's predictions closely resemble later historians' supersessionist accounts of the album's triumph over family registries, they nevertheless poignantly convey important sensibilities gaining currency in the second half of the nineteenth century: the camera was the new pen and provided a "living hagiology"—wherein likenesses were animated surrogates rather than chemical traces—in place of lifeless scribbles.[70]

A dearth of textual information in photograph albums, despite printed "index" pages in many early specimens, supports the idea that sun pictures were slowly replacing written records as the authoritative mode of genealogical preservation. Rather than eclipsing the role of the family Bible, however, photograph albums shared with Bibles the charge of resurrecting the past through inherited fragments. Throughout the nineteenth century, Bibles were important commonplace archives, designated spaces for reflection and remembrance, of which often only traces remain in the fragmented records—a date of birth, a lock of hair, a photograph. From these fragments, both albums and Bibles were charged with constructing doubtless narratives of ancestry that would instruct the present—through the beholder—and shape the future. Not merely a fiction of advertising or historical imagination, the tactility, indeed the obviousness, of the association was evident in the morphology of the two articles. The Done family photograph album from around 1860, for instance, is a leather-bound, gilt-edged volume that was once secured by a metal clasp. The portraits are placed in apertures that are nearly identical to those in family Bibles, although the leaves in the Done family album contain only one portrait per side. An album published by F. Heppenheimer in New York later in the decade also resembles a Bible, with its embossed leather cover and brass clasps, though the spine is this time marked "Album." Following current trends, this album of twenty-five leaves, with four openings per page, includes the likenesses of many famous figures — Lincoln, Henry Ward Beecher, Ulysses S. Grant, Jefferson Davis, Henry Wadsworth Longfellow, among others — alongside those of friends and family. Invoking the premise of moral suasion in Mathew Brady's *Gallery of Illustrious Americans*, card portraits of famous figures were deemed to inspire beholders toward personal excellence. The self-reflexive gaze supposed to have been occasioned by likenesses of society's leaders, however, was instead conditioned by the archival context of the portrait album and was thus extended to photographs of more familiar figures.

Also in the pages of the Heppenheimer album are three fund-raising photographs of children posed on the Union standard, from which the "nett proceeds . . . will be devoted to the education of colored people in the department of the Gulf, now under the command of Maj. Gen. Banks" (fig. 9) The inclusion of these fund-raising card photographs demonstrates both the racialized sensibilities of photograph albums and the instructive capacity of familiar shadows, both of which played out in the context of family Bible galleries as well. Recently freed from enslavement by Union forces in New Orleans, the children in these card photographs — Charles Taylor, Rebecca Huger, and Rosina Downs — were on a tour of northern photographic studios coordinated by the American Missionary Association and the National Freedman's Relief Organization during the winter of 1863–64 to raise money for the fragile freedman's schools through abolitionist support. Kathleen Collins has argued that despite the tour's main purpose of raising funds for recently freed slaves' education, the promoters, including C. C. Leigh of the Freedman's Relief Organization, accommodated northern racial prejudices "by selecting for a Northern photographic tour children with white features."[71] In an 1864 letter published in *Harper's Weekly*, Leigh described Rebecca as an eleven-year-old who, "to all appearances . . . is perfectly white. Her complexion, hair, and features show not the slightest trace of negro blood," and Leigh concluded of eight-year old Charley that "three out of five boys in any school in New York are darker than he."[72] As Nicholas Mirzoeff has argued, "the selling point and scandal" of the series "was precisely the fact that all the children, by virtue of their status as former slaves, were African American. The very whiteness of the children's skin was the sign that they had no place in slavery." In short, the message to Union sympathizers buying these photographs and placing them in albums alongside likenesses of Beecher, Lincoln, and unnamed kinfolk and acquaintances was that "slavery was to be abolished . . . not only because it was violent and inherently immoral, but because the 'wrong' kind of people were being en-

                                    When I Awake with Thy Likeness

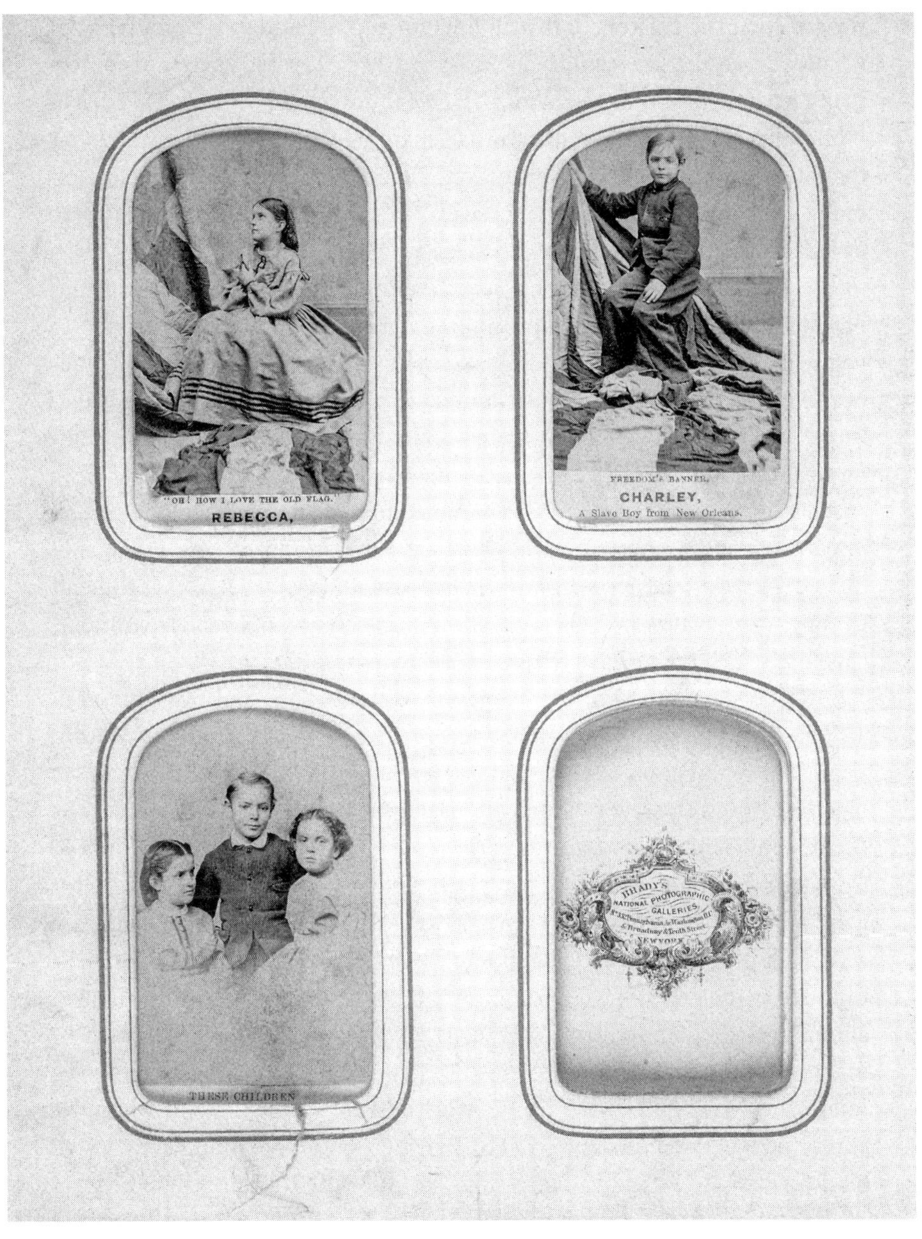

Figure 9. Fund-raising card photographs in Heppenheimer photograph album.
Graphic Arts Collection, Princeton University Library. Used with permission.

slaved." That the creators of this album chose to include the photographs of Charley and Rebecca—children who are marked as visibly white and contextually black—speaks to the album's tacit reinforcement of racialized sensibilities that prioritized "rampant miscegenation by the Southern planters" as the rallying moral infraction, even as it raised support for the emancipation of the minds and bodies of former slaves.[73] Had they been encountered three decades later, the photographs may also have reinforced G. W. Dial's insistence on thorough "genealogical searches" and his not-so-subtle suspicion of visual cues alone. Photograph albums were thus cultural sites primed to negotiate narratives of race and nation no less than those of individual families. Or rather, within the archival context of photograph albums, family pictures were inevitably wrapped up in narratives of race and nation. Furthermore, the common practice of positioning "society's leaders" alongside more familiar likenesses as well as those designed to animate the beholder's moral or patriotic sensibilities—both of which freighted racialized connotations—indeed, of binding them within the same visual narrative, makes it difficult to compartmentalize the portraits into "morally instructive" and "memorial" categories, as scholars have frequently asked us to do.[74]

The practice of collecting likenesses of the famous and the familiar in a single volume was sure to ruffle a few feathers, a fact that further demonstrates the ambiguities of visual habits. The same year that the *Saturday Evening Post* noted the recent publication of a family Bible that included "any convenient number of card cases" for photographic likenesses, a humorist for *Vanity Fair* published a scathing critique on the recent surge of "photographalbumanie" among Americans, writing that "of all the forms of insanity . . . we know of none . . . more deplorable in its effects upon the social constitution than the prevailing mania for *carte-de-visite* likenesses and a gilt-edged album to stick them in." Evidently unaware of things afoot in Bible publishing, the author goes on to consider the effect of these new social nuisances upon "the serious man, the man of truly religious principle," for whom he conjectures "a shock administered by the photographic album that may well be described as extremely distressing." To illustrate the paroxysmal effects of the album upon those with heightened religious sensibilities, as well as the unmistakable similarities between Bibles and albums, he fancies a scenario in which his killjoy Calvinist "sees before him what he supposes to be a family Bible out for a holiday, and, reverently unclasping it, is shattered into epilepsy by beholding himself sandwiched between—well, suppose we say between the Esquimaux Woman and GEORGE FRANCIS TRAIN. What can be more dreadful than this?"[75]

			When I Awake with Thy Likeness

The horror of seeing oneself within the same visual narrative as an indigenous woman and a railroad magnate demonstrated through farce the haphazard racialized ordering that photograph albums could construct by combining the contents of a cabinet of curiosity, a commonplace book, and a family record in a single artifact. Each common enough within the home and one hardly hermetically sealed from the other, the author of "Photographalbumanie" seems to have exaggerated for dramatic appeal the difficulty of recognizing the place of each photograph within the visual ordering of race. But if he was tongue in cheek in this regard and wrong about religious Americans' responses to the introduction of photograph albums—or at least wrong in his representation of "the man of truly religious principle" as the paradigmatic opponent of their staggering popularity (indeed, he went so far as to introduce a sort of sectarian conflict by designating albums as the "new religion of the *carte-de-visite*")—he was nevertheless correct to note the morphological similarities between Bibles and albums as well as the interpretive fecundity of the archival context. In other words, while portrait albums and Bible galleries shared certain attributes—leather binding, metal clasps, album leaves, photographic media, conventions of portraiture, ideologies of representation—the archival context of the family Bible differed from that of the family album in important ways. Bible portrait galleries, to put it bluntly, were not just albums inside Bibles. One important variation is that, from the beginning, the only likenesses preserved and displayed in family Bibles were those of the family, thus avoiding the "extremely distressing" scenario imagined by the *Vanity Fair* columnist. Just as important, if obvious, Bible galleries were positioned *within* the family Bible—alongside its copious illustrations, essays, family records, temperance pledges, not to mention the scriptures themselves—and thus prompted different modes of interaction. If, for instance, Bibles and albums competed for the title of the family archive and drew upon common strategies in making such claims, the genealogies that they recorded did not always map onto the same narrative aims. Recognizing the distinction does not, of course, require us to dismiss the morphological and narrative similarities between the two contexts as peripheral. Rather, it reinforces the need to situate counterarchives within their historical contexts if we are to get any closer to understanding not only how photography was absorbed into religious practices or artifacts but also how it shaped the contour and direction of American religion.

That photography was considered at least a complement to conventional familial records is evinced by new photographic methods of recording family lineages, such as the lithographic "Family Photograph Tree" published by Currier & Ives in 1871 (fig. 10). Set against a bucolic vista of a wooded village, the foreground tree features two open vignettes at the roots and twelve additional spaces in the branches — hardly a scientific chart of descent, but one highly suggestive of the narrative inventiveness of family histories. A meetinghouse in the distant background could perhaps lend credence to interpretations that privilege the displacement of religious authority in the face of scientific advances, but it is equally likely that the lithograph, which also included a schoolhouse and a farm, was making a visual claim to the institutions that nurtured a verdant lineage: church, school, and home. In any case, what is remarkable about the lithograph within the history of photographic Bible albums is that it marks one way in which a vernacular artifact designed to display the likenesses of one's own flesh became the basis for constructing a "living hagiology" that, by definition, interwove biological descent with grander narratives of race, nation, and (sacred) progress.

In her account of the growing popularity of "baby's picture" at the end of the nineteenth century, Shawn Michelle Smith has argued that, from the earliest daguerrean period, photographs were mechanisms "of preserving family history and of documenting family genealogy." Photographic likenesses, in other words, registered both retrospective and prospective modes of beholding — they were made to record the present for persons in the future to enter the past, however obliquely their admittance. For Smith, this mirrored process of memory had especially racialized implications. The "early function of the photograph as heirloom," she writes, "connects the photograph, through inheritance, both materially to the circulation of goods and the preservation of likenesses, and ideologically to the continuation of the family blood line." As the century progressed, she argues, the portrait that "was first circulated *as* a family heirloom . . . was later exchanged as a document that *recorded* an ancestral heirloom," namely, "inherited character."[76]

Smith locates such a shift in the growing popularity of Francis Galton's definition of "heredity," which provided a foundation for the racial theory of eugenics that shaped public discourse — including hereditary societies' interest in genealogy — in the United States for the first several decades of the twentieth century, affecting legal actions and legislation no less than popular sentiment. Smith argues that while Galton published his study *Hereditary Genius* in 1869, it was not until the volume was reprinted in the 1890s that "eugenics" — a term that he first defined in 1883 as "a brief word to express the science of improving stock" — became a dominant racial discourse in the United States.[77] His notion of heredity, however, resonated with theories circulating earlier in the century, particularly among portrait photographers.

	When I Awake with Thy Likeness

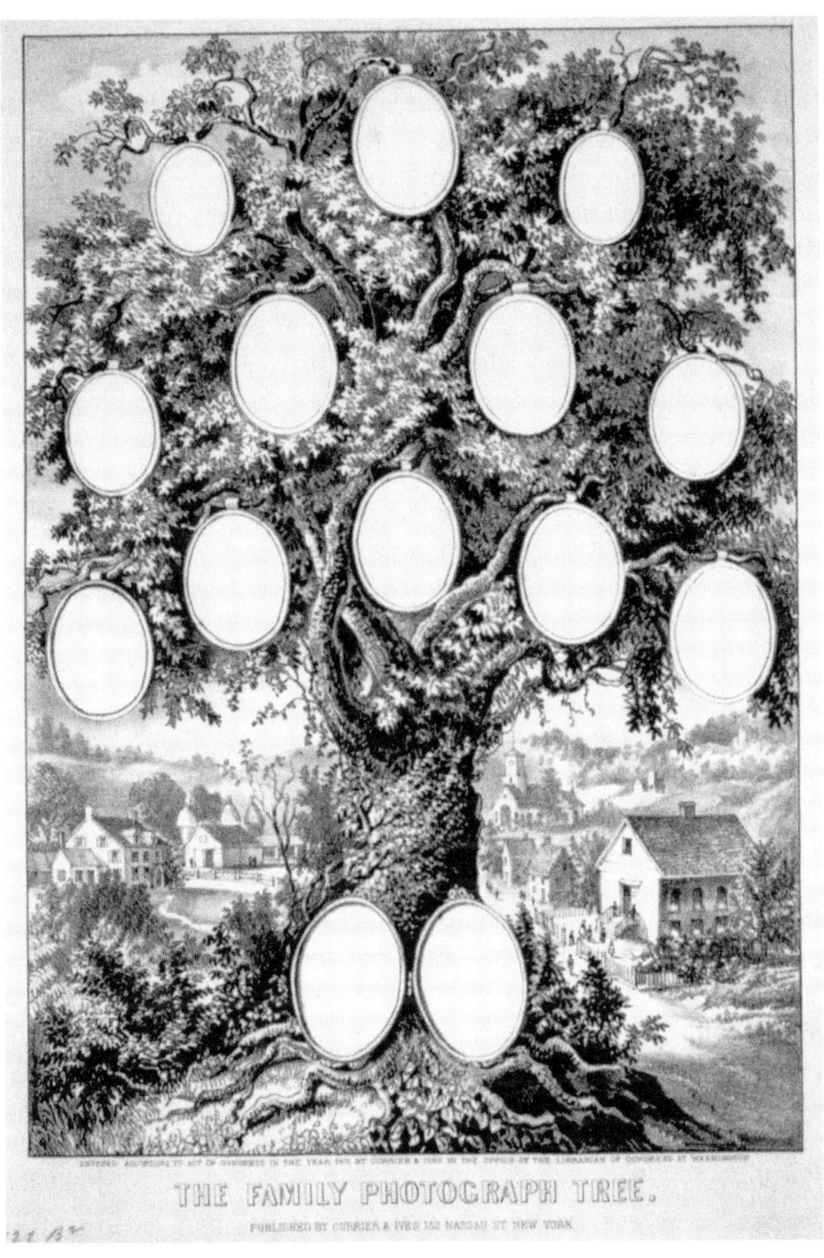

Figure 10. "The Family Photograph Tree," Currier & Ives, 1871. Library of Congress, Prints and Photographs Division.

Noticing during the course of his ethnological researches "into the mental peculiarities of different races" that certain "characteristics cling to families," Galton determined to investigate "the kindred of about four hundred illustrious men of all periods of history . . . to establish the theory that genius was hereditary." This objective did not prevent him, however, at the conclusion of his study, from writing on the "comparative worth of different races," using the data gleaned from his statistical inquiries as a rubric for comparison. Even if his work was not widely known in the United States for several decades after its initial publication, his association of mental faculties with *individual* lineages that could then be extrapolated onto races and nations—differentiated on a basis of corporeal difference guised as geographic or national variance—mirrors contemporary photographic discourses of likeness. "In fact," wrote the Philadelphia photographer Marcus Aurelius Root in 1864, "the keen-eyed physiognomist may find in every nation a cast of countenance peculiar to itself; and, still further, may discover in particular districts and even families faces or single features distinctively marking them."[78]

If photographic portraits were early measures of both national and racial identity, these were ciphered not in isolated portraits but through economies of exchange and the compilation of visual narratives inseparable from religion. Galton's *Life History Album*, first published in 1883, was "designed to contain the Chart of your Life, and to be a record of your own Biological experience," not only for one's own amusement or benefit but also because such a document "will further be of great value to your family and descendants." In addition to a genealogical record, descriptions of an infant at birth, medical history, and anthropometric observations at regular intervals, among other intended data, there were "two pages . . . left in the portion of the album devoted to each successive five years to receive photographs of the owner that have been taken during the period."[79] What is striking about Galton's album is how closely it resembled practices that had been at work in Bible galleries for nearly two decades. Although not systematically executed in the way that Galton advised—he went so far as to provide specific dimensional instructions regarding reductions "of the original face" and the distances between the pupils of the eyes—family Bible portrait albums frequently included multiple photographs of its members at various stages in life. In the Nash Bible, for instance, one page features two card portraits of a middle-aged woman and man positioned over two tintypes of what appear to be younger versions of the same couple, most likely James and Mary Nash (fig. 11). Similarly, the Hemenway Bible includes several photographs

When I Awake with Thy Likeness

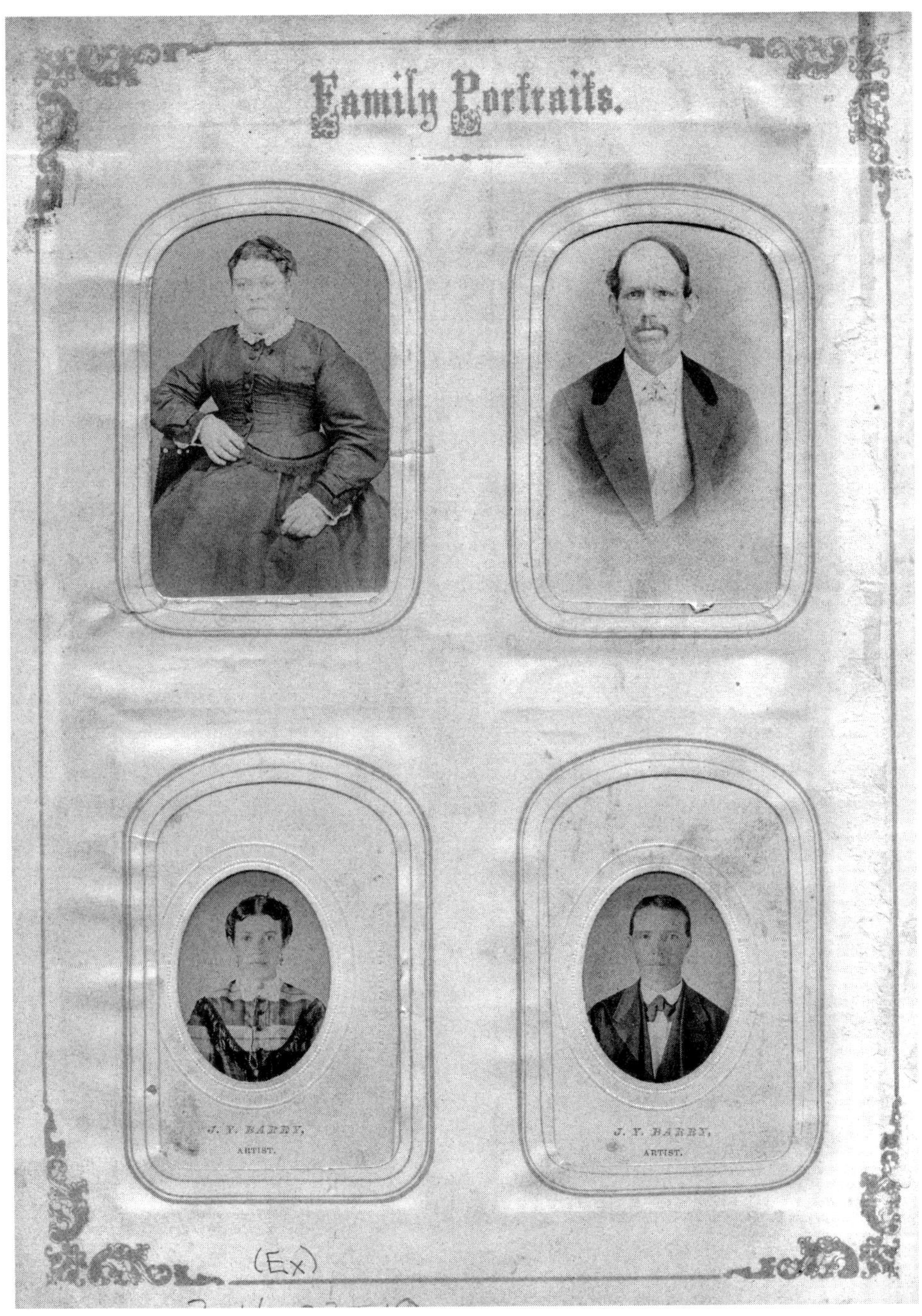

Figure 11. "Family Portraits," Nash Family Bible. Princeton University Library. Used with permission.

of Bertha from infancy through girlhood, effectively collapsing Galton's "record of . . . Biological experience" into a biblical frame.

Contemporary discourses of likeness, theories of descent, and practices of genealogy point to ways in which we can imagine the interpretive context of family Bible photograph albums. We can also look to the pages themselves for an indication of how they were understood within the context of the Bible. Oftentimes the only script on these elaborately engraved pages was "Family Portraits" or "Family Portrait Gallery," although occasionally these leaves would have more extended textual material. The National Comprehensive Family Bible, an Authorized translation published in Manchester, England, in 1870, and also circulated in the United States, for instance, included the phrase "Thine own friend and father's friend forsake not" between the open frames at the top of each page of the "Family Portrait Gallery" and the phrase "Behold how good and how pleasant it is for brethren to dwell together in unity" between the two open frames at the bottom of each page. The inscriptions were positioned on open scrolls, seemingly fastened to the page with stylized tacks. Their placement on engravings of parchment works to order the visual plane into photographic and scriptural demarcations, as both phrases were direct quotations of scripture—the first from Proverbs 27, the second from Psalm 133.[80] Because this is one of the only instances of scripture having been explicitly associated with the album section, it provides some indication of how publishers worked to regulate the relationship between photographic portraiture and biblical verse, on the one hand, and fleshly and sacred lineage, on the other. Such verses are positioned as interpretive prompts for the inclusion of portraits—do not forget these people, Proverbs commands, while the Psalm sets up the page as a gallery of "brethren . . . dwell[ing] together in unity," a model for subsequent beholders to esteem and to emulate. This ordering of interpretive authority, moreover, was replicated through the iconography of the engravings on the page. The portraits were to be placed within rectangular frames whose ornamentation mimicked daguerreotype casings of an earlier era, whereas the scriptural references were seemingly inscribed on parchment, and yet the frame surrounding the entire page indicated that the photographs and the verses were to be considered in relation to one another.

During the 1880s, John Potter & Co. of Philadelphia, which produced a number of Douay-Rheims editions throughout the decade, placed a medallion in the upper-left corner of its "Family Portraits" section, with the phrase "The LORD THINE EVERLASTING LIGHT" encircling an opened flower. Taken from the Prophecy of Isaias, the phrase portends a coming glory for

        When I Awake with Thy Likeness

those whose likenesses are therein revealed: "Thy sun shall go down no more, and thy moon shall not decrease: for the Lord shall be unto thee for an everlasting light, and the days of thy mourning shall be ended."[81] In this gallery, at least, the portraits were intended to be memorials to the deceased. This form of photographic memorialization was repeated in other contexts as well, including Jane Stebbins's popular consolation book, *Our Departed Friends*, first published in 1867. Examined more closely in the following chapter, like family Bibles, subscribers of *Our Departed Friends* had the option of including photograph leaves at the end of the binding. Like the Potter Bible, moreover, these leaves were captioned with scriptural excerpts intended to guide the beholders' interaction with the portraits. The National Comprehensive Bible and the Potter Bible are exceptional for their explicit association and ordering of biblical text and photographic likeness, and yet they only state clearly what other Bible portrait albums suggest more obliquely. Bible portrait galleries were spaces where individual likenesses became touchstones for ancestral legacies, which were in turn woven into narratives of biblical lineage that disrupted the constraints of time and positioned every soul within that "monstrous album" of celestial design fancied by the inquisitive young Tom in the pages of *The Little Gleaner*. Conditioned by emerging photographic technology and visual habits informed by racialized theories of representation, Bible galleries at once reflected the construction and influence of photograph albums and at the same time set their focal point on a yonder horizon. That likenesses were more impervious to the ravages of time than their fleshly referents seems an obvious enough point, but it was one that spurred much interest in the latter decades of the nineteenth century. Over the course of the century, photographic operations were frequently understood as memories etched in glass or silver, translated onto paper, and available to the senses no less than to the mind. Whether this memory work necessarily translated into theological work is tricky to determine, and yet it seems especially significant that the Bible's arc of history, linking a hopeful past to a redemptive promise, was so clearly mirrored in the likenesses of the saints.

HERE IS MY NAME
WHEN I AM DEAD

In the autumn of 1862, Molly Stilwell waited anxiously for news—any news—from her husband. Twenty-two-year-old William had enlisted in the 53rd Georgia Infantry in May, and as news rolled in of the carnage that had taken place near Antietam Creek in mid-September, Molly's thoughts drifted to darker and darker prospects for herself and two-year-old John Thomas, whom William playfully called Tommy. Would she ever know his fate? What would become of the farm? No doubt she knew of women who had received the dreaded news secondhand, who would never see their soldier's mortal remains, would never know for sure how he died: Was he brave? Was he frightened? Was his soul assured? Finally, her letter arrived. "Great God, what awful things I have to chronicle this morning!" William wrote. For two days, while he stood guard at the field headquarters of Confederate brigadier general Paul Jones Semmes in Harper's Ferry, Virginia, his brigade "fought and fought like men" in one of the bloodiest battles of the American Civil War. "Molly, I have not heard who was killed and wounded in my company," he wrote from the troubled uncertainty of the front, "though I learn that the regiment was almost cut to pieces. . . . I have no doubt but some of my friends is lying cold on the ground now." The blood-stained ground at Antietam Creek would prompt many Americans to consider the toll of the war as well as what such carnage ought to purchase—preservation of the Union was no longer singularly motive enough. But before the great battle would become politically sanguine, it prompted innumerable personal confrontations with death, both for soldiers surveying the field of battle and for their beloved confined to the lonely corners of their imaginations.[1]

In William's letter to his wife, mortality is the dominant motif. Although his experiences of battle were certainly not representative of all soldiers engaged in the war, the intimacy of his letter does gesture to the frightening realities that soldiers on both sides endured as well as to the theological work that their situations prompted. It also points to ways soldiers devised to bridge the caress of affection across time and space through material artifacts. William knew that there were few assurances of his prospects — "I don't know now that I will ever get to send this [letter] off, but will have it ready" — but rather than wallowing in terror, he understood what the theological circumstances of his condition required, even amid the unforgiving haste of war. "I know that you are uneasy about me," he consoled Molly, "but you know that it will do no good to grieve. It is best to be cheerful as you can, for we ought to be willing to say the will of God be done. If it is His will that your best friend should die away from home, let us submit to it." Despite discouraging Molly from grieving over his corpse and reminding her of the inscrutability of the "will of God," William nevertheless confessed to his wife what he hoped for should he, like the ranks falling around him, die in battle. "I think of you while the cannon roar and the muskets flash," he scribbled in his stolen moments of solitude. "Never have I been so much excited yet but what I could compose myself enough to think of you, and I have often thought that if I have to die on the battlefield, if some friend would just lay my Bible under my head and your likeness on my breast with the golden curls of hair in it, that it would be enough. Molly, I shall have to close, for my eyes is bathed in tears, 'till I can't write."[2]

William's letter to Molly — would it be his last? — demonstrates ambivalence about the relationship between tokens of remembrance and a culture of mourning largely defined by theologics of redemption. Stilwell's struggle to "submit" to God's will, though it cost him his life, and also to comfort Molly's grief echo motifs from consolation literature earlier in the century that positioned mourning as a matter of not only social decorum or even personal sorrow but also religious discipline. The Civil War changed the ways that nineteenth-century Americans experienced death, corpses, and mourning. But the developments that war accelerated were rooted in traditions of mourning, including representations of the deceased, that preceded the cannon fire on Fort Sumter. The ostensibly public experiences of war, moreover, were frequently undermined by moments of intimacy facilitated through material artifacts tucked into uniforms — letters, lockets, likenesses — or stowed alongside necessary provisions. William's letter, in short, invokes a shifting memorial culture that was rooted in historical modes of representation and theologies of redemption even as present circumstances — war, in particular, but also recent developments in photography and social practice that the war would accelerate—prompted a revision of their application to experiences of grief, mourning, and remembrance.

As material artifacts, photographs were related to an archive of mourning whose theological moorings had been debated for centuries. Rings, tombstones, portraits, printed sermons, and consolation books had long been exchanged and commissioned as memento mori: objects intended to remind the living of their mortality and their own quick succession to the grave. The danger that ministers and other consolationists feared was that these articles, which were designed to encourage introspection among the bereaved, were in fact nurturing injurious allegiances to mortal conditions. Grief was, of course, to be expected of the bereaved. British consolationist Richard Cecil, whose *Friendly Visit to the House of Mourning* was reprinted in the United States through the 1840s, acknowledged in 1793 that "our heavenly Father, who *knows our frame, and remembers that we are but dust* allows us to mourn when he afflicts us; he often, in his providence, calls us to it, and charges us to *weep with them that weep*." Indeed, "there is something sacred in grief," he wrote, when it draws mourners into awareness of the "unerring Providence [that] presided over the whole, yea, actually *conducted* every part on reasons as right as inscrutable." And yet there were dire consequences for failing to submit to this unerring Providence, even in the midst of personal anguish, even, as William no doubt understood, in war: "All allowed repugnance to the determinations of his [God's] government, (however made known to us) is *sin*."[3]

Even though there is no way of knowing whether or not William had read Cecil's treatise, his seemingly impossible instruction to Molly not to grieve—"it is best to be as cheerful as you can"—betrayed a long-rooted gendering of grief in which material objects nurtured effeminized grief to a point of soul-damning doubt. Cecil's models of properly submissive mourning were the biblical patriarchs Aaron, Eli, David, and Job, and his vocabulary evinces a gendered understanding of unregulated, indeed sinful, grief: "There is such a thing as nursing and cherishing our grief; employing a 'busy meddling memory to muster up past endearments,' and personate a vast variety of tender and heart rending circumstances."[4] Fathers, husbands, and brothers grieved as well, but their sorrow, when "nursed," "cherished," or "meddlesome," signaled a decidedly effeminate lack of discipline. As late as 1855, in fact, no less a cultural authority than Horace Greeley summarized gendered dimensions of unholy grief familiar to his contemporaries when he declared that "it often seems to me that the bitterness of our anguish by the

   Here Is My Name When I Am Dead

death-bed and the open tomb, is exaggerated and un-Christian" and admonished his readers to "stop this unmanly howling, evince some fitting trust in God, and exhibit a deportment becoming our faith."[5] But whereas William encouraged his wife to receive unerring Providence with due humility, his own deathbed reverie indicates a more tormented relationship with material tokens of transcendence than declarative theologies could possibly encompass. What this chapter offers, then, is an account of the ways in which material objects, especially photographs, became contested sites of religious discipline in the throes of grief. On the one hand, as memento mori, photographs were objects that prompted meditation on the "divine life" through the cipher of the past—"death at hand . . . should be death in view, and lead us to consider next / our PROSPECTS from this House of Sorrow, as inhabitants of a present and future world"—and, on the other, shackles that bound the bereaved to recurrent bouts of sinful woe. "There is a tearing open the wound afresh by images and remembrances," Cecil warned, "and thereby multiplying those pangs which constitute the very [b]itterness of death itself." The consequence of submitting oneself to such "voluntary torture" was dire, for it "unfits the mourner for the pressing duties of his station, [and] leads to that *sorrow of the world which worketh death* to his body, soul, and Christian character."[6] By the middle of the nineteenth century, photography was as wrapped up in this internal struggle over the theological utility of material artifacts of mourning as were printed sermons, mortuary portraits, painted miniatures, gift books, hairwork, and innumerable other tokens treasured by the bereaved. But whereas these previous articles had been used to invoke recollections of the now-absent body, photographs became increasingly identified with the body of the deceased itself. Whether or not Stilwell was familiar with Cecil's text, which was printed as late as 1848 by the American Tract Society, we can almost see his face twisted in deep contemplation, struggling to reconcile his own desire for one more touch, one more look, with God's inscrutable demand for resignation to his will.

At the heart of this story is the ascendancy of the photographic portrait as both the preferred iconography of mourning in nineteenth-century America and as a relic of the departed that disclosed future glory to the bereaved. If sermons, consolation literature, and commemorative verse worked to subordinate or even malign material archives of remembrance in favor of the perfect will and righteousness of God's inscrutable timing, these same sentiments were often facilitated through material artifacts. Consolation literature, for instance, was frequently structured around material references, from John Flavel's *A Token for Mourners* (1674) and John Dunton's

The Mourning Ring (1692) in the seventeenth century to nineteenth-century volumes bearing such titles as *The Cypress Wreath* (1844), *Agnes and the Key of Her Little Coffin* (1857), and *The Empty Crib* (1868). By reproducing engravings of the deceased, these latter volumes and others silently testified to the portrait photograph's increasing prominence as memorial iconography even if they fail to comment directly on the particular circumstances of its ascendancy. What is more, even as photographs of the dead invited reflection on the temporal existence of those now absent, thereby encouraging conditions of protracted sorrow, postmortem and memorial photographs were nevertheless deliberately positioned to prompt meditation on the vanities of corporeality and assurances of immortality, frequently by attaching photographs to snippets of scripture and promises of future reunion. In short, at a time when prevailing sentiments nurtured filial affections amid high mortality rates, the tension between cultivating fondness for one's relations—most especially one's children—and, as one midcentury consolation book put it, "view[ing] the FATHER's dispensations with resignation" produced a culture of mourning that both lamented and celebrated death even as it cherished and scorned material tokens of remembrance.

At the center of this ambivalent memorial culture was the body of the deceased. The whole business of photographing likenesses was to one degree or another concerned with immortalizing human form, but nowhere was the association between substance and shadow more acute than in the vast archive of memorial photography. Postmortem portraits, pictures taken in life and repurposed for memorialization upon decease, and even spirit photographs each worked in different ways and to different effects to strengthen bonds between photographs and bodies of the deceased. As material tokens that not only represented but verily mediated the presence of the dead and dying, in other words, photographs were fraught with the potentially dangerous capacity of protracting devotion to the "emptie carcasse" as they began to displace conventional figurative representations of death. In short, as photography began to supplant previous iconographies of death and mourning, corporeal representation became increasingly theologically significant among communities of the bereaved.

For generations before the daguerreotype, previous modes of representation—most notably hairwork—had invoked the body of the deceased, and the moldering body had been a common trope in funeral sermons since the seventeenth century. But whereas photography in a large sense collaborated with these previous modes of representation, it also invited new forms of scrutiny, both corporeal and theological. For instance, around midcentury,

Here Is My Name When I Am Dead

"recognition" became a concern among Christians interested in heavenly reunion: Will we recognize relations and others in heaven? Will they appear the same as the faces in the daguerreotypes or as the strangely familiar likenesses in the family Bible? In some ways more fundamental than notions of photography's representational exactitude, however, was the widespread conviction that photographs mediated presence in spite of corporeal absence. It was surely this underlying belief that prompted William Stilwell's desire for his wife's likeness in the moment of his demise. Whereas hair had previously accompanied portraiture to authenticate the presence of the deceased, with photographic portraiture it came to signify the commemorative operation of the photograph itself. In other words, hairwork silently instructed beholders not only to see the photograph as a representation but also to identify in the likeness the very body of their beloved.

Over the course of the first two decades of photographic portraiture, bodies of the deceased were commonly represented in death, a practice that invoked a tradition of posthumous mortuary portraiture.[7] In this sense, postmortem photography was an attempt to preserve the literal face of death for spiritual reflection via physiognomic inspection, a practice common to generations before the introduction of the daguerreotype. "I closed her dying eyes, and we sat for a moment in solemn Silence," Deborah Logan wrote of her cousin, Hannah Griffitts, in 1817, "each, I believe, contemplating the joyful landing of her Soul upon the celestial Shore, a sweet evidence of her happiness resting with us."[8] Locating "sweet evidence" of the soul's triumph in the form now "resting with us," Logan points to a long-standing tradition of corporeal inspection that postmortem photography would invoke among later generations. Postmortem photographs were certainly complex cultural documents, hardly explained by any single motivation or precedent.[9] And yet, whatever else they were, photographs of dead people, whether taken posthumously or from life, were associated with practices of inspection that promised both the corruption of the flesh and the triumph of the soul.

Municipal authorities and a rising funeral industry increasingly regulated the conveyance and disposal of the dead between 1840 and the end of the century, and as a result postmortem photographs became less frequent before becoming rare in the twentieth century. Far more ubiquitous, however, were photographs taken in life and repurposed as tokens of remembrance after death. By the end of the daguerrean period and into the early years of albumen paper prints, photographic methods began to claim status not only as representation but also as identity itself. Catharine Christ of Berks County, Pennsylvania, summarized this sentiment well when she slipped a snatch of verse beneath her daguerreotype likeness in 1859, concluding with the statement, "Here is my name when I am dead."[10] Three years later, in October 1862, a correspondent for the *New York Times* fancied that pedestrians "would jostle less carelessly down the great thoroughfare, saunter less at their ease, were a few dripping bodies, fresh from the battlefield, laid along the pavement." While survivors of fallen soldiers were increasingly bringing bodies home for burial, when such a course was possible, this correspondent was not referring to embalmed corpses but to the recent installment of photographs at Brady's gallery. "If he has not brought bodies and laid them in our door-yards and along the streets, he has done something very like it" by exhibiting for the public "views of that fearful battlefield, taken immediately after the action." The photographs of slain Confederate soldiers taken by Alexander Gardner and exhibited in Brady's gallery may have been artfully arranged, as later scholarship has determined, but they still carried the weight of carnage for their pedestrian beholders.[11] If few Americans would have had the opportunity to view this series in Brady's gallery, many thousands more witnessed the carnage in three-dimensional relief through the circulation of Gardner's stereographs, such as one of crumpled Confederate bodies, bloated from exposure to the balmy September climate (fig. 12). Pairing crumpled Rebel bodies with a crumpled Union standard was no doubt Gardner's deliberate compositional maneuver, but whatever the ideological motive, like Christ's instructions to beholders of her likeness, the view's effectiveness was related to the assumption that the image was tied viscerally to the referent.

Of course, even if beholders were conditioned to perceive photographs as immediate references to the body, they were nevertheless mediated representations. The association that William Stilwell made between the Bible, photographic portraiture, and hair in his intimate reverie demonstrated how each of these artifacts could be used to mediate haptic experiences beyond corporeal measure. William survived the war. He suffered a foot injury in the battle of Cedar Creek, Virginia, in 1864, "which necessitated an amputation, leaving only the ankle and heel," according to a pension application filed later in the century, but was able at long last to return home to his wife and son.[12]

All too many were not so fortunate. In the weeks and months after Gettysburg, a "feeling of tender sympathy and interest" swept over northern citizens as efforts were made to identify "the unknown soldier who died in the field . . . clasping in his hand the picture of his three little children." By late November it was confirmed that the soldier was Amos Humiston of New York and that the treasured ambrotype had been sent to him by his

     Here Is My Name When I Am Dead

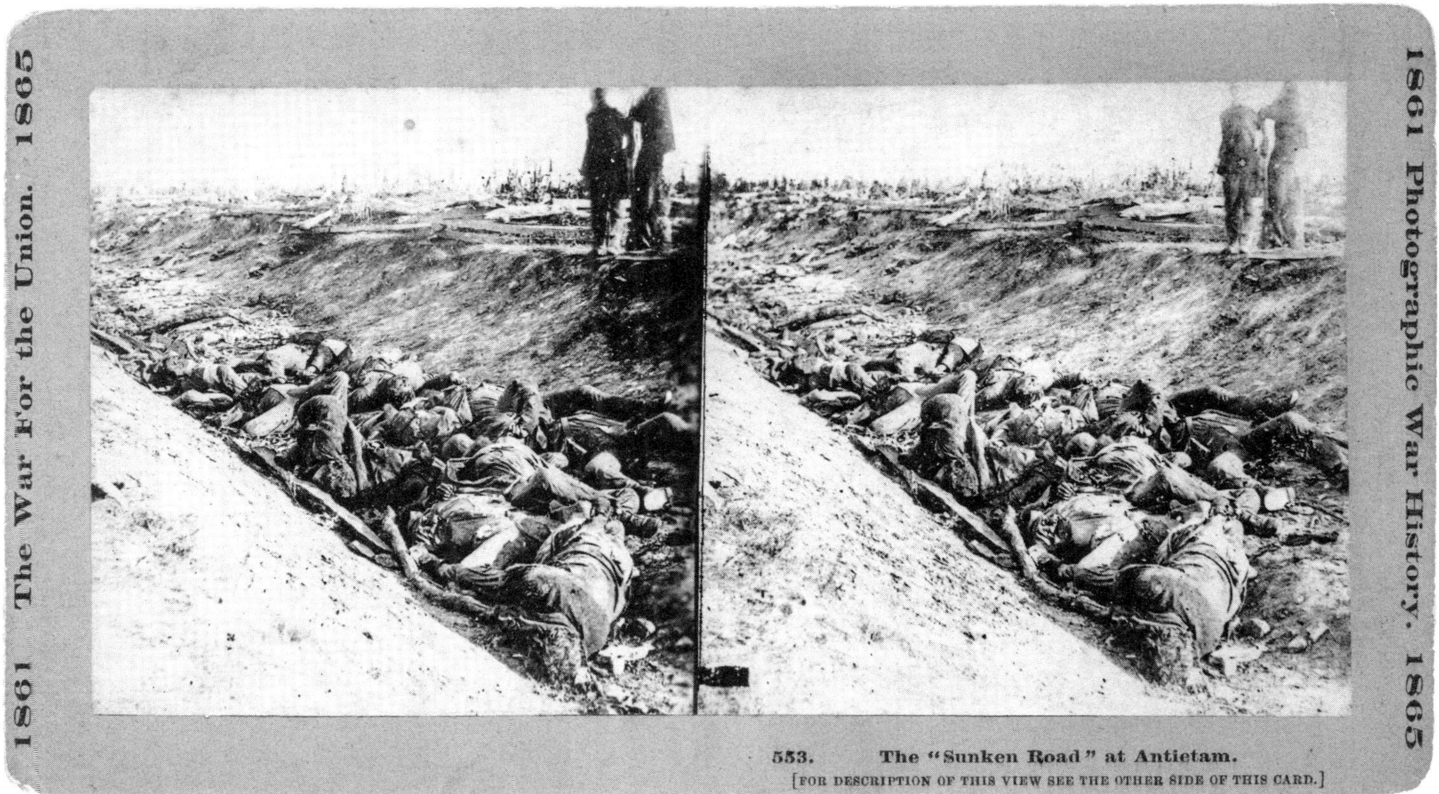

Figure 12. "The 'Sunken Road' at Antietam." Alexander Gardner, 1862. Stereograph, Taylor & Huntington, ca. 1885–89. DeGolyer Library, Southern Methodist University. Used with permission.

wife shortly after he enlisted in the Union army in July 1862.[13] The soldiers' desire to hold these likenesses in the moments of their own death mirrors, through the looking glass as it were, the more common use of photographs as tokens of reflective promise—a kind of future-oriented memory—among the living. If Molly could not be with William to cradle his broken body during his final earthly moments, then her likeness would suffice to ease his soul through the transformative power of imagined reciprocal touch as he fingered her golden curls—her likeness and her hair, in other words, mediated her presence in spite of her corporeal absence. More than any other media, in fact, as the century progressed, hair and photographs were used to evoke the moldering body in nineteenth-century memorial culture. But rather than signaling a morbid obsession with putrefaction and decay, they promised the triumph of immortality that awaited the souls of the faithful.

Nineteenth-century Americans who listened to funeral orations and perused any number of consolation books knew that material tokens— fragments of belongings, photographic or painterly representations, and even corporeal relics—could nurse morbid myopia of grander schemes, a shortsightedness unable to see through the present pale of sorrow to the tableaux of redemption. Worse, they could bind feeble or susceptible—in a word, effeminate—mourners to a perpetual or recurring state of melancholy that stunted the spiritual fortitude that such affliction, many believed, was intended to produce. But they were equally convinced that these same articles could procure healthful meditation on the human predicament and on assurances of corporeal frailty that led to submission to the providences of God and induced personal reforms necessary for favorable judgment at the moment of their own reckoning. Striding alongside the theological ambivalence of a material culture of mourning was the development of a photographic culture of remembrance that positioned the bodies of the deceased at the center of a new iconography of spiritual promise.

"A Story Too Deep for Tears"

The poem "Wilbraham Is in Mourning" evinces a material culture of mourning that was familiar to many Americans in the early decades of the nineteenth century. Printed between 1830 and 1840, the poem opens with a scene of mourning that enveloped the town of Wilbraham, Massachusetts, "girded in sackcloth, and the cries ascending," after the watery deaths of six young inhabitants. The verses move back to a moment of youthful bliss—"Just now, all active, little thinking danger"—and then rush forward to the unthinkable

   Here Is My Name When I Am Dead

turn of events — "Now hastening, judgment from the Great Eternal / Not to be altered." After pausing for a moment on the "mournful shores [where] the corps are lying" to "see tender mothers wipe the drowned faces," the author turns from verse elegiac to a prayer of resolve:

> Wisdom has mingled this our cup of trembling,
> May we not murmur, but in silence drink it;
> Parent of heaven, while we wade the billows,
> Hold us from sinking.
> Just are thy dealings, thy decrees eternal;
> May sinful mortals never question wisdom,
> Nor wish to turn a leaf of heaven's secrets,
> Waiting contented.

This turn from trembling grief to contented resignation echoed theological modulations of purposeful sorrow from generations past. Marking developing theological interest in celestial reunion, moreover, the final stanzas move readers through the funeral proceedings and interment of the six drowned youths in their "silent mansions . . . Borne up by bearers" to a lugubrious farewell limned with a mournful promise of future embrace:

> Farewell, our children, till the great Archangel
> Shakes the creation with the trump of heaven,
> Then hope to meet you joined with Saints and Angels;
> Hail the Redeemer.[14]

The verse itself points somewhat obliquely to the material culture of Christian mourning of the early nineteenth century. "Sackcloth" signaled the mourning garb draping persons, while elsewhere in the poem "tidings spreading clothed the streets in mourning" suggested the town itself was draped in heavy somber fabrics, most of which would still have been woven in the homes of the bereaved.[15] "From the desk a solemn warning given" refers to the pulpit from which the funeral oration was delivered and "silent mansions" to the "string of coffins" that preceded the "trail of mourners." But what is less apparent is how the poem itself was part of a memorial culture that was facilitated in large measure through material artifacts. And completely absent is any sense of the context of the actual event.

Indeed, the elegy did not refer to a recent event but to an accident that had transpired decades earlier. Gordon Bliss, his brother Leonard, their unnamed sister, "a daughter of Dr. Merrick," Catherine Warrener, and Guy Johnson drowned in a pond outside of Wilbraham in the late spring of 1799.

They were "visiting at a house near the Pond," the *Connecticut Courant* reported in May, when "ten set out, in haste," to a small boat. The "three young Gentleman and three young Ladies" who succeeded in securing passage were "but few rods from the shore, when a sudden gust of wind upset the boat," resulting in their deaths.[16] Thirty years later, their tragic demise was still used to negotiate theologies of mourning through the circulation of a commemorative poem. Rather than signaling a contradiction—Do we mourn, or do we submit to the inscrutable will of God?—the poem, like consolation books and memorial photographs, succeeded in demonstrating the theological complexities of a culture that was deeply committed both to soteriologies of redemption and to remembering the past, largely through material artifacts.

In the mid-nineteenth century, death was a far more regular feature of Americans' daily lives than it would be among later generations. Mortality rates, particularly of children, were staggering by modern comparison, and rituals of death and mourning transpired in private homes rather than in hospitals and businesses dedicated to the care of the deceased.[17] Harriet Beecher Stowe's vignette of little Eva's deathbed in *Uncle Tom's Cabin* was but a paradigm of countless other such scenes that transpired in American homes during the 1850s. In fact, Stowe's iconic scene, in which the prevailing temperament is confident resignation rather than anxious disquietude, may have been influenced by her father's recollection of his wife's reaction to the death of their infant daughter, also named Harriet, half a century earlier in March 1809. The babe, who was "seized . . . with the hooping-cough," died while her mother slept. Stowe's father, Lyman Beecher, later recalled that when his wife, Roxana, awoke to find that her month-old daughter had succumbed during her slumber, "there was no such thing as agitation. She was so resigned that she seemed almost happy. I never saw such resignation to God; it was her habitual and only frame of mind; and even when she suffered most deeply, she showed . . . an entire acquiescence in the Divine will."[18] And yet, using such authoritative reminisces as interpretive bellwethers is a tricky undertaking. Indeed, even if the frequency of death allowed a certain level of expectation and even if the trope of the "good death" in popular literature provided a model for Christian response, this proximity to death hardly soothed its bitter sting for many Americans. Kneel, for a moment, with the minister in the darkened bedchamber as he read "heavenly messages of consolation" to the recently bereaved as they "rocked and trembled under the tempest of their agony."[19] Stand with a father in the doorway of the empty nursery, tears coursing down his cheek as he examines the dead child's playthings. No matter the promise of celestial reunion, for many Protestants and

Here Is My Name When I Am Dead

Catholics throughout the nineteenth century, death was still a cross to bear, a burden of seemingly impossible magnitude that demanded spiritual resolve and, in the common idiom, manly fortitude.

Material artifacts straddled this seeming gulf between celestial promise and terrestrial grief. On the one hand, they were emotive tethers to the "vapours" of fleshly existence. "In almost every home," wrote one consolationist shortly after the Civil War, "there are stored away, among its most cherished treasures, a little photograph, or a box of toys, a torn kite, a half-worn cap, or a pair of tiny shoes. They all tell a story too deep for tears."[20] On the other hand, they were the very brick and mortar through which spiritual discipline was effected, that is, clothing, jewelry, repasts, coffins, tombstones, and portraits, were all ways of prompting spiritual reform even as they threatened to nurture soul-damning doubt. And while the social form of mourning shifted over the course of the nineteenth century, mourning continued to connote a particularly tenuous period of time that demanded close regulation of ardent passions that threatened to disrupt both theological and social fabrics.[21] In the late seventeenth century, for instance, British minister Richard Allestree instructed in his *Whole Duty of Mourning* on "how to comfort our selves with Spiritual Remedies against immoderate Grief for the Loss of Relations and Friends." As Richard Cecil would do a century later, Allestree subordinated grief to spiritual promise: "Let not, I beseech you, immoderate Grief too much overwhelm you; but when you have shed your solemn Tears, and paid your due Sighs to the memory of your Friends, then wipe your Eyes with Comfort of Hope, and change your Grief into Charitable Joy." Such an exchange was not only a matter of calming mental tempest, it was the essence of Christian confidence: "Excessive and immoderate Sorrow, implieth a diffidence or distrust we have of our Soul's immortality, Resurrection, and Glorification."[22] In explaining scriptural injunctions to "moderate the mourning of Christians for the Death of Others," John Dunton explained to his readers in 1692 that because death "*is the end of all men*, it is that that is the common condition of all men, it should not be too grievous, nor too doleful to any man."[23] Twenty years earlier John Flavel's enormously popular *A Token for Mourners*, which was reprinted as late as 1818, was a sermon to "a distressed Mother" upon the death of her son "wherein, the Boundaries of Sorrow are duly fixed, Excesses restrained, the Common Pleas Answered, and divers Rules for the support of Gods afflicted ones prescribed."[24]

And yet, somewhat ironically, in addition to their intended task of moderating grief as spiritual discipline, these tracts also constituted a material archive of mourning that was in danger of participating in the very dolor it intended to circumscribe. Allestree deemed that his tract was "necessary to be given at all Funerals," whereas Dunton was more reserved, claiming his treatise was "recommended as proper to be given at Funerals." Dunton, in fact, explicitly associated his work with tokens more commonly associated with funerals, such as gloves and rings sent as invitations and distributed as memorials.[25] Having been asked "whether Books are not more proper to be given at Funerals, than Bisquets, Gloves, Rings, &c.," he confidently retorted that "undoubtedly a Book would be a far more convenient, more durable, and more valuable a Present, than what are generally given, as much exceeding them, as the Soul does the Body." Addressing "the Sorrowful" in 1709, Cotton Mather evinced a similar orientation to printed texts as appropriate mourning articles in his published sermon, *The Cure of Sorrow*: "If this *Book* in thy closet help thee, in those Methods of Piety, which will afford Rest unto thy Mind, under any uneasy Occurrences, the End of it will be happily answered."[26] These printed texts were supplemented by an even vaster archive of letters, diaries, and memoirs that, according to one historian, "often substitute[d] as the only *memento mori* possible," especially in the years prior to photography's invention.[27] Even as they worked to moderate grief and sorrow, then, by training mourners' eyes on grander dramas of redemption than present predicaments could possibly comprehend, these texts drew upon material vocabularies—tokens, rings, and the like—that muddied the very distinctions they were trying to maintain. It was against this historical backdrop of mourning as a catalyst of spiritual regeneration, rooted in material sensibilities and gendered ideas of grief, that nineteenth-century mourners worked to reconcile theological aspirations with circumstances of impossible personal anguish.

But even with a vast material record of mourning, it takes an interpretive sleight to move from these articles to the mourner. For Nehemiah Adams, a Congregational minister in Boston, the material link with his daughter, Agnes, who died just before her first birthday, was the "key to her little coffin." His tormented relationship with the key in many ways unearths an entombed historical silence surrounding memorial culture more broadly considered, including photography. To wit, material articles of mourning seldom speak directly to what they meant for the people who held them. Finding it in his trouser pocket the night after the burial, the diminutive token that had "supplant[ed] the remorseless screw and screw-driver" nevertheless prompted great anguish: "I could neither keep it nor part with it. I abhorred it, and idolized it. I wished to be rid of it, and I clung to it. There was a fear-

     Here Is My Name When I Am Dead

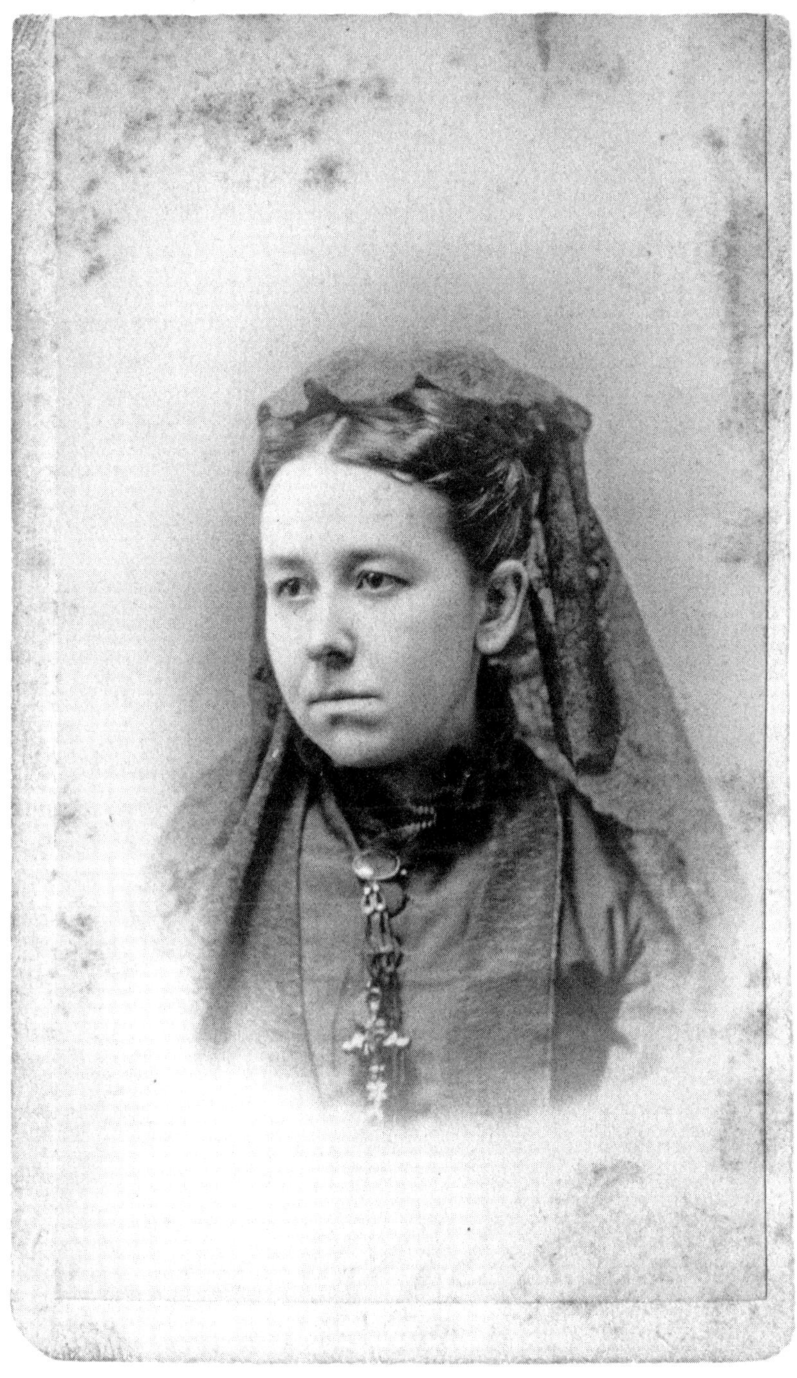

Figure 13. Carte de visite of woman in mourning attire. Lowell, Mass., ca. 1863. Author's collection.

ful spell about it; and yet it was a charm, a precious treasure, and at the same time a symbol of my agony." As the months went by, though still a tangible link to "her little form . . . mouldering back to clay," the key began to unlock many a door to heaven through Adams's ministrations to the dying and bereaved, opening, as his wife put it, "a way for us to sorrowing hearts."[28] In charting this history of mourning, then, we would do well not to be too confident in the power of the object to disclose experiences of sorrow.

Despite an expansive archive of memorial tokens, perhaps the most publicly (and historically) visible mode of mourning during the nineteenth century was attire. Richard Allestree had advised in 1695 that "our Garments [are] being Badges of Mortality, and Cognizances of Death, so as we look upon them, we are called of God to remember Death." By the nineteenth century, Allestree's point that all clothing should be a reminder of "when by our Sin we came first into the world to the state of Death" was more explicitly rendered through the corpse's winding sheet and the mourning dress of the bereaved.[29] Despite passage of sumptuary laws in many colonies during the colonial period that prohibited the wearing of mourning attire—it was, after all, an undeniable signal of wealth and status—by the nineteenth century mourning garb was a central component of mourning ritual across a broad swath of Americans, middling and otherwise.[30] In the 1820s, Charles Winslow of Boston had "mourning articles constantly on hand" among his store of "English, French, and Canton GOODS."[31] Around the same time, Mrs. M. D. Chapin, also of Boston, advertised her "fashionable millinery and mourning bonnets, of all kinds, ready made."[32] Among the "spring importations" of mourning articles available at Besson & Son of Philadelphia in 1851 were twenty-four varieties of black fabrics—chaly, silks, grenadines, bombazines, "Mousseline de Laines," and crapes—intended for a variety of different articles, including gloves, shawls, "mode or love veils," and, of course, dresses and petticoats. Also for sale were a number of fabrics and articles specifically designated as "mourning": siciliennes, poplins, lawns, ginghams, chintzes, "collars and cuffs," and "bordered hdkfs, &c."[33]

In contrast to widowers, who officially mourned for six months, the regulated duration for widows was two and a half to three years, although many women, following the lead of Queen Victoria, mourned in perpetuity. Significantly, although widows in first mourning, whose resources permitted, were to restrict their presence in public, many took time to have their likeness made in photographic studios. This card photograph (fig. 13) of a young woman by the Kimball Brothers of Lowell, Massachusetts, not only demonstrates the mourning garb all too frequently worn by her generation—the

   Here Is My Name When I Am Dead

presence of the black mourning cap and draped veil indicating that she was in full mourning—but also something about her desire to be remembered in her state of mourning. Another widow from the same period who distributed her likeness in full mourning attire signed the back, "Your friend in distress, Sue."[34] In addition to the fact that the ostensibly secluded mourning period was frequently documented through photographic means, that these studio portraits of widows were also circulated, and not merely stored for posterity, simultaneously announced a recent loss (and perhaps a patriotic sacrifice) and worked to maintain ties among the living through established circuits of social exchange.[35]

A similar desire to document grief was at work in postmortem portraits wherein bereaved parents held the remains of their children. The latter convention has been explained in part as an urgent acquisition of a family picture.[36] And yet these photographs were not just records of existence or markers of status.[37] Not unlike the winding sheets and coffins among previous generations, photographs of the dead and of the bereaved demonstrated what Susan Stabile has identified in another context as "the shared identity between corpse and mourner as death's remains."[38] Rather than being completely concerned with remembering the deceased, photographs of the widow sitting in her weeds and the mother holding her dead child signaled an identification between the mourning body and the corpse as parallel testaments to what death had wrought. In her study of an eighteenth-century coterie of Philadelphia women, Stabile demonstrates how these women "created a specifically material aesthetic of mourning that preserved their corporeal connection to the dead" by "embodying grief in tangible artifacts that represent the absent body."[39] Although coffin keys, empty cribs, mourning garb, and "india-rubber rings, with prints of small teeth in them," were common articles of commemoration in the nineteenth century, likenesses and hair became staples in the material archives of mourning. Frequently worn close to the body in the form of pendants, lockets, and pins, moreover, photographs and hair were more deeply entrenched in practices of display that reinforced the association between the body of the deceased and the body of the bereaved.

The relationship between corporeality and commemoration at work in daguerreotypes, ambrotypes, and card photographs echoes the cultural work of the painted portrait miniatures that were popular among affluent classes between the mid-eighteenth and mid-nineteenth centuries. Frequently, however, these earlier "miniature pictures" were not likenesses of individuals but anthropomorphic representations of death and mourning. A common motif was a figure bent over a fresh grave with an urn in the background documenting the date of death and willow branches hanging over the scene. While photography did not entirely displace these figurative representations, by the end of the nineteenth century memorial iconography centered on photographic likenesses of the deceased. The availability of photographic modes of representation did not, of course, unilaterally induce this broad shift in memorial iconography, nor, more broadly speaking, was photography alone in elevating ideologies of individualism during the nineteenth century. Firmly ensconced in Jacksonian political sensibilities, ecclesial disestablishment, the philosophical sensibilities of Scottish common sense realism, revivalism, rising mercantilism, and rapid advances in printing technologies, steam power, and telegraphy — each of which elevated individual experience and agency, even within corporate contexts — the years preceding the daguerreotype's introduction to Americans were undergoing rapid transformations that were continually refiguring epistemologies of individualism across political, social, and theological spheres. Yet even if photography did not solely determine the ontological contours of personhood (which it did not), the medium worked to negotiate and entrench abstract ideologies into material forms.

"He Shuts His Eyes to See"

After the death of his wife in 1848, A. J. MacDonald of Albany, New York, reflected on the "custom of this age" for dealings with corpses. "She died, and was . . . enclosed in a coffin, and buried in the earth, in a place called a graveyard, where there was a great display of tomb-stones and monuments." It was not the promise of the decay of his wife's remains in the "bosom" of earth that troubled MacDonald. Rather, it was "the custom to place a tomb-stone or monument over the grave . . . which agitated my mind for a long period." When he decided not to place a marker over her grave, friends predictably asked why — did he not respect his wife? Such queries, MacDonald replied, missed the point. Of course he respected his wife, whom he called "the partner of my home." But costly monuments and grave markers would hardly benefit her and they were equally incapable of comforting him as they gave "no consolation for my loss." "To me it looks like heathenism and idolatry!" was the widower's unguarded judgment on the subject.[40]

But then MacDonald considered what monuments were intended to do for communities of the bereaved, namely, to prompt recollections of the deceased so as to quicken sinners to mend their ways. A consolation book

Here Is My Name When I Am Dead

printed a couple of decades later was insufferably optimistic in this regard: "The grave should be a place to inspire high and holy purposes, to beget pure and benevolent desire, and to inspire rapid preparation for the fulfillment of our mission which remains on this side."[41] In addition to individual graves as sites of contemplation and reform, the bucolic landscapes and grand architecture of rural cemeteries that had become fashionable in America after the opening of Mount Auburn outside of Boston in 1831 were also intended to invoke the sublime.[42] Frequently restricted to the wealthy and refined citizens, even this guarded access provided an instructive allegory of things to come. Reflecting on the Greenwood Cemetery outside of Hartford in the 1860s, Jane Stebbins described a "magnificent gateway, or entrance, at which stands a porter mindful of those who seek admittance there," and she then proceeded to ask, "Who can enter and not think of another porter and another gate?"[43]

To such sensibilities regarding the inspirational capacities of remembrance, MacDonald had a measure of sympathy, but he nevertheless deemed their association with graves misguided folly. "Fancy a man *alone* on the earth, whose wife is buried in a wood," and who, because his memory fails him, marks her grave so that he can distinguish it from the surrounding foliage. "But is it because he loves the loathsome, putrifying flesh and decaying bones, that he wishes to remember the spot where they lay? Would he not be horror-struck to have them come in contact with him? How can he love that which is so unlovely, and which we really look upon as being so horrible? No! he cannot." In truth, then, MacDonald reasoned, the object of remembrance was not synonymous with fleshly form, which is subject to decay: "It is the image, the form which that dreadful mass of corrupt matter once presented, that he loves; that being whose bright eye, in reality, shines no more—that gentle smile which always gave him joy, but which now he shuts his eyes to see . . . yes! he loathes the putrid carcase, but the dearly loved image remains to be loved still." For MacDonald, it was not that the body itself was to be categorically derided or that the motives behind monuments and memorials were unsound. Rather, physical form was a hieroglyph of the soul so long as it was properly portrayed. "Create whate'er you please," MacDonald wrote, "there is no memorial like a portrait, for in it I see the nearest image of herself; her smile is there, her deep dark eyes, and the sweet bloom upon her cheeks; her lips, they even now would seem to speak, and almost whisper comfort to a grief-torn heart." Grave markers, in short, were poor monuments to the memory of the departed because they associated acts of remembrance with the site of putrefaction and decay—inevitable natural processes that, when dwelled upon, interfered with maintaining memories of form "once presented." A truer monument, an artifact that more closely associated the object of remembrance with a material token, was a portrait.[44]

Unlike "likeness," which, by the middle decades of the century was increasingly understood as a pictorial convention that vaulted representational similitude, portraiture had historically been less interested in fidelity to fleshly form than to the portrayal of imperceptible — at least to the untrained eye — traits. Even Charles Bell's enormously popular 1809 treatise *Essays on the Anatomy of Expression in Painting*, which lauded anatomy as the "grammar" necessary for those who would "show the working of human passion," nevertheless scorned those artists, so-called, who possessed only "the merit of accurate imitation" and who were "satisfied merely to copy and represent what he sees."[45] The issue also haunted early champions of the new art. Recall Marcus Aurelius Root's defense of heliography as a godlike art rather than a mere mechanical trade in his early history of American photography. Fearful of the daguerreotype's precarious social pedigree, moreover, charter members of the state's photographic association at a New York daguerrean convention in July 1851 wrung their hands over the "mere catchpennies who hold themselves up in the world as artists, when they are not." While still considered "more faithful to nature than any other style of portraits," the reputation of the daguerreotype as art was in jeopardy, the gentlemen fretted, by so "many imposters" flooding the cities with "caricatures" rather than true portraits, the latter being likenesses that conveyed inner form as well as outer lineament.[46] As for MacDonald, the issue in all of this was not imitation (the "putrid carcase") but representation (form "once presented"). By the 1840s when MacDonald mourned his dead wife, portraits had long been used as memento mori. Painted miniatures and portraits commissioned in life with one's progeny in mind as well as postmortem portraits that improved upon death's inevitable somatic alterations in order to "preserve these bodies in that high perfection of form," in the words of celebrated portraitist Charles Wilson Peale, had comprised an archive of memorial portraiture since the eighteenth century.[47] Yet it was not until photographic methods increased in popularity beginning in the early 1840s that memorial iconography increasingly exchanged figurative representations of death for representations of the deceased either in postmortem photographs or, more commonly, in likenesses taken in life and repurposed for commemoration upon decease.

As early as 1844 the Langenheim brothers of Philadelphia were quite candid with this latter application. "SOME time or other we all have to leave this world," they declared, "anyone whose parent, whose wife, whose husband, whose friend, whose child has died, what would he not give to possess

                                    Here Is My Name When I Am Dead

a likeness of them as they appeared in full life and bloom." Indeed, "NOTH-ING can be more affecting or exciting to the feelings of our hearts," they proclaimed in another advertisement from 1844, "than to take to hand an excellent Daguerreotype portrait of a parent, a brother or sister, a child, a friend or anyone else we love, after they are 'far away' or dead." While Marcus Aurelius Root would defend heliography in a language familiar to pictorial conventions of portraiture in his early history of photography, contemporary proponents such as the Langenheims ballyhooed the daguerreotype's greater exactitude of representation than any other medium, especially painted miniatures. "No limner's brush, no engraver's steel, no lithographer's ink is able to produce a likeness so striking-pleasing and lifelike as the Daguerreotype, which is not done by the hand of the artist but by the *Pencil of Nature*."[48] In this context, then, as photographic modes of representation came to displace painted portraits as signature tokens of affection and regard, the discourse of exactitude espoused by champions of the new art nevertheless confused the distinction between likeness and portrait, between imitation and representation. Indeed, as with the defenders of the artistic merits of portraiture, rather than merely becoming a transcription of fleshly form for future generations to inspect, memorial likenesses sutured relics of the past with a discourse of celestial reunion, wherein the body of the deceased, represented through relic and shadow, became a mirror into the beholder's soul.

It is unclear whether MacDonald had a painted miniature of his wife or a tinted daguerreotype or, for that matter, whether he describes an actual likeness or only the one he saw when he closed his eyes. In the late 1840s he could easily have secured his wife's likeness on either ivory or silvered copper, and in many respects either article would have performed a similar commemorative function, although they would have signaled different relationships to the market and social status. What is most important here is that regardless of the compositional or formal similarities between painted miniatures and photographic likenesses, MacDonald identified an important shift in the memorial culture of the mid-nineteenth century: a move away from meditations on the decaying corpse and toward a culture of memory that prompted self-reflection through the mediated presence of expired loved ones. And yet, ironically, the body of the deceased remained central to this changing memorial culture.

MacDonald's evaluation of portraiture and gravesites as artifacts engaged in the common pursuit of memorial, although sponsoring different associations with the body of the deceased, was also evinced in a common bit of doggerel inscribed, stitched, and scribbled on other "monuments" during the period. Tracing iterations of a verse in the context of differing material presentations demonstrates fluctuating relationships between corpses, memory, and presence. In October 1859, Catharine Christ scripted a verse in her own hand before carefully entombing it behind her daguerrean effigy:

> Fetherolfsville [Pennsylvania] October 29 AD 1859
> This is the likeness of
> Catharine Christ
> When I am dead and in
> my grave And when my bones
> are rotten Remember me
> When this you see or I
> shall be forgotten. The grass
> is green The rose is red here
> is my name when I am dead.

In the sixth-plate daguerreotype, which fits comfortably in the palm, Christ — very much alive — sits in a rather plain chair, hands crossed over her lap, and looks to the left of the compositional frame. For Christ, whose explanatory note, sequestered in its sarcophagic casement, was removed from view of all but the most inquisitive beholders, her portrait became her name, her identity, in her absence. In this context, then, the verse indicated the photograph's increasing surrogacy for corporeal presence by positing that, through her likeness, her presence continued beyond her bones' decay. The verse is also significant for what it omits.

This verse was not unique to photography. As early as 1797, twelve-year-old Martha Taylor stitched this chime into her girlhood sampler: "Martha Taylor is my name Lancaster is my Habitation Octorara is my dwelling place & christ is my Salvation the rose is red the leaves are Green the days are past [that] I have seen when Im dead & in my Grave & all my bones are rotten when this you see remember me Adieu."[49] Eighty years later, in a recurring "Gazette Museum" segment featuring "curious facts, fancies and figures . . . for inquisitive readers," the *National Police Gazette* described the "lonely grave" of one Margaret Hurley in Gratton Township, Michigan, whose epitaph read:

> Margaret Hurley is my name,
> Ireland is my nation;
> Vergennes my residing place,
> Heaven my expectation.

The grass is green, the rose is red,
This tells my name when I am dead
When I am dead and in my grave,
And all my bones are rotten,
This little stone will tell my name
When I am quite forgotten.[50]

Whereas Christ's portrait signaled presence, these other artifacts signaled absence. In 1870 Margaret was an eleven-year-old girl in a large family of Irish emigrants to western Michigan. What made her grave a curiosity a decade later could not have been the verse's novelty but rather its incorporation of somber mirth into the familiar scene of woe. More to the point, whereas Christ was still very much alive when she penned the verse and tucked it into the daguerreotype case, the same singsong verse on Hurley's grave operated less as lilt to remembrance than as a marker of identification. But, unlike MacDonald's anguished meditation on his wife's grave, the verse had the peculiar effect of dissociating Hurley from the residing place of her corpse. Here, the verse reminded mourners and visitors to Hurley's grave of her absence. Associated with neither her corporeal form nor her grave, in the case of Martha Taylor the token of remembrance is the product of her labor, which, unlike later memorial commodities, still referred back to the hands of the one who crafted it.

The fact that Christ's daguerreotype lyric lacks reference to her "salvation" or her celestial "expectation" may be attributable to the limited space provided by the diminutive likeness. Or it may have been intentionally omitted. Regardless of Christ's intentions, it is likely that the verse's celestial chimes would have rung in her ear if not for those who dared to lift her likeness out of its thermoplastic case. Yet even if Christ's daguerreotype — which, as an artifact, necessarily included the case and the note — omitted common religious references, it nevertheless gestured to the theological significance of presence in nineteenth-century memorial culture. Oftentimes, when treated at all, the notion of continued presence is relegated to the curio cabinets of historical inquiry — apparitions, ghosts, spirit photography are all well and good but hardly the stuff of, well, material history.[51] But presence was not a curiosity for nineteenth-century Americans. Thus, whereas the inscriptions on Taylor's sampler and Hurley's grave gestured to the theological significance of absence — saying, as it were from beyond the grave, that I was as you are and you will be as I am — Christ's portrait suggests that presence was also part of a nineteenth-century interpretive apparatus of beholding.

Photographs in particular communicated the importance of continued presence by providing a vehicle for the deceased to interact in the daily affairs of the bereaved. Presence was also a familiar aspect of nineteenth-century American piety. Landscapes and babies were christened with biblical names—Enoch and Zipporah alongside John and Rebecca—and even if there was disagreement on the degree to which human sensoria facilitated divine presence, most agreed that God and his emissaries, whether incarnate or discarnate, commingled daily in human affairs. Indeed, presence was something of a prism, reflecting both biblical past and celestial future through the embodied present. Naming newborns after biblical figures and newly discovered territories and new municipalities after biblical terrain—Jordan, Bethlehem, Shiloh, Mount Sinai, Jericho—was not merely to commemorate the past but to shape the future. Likewise, photographs of the now-dead were not intended only to memorialize but to prompt regeneration. Christ's daguerrean likeness, taken in life, eulogized in her own hand, and intended to facilitate her transformative presence after death, parallels the temporal slipperiness of presence that was familiar to many nineteenth-century religious Americans. Photographic and religious notions of presence were not exact analogues, of course, but they each gestured to the ways in which both beholding and believing were capable of seeing beyond sensorial referents.

In its capacity to evoke not only the image of form once seen but also the whisper of a voice once heard, a touch once felt, a scent once breathed, a likeness of the deceased depended on some fidelity to somatic representation in their commemorative operations. But in addition to depending on the corporeality of the deceased in acts of remembrance, portraits also anticipated the corporeality of the beholder. Declaring that "a portrait is without doubt the greatest of monuments," MacDonald continued to meditate on its unique ability to facilitate continued interaction between the two bodies. "You can hide it in your chamber, or mayhap in your bosom; you can gaze upon it with love; you can press it to your lips, and in imagination, you can find in it, one who watches your actions, and keeps you ever humble in your path."[52] By endowing his dead wife with a form of agency that was animated through her visual representation, MacDonald touched on the theological and social work that photographic jewelry, among other modes of memorial photographs, performed as articles of personal adornment. I consider the corporeality of the beholder more closely in later chapters, but the corporeal relationship between the mourning body and the absent body was also articulated in other modes of mourning-work. A quick look at how these two

                                    Here Is My Name When I Am Dead

bodies were associated in the broader sweep of nineteenth-century mourning culture sheds light on the visual habits of photographic memorial portraiture.

A year before he published his treatise on monuments, MacDonald
edited a giftbook comprised of poetry and short stories by authors representing nineteen states, including an original poem by Mrs. Frances H. W.
Green of Rhode Island. Although death was a prevailing motif throughout
the volume, Green's poem, entitled "My Still-Born Babe," offers the most
intimate experience of grief in the collection. Written as a meditation on the
body of her lifeless daughter, whom she has enfolded in "these bereave-ed
arms," Green begins with a cry of helpless disbelief: "Unfolded Bud of Life,
oh can it be / This lovely form is *all there is* of thee?" Her soul-heavy response
is that the limp form is not—could not be—all that remains of her child and
consoles herself with the promise of a future embrace denied "when Birth
and Death were gathered face to face": "The sweet maternal office yet is
mine— / The human all engrossed in the divine; . . . Through all the Courts
of Heaven my ear shall greet / The bounding music of thy little feet." Though
the promise of heavenly reunion that limns Green's verse may at first reading
suggest a devaluation of corporeal form, it is in fact her mournful scrutiny of
the tiny features that enables her to imagine their expression in the Courts
of Heaven:

> These mute lips ne'er shall utter baby moans;
> . . . Love shall teach
> To thee the music of an angel's speech—
> When from this curving mouth sweet words shall part
> With deep a blessing for thy mother's heart.
>
> . . . .
>
> Rich "Gems of Life" to crown thy flaxen hair;
> And all the beauty of these soft blue eyes,
> That woke not here, shall brighten Paradise—
> Till in their peerless depths my Soul shall see
> A picture of our love's eternity.
>
> . . . .
>
> Once more in these bereave-ed arms I hold thee—
> Once more to this lone bosom I enfold thee—
> My First-Born, and my Precious! for I know
> The time has come when even *this* must go;—
> Yet tell me not my clinging hope is in vain!—

Dear little Mary, we shall meet again!
I am denied *one* living, warm caress;
Yet these cold lineaments have power to bless,

.   .   .   .

But for a season I release thy hand,
I will not keep thee from the Spirit-Land.[53]

As she examines the limp frame of her baby, who was so recently a part of her own living body, Green's elegy poignantly summarizes the corporeal identification between death and mourning that shaped experiences of grief. The image her poem elicits, of a mother cradling her dead child, also recalls innumerable postmortem daguerreotypes of small children being held by their grieving parents. During the daguerrean period, parents of deceased children often posed with the corpse in a manner that invoked the Pietà. Although Protestants esteemed Mary differently from their Catholic counterparts, the mother of Jesus nevertheless provided a model of mourning for the grief-stricken as well as a way to identify their personal sorrows with the pageantry of salvation. Reflecting on the recent death of her daughter, Ruby, Mildred Mifflin wrote in her journal how "this mourning for my firstborn child brings me into nearer sympathy with that unexampled grief which must have rent the heart of Mary, the mother of Jesus, as she beheld him, in whom was the hope of her race, dying the ignominious death of the cross!" Mifflin's liberal strand of Christianity may not have reflected the theological sensibilities of many of her companions in mourning, but she saw in Mary's trials an "experience which must ever sanctify the mother-love and dignify the mother-grief" of all women who shared in her lot of despair.[54] In this sense, then, postmortem likenesses performed a kind of theological work by sacralizing sorrow as a religious experience.

Lastly, Green's poem also makes explicit the necessary relationship between form and memory that underlies MacDonald's critique of contemporary memorial practices, while at the same time pitching the function of memory less to records of the past and present than to future glories limned in her babe's "cold lineaments" and visible to the soul if not to the organ of sight. In this sense, her meditation closely resembles earlier practices of visually inspecting corpses for signs of heavenly rapture. In other words, while full of sorrow, Green is also full of hope — gazing into "these soft blue eyes" Green sees not an unforgiving grave but "a picture of our love's eternity." The prevailing language of mourning culture in the mid-nineteenth century was one that celebrated a future heavenly reunion. In this context, the human

   Here Is My Name When I Am Dead

form, represented in portraiture, became increasingly important throughout the century. The portrait was an abundant referent, signaling not only the realness of what had passed before the camera's lens but also the continued presence of the departed as well as promises of glories to come.

"Prepared to Meet You There"

The relationship between the body corruptible and body glorified prompted a great deal of soul searching during a century when one's physical likeness became increasingly associated with one's soul and when corporeal decay was increasingly stayed by advancements in mortuary practices.[55] A number of consolation books commented on the prospects of "recognition" in heaven. In 1855, Presbyterian minister James Madison MacDonald defended the position that "the Scriptures plainly teach that the redeemed are to possess bodies so far resembling the bodies they had on earth, and which were 'sewn' in the grave," that loved ones would have no trouble recognizing those who had gone before. Evidence of this was in the Bible, he argued, as a necessary requisite for communing with the ancients and rejoicing in the bounty that each individual prepared for glory. It was also, of course, superlatively "soothing . . . to the Christian, mourning for those who 'sleep in Jesus.'"[56]

Books of consolation had been popular since the late sixteenth century, and such volumes as John Flavel's *A Token for Mourners*, first published in 1674, were in print well into the nineteenth century, including an abridged version for the New England Tract Society in 1818. While many motifs remained constant over the years, such as, in Flavel's words, the desire that "these searching afflictions may make the most satisfying discoveries," the idea that heaven was a place of reunion made possible by the continuance of social ties was influenced by the eighteenth-century theologian Emanuel Swedenborg.[57] By the middle of the nineteenth century, recognition of relations, especially children, in heaven had become a subject of much theological interest in both England and the United States and a popular topic in books of bereavement. Books under titles such as *The Recognition of Friends in Heaven* and *The Recognition of Friends in Another World* were in print from the 1830s through much of the rest of the century, and chapters on the subject were included in books by Spiritualists and Universalists as well as Presbyterians and Baptists.[58] In *Agnes and the Key to Her Little Coffin*, Nehemiah Adams mused on "what scenes there must be in heaven, every day, in the meetings of parents and children, and relatives and friends."[59] The certainty of Frances Green's reunion with her stillborn daughter — "Dear little Mary, we shall meet again!"—was predicated on the knowledge that she would recognize the child whose eyes were to "brighten in Paradise."

The relationship between a developing theological interest in recognition and the popularization of photographic portraiture was neither causal nor consistent. But by accelerating the portrait's surrogacy for corporeal presence and thus personal identification, photography certainly had a hand in these developments. In her 1867 consolation book, *Our Departed Friends*, Jane Stebbins described memories of friends and, especially, children as "daguerreotypes" provisioned by God. However, for Stebbins such daguerreotypes did not refer to a material likeness but rather to a divine impression, "chiselling the features in substance more enduring than marble, and dwelling upon and preserving every look, tone, and word with careful exactness, thus creating a likeness that in after years is recognized as *the* one that was once a reality to us."[60] This figurative use of the daguerreotype as a synonym for memory was, by the late 1860s, a somewhat dated usage of the term. During the 1840s and 1850s, "daguerreotype" was bandied to denote precision rather than impression, as in the Boston magazine, the *Daguerreotype*, which published foreign news rather than developments in the field of photography. That Stebbins used a photographic metaphor to describe divine impressions upon the mind worked to associate the operations of memory with the daguerreotype's marvelous detail and tonal depth—even if she failed to account for its well-known fragility and mercurial image. In any case, relying on the "daguerreotype" impression of mortal associations, Stebbins assured her readers that "surely we may count upon the joyful recognition of friends, upon meeting the loving ones in the streets of the New Jerusalem, and walking with them 'in white' on the holy errands on which our Lord may send us."[61]

Although there was hardly consensus on the nature of the glorified body in the communion of shadows, memorial culture throughout the century commonly assured the bereaved that heavenly reunion awaited them after a brief separation. Funeral cards, such as those provided by the company of H. F. Wendell of Leipsic, Ohio, at the turn of the century, often paired verse with images—a common motif was the name of the deceased inscribed on a Bible—in addition to the details of birth and death that reminded the bereaved that their separation was temporary. The family and friends of Catherine Mumma, who died in 1901, were reminded that though "we must lay thee / In the peaceful grave's embrace," Catherine's "memory will be cherished / 'Till we see thy heavenly face." And when seventy-year-old Ivory Jones died in 1890, her mourners were heartened by the promise

     Here Is My Name When I Am Dead

that "One by one our hopes grow brighter, / As we near the shining shore, / For we know across the river, / Wait the loved ones gone before." Most of these cards employed text and memorial iconography to comment on the soul's safe journey to heaven: a common visual motif was a dove, the conventional symbol of both the soul and the Holy Spirit. But by the end of the century, several suppliers provided spaces for photographs of the deceased as well, such as the one for Jonathan W. Osborn using a card from the Ideal Memorial Card Company of Bluffton, Ohio, to which a salt print medallion was affixed (fig. 14).

If the association between likeness and the soul's sweet embrace was in these cases rendered visually explicit, other memorial photographs used more cryptic visual cues to identify the depicted individual as deceased. Black borders around the portrait, for instance, designated the image as a memorial photograph. Another common method of rendering a portrait as a memorial was the application of studio retouching. Since the 1860s when wet-plate glass negatives had all but replaced single-exposure daguerreotypes and ambrotypes as the dominant commercial method of photographic portraiture, studios had been storing negatives so that patrons could order additional prints—a practice that earlier photographic techniques simply did not allow. Now the bereaved could issue memorial cards of the deceased from negatives taken in full health. Display practices and iconographic studio embellishments, such as wreaths or flowers, would signal the occasion to beholders.[62] A generation earlier, display practices signaling the death of the pictured individual could involve trimming a portrait to fit commercial mounts that had been embellished with visual cues. During the card photograph era of the 1860s, one such mount featured a tasseled vignette frame (fig. 15a). Absent any textual cues, these modes of memorialization required a sort of visual literacy, especially when placed into albums or other contexts that limited the beholder's ability to handle the photograph. Here there were no textual cues prompting mourners to reflect on celestial reunion, no stylized Bibles embracing the name or likeness of the deceased. In such contexts, the memory work of photographic portraiture relied heavily on practices of display.

After receiving memorial portraits at funerals or wakes or upon visiting the house of mourning, memorial photographs were often archived in Bibles, albums, or other designated contexts. Like other forms of vernacular photography in the communion of shadows, the relationship between a memorial photograph and a beholder was conditioned by circumstances of encounter. When seventeen-year-old Charles Hall died in 1867, his bereaved parents

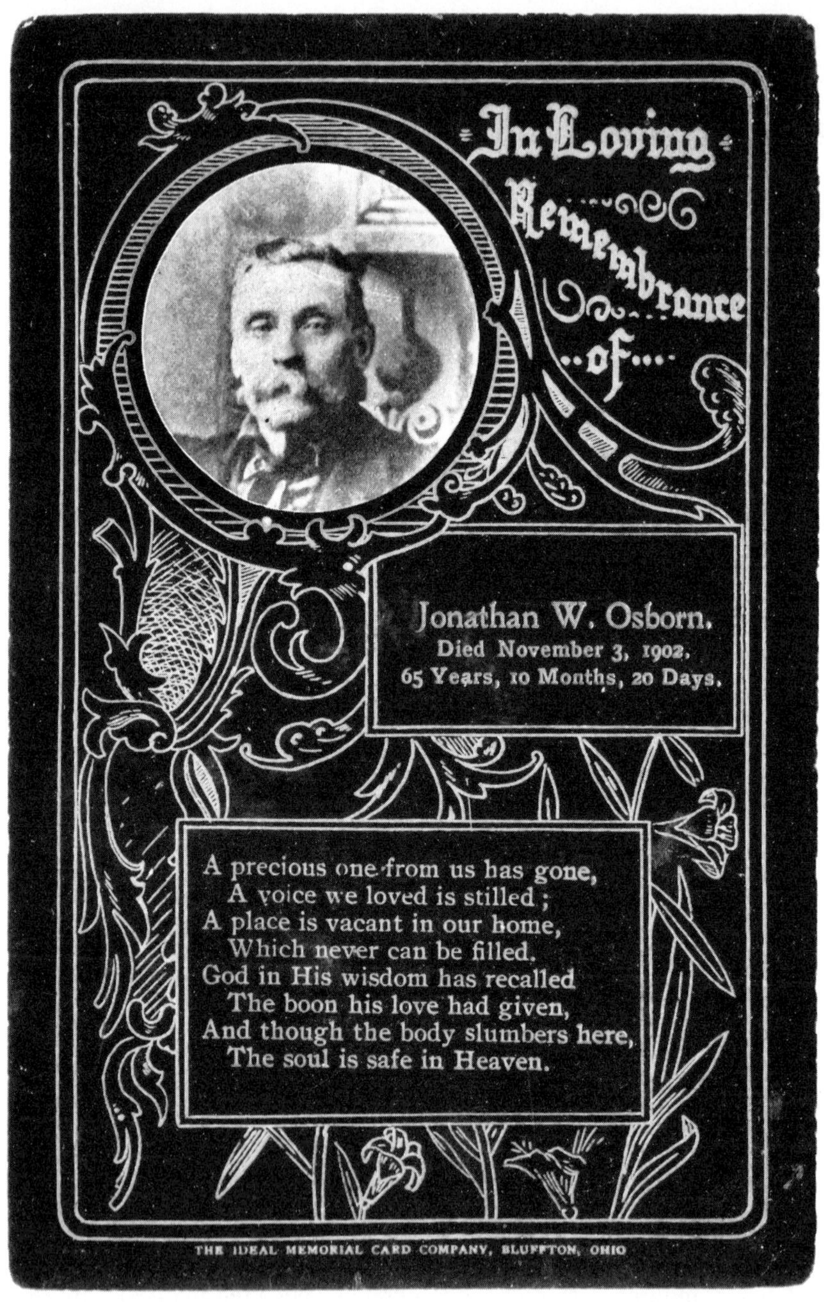

Figure 14. Memorial card for Jonathan W. Osborn, ca. 1902. Salt print.
Author's collection.

placed a recent photograph of the young man on commercial memorial cards to distribute at his funeral and as friends and acquaintances called at the house over the coming weeks and months (fig. 16). Like the unidentified man in figure 15a, who was memorialized on a similar format, the cards were of ordinary carte de visite dimensions and featured an elaborately tasseled frame in gold ink, suspended from a point near the top center of the card. Charles's youthful likeness was trimmed to fit the blank oval in the center of the frame. But unlike the other likeness, beneath Charles's portrait someone wrote with mournful promise the dead child's final admonition to the land of the living: "I am gone to the better land / Prepared to meet you there."

Drawing on a discourse of heavenly recognition, Charles Hall's memorial photograph demonstrated how portrait photographs were used to bridge body and soul, heaven and earth, susceptible flesh and incorruptible spirit in the changing memorial culture of mid-nineteenth-century America. If in life one's likeness was perceived as an index of character, in death it became a cipher of the spirit, not merely a record of "a form once presented" but also a promise of what was to come in "the better land." But Charles's photograph was not simply distributed. It was received and, for many, would likely have been cherished, placed shortly after receipt within a popular consolation book in pages specifically designed for cartes de visite.

In 1867, Jane Eliza Stebbins, a temperance woman from Hartford, Connecticut, published her "proofs of the great doctrine of immortality." Sold by "agents, ladies, and Clergymen" from Hartford to Cincinnati, *Our Departed Friends, or Glory of the Immortal Life* was a consolation book that was commended by ministers from across the Union — ranging from glowing reviews, as when H. D. Kitchell, the President of Middlebury College, deemed it "worthy to lie by the side of the Bible as a family book," to weak endorsements, such as that of Rev. S. D. Willard who "read some portions of [the] new work" and thought "well of the subject and spirit of the book." Kitchell's association of Stebbins's book with the Bible was echoed both in its structural similarity to recent Bibles that also included photograph albums as well as in an advertisement in the *Christian Advocate*, which described the volume as "a religious work of the highest type, is in harmony with the Bible, not sectarian."[63] If the book was "not sectarian" in religious terms — which it was, as its Protestant bias betrays — it was more clearly tilted in its sectional prejudice. Before readers even opened the book to see that she had dedicated it "to the Friends of the 341,670 (Official Report) Deceased Soldiers, who volunteered in Defence of the Union . . . sacrificing their lives in the prime of their manhood, for the good of their country," they would recog-

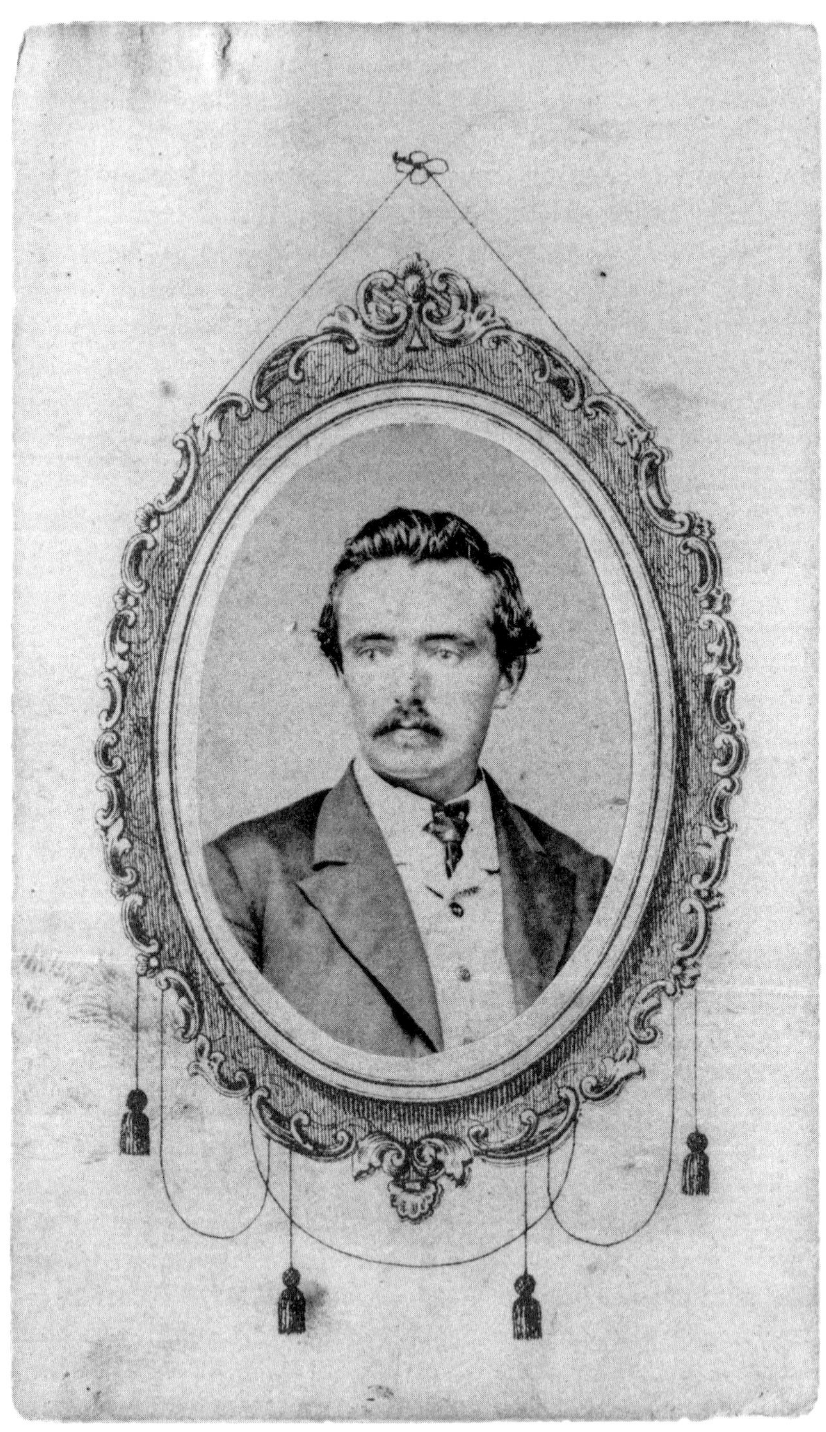

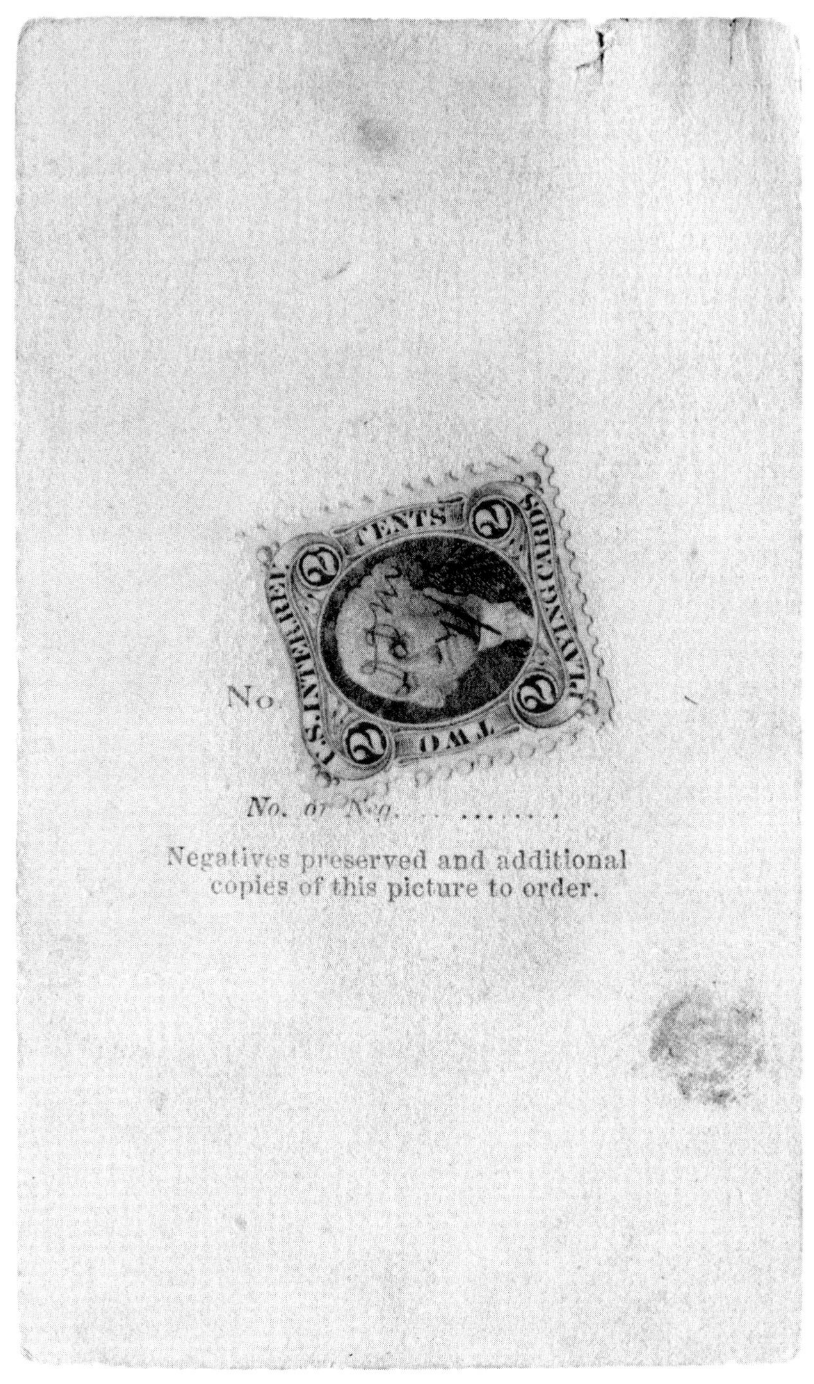

Figures 15a (*opposite*) and 15b. Memorial card (front and back) for an unidentified man, ca. 1865. Carte de visite. Author's collection.

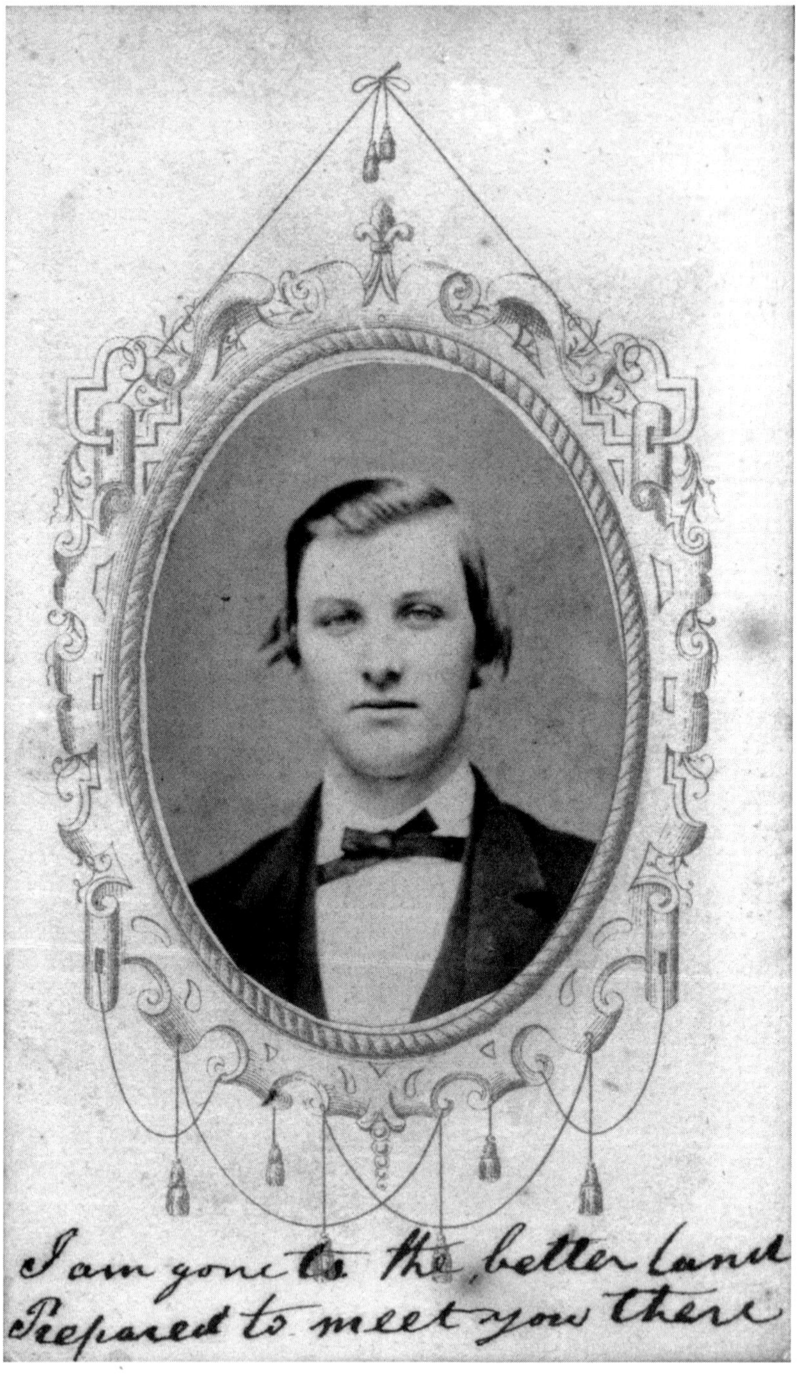

Figure 16. Memorial card for Charles E. Hall, ca. 1867. Carte de visite. Andover-Harvard Theological Library, Harvard Divinity School.

nize in the Union-blue binding and embossed gold decorations the Federal uniforms that paraded through the streets and haunted the battlefields of recent memory.[64]

First published by her uncle, Lucius Stebbins of Hartford, Stebbins's book was reprinted as late as 1880 under different titles, including *Glory of the Immortal Life* (1871) and *Earthly Trials and Glory of the Immortal Life* (1879). Although it was an unapologetically verbose examination of the soul's immortality, Stebbins also saw her consolation book as a work of art. By positioning herself in the pictorial tradition she hoped to convey "glad conceptions to all who look upon this picture of the *glories of the immortal life*," adding modestly that her success was only "inasmuch as its brightest . . . tints have been borrowed from the sketches of divinist models—*the sacred artists*."[65] In a sense, then, Stebbins used the sacred artists to subordinate her own toils in composing an elaborate excursus on "the great doctrine of immortality." She was, in effect, preemptively deflecting critics who would accuse her of transgressing established roles of religious authority in American Protestantism. But her application of the pictorial motif was not only to establish a deflective maneuver. It also spoke to transitions in memorial iconography that brokered the communion of shadows.

From cover to cover, *Our Departed Friends* demonstrated how photography was transforming the iconography of mourning during its years of publication. Not all copies would have included photograph leaves at the end of the binding. Indeed, much like Bibles during the period, Stebbins's book was sold by subscription, and purchasers would have had the option to include albums for a premium charge. Among extant copies, few more than a quarter of subscribers purchased album leaves, and only a fraction of these remaining copies still include photographs. Despite a paucity of surviving archival evidence, however, Charles was hardly the only one whose likeness was displayed within the pages of the consolation book. The difficulty of identifying precise subscription records and the impossibility of cataloging every instance of photographic display hardly diminishes the fact that the very availability of album pages marks an important development in iconographies of mourning that were increasingly attentive to theologies of recognition, evident in the process of displacing figurative symbols with likenesses of the deceased.

The front cover and frontispiece of *Our Departed Friends* feature conventional funereal iconography. On the blue cloth cover, an embossed angel with outstretched hand is surrounded by four stems of lily, one in each of the four corners. Both were traditional funerary icons. Angels were depicted as messengers between heaven and earth, and the outstretched hand figuratively reaching toward heaven also pointed to the embossed gilt circle bearing the phrase "Glory of the Immortal Life," effectively highlighting the triumphant rewards awaiting the souls of those dearly departed. Similarly, the lily was the traditional symbol of the resurrection of Christ and the promise of the restoration of the souls of the faithful. More densely iconographic than the cover, an engraving of a cemetery scene on the frontispiece continues to invoke conventional tableaux of grief and mourning. Two women kneel beside a freshly covered grave, while a man in uniform stands behind the simple internment. A bouquet of flowers, symbolizing the brevity of life, has been set upon the heap of earth, and a willow tree, symbolizing both body-bending grief and resurrection—the willow will regenerate from a cutting—embraces the three figures. Again, an angel, mediating one's passage between heaven and earth, watches over the whole scene. Simple grave markers, urns, an obelisk, and a monument comprise the background, each of which was associated with conventional funerary iconography.

Illustrations throughout the text also rely on memorial iconographies. In an engraving entitled "Raising of Jarius Daughter" in her chapter "The Resurrection"—in the copy I now hold, someone has folded in this page a single flower, now crumbled—the empty shoes below the bed signified death. The same motif was reiterated several chapters later in a print of a modern deathbed scene. Here, the good death is modeled by prayerful resignation. The dying man's ailing body is bent in prayer as the cleric administers his last rites, and the executor, still blinded by mortal concerns, reaches into his breast pocket for a pen to sign the mess of papers spilled on the bed. The finality of the moment is signaled both by the empty shoes and by the abandoned spectacles. "What glorious appearances will greet the organ of vision in the world of light!" Stebbins declared on the preceding page. "Something of this power seems to be given to the dying, as they gather up their feet at the close of their mortal journey."[66]

At the other end of Stebbins's ambitious account of "the prophecies and proofs of the great doctrine of immortality," optional die-cut-decorated album inserts paired photographic likenesses with scripture. Unlike the book's previous invocations of mourning iconography, the photographs benefit from deliberate scriptural framing. This captioning of the die-cut album frames was, in part, because the photographs referred to specific individuals—whose present circumstances could be witnessed through scripture—rather than to grand literary or painterly motifs. Turning to the end of the volume in which Charles's picture was preserved, the two album leaves,

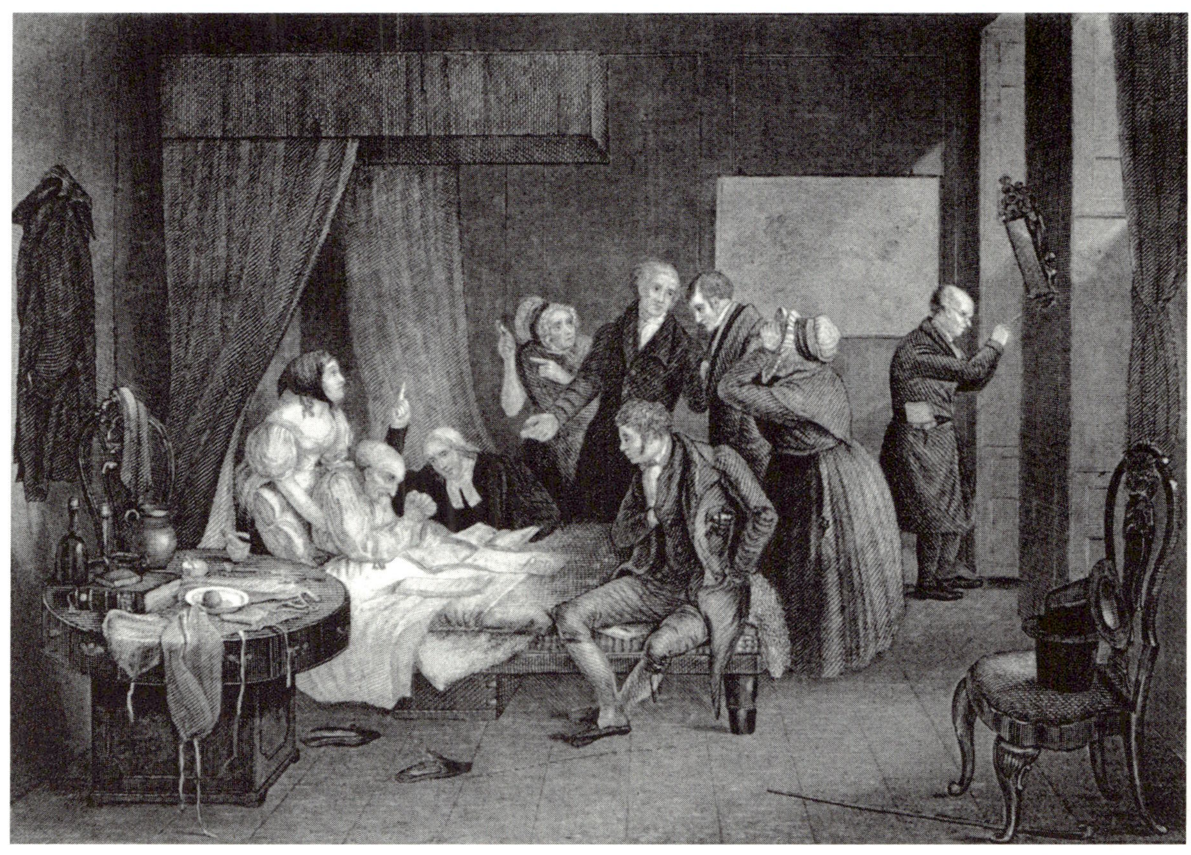

Figure 17. "Then Shall the Righteous Shine Forth as the Sun." Engraving from *Our Departed Friends* (Hartford, 1867). Author's collection.

with spaces for a total of eight card photographs, include four likenesses. Below a studio portrait of a young man with a full beard, perhaps a soldier, is a line from the Revelation of John, "And God shall wipe away all tears from their eyes," a verse that speaks both to the promises of heaven and to the community of the bereaved (fig. 18a). The words of the prophet Daniel, "The wise shall shine as the brightness of the firmament," was paired with a carte de visite of a Union infantryman, and a photograph of a baby girl—her gender indicated by her hair's center part—was coupled to a verse from Paul's epistle to the Galatians with apparent deliberation: "An heir of God through Christ" (fig. 18b). Beneath Charles's youthful visage (fig. 18a) is the heartening promise from the Gospel of Matthew: "Of such is the kingdom of heaven." The portraits are not identified in their setting by name, simply by their likenesses. Only by removing the likenesses from their ensconced position—an action that risks compromising the integrity of the album—do we learn the identity of those whose names have been recorded. Even the inscription below Charles's likeness is obscured when it is in the album, a fact that gestures to the photograph's other display contexts. Not unlike Stebbins's figurative "daguerreotypes," the studio photographs placed at the end of the book also facilitated this divine impression of redemptive promise through material form. By invoking the body in ways that the conventional iconography in her book's frontispiece and illustrations could not, moreover, the likenesses prompted more urgent reflection on the temporality of mortal life. Indeed these "daguerreotypes" were also designed to remind the living that their names were on the roll call too. By opening with figurative representations of death and concluding with photographic representations of the deceased, Stebbins demonstrated a moment when likenesses were in the process of displacing figurative iconographies in becoming dominant modes of remembrance.

"A Relic Which Becomes You Well"

"On many a shelf at home," wrote the Massachusetts Baptist minister Daniel Clarke Eddy in his 1857 gift book, *The Young Woman's Friend*, "is the silver plate snatched as a memento from the coffin ere it was lowered into the ground; the miniature form taken just before the loved one died, or while it was in its little shroud; full many a relic which becomes you well, is worn in memory." Notwithstanding Eddy's religious affiliation or political orientation—in 1854 he was elected by the Know-Nothing Party to the Massachusetts legislature—his description invokes the ubiquity of postmortem and

Here Is My Name When I Am Dead

memorial daguerreotypes of children in mid-nineteenth-century American homes. He also marks a changing understanding of relics among American Protestants.[67] A quarter of a century earlier in the first edition of his *American Dictionary*, Noah Webster defined "relic" as "that which is left after the loss or decay of the rest" and, more specifically, as "the body of a deceased person; a corpse." In this definition, a relic signified absence; it was what remained when, according to another period definition, "the body [was] deserted by the soul." Corpses were relics. And yet even though Webster did not alter his definition in the 1857 edition of his dictionary (published the same year as Eddy's book), Eddy's use of the term nevertheless suggests an interest in presence — "full many a relic which becomes you well, is worn in memory." Sixth-plate daguerreotypes — the "silver plate snatched" — could easily be worn in vestments, tucked into folds or pockets. But Eddy was likely here referring to articles intended for ornamental wear. And if the nativist Baptist minister may have scoffed at the idea that these likenesses mirrored the devotional habits of Catholic immigrants, the category of the photographic relic nevertheless resonated for many of his contemporaries as articles that are "kept in memory of another with a kind of religious veneration."[68]

American Protestants beheld photographs as relics of the departed that signaled the wider canopy of the communion of shadows. They accomplished this role by wedding fragments of the deceased body — namely, hair — into presentments of likenesses before fully subsuming the role that corporeal fragments had previously performed. Mourning jewelry had been popular well before the mid-nineteenth century when photographic technologies began to recenter memorial iconographies on visual representations of the deceased. In 1693, a gold band manufactured by the Boston jeweler Jeremiah Dunner became the first article of mourning jewelry made by someone born in the colonies.[69] A century later in Philadelphia, Joseph Anthony, a prominent "goldsmith and jeweller," advertised "Miniature Pictures set . . . in Hair" and "mourning rings & lockets Made on the shortest Notice" among his "General assortment of Gold, Silver, Plated Wares, & Jewellery of the newest Fashion and most elegant taste."[70] If hairwork and photographs were not considered relics in the sacramental sense familiar to Roman Catholicism and Eastern Orthodoxy, they were nevertheless highly charged articles that traversed similar theological and social registers. In this case, the communion of shadows opens a window into the material theology of American Protestantism.

Not all articles of photographic jewelry were worn in mourning. Collectors Larry West and Patricia Abbot have identified no fewer than fifteen

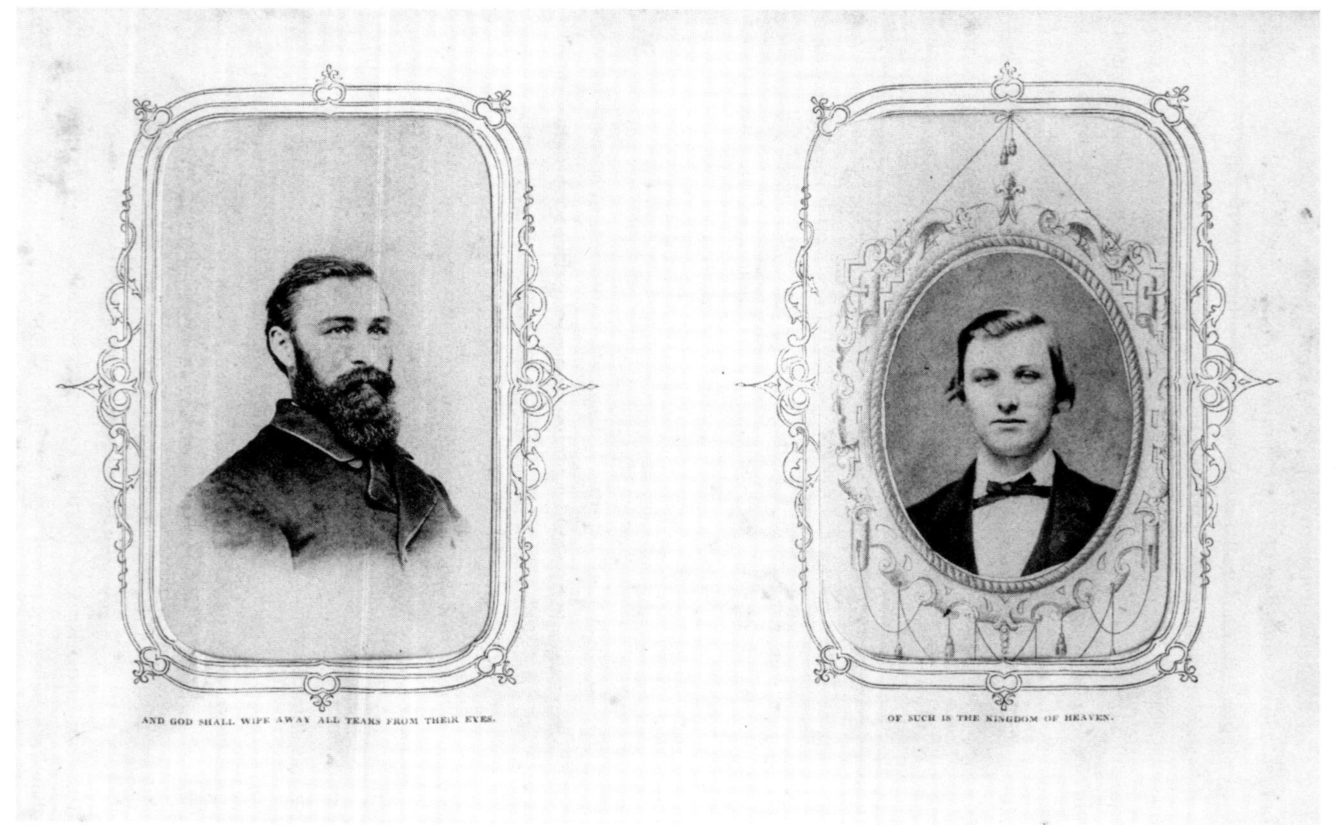

AND GOD SHALL WIPE AWAY ALL TEARS FROM THEIR EYES.

OF SUCH IS THE KINGDOM OF HEAVEN.

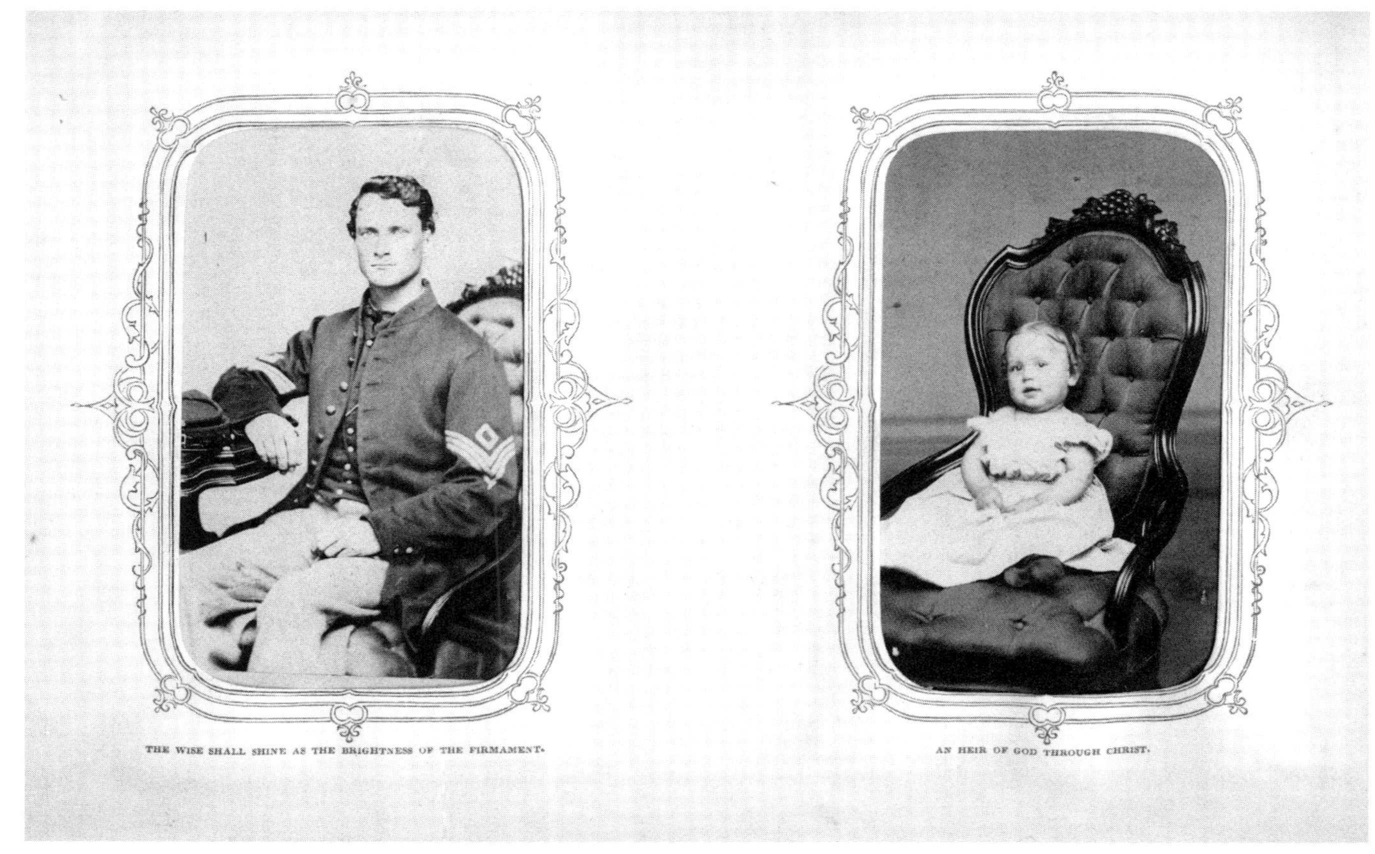

Figures 18a (*top*) and 18b. Carte de visite photograph album from *Our Departed Friends* (Hartford, 1867). Andover-Harvard Theological Library, Harvard Divinity School.

categories of nineteenth-century photographic jewelry, from bracelets and buttons to stickpins and watch fobs, of which they have classified one as mourning pins and badges, although they also recognize that any article could have become "commemorative."[71] Photographic jewelry could be worn for a variety of reasons—to commemorate a birth or christening, a marriage, an anniversary, or a holiday; to announce political or social allegiance; or simply as novelty ornamentation. And yet, when articles depicted someone who had died, they seemed to become all the more precious. Imagine the sense of urgency and renewed loss that would envelop a grieving widow, parent, or sibling if the very object designed to provide a tangible link with their beloved was suddenly gone. In late April 1853, William Catchcart of Baltimore lost "a GOLD LOCKET, with a male Daguerreotype likeness and plait of hair in the back." We can imagine the hair belonging to a son lost in the Mexican-American War or a brother who headed west in search of gold and adventure, never to return. Perhaps the man in the daguerreotype was felled by something more mundane—a fever or an accident. Whoever it was, the cost of its absence far outweighed the article's market value. The locket, Catchcart pleaded, "is of little value to anyone but the owner, by whom it is highly prized as a memento."[72] Newspapers commonly ran ads for these lost relics throughout the middle decades of the century. In October 1856 a citizen of Baltimore offered a "liberal reward" to anyone who would return "a HAIR BRACELET, with Gold Locket," that had slipped off her wrist earlier in the week.[73] Two years later in New York, a thief lifted "one Gold-Linked Chain, with cross and large locket attached, containing a lady's likeness, marked M.A.P." and "a lady's mourning pin, containing hair," among several other articles.[74] In addition to demonstrating the precious nature of these articles, worn close to the body, intended not merely for display but for communion, these classifieds also point to the association of hair and likenesses, especially in memorial photography. If over the course of the nineteenth century photographs became increasingly identified with absent bodies, nowhere was this more evident than in the common association of hairwork and photographic likenesses.

In the eighteenth and early nineteenth century, hairwork—a variety of fancywork created from human hair worked into jewelry or ornamental display—was popularly used to materialize bonds of affection and to memorialize those who had died through a relic of the very body that had once commingled with those now bereaved.[75] Far from becoming obsolete after the introduction of photography, hairwork in fact became even more popular as a parlor entertainment, and hair jewelry became a common form of adorn-

Here Is My Name When I Am Dead

ment. Throughout the 1860s, *Godey's Lady's Book and Magazine* published notices of recently mailed articles that women could expect to arrive over the coming days and weeks. Out of twenty-six such notices in September 1863 were five hair rings, one cross, one hair pin, one hair chain, and one unspecified "hair-work."[76] The two "braiding patterns" that were mailed were most likely for women who endeavored to create their own hairwork at home. "Hitherto almost exclusively confined to professed manufacturers of hair trinkets," *Godey's* had written in 1850, "this work has now become a drawing-room occupation, as elegant and as free from all the annoyances and objections of litter, dirt, or unpleasant smells, as the much-practiced knitting, netting, and crochet can be." Although its readers surely excused themselves from such deceptions, this earlier piece instructed them that by "manufactur[ing] the hair of beloved friends and relatives into bracelets, chains, rings, ear-rings, and devices" at home, they would "insure that they do actually wear the memento they prize, and not a fabric substituted for it, as we fear has sometimes been the case."[77] Hair bracelets had been a popular mourning accessory since at least the seventeenth century, and during the eighteenth century girls' academies instructed pupils in the art of palette-worked hair, which consisted of either finely chopped or dissolved hair that was painted into memorial tableaux.[78]

By the 1850s, loupe work had become fashionable, which was made by curling the hair on a hot iron and then arranging it into feather-like plumes, such as the one demonstrated in a "catalogue of artistic hair work for mementoes and souvenirs" published by the National Artistic Hair-Work Company in 1886.[79] This catalogue was composed of a variety of patterns for memorial hairwork, including several for pins, pendants, and rings. The majority of these patterns featured conventional memorial iconography—urns, anchors, willow trees, angels, crowns, wreaths, crosses. Two of the patterns in the 1886 catalogue, however, were intended to incorporate photographic likenesses into the design . In the first, a wreath of willow and blossoms encircles a photograph of a young man (fig. 19a). The "negative" for this pattern, as the catalogue termed their designs, was mounted on an 8- by 10-inch plate of glass, which would have been suitable for a large wall frame. The second design features a young girl, surrounded by an open wreath, although the negative for this pattern was on a much smaller 4- by 6-inch plate (fig. 19b). Despite the variation in size, the photographs in both patterns would likely have been card-size portraits, as indicated by the proportion of the likeness in relation to the hairwork. In the second pattern, the girl is wearing a locket. Although these were merely patterns that would be modified by con-

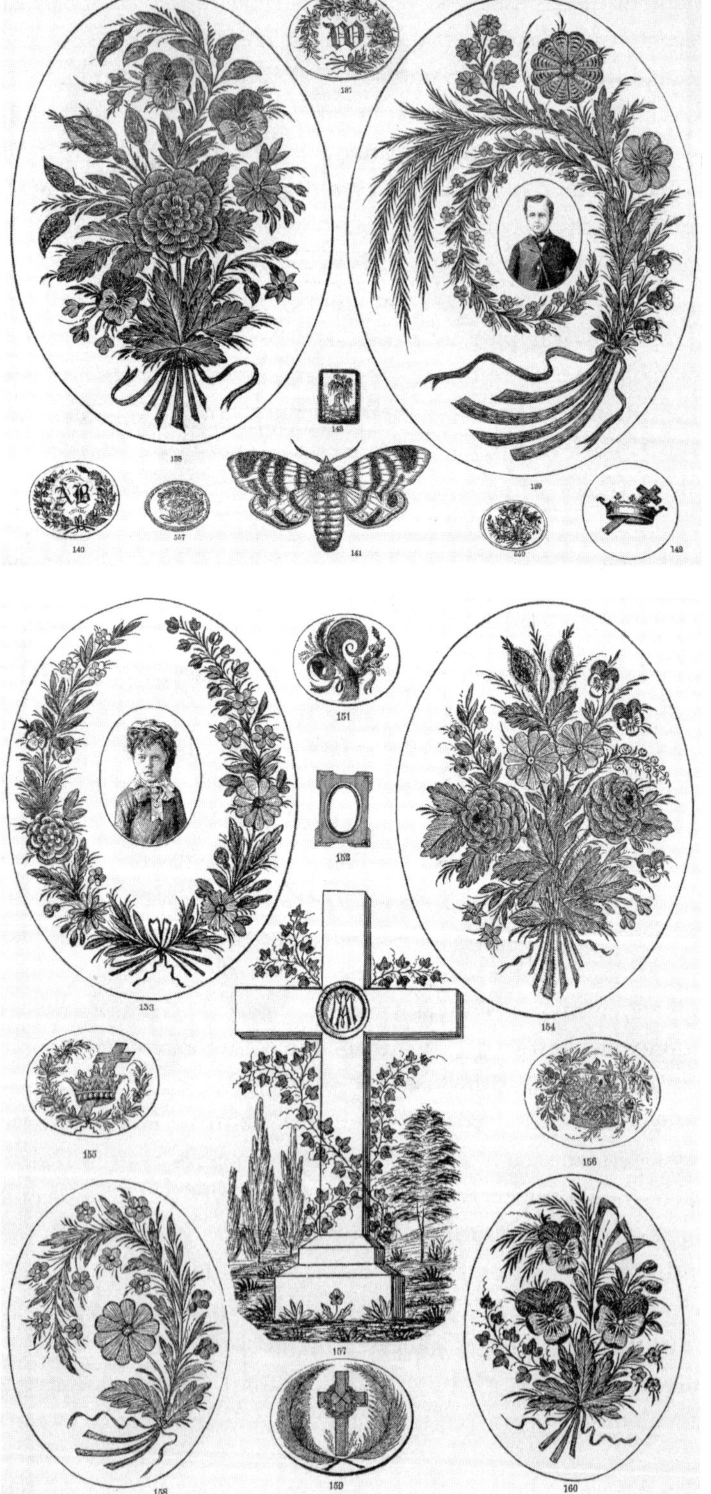

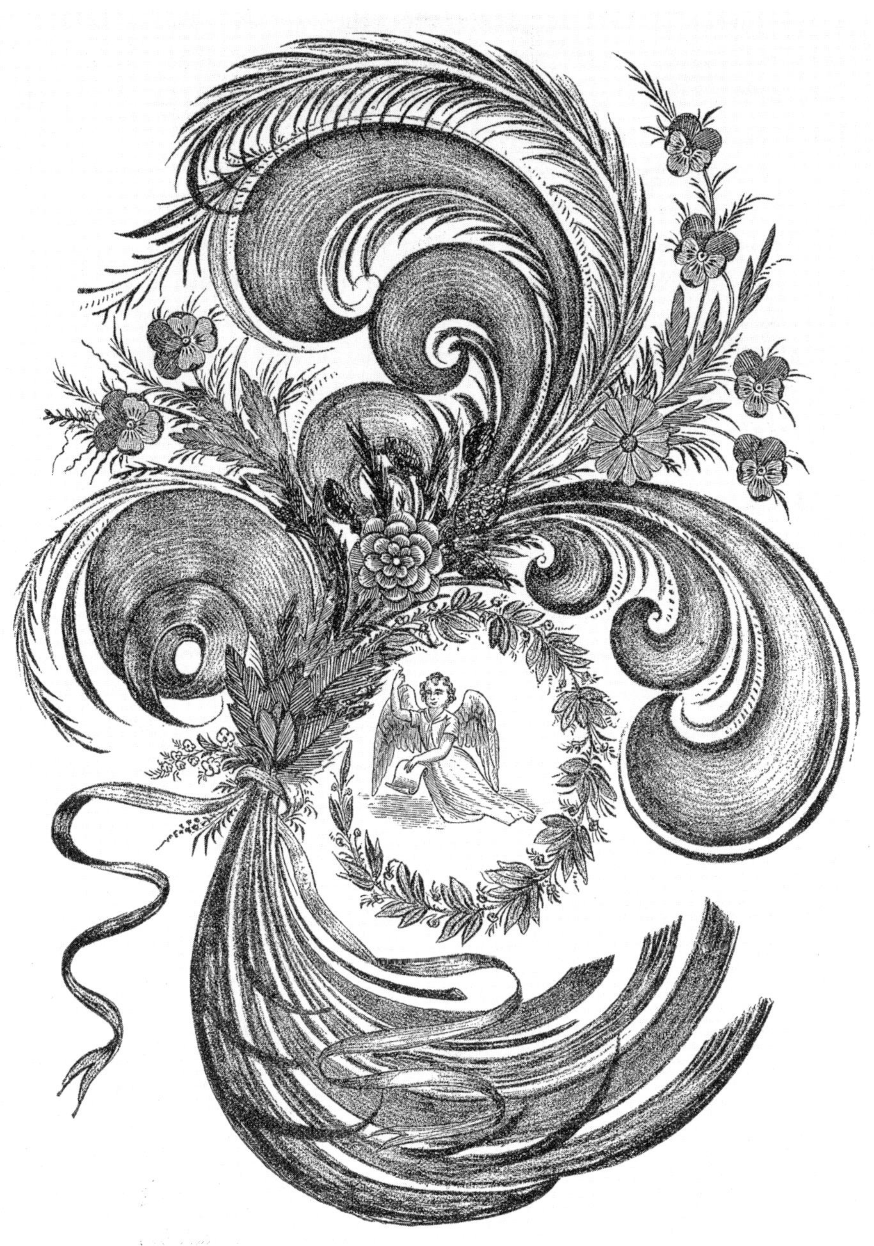

Figures 19a (*opposite, top*), 19b (*opposite, bottom*), and 19c. Hairwork "negatives,"
including two samples for incorporating photographs. *Catalogue of Artistic Hair
Work for Mementoes and Souvenirs*, Library of Congress.

sumers, the inclusion of a portrait in which the depicted individual is wearing a locket—which could have held a likeness or a lock of hair, or both—demonstrated the deep entanglement of photography and hair in memorial culture toward the end of the century.[80]

If the catalogue only gestures to probable associations between likenesses and hairwork, another artifact more surely demonstrates their representational collaboration. Notice, for instance, how in this album of card photographs (fig. 20) the hairwork is situated in sequence with other likenesses without any further remark than the identifying inscriptions: "Mother / Died Dec 16th 1867 / Aged 56 years" and "Father / Died May 31st 1872 / Aged 64 years / Born March 16th /1808." Flipping through the album, it is as if the worked hair was reiterating if not replacing the albumen prints (absent any further written commentary, later beholders do not know if Mother and Father are found elsewhere in the album). And if the hair prompts revulsion in a way that photographs do not, their common association in nineteenth-century artifacts suggests that this responsive discrepancy was not shared by their crafters or earliest beholders.[81]

This album's deliberate orchestration of relics invites beholders to reflect not on life generally but on specific saints in glory. Here, the worked hair is positioned deliberately as a compositional analogue to the surrounding photographs. Far more readily available for researchers are articles of jewelry that feature both hair and likenesses.[82] Significantly, however, in both forms of display, hair and photographs were presented as compositional analogues. The visual habits of photographic beholding were caught up in modes of representation and recognition that were distinct from the legacy of hairwork. Nevertheless, the relics' ubiquitous association demands they be treated as, in the terminology of Geoffrey Batchen, "hybrid" artifacts rather than competing modes of representation.[83] As early as 1844 daguerreotypists were advertising their ability to set daguerreotype portraits "in a breast-pin, bracelet, locket or finger ring."[84] When Millard Fillmore sat for the Boston daguerreotypist John A. Whipple in 1851, Whipple made duplicates for the president's wife and daughter, the latter of whom received a "beautiful little miniature of the same in a locket" and was "greatly delighted with it."[85] Around the same time a jeweler in Providence, Rhode Island, named Cornelius Cunliff began manufacturing swivel box pins, which, according to an 1892 retrospective on the jewelry industry, placed a "regulation" box pin design on a pivot "to contain hair in one side and a miniature in the other." A brooch containing a tintype of a Union soldier (fig. 21) exemplifies this common type of photojewelry. Notice how the ring for a chain, or perhaps a black ribbon, as was

Here Is My Name When I Am Dead

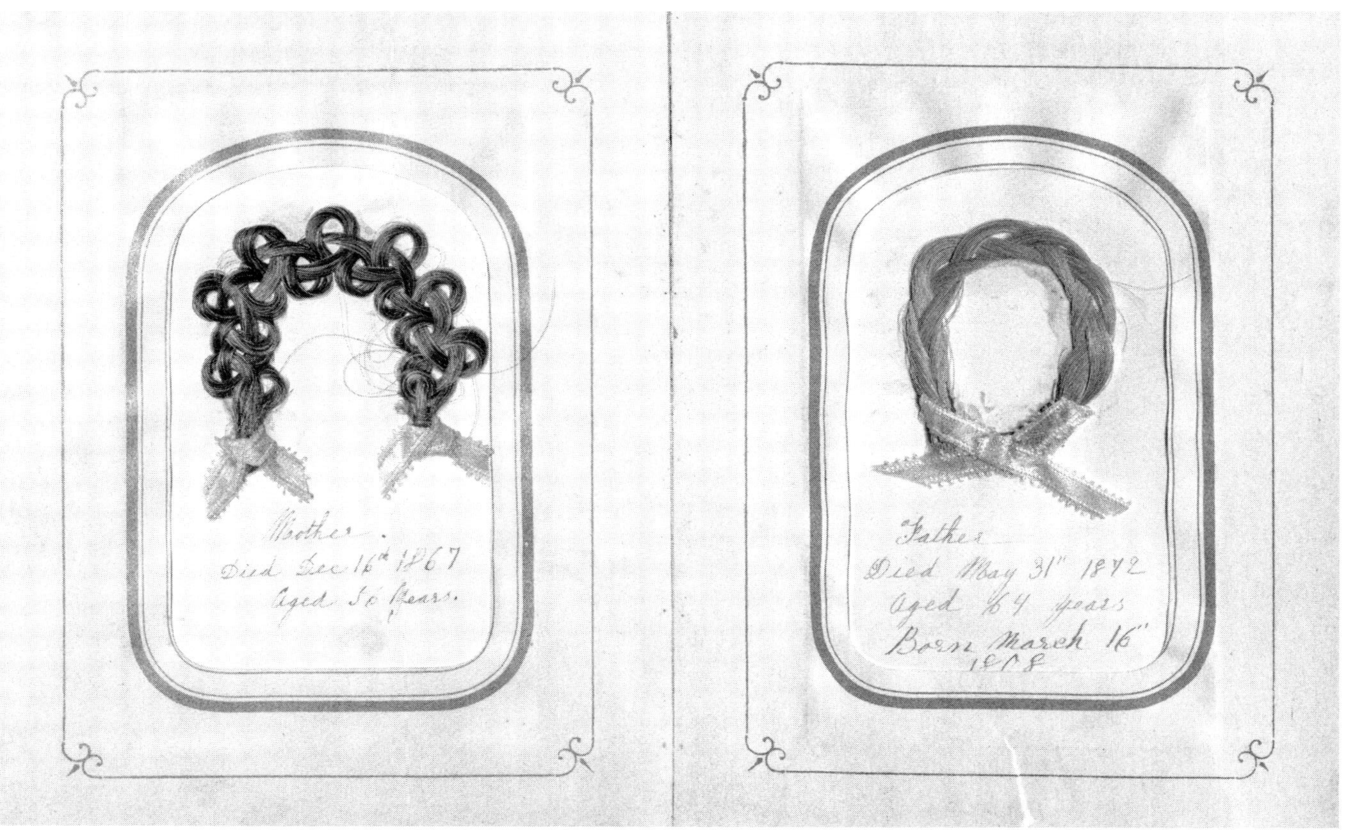

Figure 20. Hairwork "likenesses" from carte de visite album, ca. 1865–75. Author's collection.

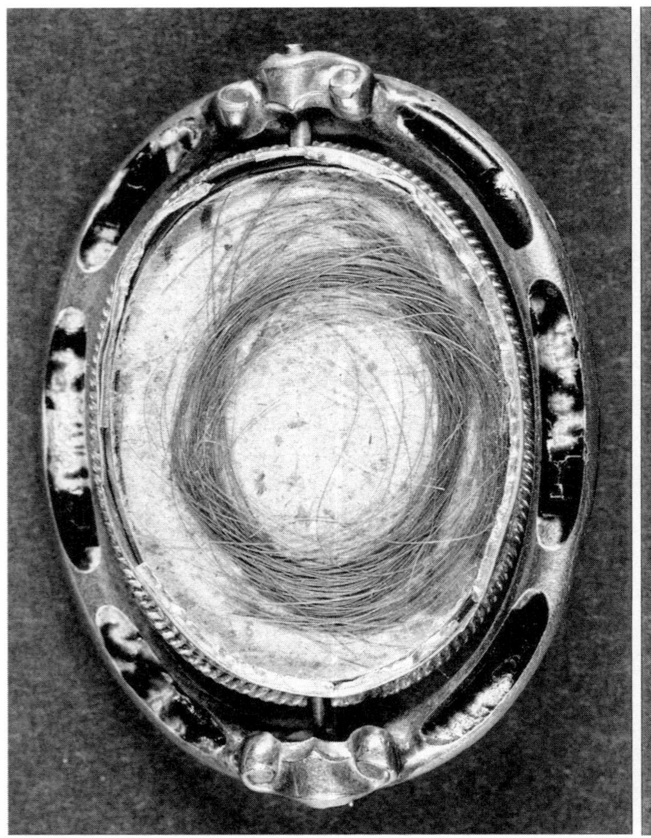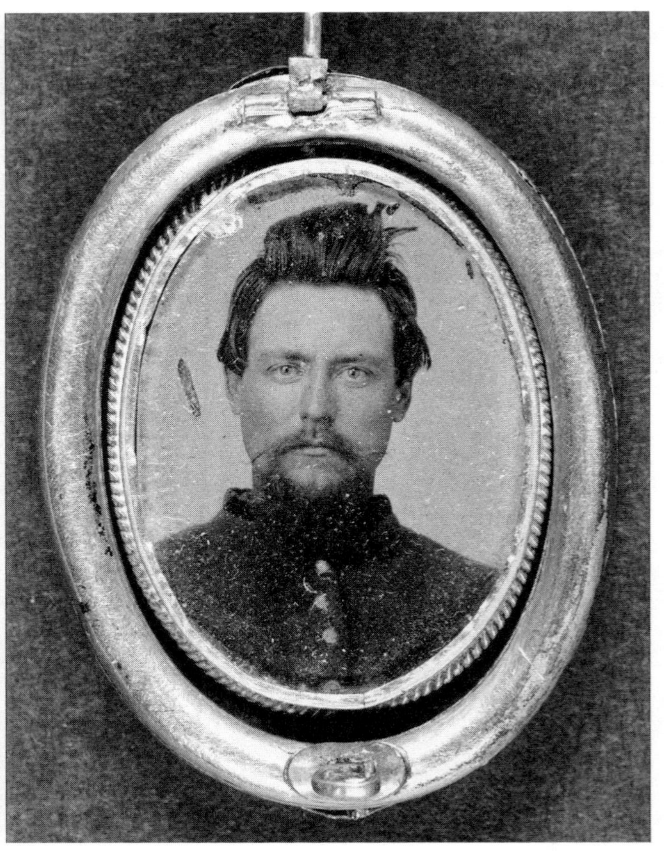

Figure 21. Swivel brooch of unidentified Union soldier. Oval sixteenth-plate tintype, 4.6 by 3.4 cm (case), ca. 1861–65. Library of Congress.

common during periods of mourning, was positioned below the likeness, demonstrating that the intended beholder was the wearer rather than the public. Standard box pins were also intended to contain "mementoes in the shape of hair, picture, or the like," and patrons often tucked a lock of hair beneath a likeness when an article could not easily display both. According to the same retrospective, the intended "purpose" of lockets attached to long chains, popular among women in the mid-nineteenth century, "was to contain hair or a miniature."[86]

Worked hair and photographic likenesses may not have carried the theological weight of relics of Jesus, the apostles, or the saints, but for many American Protestants during the nineteenth century, struggling to reconcile the untimely demise of their beloved with a desire to fulfill the expectation to resign to God's inscrutable will, these articles each allowed a continued mode of presence and communion with the absent body. The practice of working hair preceded the theological emphasis on recognition that developed during the middle decades of the nineteenth century, and yet as a cultural practice, it continued into the early twentieth century when changing attitudes and aesthetics contributed to its decline. As a prephotographic mode of authorizing the historical presence of individuals depicted in portrait miniatures or memorialized in iconographic tableaux, the continued association with commemorative and memorial artifacts after the introduction of photography suggests that hairwork silently instructed the visual habits of memorial photography. In other words, as a conventional signifier of presence, hairwork contributed to the photograph's co-option of that function for later generations. Moreover, as a somatic survival of the deceased's body, hair succeeded in the task of immortalization that photography could only pretend to accomplish. Whatever the precise nature of the relationship between photography and hairwork, these entangled relics were significant components of a memorial culture that was increasingly concerned with the body of the deceased as something more than memento mori for the bereaved.

Conclusion

In his lively study of northern Protestant notions and experiences of death, Gary Laderman has argued that nineteenth-century evangelicals "did not grieve the corpse — it simply began to serve a new purpose of functioning as an instrument for healing the pain of survivors." This assessment can surely be arrived at by attending to theological instructions and popular literature that modeled both good death and proper resignation to God's own time. But perhaps the issue is not that Protestants did not grieve but that the rituals and rhythms of grief changed during the course of the century. For Laderman, the corpse was a "symbolic object," abundant with potential meanings for different situations and persons. "In spite of the rather uniform ritual structure that managed the elimination of the dead from living society," he writes, "there was no fixed meaning for the remains."[87] Nor, we might add, following Stabile, were the "remains" of death limited to the corpse. The communion of shadows extended the reach of earlier memorial customs even as it transformed inherited mourning practices by making visual representations of the deceased—rather than traditional iconographies of death—a central feature of the deceased's memory. While portraits did become the increasingly dominant mode of commemoration, the rising popularity of photographic memorials neither displaced traditional iconographies entirely nor signaled movement away from religious motifs or sensibilities. If a central function of memorial photographs was to trace the silhouette of the soul's survival after the body's demise, to behold in the mortal frame the promise of celestial glory, another development in the communion of shadows amplified these claims by surfacing the spirit on plates of glass. Spirit photography is often approached as a curiosity on the fringes of nineteenth-century religion and culture. But when placed alongside the vast culture of memorial photography, we begin to see it in a new light.

Here Is My Name When I Am Dead

THREE

AGENTS OF A FULLER REVELATION

On a rainy New Year's Day, 1863, readers of the *Daily Evening Telegraph* of San Francisco who found themselves skimming through the latest financial reports, war information, and advertisements for sundry elixirs to cure coughs, purify blood, and restore hair may also have noted the birth of a daughter to Philip Quigley, as well as the deaths of three young boys during the preceding week. Just below the death notices of Hyatt James, aged two years, nine months; Henry de Courellion, aged ten months, and Michael Edward Monahan, nearly six, the paper gave notice of some curious information trickling in from the East Coast. "Believers in spiritual manifestations are now greatly excited in relation to alleged discoveries of a Mr. Mumler of Boston," the *Telegraph* reported, who is reputedly "enabled to produce photographs of spirits around his human sitters." Suspecting "some humbug about the affair" when news of William Mumler's apparent discovery began to buzz through the cables the previous fall, a committee "from this city" was sent to Boston "to investigate the matter, and report that there is something in it." "The pictures of real flesh-and-blood individuals in such pictures, are opaque," the paper explained, "but those of the spirits are so thin and transparent, that curtains may be seen through them, yet they are alleged to be recognizable likenesses of the deceased."[1]

The guarded optimism in this titillating report entitled "Pictures of Dead Men," printed just below the week's death notices, exposes a seam in the communion of shadows, a fissure, perhaps, between fraud and faith. For hosts of Americans across a spectrum of religious affiliations and social stations, Mumler's pictures, as he would later put it in his autobiography, offered "evidences of a future existence" that were recognized by the bereaved as "actual likenesses of those who have passed to spirit life."[2] But what Mumler and others advertised as spiritual revelation, others would decry as hokum. "Mr. Rufus Elmer, of Springfield, Mass., was swindled out of seven dollars and fifty cents, by Mumler and his woman," railed one agent of disillusion, "and Elmer is no fool."[3] Still others placed blame on "the amount of credulity a man must have, to believe that the picture of a spirit can be taken by a photographist, the same as he would take the likeness of a human being."[4] By early 1863, the photographic profession was also weighing in on the pictures. In January, the *Photographic News* of London nervously described the "considerable interest" that was "excited in certain circles in America by the alleged production of photographs of disembodied spirits" and reminded readers that a previous issue of the paper had "alluded to the subject . . . as a *canard*." Now the pictures were being defended in numerous papers by presumably reputable sources, including "practical photographers," who investigated the process and, in the words of one William Guay, were "obliged to endorse its legitimacy." By early February the paper had had enough. The American Photographic Society had recently "solemnly resolved that the spirit likenesses are a fraud and gross deception," and their counterparts in London in turn renounced the pictures as "pitiable delusion originating in shameful fraud or mischievous trickery," especially grievous as a form of Spiritualism "in which our own art is prostituted to purposes of imposture."[5] What is more, hinting at mounting disagreement within the ranks of modern Spiritualists, Guay had been commissioned by Andrew Jackson Davis, the celebrated Seer of Poughkeepsie and architect of modern American Spiritualism, "to make a strict investigation of the process."[6] So convinced was Guay of Mumler's gift — or so enticed by the profits of the trade — that by the end of the decade he had become Mumler's assistant. In the 1860s, scientific discoveries, from microorganisms to fluorescence, had made it possible to see new depths in the fabric of creation (the latter described by the British physicist who discovered it in the early 1850s as "literally darkness visible").[7] If arrangements of chemicals and lenses in other contexts could prove the existence of things as yet unseen, the notion that cameras could also record the existence of the soul's survival after death was, for many, entirely plausible. For many others, spirit photography represented the worst qualities of deception and greed in a decade of tremendous death and unimaginable grief. Even as harsh skepticism warmed into cautious acceptance among many investigators, more than a decade later Mumler still bristled that "many of my strongest opponents have been professed Spiritualists."[8] Whatever Mumler's motives may have been, and no matter the sincerity of

Agents of a Fuller Revelation

his claims, the dramatic debut of spirit photography in the United States in 1862 staged the pageantry of beholding under a spotlight that better illuminates the wider cast of the communion of shadows.

Haunted by accusations of humbug from the beginning, spirit photography was also approached by the bereaved—be they Methodists from Boston, Jews from Louisville, or Baptists from Richmond—as evidence of their beloved's continued existence after death and as a material disclosure of the life they would, in due time, again share. Over the course of the next four decades, many claims would be made as to what, precisely, spirit photographs disclosed. The spirits would also change appearance over time, transitioning from recognizable likenesses in the 1860s to a variety of effluvia and, in the developing terminology, "ectoplasm" by the turn of the twentieth century.[9] Mumler's photographs were limited to the former category, those of recognizable likenesses. Still, within this category, the spirits could communicate through a variety of manifestations. In an undated pamphlet published at the end of the century, R. L. Green, "Spirit Photographer" of Onset, Massachusetts, provided a "rough classification of what are called Spirit Photographs." They could include, as Mumler's did, portraits of "psychical entities not seen by normal vision," as well as "pictures of objects not seen nor thought of by the sitter or by the Medium or operator." By this Green was referring to the "flowers, words, lights and various emblematic objects" that appeared in many portraits. In this portrait (fig. 22) of Colonel W. H. W. Cushman of Chicago, for example, the Quaker spirit brought with her a bonnet and lock of hair that settled into his lap (someone—the spirit or Mumler—emphasized these objects by writing "hair" on a placard just below Cushman's folded arms). A third category of spirit pictures were those "portraits on plates which developers have failed to bring into view, but which can be seen and described by clairvoyants and by mediums when in trance." Just as different waves of light, manipulated by chemicals and lenses, could reveal unseen truths in laboratories, so too, such advocates held, could mediums, whom one prominent Spiritualist likened to "the sensitized plate of the photographer," see what remained invisible on the glass.[10] Throughout his career, "entities not seen by normal vision," as well as the objects they bore from the beyond, populated Mumler's pictures.[11] Even as the profile of spiritual manifestations changed over the course of the nineteenth century, the debate that Mumler's pictures sparked would define encampments in the communion of shadows well beyond his own blustery career.

The seam in the communion of shadows was, in turn, less between Spiritualists and anti-Spiritualists, or between religious orthodoxy and hereti-

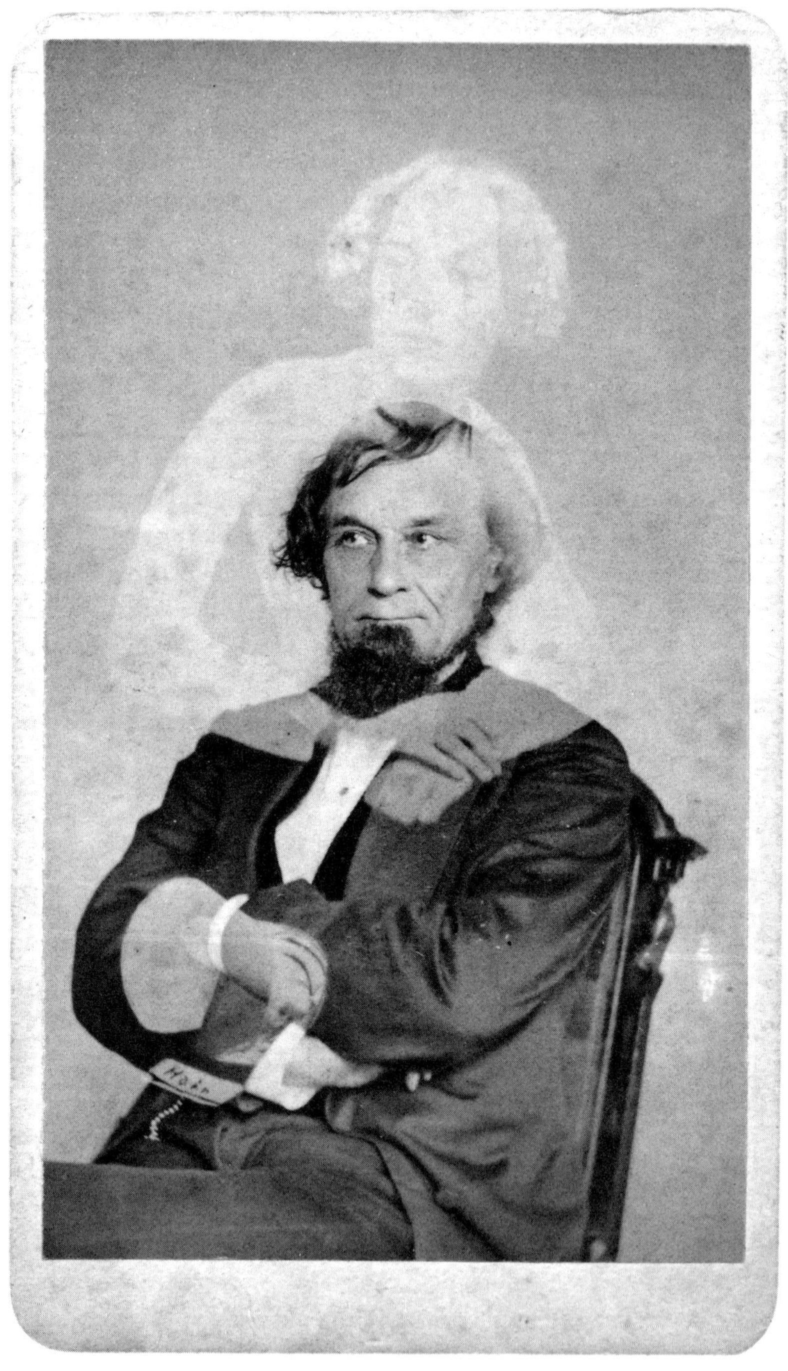

Figure 22. Colonel Cushman. Albumen silver print. William H. Mumler, ca. 1870. J. Paul Getty Museum. Used with permission.

cal humbuggery, than in the confidence invested in the visual authority of photographs in modern America. What did they—what could they—disclose? Mumler's pictures at once provided evidence of future existence and, as one columnist later put it, "a revelation that they may be made to lie with a most deceiving exactness."[12] Shrill debate around these curious artifacts in the 1860s frames historians' investigation of habits of beholding that unhinged photographs from what people saw in them. In early 1869, the tensions surrounding mechanical deception, scientific empiricism, and divine revelation would lead to Mumler's arrest and a very public trial that scrutinized the religious and historical authority of photographs. Mumler's career, trial, and demise is not the only story to tell about the rise and decline of spirit photography in nineteenth-century America. But it is an opportunity to explore competing habits of beholding surrounding a specific set of photographs and the larger cultural debates around religious authority in the modern world that they elicited. To a level previously unmatched, the curious case of William Mumler stages cautious, suspicious, and at times caustic practices of beholding, practices so fraught that they culminated in a public hearing that quite literally positioned the Bible and the camera as competing mechanisms of religious authority in modern America. In this unfolding drama, spirit pictures emerge within the communion of shadows as a hinge between the corporeal referents of bodies in studio portraiture and mourning photographs, on the one hand, and the practices of biblical beholding, on the other, that asked beholders to see what was really there, truths invisible to the eye that the camera had disclosed.

258 Washington Street, Boston

In 1862 William Mumler was an engraver by trade, employed by the silver firm of Bigelow Bros. & Kennard, when he was called to 258 Washington Street in Boston to investigate a recent spate of anomalies disfiguring a local jeweler's wares. Mrs. Stuart was best known for her hairwork, "the weaving of hair into bracelets, lockets, and similar articles" as "mementos of friends, both living and deceased." At her clients' request, many of these articles contained "provision for a photographic likeness of the person to be remembered." To make the likenesses "in the size and form required" of the jewelry, Mrs. Stuart employed a photographer who had "learned enough of the art to do it tolerably well." Of late, however, the pictures began "coming out blurred and confused, [with] inexplicable figures like stars and comets showing themselves, instead of the image of the sitter." Suspecting a chemical culprit, Mrs. Stuart sent for Mr. Mumler, whose profession required "some chemical knowledge" and who sometimes claimed to be an amateur photographer. Whether or not he had tinkered with photography before, during the course of his investigation, Mumler observed the tedious process of wet-plate photography—selecting, cleaning, and sensitizing the glass plate; making the exposure in the correct light and at the right focus before the plate dried; and developing the image on the plate through another alchemy of chemical solutions. This was to say nothing of the subsequent process of using these glass negatives to make positive exposures on paper. One Sunday in early October, "while entirely alone in the gallery," he "attempted to get a picture of myself" in the manner he had observed countless times before. Upon developing the image, he instantly discovered that "a second form appeared upon the plate." Perplexed and bemused, he showed it to Mrs. Stuart, who "instantly pronounced it the portrait of a spirit who had taken this method of communicating with mortals on earth."[13]

Mrs. Stuart was, in fact, one Hannah Green Stuart, who, in addition to owning the jewelry shop, was also a medium and, like her mother, a clairvoyant physician. Modern Spiritualism had emerged onto the American scene some fourteen years before Mumler's discovery. Over the preceding decade it had attracted both a large and discordant following as well as untold seekers of curiosity and armies of skeptics.[14] William Mumler held throughout his life that he was not a Spiritualist in 1862—that he had "never believed in spiritualism, but has opposed and ridiculed it"—though others had often told him that he was a "powerful medium."[15] It was a title that he wore awkwardly throughout his career. Hannah, by contrast, embraced Spiritualism throughout her life, which marked her for scrutiny by disbelievers. Within a few weeks of Mumler's discovery, Hannah's role in the affair was handily censured in the *Boston Investigator*, a freethinking periodical. "The business had *originated* in her office, and she meant to have the benefits accruing from it secured to her place," the skeptical inquirer reported, adding that she "would not consent, upon any considerations, for Mr. Mumler to go to any other office once" to examine the claims.[16] In those first weeks in the autumn of 1862, Hannah refused to allow Mumler to attempt to replicate his process in other studios. The *Investigator* clearly discerned a swindle in this quarantine, though it is also possible that Mrs. Stuart, as the proprietor of her business, saw a market that she wanted to corner. When the two married in 1864—his first marriage and her second—her role as medium was subsumed in press coverage into Mumler's practice, and beyond the occasional reference to "Mumler and his woman," she became the ghost in the

   Agents of a Fuller Revelation

picture of Mumler's life. During the trial in 1869, the prosecution pressed for a further account of her role in the operations for a time, but bored quickly when witnesses yielded little detail beyond her presence as a bookkeeper. Still, in the wake of Mumler's arrest and the effect it had on his practice, it was Hannah who continued to advertise and practice as a "clairvoyant physician." After the trial, when William and Hannah returned to Boston, Hannah used her husband's talents to advertise her own bona fides in a carte de visite, "taken while entranced," of her "controlling power, DR. BENJ. RUSH" (figs. 23a [front] and b [back]).

The photograph depicts the prominent early American physician behind an entranced Hannah Mumler, his right hand cradling her head and his left hand reaching around her side, as if transferring energy from his hand to her hands, clasped and resting on her lap. Like many of Mumler's photographs, the head and torso are the most distinct parts of the spirit body, fading into disappearance lower in the frame. Ann Braude has mapped the contested terrain between medical "regulars" (physicians, usually male) and healing mediums (usually female) in nineteenth-century America, a period when medical therapies too frequently failed to heal and often induced further physical ailments.[17] Through the controlling power of Benjamin Rush, Hannah Mumler's remedies—including "Mesmirine for the Blood," a tonic that "acts on the blood" and is effective in "displacing the many different diseases the flesh is heir to"—were imbued with the imprimatur of male oversight, at the very least, and also the seal of one of the most famed medical authorities in early America. Hannah may have questioned the healing power of regulars, but she recognized the social power Rush freighted. The photograph was so vital to this message that, as an advertisement in the *Daily Cleveland Herald* promised, it "will be given away on application at the principal Drug Stores in the United States."[18]

The spectral likeness of Benjamin Rush was valuable currency among those seeking Mrs. W. H. Mumler's "clairvoyant remedy," but another symbol in the picture registered a different order of authority. The cross around her neck is in stark relief against her pale skin, as if to signal her continuity with, rather than rupture from, Christianity. This was a message that Mumler had worked to communicate from the beginning and that many of his patrons silently defended through their refusal to identify as Spiritualists. Americans with backgrounds as Universalists, Quakers, and Swedenborgians, among other liberal religious traditions, comprised the rank and file of antebellum Spiritualism. And yet, as many historians have noted, Spiritualism also "remained within the broad spectrum of religious belief."[19] Some

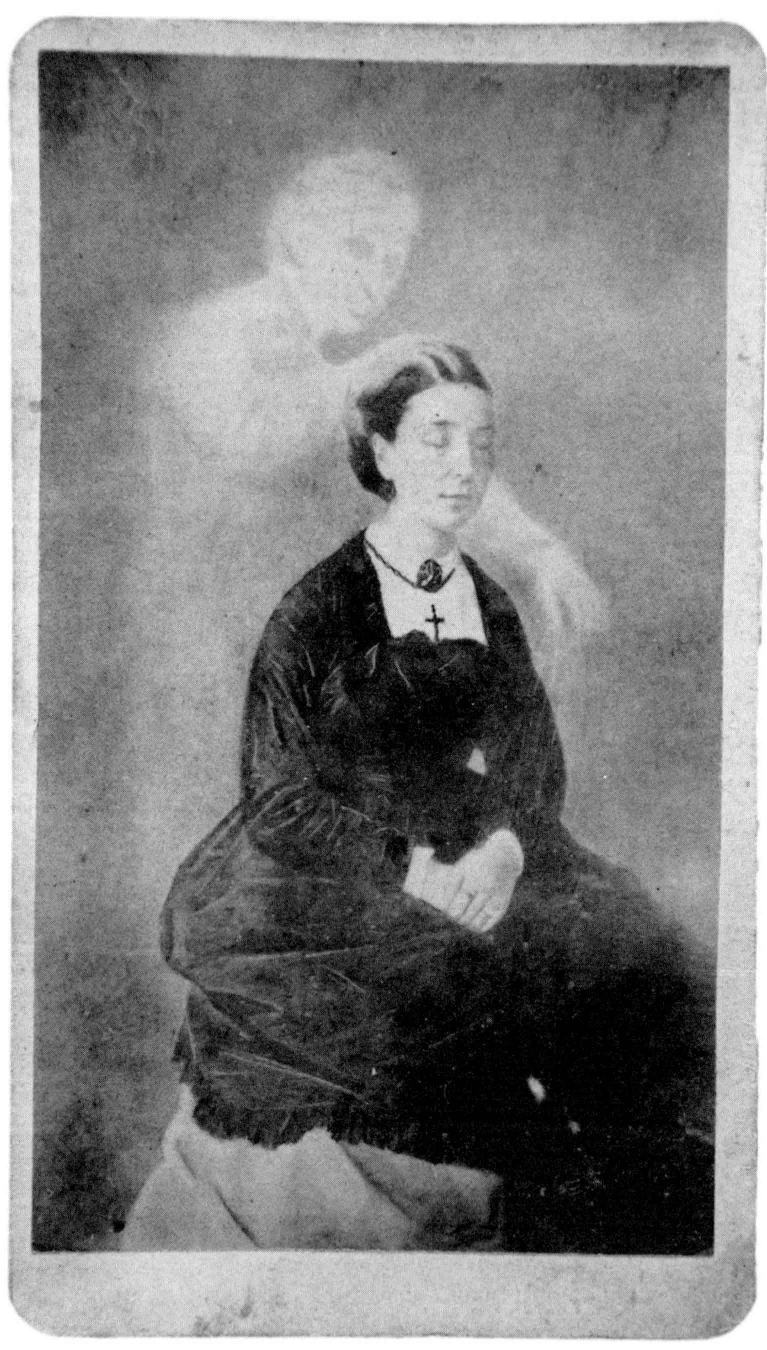

Figures 23a and 23b (*opposite*). "Hannah Mumler with the Controling Spirit of Benjamin Rush." Carte de visite (front and back), ca. 1870. Ackland Museum, University of North Carolina. Used with permission.

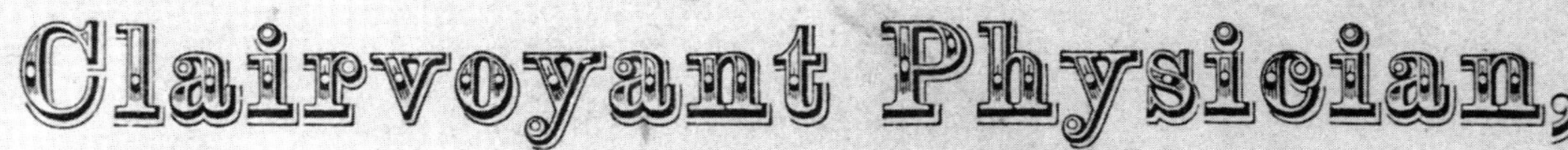

MRS. W. H. MUMLER,
Clairvoyant Physician,
170 West Springfield Street,
BOSTON, MASS.
N. B.—The Photograph on the reverse side is of Mrs Mumler, taken while entranced, and showing the controlling power, DR. BENJ. RUSH.

believers advocated "Christian Spiritualism" as a modern proof of the Bible (and indeed this language would be invoked in connection with Mumler's pictures), whereas others understood the spirits to convey a much stronger indictment of biblical claims. While the constellation of modern Spiritualism was vast, a central premise was that, from biblical time to the present, spirits had never ceased to address the living even as organized religion had stifled and at times demonized this communion. Revivalism and the rise of "resto-rationism"—the restoring of the early church—had transformed American religion in the early nineteenth century, and the emergence of modern Spiri-tualism was informed by this broad undercurrent of restoration.

Antebellum Protestant reform had advanced practices and pieties of individual redemption through biblical reading and personal sensations of "rebirth," and Spiritualists took this message further by teaching that, al-though evidence of spiritual knowledge, the Bible was not the only record of such assurances. Methodists and Baptists in the throes of revival testified to experiencing atonement in their flesh, to visions of glory and the trumpets of heaven. Many Spiritualists were further assured of future glory by per-sonal communication with those whose "physical bodies have been removed by death, yet live on as immortal entities by virtue of the 'spiritual body' ... enumerated in Paul's compend of humanity."[20] By the conclusion of the Civil War, the restorationist message of Spiritualism was, if not supported by, then echoed in the popular theology of the Christian afterlife, most famously and enduringly in Elizabeth Stuart Phelps's novel *The Gates Ajar*. The novel was set around the death of a young soldier in the Civil War and the crisis of faith that his grieving sister, Mary, thus endured in the confines of the re-strictive theology of Dr. Bland and Deacon Quirk, her church elders. Relief is found through the companionship and counsel of her mother's youngest sister, Winifred Forceythe, who explains that her beloved brother Ray is *only out of sight*, you remember, not lost nor asleep, nor annihilated, he goes on loving."[21] Confident in her own study of scriptures, her reading of church fathers and later theologians, and through the intuition of her faith, Aunt Winifred "went on, speaking low, — 'I cannot doubt that our absent dead are very present with us. He [Jesus] said, "I am with you always," knowing the need we have of him even to the end of the world. He must understand the need we have of them. I cannot doubt it.'"[22] For her part, Mary repeatedly balks at Winifred's "beautiful heresies," only to be assured that "as I hold fast by the Bible, I cannot be in much danger."[23] *The Gates Ajar* was not a Spiritu-alist novel, and there was a limit to the novel's theological elasticity, and yet the inkling that the presence of "our absent dead" was supported by scrip-

                                    Agents of a Fuller Revelation

ture confounded harsh lines between Spiritualist claims and Christian orthodoxies in the communion of shadows. The Bible was repeatedly marshaled to support Spiritualist claims, and increasingly the camera was called on to replicate biblical truths in modern times. Both these threads came together explicitly in Mumler's trial.

Even under Hannah's close guard, news of the wonder spread quickly. From Honolulu to London, papers described these "pictures of dead men" and recounted the remarkable story of the "high priest of this art."[24] The famously irreverent *Spectator* of London seized upon this meaty departure from the "stray crumbs from the loquacious religious intellect of America" and the exhausted novelty of reporting knocking table legs among other pieces "of nineteenth-century joinery." The description of Mumler's ghost, sitting "gratuitously, of course," brims with bemusement but, the paper noted, was nevertheless based on "a very good [photograph] now before us."[25] As news spread from spiritualist and skeptical periodicals to popular and trade presses, readers of the *Photographic Journal* heard that "the forms are not as distinct as we could desire, yet they are sufficiently marked to prove individuality to friends."[26] As time went on, Mumler's pictures were more commonly noted for being of a rather "inferior quality" than examples of superior craftsmanship. And in 1865 the pictures received the distinction of an entire chapter of P. T. Barnum's compendious survey *Humbugs of the World*, an association that Mumler would never shake.

As was the case with other modern manifestations of the spirits — rapping, writing, caressing — accusations of fraud were frequent. As early as March 1863, reports began circulating that spirits in Mumler's photographs were not only detected in multiple instances but were recognized as Bostonians who were *"alive and well!"* The *Investigator* played a large role in amplifying these reports, but spiritualist papers were also cautious in their defense of Mumler's pictures. Apart from the high fees he commanded — many times the going rate for studio portraits, often with disappointing results — the basic premise of the craft posed a challenge. "If a spirit has substantiality enough to go through this process," that is, to be photographed according to the known scientific principles behind wet-plate photography, "it can be caught and put in a box" huffed one unapologetic critic above the haughty signature Nuf Sed.[27] In other words, short of deception, how could the camera record something that the eye failed to detect? Defenders of spiritualism shot back that they had demonstrated "continual caution" in their efforts and, to their readers, "warn[ed] against hasty conclusions on the subject."[28] Indeed, the very practice of investigation, Ann Braude has noted, more than the manifestations themselves, "provided the content of the new religion" of modern Spiritualism.[29] Dr. A. B. Child minced no words on the matter. "The *modus operandi* of producing these spirit-pictures is a mystery." But after asserting that "there is no appearance of deception—that the pictures are real pictures of real spirits," he nevertheless pondered how it was so. "There is no spirit seen standing by the side of the person who sits for a picture, which shows that the picture of the spirit is not made like the picture of the mortal—by reflection on the camera." The spirits, in other words, were not bouncing light onto chemically sensitized plates of glass. There was another action afoot. Child concluded that the spirit pictures must instead be "made inside the camera," but by what means he did not know. "How it is made, neither deception, investigation, nor philosophy can answer."[30] Echoing Child, other commentators held a middle ground between zealous evangelism and cynical denunciation. Whether one saw in Mumler's ghosts a "singular freak in chemical art, . . . or the new manifestation of spirit power," as one commentator wrote in 1863, the matter surely "commands most earnest attention and inquiry."[31]

The pictures themselves were offered as proof of each of these positions—revelation, manipulation, fraud. Improperly cleaned plates could produce faint outlines on new negatives, some argued, while others asserted that this was no darkroom accident, that Mumler and others were perpetrating a swindle on the bereaved and credulous. Still others held steadfast to their belief that the Boston engraver had become an unwitting instrument of the spirits, who were, in the words of one aging Spiritualist in 1882, seizing upon the camera to unveil "a fuller revelation to redound to the glory of God."[32] Thus assertions of fraud echoed in a chamber of belief, of anticipation of a glorious communion that modern technology was now revealing to a troubled world. By century's end, more Americans were likely to see spirit photographs, at best, as relics of beguilement than as agents of revelation. But this position came on the heels of more than a decade of attention and inquiry from American Spiritualists, photographers, chemists, physicians, and believers across the religious landscape.

Within months of Mumler's discovery, his patrons began writing to the *Banner of Light*, Boston's premier Spiritualist periodical, with accounts of their experiences, leavening cool observations of technique with moving tales of widows "weeping at the truthful likeness of a spirit." Mumler's own register of clients is the most complete record of his early patrons. Certainly he played the role of ventriloquist when he published selected accounts, giving his own voice to distant encounters, and yet we can still read these

                                    Agents of a Fuller Revelation

records for what they reveal about his own framing of spirit photography in the communion of shadows. In his autobiography, published in 1875 after the heat of his early reputation had fizzled, he recalls thirteen visitors to the studio at 258 Washington. Mr. Alvin Adams, of railroad shipping interest, dropped in unannounced and provided a "pretty good test" when he found his guardian spirit, Daniel Webster, "exhibited in the negative." While spirits of dignitaries and Native Americans and other guides were not uncommon in Mumler's studio, he and the press preferred to emphasize likenesses of relatives and friends who visited their bereaved. John Ewell's sister appeared in his photograph in the same position she was when she died of consumption; Horace Weston recognized his father; Mrs. Babbitt received "the unmistakable likeness of her husband," and Mr. Thomas R. Hazard, a year after receiving his print, "unexpectedly discovered in it a perfect likeness of my wife"; and Mr. Miller "requested mentally . . . that his little son would appear sitting on his knee" and found "an unmistakable likeness of his boy" in the proofs. "All likenesses of spirits thus far taken are not recognized as those of deceased friends," A. B. Child wrote for the *Banner of Light* in 1863, "though most of them are fully recognized as such."[33] As in other studio portraiture, the discourse of recognition indicated theological claims lingering just beneath the surface. Not only were spirits manifesting in photographs, but they were manifesting *as in life*. Well after Mumler's own mortal demise, the discourse of recognition would remain strong in the world of spirit photography. Mr. Lane of Boston was somewhat less than enthusiastic when he received a picture in January 1894. The young man who he beheld was "no doubt my son," he wrote, "though [it was] very indistinct." That same month, a reporter from Boston described two sittings from which nine ghostly lineaments had appeared, "ALL OF WHICH WE RECOGNIZED." A sister, a brother who died at the battle of Fredericksburg in 1862, and "also a Methodist Minster" were among those deceased relatives whose pictures were "transferred . . . through the instrumentality of the lens."[34] Even as the Spiritualist afterlife of the "Summerland" departed in important ways from Christian expectations of heavenly glory, for many of Mumler's patrons—through the filter of his own account—photographs offered evidence of the communion of saints that transcended the frontiers of mortality.

One of Spiritualism's earliest converts was William Lloyd Garrison, publisher of the abolitionist paper the *Liberator*. A little more than a year after Mumler's discovery, the paper provided readers with "more details from Boston" on the matter of spirit photographs, mostly through copy originally published in the *Herald of Progress*. But Garrison also included "a few details from a reliable friend" who had gone to Mumler at Garrison's request to investigate the process and the medium. The investigation was a bust. Having attended three "sittings," the trusted correspondent reported, "at each of these there was no report. The medium became so anxious, disappointed and disheartened, that he gave up for the day." And yet, even if Mumler was unable to manifest the spirits during this investigation, the unnamed correspondent was nevertheless convinced of his sincerity. The history of Spiritualism, after all, had been a series of false starts and long waiting. Circles (séances or other gatherings) in the early 1850s had waited weeks, even months, on end with no demonstrations before the spirits made their appearances. Mumler's disappointment was a recognizable disposition among early mediums. But for this investigator, the absences in Mumler's pictures — conspicuous absences — were no match for the "*real* look" of his successful photographs. "I have seen several pictures," Garrison's correspondent reported, "and there is a *real* look about them all. I examined the process of taking, and could find no sign nor shadow of trickery. The medium's air and manner, his non-success, his disappointment, all indicate *reality*."[35] The "reality" of the photographs was, of course, in dynamic exchange with the stories they were made to tell. Two decades later, Garrison wrote to fellow abolitionist Oliver Johnson, inquiring whether "Wendell [Phillips] put in your hand a card photograph of me, . . . on the negative of which appear the form and features of Charles Sumner." Nine days after the prominent antislavery Republican died, Garrison had visited Mumler himself and had received the likeness of Sumner, "holding a broken chain over my right breast, symbolical of the slaves' liberation."[36] By 1874, American slaves had been emancipated and the "*reality*" of Mumler's camera was to overwrite black suffering and liberation with a visual record of white political accomplishment (fig. 24).

Claims to the reality of photography, to the empirical conceit, had been, as we have seen, claims running through the communion of shadows and would become even more amplified as the century continued. But what was "real" was a subject in flux. Writing to the *Investigator*, the freethinking organ, in June 1868, A. G. D. announced herself as a Spiritualist who had "taken my first lesson in the Fox family twenty years ago." In her letter, she recalled a woman who had her photograph taken by Mumler years earlier and had "recognized the picture of her own mother by the side of her own." At some later time, it was discovered that Hannah had a photograph of "another old lady" in her studio from which, it was alleged, "the 'lady's mother' had been taken." Even so, A. G. D. continued, "the lady still insisted that it was a veritable picture of her *spirit* mother!" The point in recounting this "Spiritual

Agents of a Fuller Revelation

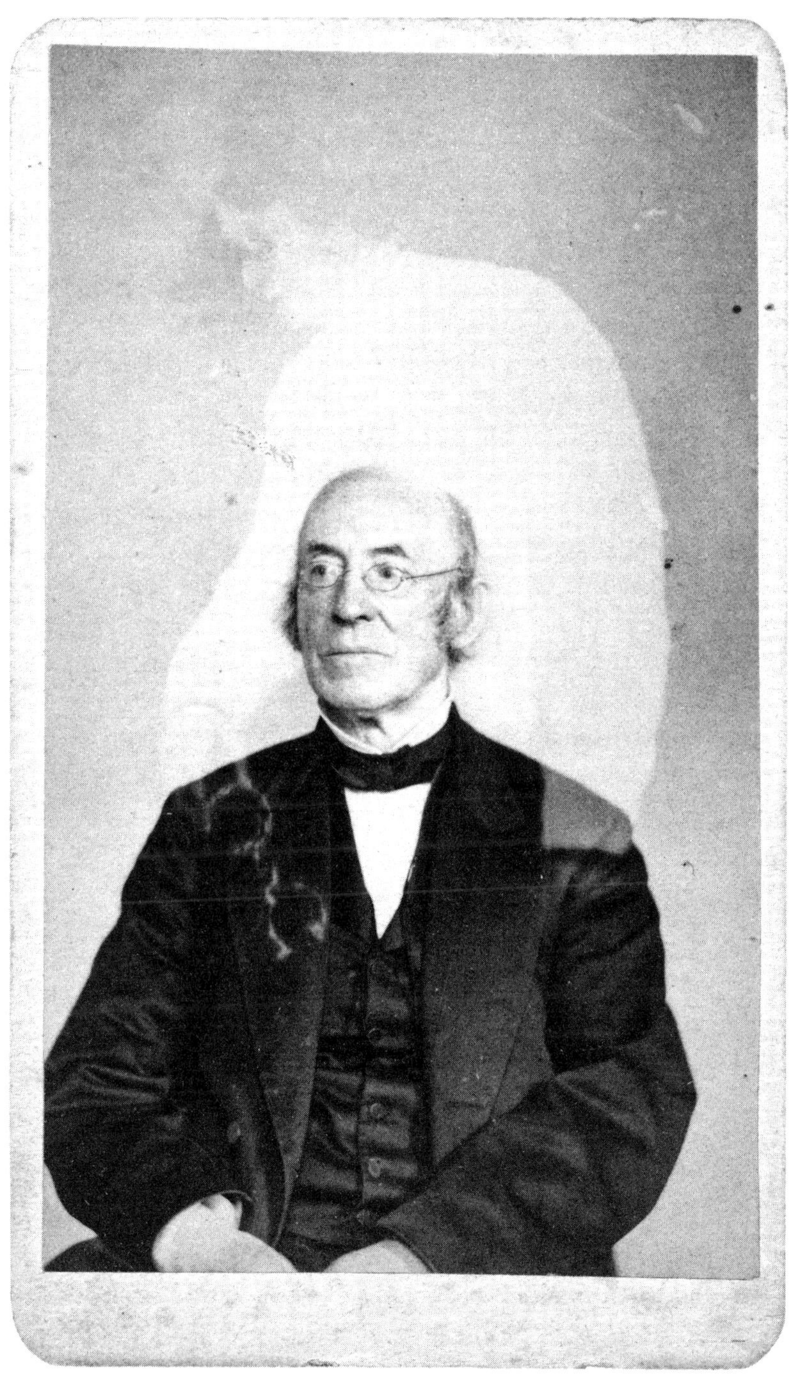

Figure 24. William Lloyd Garrison. Albumen silver print. William H. Mumler, 1874. J. Paul Getty Museum. Used with permission.

fraud," she concluded, was to discern that of those many recognitions of mothers, fathers, children, and spouses, "they are truthful, albeit they may be more or less fictitious."[37]

Six years after his discovery, Mumler's business was booming. He commanded among the highest fees for studio portraits: ten dollars for a dozen likenesses. The going rate among studios whose clientele was limited to mortals was around two dollars per dozen. When inquirers asked about the soaring costs of his technically inferior products, Mumler coolly replied that money was no object to him, beyond the necessities of a comfortable life, but that "the price was so fixed because the spirits did not like a throng and that to exclude the 'vulgar multitude' the price was fixed at the high rate, &c." Mumler's clients paid high prices to procure the misty profiles of the dearly departed who manifested on otherwise unremarkable portraits. Despite his extensive list of clients and supporters, most of whom would claim no affiliation with the institutionally diffuse spiritualist movement, others remained skeptical. In late 1868, William and Hannah moved their family to New York to start afresh. True or trumped, accounts of living Bostonians showing up as spirit likenesses had tarnished his reputation, and New York was a city rich with promise. But his demons followed him south. By March his critics would earn their day in court when William Mumler's inferior likenesses came under legal scrutiny in a trial of religious authority in modern America.[38]

630 Broadway, New York

"I arrived in [New York] with my family, having scarcely money enough to sustain ourselves for a week, and began to look around for business," Mumler later recalled, "but I found that my reputation as an alleged trickster had preceded me, and it was with difficulty I could obtain the use of a gallery."[39] This rejection by the photographic guild "reduced [him] to the direst extremity," but after much searching Mumler finally secured a studio at 630 Broadway, in the rooms of William W. Silver, where he could practice his trade. Like other photographers, Silver was skeptical of Mumler's supernatural claims at first but was convinced after a series of demonstrations that there was no trickery in the production of his pictures. New York Spiritualists had been among the first to hear of his pictures when they first surfaced in 1862, and his reputation preceded him there, too. Not long after setting up his Broadway operation, Mumler decided to advertise his new studio by posting some of his pictures in lecture halls where he knew Spiritualists gathered. Upon

                                    Agents of a Fuller Revelation

petitioning for such a privilege, however, he was refused and sent home. Despite such a humiliating rebuff as he struggled to build a local clientele in New York, Mumler was quickly successful and by March was able to buy Silver out of his share of the gallery, including his entire store of equipment.

The timing was terrible. In February a reporter for the *Sun*, "ever on the alert for new and interesting intelligence," was sent to the studio on Broadway "in company with an eminent photographer of this city" to investigate the "wonderful mystery" (a former Wall Street banker also tagged along). The paper, which had early acquired a reputation among the penny presses for questionable publishing ethics, wasted no time in printing the "remarkable story" in full, along with a hasty caveat that they did so not as an endorsement but rather as "simply a matter of news." Upon entering the gallery, the reporter first inspected scores of specimens Mumler had preserved of previous sittings. Ladies and bankers, elderly gentlemen and young mothers, real estate moguls and painters, people from New York and Arkansas and Illinois, each had sat for Mumler and each had received a spirit likeness. His curiosity piqued, the reporter, naturally, wondered what ghosts "would sit along with him" and proceeded to sit for Mumler himself. The eminent photographer in his company, under the pseudonym Brown, inspected the instruments and materials and even prepared the plates for exposure. There was some confusion when a "middle aged man, with dark beard," appeared alongside portraits of both Brown and the reporter, and the trio decided to wait for "sun proofs" of both negatives (that is, for positive prints) to discover their unknown mutual acquaintance. Dramatically, in the process of drying the reporter's negative, the glass "shivered to pieces," making it impossible to develop a proof. The intrepid reporter thus requested another sitting, this time calling to mind "the appearance of his father, as he lay dying, some eleven years ago." The resulting image was a dim profile, but "in general outline . . . much like his father as he thought of him."[40]

As a result of the publicity, a city employee brought Mumler to the attention of Mayor A. Oakley Hall, who in turn ordered his own investigation of the process.[41] When Hall's chief marshal Joseph H. Tooker called upon Mumler in March under a false name, he was shown a negative that was said to contain the spirit likeness of his father-in-law. Tooker, however, "failed to recognize the worthy old gentleman" and insisted that the picture failed to represent "any person whom he had ever seen or known."[42] Soon after, Mumler was arrested for the felonies of defrauding and cheating the public, as well as misdemeanor larceny. Within a few weeks of having purchased the studio on Broadway, Mumler and his pictures had become the subject of a bizarre public interrogation of spirit photography, religion, and biblical authority.

Mumler was arraigned in police court before Justice Joseph Dowling on Monday, April 12, 1869.[43] The charges read against him were three: two felony counts of fraud and one count of misdemeanor larceny. In the eyes of the prosecution, Mumler had "defrauded and cheated" his patrons "through trick and device and by false pretense, in furnishing certain . . . cards said to have been produced by spiritual and supernatural agency, but which were in fact the result of ordinary scientific and chemical means, in common use by persons engaged in the photographic art."[44] A crowd of "motley and hetero-geneous classes" had filled the gallery, from "legal gentlemen, curious to note the points of law which might arise" during the proceedings to "a sprinkling of middle-aged ladies" whose interest in the case was "scarcely exceeded by that of the party principally concerned."[45] The charges were as imposing as the building in which he sat. The massive Halls of Justice building facing Centre Street occupied an entire block at the edge of the city's infamous Five Points. Despite the impressive Egyptian-style architecture, intended to invoke the scale and might of that ancient civilization, there was a reason the building was better known as the Tombs. Built in the 1830s on the former site of the city's Collect Pond, which had provided the main supply of drink-ing water to citizens of New York, the granite behemoth seemed to extin-guish any light that crept under the portico or through the tight iron bars of the prison's two hundred cells. Thirty years later, when Mumler had the misfortune — many would say due justice — of gracing its halls, the prison frequently held double its intended capacity. Damp, poorly ventilated, and dark, the Tombs was, without doubt, "a terribly sickly and dreary abode."[46]

After hearing initial depositions, Dowling "held the accused for exami-nation" and remanded him to the Tombs "for want of bail." Mayor Hall had intended to prosecute the case himself but had to bow out at the last minute. When the examination convened on Friday, April 16, in his stead for the prosecution was the rising moral crusader Elbridge T. Gerry, grandson of the vice president to James Madison with whom he shared a name, and noted by his peers as one of the law's "most careful, scholarly, and eloquent followers." Among the routine offenses that came before Justice Dowling in the ordi-nary ritual of police court, special sessions was reserved for crimes of greater severity, conduct not to be dispatched with the regularity of drunkenness or disorder. Here, cases were entitled to counsel and witnesses. This was not a trial before a jury of Mumler's peers but rather an examination of whether the charges of fraud and larceny were supported by law and evidence. If the

　　　　　Agents of a Fuller Revelation

prosecution prevailed, Mumler would stand trial before a grand jury and likely be convicted of fraud. If it did not, he would walk out of the Tombs a free man, cleared, if not blameless, in the eyes of the law. Given the nature of the charges, the legal framework of Mumler's defense would make every difference in the outcome of the case, and Mumler had selected his counsel wisely and at considerable expense. The top-notch defense attorney John D. Townsend was three years Mumler's junior and had already traveled the world over as a seaman, served as state representative for Queens County, and gained a reputation as "the Fighting Lawyer."[47] Townsend was his best bet. Reporters from the leading New York dailies followed the case closely from the beginning, feeding a growing public appetite for the proceedings taking place within the packed gallery of the Court of Special Sessions, and as the hearing continued week after week, correspondents from around the country had been sent to cover it as well. Legally speaking, this was a minor case in the lowest court in the land. Accusations of fraud, especially among Spiritualists and others on the perimeters of American religious life, were not uncommon. Yet the pictures at the heart of this trial had struck a nerve that went straight to the heart of religious authority in modern America.

The charge of fraud required that the prosecution prove Mumler had *knowingly* deceived his patrons, promising a product he knew to be delivered under false pretenses. Gerry had Mumler on price inflation, perhaps, but proving fraud was another matter, especially when the prisoner's defense hinged on the supernatural, and try as he might, none of Gerry's witnesses could prove just how Mumler had made his photographs. There were theories, of course, and the prosecution's witnesses introduced nine possible methods of producing the so-called spirits by mechanical and chemical means, but no one had caught Mumler in the act. Throughout, this remained a battle of beholding, of determining what the pictures disclosed. But without a smoking gun, the focus of the prosecution shifted back and forth between Mumler's character—What kind of depravity would entice someone to capitalize on the credulity of those stricken with grief?—and the threat of Spiritualism to the American legal and social fabric in, as Gerry phrased it in his remarks, "these degenerate days." The measure of success on both sides of the case fell on a body of evidence relatively new to American jurisprudence. Were the spirit pictures themselves evidence? If so, what did they— what *could* they—prove?

On the first day, the court heard depositions from Tooker; a science reporter from the *World* who had attended a recent meeting of the Photographic Section of the American Institute at Cooper Union, where speci mens of Mumler's cards had been exhibited; the Secretary of that Photographic Section; and an "inventor, expert and professor of the photographic art."[48] From the beginning, debates around how to see photographs that claimed to provide evidence of a future existence were at the center of the investigation. Charles Boyle, the "expert and professor," had been keeping tabs on Mumler since early 1863, when he first proposed to go to "Mr. Mumler's rooms with a committee of disinterested men and an honest reporter" to "discover and exhibit the trick of spiritual photographing."[49] When Dowling ruled for further examination of the claims made in these original affidavits, court was recessed until Friday, April 16. Mayor Hall requested an adjournment until he could prosecute the case—Friday was "a most inconvenient day for him"—but this request was rebutted by an ally of the defense who reminded the court that the press had been having a field day with statements made on Monday and that it would behoove the pursuit of truth for the examination to continue. Under the headline "A Stupendous Fraud," on Tuesday, the *New York Times* had reported that the prisoners (Mumler's former associate Silver had been arrested too but was soon released) had "been in the habit of producing pictures . . . with the shadowy outlines of a human face in the background, which they pretended had been produced by spiritual or supernatural means, the faint portrait being, as they always alleged, the features of some deceased person then unknown, and who was in some way connected or related to the person sitting before the camera."[50] The ally redressing such unbridled aspersions was Judge John Edmonds, formerly of the State Supreme Court, who had retired from his profession in 1853 to devote himself fully to the study of Spiritualism.[51] Dowling assented to the defense's petition, and the show went on. Now it was up to Townsend and his team "to prove that there is no trick, fraud or deception in what are called spirit pictures by the accused." When the papers ran on Saturday, they had a counterargument to Monday's scathing testimony of fraud: "There are many intelligent men and women who, after careful investigation, are firm believers that the pictures are really likenesses of the spirits of the departed, and that the taking of such pictures is a new era in photography, an art still in its infancy."[52] The battle lines were drawn.

Even as Mumler was himself subject to the decision of the court, it became clear quite early in the proceedings that, as one concerned commentator put it, "the questions raised in this trial do not turn on the innocence or guilt of one man."[53] Mumler's supporters, including Amelia V. Brooks, who had pleaded with Dowling to provide "suitable accommodation" for women to attend the proceedings, recognized the case as "the first time that our be-

    Agents of a Fuller Revelation

lief has been made the subject of judicial determination." Although hardly in sympathy with Brooks, prosecutor Gerry similarly seized upon the scope of the case as he worked to expose the "photographic curiosities" and "pretended miracles" effected by what could only have been, in the estimation of his many expert witnesses, artful manipulations of the camera at the considerable expense of his patrons' grief and pockets. William Mumler stood trial for fraud, but the real crime, in the estimation of the people, was "an old form of infidelity in a new dress."[54]

At the center of these nested trials, both the specific case of William Mumler and the broader theater of religious authority, were the photographs. Although photographs had begun to be introduced into legal proceedings in the previous decade, Mumler's trial was among the first cases in which photographs came under sustained scrutiny as evidence in their own right, rather than as assisted testimony to, for instance, geographic features (as in land grant disputes) or alleged forgeries (via comparison of handwriting samples).[55] At issue was not only what the pictures were of—allegedly incorporeal spirits—but also the process by which they were made and thus the credibility of their testimony. From a technical perspective, it is important that Mumler had repeatedly described his pictures as "spirit forms [that] appear upon the negative."[56] The negative, in this case, was a glass plate that had been inserted in the camera and received the exposure. From the glass negative, Mumler or an associate created any number of prints. If the spirit appeared on the glass plate, he subtly asserted, then it was not the product of darkroom manipulation. Photographers for the prosecution retorted that such an assertion was smoke and mirrors. Alongside the photographs entered as evidence, the recent technical history of photography played a key role in determining the outcome of the case. Because of the long exposure times required of landscapes and architectural details, these subjects occasionally featured passersby who had entered the camera's field of vision long enough to register an indistinct image. This accidental haunting was seized upon by the British philosopher Sir David Brewster, who offered a how-to guide to "regions of the supernatural." Noting that even the most rigorous scientific theories could be "employed for purpose of amusement" as a means of instruction, he jested that "while a party is engaged in their whist or their gossip," a spiritual appearance was created when a "female figure, suitably attired, walks quickly into the place assigned her, and after standing a few seconds in the proper attitude, retires quickly." When this procedure— later known as Brewster's method and introduced as such in the course of Mumler's examination—was properly executed, "all the objects immediately behind the female figure . . . will be seen through her, and she will have the appearance of an aerial personage."[57] Brewster's jest sat curiously against Mumler's claim, and it was up to the court to determine not only who was to be believed but also what testimony might be derived from the photographs.

Witnesses for the defense were called on April 21 and included a photographer from Poughkeepsie who claimed that Mumler had taken spirit pictures in his studio, with his equipment; Mumler's assistant William Guay (who had been among the first to investigate him in 1862); Judge Edmonds; and the photographer Jeremiah Gurney. The defense aimed to demonstrate from the outset that the charge of fraud failed to apply because no one, not even the city's best photographers, could discover any trick. But their testimony also established the case as a trial of beholding, of what the pictures, in truth, were. Gurney had been a photographer for twenty-eight years, which meant, in 1869, he had been practicing since the medium's beginning. He observed the process and found "nothing which savored of fraud or trickery" but concluded that "I have unbelief as to the spiritual emanation of these photographs." "On the contrary," he continued, "I believe, although I cannot assert positively, that they are produced by purely natural means."[58] Despite this early seed of doubt, the assertion from someone more knowledgeable of photography than perhaps anyone else in the proceedings that the photographs were themselves imperfect witnesses, both the defense and the prosecution introduced photographs as evidence of their respective charges. In all, twenty-two photographs were introduced as evidence over three weeks.[59]

On the fourth day of the investigation, Friday, April 23, Gerry stuck his toe in a door that Townsend would soon yank open. The undercurrent of religious belief had been coursing throughout the investigation, but when Gerry cross-examined the defense witness David A. Hopkins, he made it explicit. The papers described Hopkins as "a gentleman of unmistakable New England birth" who "gave his testimony in a clear, straightforward manner, which impressed everybody with confidence in his honesty and sincerity."[60] "To what religious denomination, or sect, do you belong?" the prosecutor asked the railway manufacturer. When Hopkins replied "no particular sect," Gerry pushed further. "But you believe in spiritualism to some extent?" Hopkins didn't blink. Pointing to the Bible on Dowling's desk, he answered, "That . . . is full of spiritualism. As a Christian I must believe in it, or throw away the Bible altogether." The next witness for the defense was Mumler's former associate, William Silver. Again, Gerry asked, "You did not become a convert to spiritualism notwithstanding all these forms [you had seen]?" Silver replied, "I believe in the picture." The next witness, Mrs. Luthera C.

   Agents of a Fuller Revelation

Reeve, had visited Mumler's gallery in January with her nephew to procure a photograph of her deceased son, who had died at the age of eleven a year earlier. "No photograph of him had been taken for two years previous to his death," she recounted. "On my picture he appeared as in health." When Gerry asked during his cross-examination whether she believed "deceased persons revisit their friends," she replied, "I cannot say. I believe so by the pictures." None of the witnesses offered a throaty endorsement of Spiritualism as a belief system. Reeve could not "say whether or not departed spirits revisit the earth," and Hopkins declared that even though he belonged to "no sect or denomination," he "believe[d] Jesus Christ to be a perfect example for human imitation, and believe[d] in the existence of the Deity." Samuel Fanshaw declared that when he visited Mumler he "was not a believer in spirits, except as a Christian." Many of the defense's witnesses claimed that skepticism, not faith, had motivated their dalliance with Mumler's camera. Charles Livermore had been warned by friends in Boston that Mumler "was a trickster" and had "called upon him as a skeptic." Fanshaw was "entirely skeptical." All of the defense's witnesses, however, believed in the photographs. Fanshaw, a miniature and portrait painter, declared unequivocally that he was "not a spiritualist" but that "as a Christian I believe that spirits do visit the earth, and I was more convinced of it after I had my pictures." Livermore was divided, asserting that "my belief is not yet settled" and that he did "not believe these are photographs of spirits," but he was nevertheless convinced that "a picture can be procured of an object not strictly speaking material." Townsend was paying attention to Gerry's tactics, to his efforts to undermine the defense witnesses by painting a picture of deception and credulity, and, importantly, also to the responses that intimated postures of compatibility with rather than antagonism between the claims of the camera and the truths of the Bible. The defense rested. But the trial was far from finished.[61]

Gerry mounted the prosecution's case when the court reconvened the following week. On Wednesday, April 28, his associate called Abraham Bogardus to the stand. Bogardus had been a photographer for nearly a quarter of a century and had been instrumental in the earliest days of commercial daguerreotypes. He was also a member of the National Photographic Association of the United States, an organization, he reported, that had been "formed for protecting honest people in the trade from patents and for putting down any humbug we could discover." Like many of Gerry's witnesses, Bogardus represented the photographic guild and scientific authority. The prosecution lobbed a softball at him. "How many processes are there of taking so-called spirit photographs?" Answer: "I cannot say, we might count them by scores." Townsend was finished with this game. Not one of the witnesses that Gerry had called that week had caught Mumler's deception, though they all echoed the humbug refrain—there are so many ways one *could* produce these pictures by mechanical or chemical means, so Mumler *must have* used a trick or device. Instead of affirming the premise of this line of argumentation, Townsend turned the tables back on Gerry's earlier cross-examinations. What if the pictures were evidence not of trickery but of revelation?

The *Tribune* summarized the day as "a succession of pleasant surprises and dramatic situations." Indeed. Townsend spared no time in cutting to the chase in his cross-examination, asking Bogardus if he could produce likenesses of deceased persons who had had no photographs taken in life ("I cannot") and if he was a believer in the Bible ("I am"). Townsend then proceeded to read into the record 1 Samuel 28, a passage of biblical text wherein Saul summons the "witch of Endor" to "bring up Samuel" from beyond his grave. He then asked the witness, if a photographer had been present at that interview, could he not have taken a photograph of Samuel? The prosecution objected. Not to reading the Bible in court, "because he thought a person would not be injured by the Scriptures anywhere," but to the "theological questions" Townsend introduced "for the purpose of confounding the witness." The question was excluded. Undeterred, Townsend "proposed to read a number of other passages from Scripture, narrating the appearance of spirits, for the purpose of asking the same question in regard to each." The defense introduced Genesis chapters 12, 16, 17, 23; Numbers 22; Joshua 5; Judges 6 and 13; 1 Samuel 19; Ezra 1; Matthew 27 and 28; Acts 12 and 16; and Corinthians 15. His purpose, he endeavored, was not "to direct any question in regard to theology, but to question [Bogardus] as a photographer." Dowling would have none of it. The entire line of questioning was dismissed.

Even if Dowling saw through Townsend's strategy, the lawyer was playing to the packed galleries and weekly reporters as much as he was angling for a credible legal toehold. Gerry was in on it too, and his next witness was clearly called not for his professional expertise but for his garrulous mastery of public sentiment. Bogardus may have been an authority in the art and science of photography, but the city's premier arbiter of humbug was Phineas T. Barnum. If anyone was going to sniff out bunkum, it was Barnum, the prosecution contended. Four years earlier, Barnum had featured Mumler in *Humbugs of the World* in a chapter on "spiritual photographing" where he had singled out an unnamed "ingenious man and scientific chemist" who had "found it very profitable . . . [to reproduce] ghost-like pictures, ad infinitum, at the rate of five dollars each." Mothers, widows, friends, and husbands visited the photographer's studio in search of "the ghostly lineaments of some person, who, they believed, inhabited another sphere." Predictably, Barnum scoffed at the claim. "Can human credulity go further than to suppose that the departed still appear in the old clo' of their earthly wardrobe? and the fact that the appearance of 'the shade' of a young lady in one of the fashionable cut Zouave jackets of the hour did not disturb the faith of the believers, fills us indeed with wonder."[62] In Barnum's more serious moods, humbugs were not only financial swindles or false pretenses but also the bedrock of what he called "false religions." "I apprehend that there is no sort of object which men seek to attain, whether secular, moral or religious, in which humbug is not very often an instrumentality," he wrote in the introduction to *Humbugs of the World*, but "false religions are perhaps the most monstrous, complicated and thorough-going specimens of humbug that can be found."[63] In his lighter moods, humbugs played important social functions in his own museum by "putting on glittering appearances—outside show—novel expedients, by which to suddenly arrest public attention, and attract the public eye and ear." Certain professions—clergy, lawyers, physicians among them—would "not . . . be apt to succeed" with such a method, but "an honest man who thus arrests public attention" could be at once a humbug without being "a swindler or an imposter." In such cases, the test of the latter appellation lay in what the humbug did with the crowds he or she had attracted. This parsing of what humbug meant, beyond "Dr. Webster's sense of that word," came into play in Barnum's testimony at Mumler's trial.[64]

Barnum's testimony was widely reported. "The humorous manner in which this witness gave his testimony elicited considerable laughter from the audience," the *Tribune* reported. As the prosecution's witness, the showman began by testifying that he had known of a Mr. Mumler in Boston some years before who was earning a reputation as "a taker of so-called spirit photographs" and that he had solicited Mumler to "buy some of his photographs to show as curiosities" in his museum. The photographer agreed and sent some specimens. Their correspondence, Barnum lamented, was destroyed when his museum caught fire, but he was sure that it was this Mumler currently at the bar with whom he had traded. Gerry proceeded to inquire about Barnum's recent visit to the studio of Abraham Bogardus. "Do you believe in 'spooks'?" Gerry asked, to "great laughter." "Yes, Yes, I do. [Renewed laughter.] . . . It is only necessary to believe in them to see them. [Laughter],"

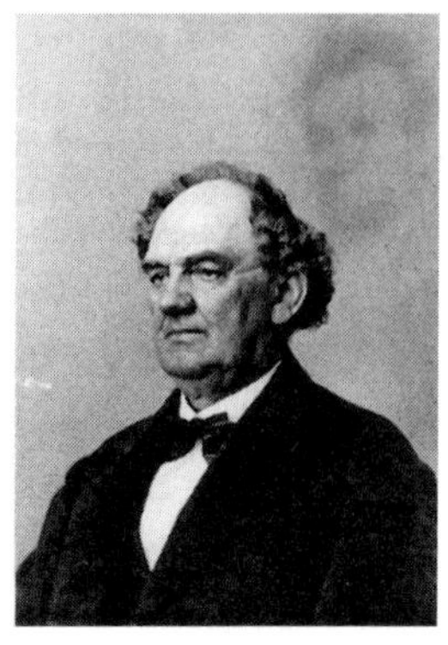

Figure 25. Abraham Bogardus, Hoax "Spirit Picture" of Abraham Lincoln and P. T. Barnum, 1869. Halftone reproduction, n.d. Wikimedia Commons.

Having established both levity in the courtroom and Barnum's willingness to play along, Gerry continued to ask Barnum about his visit to Bogardus's gallery the day before. "I went in to ask him if he could take a spirit photograph," Barnum replied, "but I told him that I did not want to have any humbugging in the matter. [Great laughter.] He said he could do it." Barnum proceeded to "examine the things" as Bogardus worked, investigating the plate glass, entering the darkroom and watching the preparation of the plate and its insertion in the camera, through the operation. The result? Barnum "had my shadow taken, and that of the departed Abraham Lincoln came also upon the glass. [Great laughter]." "Is that it," Gerry asked, pointing to the picture. "Yes, that's the critter. [Renewed merriment]." Gerry pressed the showman to identify when he first saw the hoax spirit photograph — "as soon as I came into the darkroom" — and to state whether he had detected the trick — "No." He concluded his examination of the witness by asking, if he had not seen the trick, had he been "conscious of a spiritual presence"? "I did not feel anything of that sort. [Great laughter]."[65]

With the courtroom in a titter, Townsend struggled, unsuccessfully, to reign in the mirth. "How long have you been in the humbug business?" But Barnum did not bite. "I was never in it; I never took money from a man without giving him the worth of it four times over," he testified, again to laughter. He had certainly exhibited humbug in his museum, Barnum continued, but such specimens were exhibited "as a humbug, and not as a reality." Such hilarity went unappreciated by Townsend as he tried with little success to catch Barnum in a web of his own making. There was no beating Barnum at his own game. Still, Townsend refused to give up the line of questioning, asking incredulously, of all the humbugs that he had taken money for, "did you tell the people at the time that they were humbugs?" Again, Barnum replied that he gave his patrons their money's worth. In response, Townsend

                                                    Agents of a Fuller Revelation

introduced some of the showman's headlining humbugs to test his account, starting with the famed woolly horse, "a freak of nature, and withal a very curious looking animal," that Barnum had turned into a sensation in the late 1840s by associating it with the harrowing westward expeditions of Colonel John C. Fremont.[66] "Was it actually a woolly horse?" Townsend asked. "It was actually a woolly horse," Barnum replied to "bursts of laughter, which were at once checked by the court." Barnum had clearly won over the spectators in the courtroom and the scribbling teams of newspaper reporters, but Townsend continued to press on, hoping the showman would undermine his own stated authority as arbiter of swindle. Tone deaf to the circumstances at hand, Townsend focused on the horse itself rather than the story that made it famous. Barnum's craft was to take the grotesque, the "freak of nature," and transform it through a rousing story into a patriotism that was quite literally on display. The woolly horse became famous because it captured the anxiety and triumph of westward expansion in Jacksonian America. The courtroom knew it, and we can almost see the twinkle in Barnum's eye, hear the joke under the truth of his testimony. As with the woolly horse, so it went with the mermaid. "I represented it as I bought it, and found it as I bought it." Grasping, Townsend asked in exasperation, "have you as a public entertainer presented to the mass anything which you knew to be untrue . . . and taken money for it?" "Well," Barnum replied, "I think I have given it a little drapery sometimes founded on fact. [Great laughter which was not checked for some moments.]" Townsend was stuck between a legal argument, in which humbug was a category distinct from fraud, and a witness whose art was to smudge the bright line between fact and fiction. He nearly pivoted back "to this question of Mumler" before he remembered another example of what he knew to be the uglier sort of humbug, intended to draw in the paying crowds on a false pretense of historical merit. "Oh! the nurse of George Washington," he recalled to "peals of laughter." Was Joyce Heth truly "the nurse of George Washington"? "I have no reason to doubt it," Barnum replied, explaining that he had "bought it as such" and affirming his justification to "shouts of laughter, which the court for some minutes vainly endeavored to check." After a few more moments of examination, Townsend turned to Judge Dowling, appealing for some intervention. The room was in on the joke, and so was the judge. "He has given his reasons."[67]

Barnum's testimony did not provide proof of any criminal act or misdemeanor. Even so, it was a well-played charade that amplified his previous assertions that spirit photographs were legerdemain of the grossest order. Townsend had to reign it back in. The next witness for the prosecution was Charles B. Boyle, a member of the American Institute and a photographer with twenty years' experience who had also known Mumler in Boston. Having provided an affidavit on the first day of the hearing, the prosecution recalled him to elaborate on the possibility of spirits producing their own light. It had come up in previous testimony that many of Mumler's portraits evinced conflicting, and therefore seemingly impossible, light sources. Boyle refuted the possibility; it is "impossible that the spirit form could have been in the field of the camera with the sitter."[68] Townsend found an opening. During the cross-examination, Boyle testified that he was "not a spiritualist" but he had "looked into the subject." In any case, "I have never heard that spirits are governed by their own light and form." Question: "Do you believe in the Bible?" Answer: "I believe there are some things in the Bible that are good and some are not; what appears to me to be true I believe, but I do not take it all as true." Boyle had been paying attention. Townsend then proceeded to read from the book of Matthew in the Christian scriptures, a passage recounting the transfiguration of Christ. The verses describe the scene: "His face did shine as the sun, and his raiment was as white as the light" as Moses and Elias "appeared unto them."[69] Gerry objected. Townsend countered. "Spiritualists base Spiritualism on the Bible. They form a religious denomination derived from the Bible." Astonishingly, Judge Dowling allowed him to proceed. "My belief is suspended upon all questions I cannot comprehend," the seeker Boyle continued. "I suspend my belief in Spiritualism because I cannot understand it. I say these pictures of Mumler's are not spiritual pictures." Townsend pressed on, but it was Gerry who, according to published transcriptions of the proceedings, tidied up the testimony by slipping the line of questioning firmly into biblical interpretation. "Was there anything in the passage of transfiguration," he asked Boyle, "showing that they shone by their own light?" "No." In an April 1869 court of law, a photographer was called upon to define the truths of the Bible.

It had been quite a day in Judge Dowling's court. The prosecution had worked to establish the authority of the photographic profession with regard to spirit pictures. In the words of Charles D. Frederick, referring to four of the photographs that had been introduced as exhibits, they "must have been done by mechanical processes." Townsend had detected in this line of argument a theological premise, or at least a religiously informed suspicion that spirits would not use such base mechanical means to present themselves in these modern times. Gerry had hinted as much when he had questioned David Hopkins about his belief in spiritualism the week before. Townsend's response had been to counter that suspicion by calling upon the authority of the Bible and in the process had invited himself and the proceedings into one of the headiest theological debates of the nineteenth century. By the end of the fourth day, many observers would have been asking themselves anew, who, or what, was on trial? This was, in the legal sense, not a trial at all but rather an examination of the merits of the charges against Mumler. But in a larger cultural sense, this was indeed a trial of photographic beholding, a sustained interrogation of what the camera had recorded and what people saw on glass and paper. Contemporaries to the examination recognized that the trial hinged on much more than "the guilt or innocence of one man," but the wider theater was not the truth or falsehood of modern Spiritualism. The bigger question raised, and the one that would haunt American religion far into the twentieth century, was instead around the role of modern technology in revealed religion. Mumler's hearing would not answer that question. But Townsend could be optimistic about his strategy. Despite the testimony of Barnum and leaders in the photographic establishment on this last day of testimony, the *Tribune* reported that "it is not shown that the pictures in question are not genuine portraits of spirits."[70]

After several weeks of testimony and more than twenty photographs entered into evidence, it was still difficult to discern what the subject of this case was. On the one hand, it was a rather straightforward fraud case. But determining the outcome of this charge had shifted the emphasis from Mumler to modern Spiritualism, biblical authority, and the legal burden of photographic evidence. When Mumler was called to the stand on the morning of Monday, May 3, to address the charges against him, he held his cards close to his chest. He recounted that Sunday in Boston, now nearly seven years ago, when he had first discovered the ghostly lineaments on his intended self-portrait. "I wish to state that at the time I developed the shadow or form [previously] alluded to," Mumler testified, "I was a complete novice in the art of photography, and had no experience whatever in the composition of chemicals used in the business." The spirits, he held, had chosen him. Even to this day his technical knowledge was limited, he continued, certainly nothing beyond what was "needed to take ordinary photographic pictures," and that far to the contrary of any "trick or device" alleged by the prosecution, the spirits and shadows in his pictures "have appeared in each and every instance . . . without any effort, except my will-power to produce them."[71] Mumler narrated his initial bemusement, then skepticism, and finally his conviction that the images were in fact of spiritual origin. He countered some aspersions to his character that had been raised, most notably by P. T. Barnum, but if the crowded room and scribbling reporters were holding their breath for a spectacular declaration of anything, he left the courtroom deflated. He had played his role, kept his cool. Now it was time for Townsend and Gerry to make their final arguments.

Townsend wasted no time in painting this as a trial of religion. Beginning with the assertion that public attention had not been "exclusively directed to the prisoner," he argued that "interest in the case had spread itself among those who have religious views differing materially from those entertained by the community generally." As such, he aimed to direct Dowling to the legal aspect of the case, "and subsequently he would touch upon the belief popularly known as Spiritualism." He wanted to have his ghosts and see them too. Mumler was charged with fraud, he stated, because "the prosecution cannot understand how the spirit form was produced." This ignorance, he contended, was a hazard of this marvelous age of discovery, but not a legal pretense of criminal behavior. Suppose Morse had been similarly charged before he had worked out the scientific principles of the telegraph, though he knew that "communications might be had on the instant between persons hundreds of miles apart"? Suppose some skeptic had demanded a demonstration, on the spot, and "the attempt to transmit the message should fail," would the prosecution then have intervened on behalf of the unbeliever in electronic communication? "Would such a failure be counted a fraud by any court or jury in Christendom?" Of course not. At least, not today, Townsend implied. The prosecution's witnesses, of all people, should have recognized this. Instead, Townsend lamented that "science had taught them certain facts, and they were unwilling that any one should declare anything not fully within their comprehension—they don't believe science can improve." He was just warming up. "Men like these would have hung Galileo," he moralized, and over the course of his defense of William Mumler, the "fighting lawyer" spared no punches. No complete transcripts of his argument survive, and press coverage was uneven, but for two hours Townsend exhorted Judge Dowling to consider the weight of his decision in this sensational case. He reiterated his earlier argument, as well as the scriptural proof texts, that "Spiritualists found their belief on the Bible." This time, however, Townsend pushed it squarely into the theological camp he had previously hedged. "Spiritualism came in time to fill a gap in the religious world. People were drifting rapidly toward neglect or unbelief, when Spiritualism appeared and woke them up to the importance of the great hereafter." If spirit photography had "convinced only one single person of the immortality of the soul," Townsend continued, "it had served a good purpose."[72] Here the legal, the scientific, and the religious came together: "There is no evidence that Mum-

   Agents of a Fuller Revelation

ler pretended to do what he knew to be false, and consequently the whole element of crime is wanting."[73] But that is not all; to the contrary of the prosecution's claims, "there is abundant evidence that he believed he could give a spirit picture." As for Barnum, "He is a man who smells of fraud in the very nostrils of the people of New York." For the defense, the photographs presented evidence of Mumler's belief in the immortality of the soul and of a new dispensation of revelation anchored in a biblical tradition. Surely there were those who disagreed, but this was hardly the place for those discussions to take place. "The case in a Court of Justice should be looked on simply as one of law." On those charges, Townsend concluded, the prosecution had failed to make its case.

Gerry, predictably, disagreed. For the prosecution, the photographs could not be evidence of belief; that was beyond the purview of the law. Rather, they had to signify evidence of a different order. "Now, the Law does not deal with the supernatural, nor recognize it as an element in its dealing with facts," he asserted. Thus "the *onus* . . . rests on him who asserts that supernatural means did produce a natural result." In other words, if the entire defense strategy was built on the premise that the pictures were produced by supernatural means, and that Mumler was not intentionally deceiving his patrons, then the burden of proof was not met. Referring to Exhibit No. 10, the "yellow book" Mumler had circulated soon after arriving in New York to describe and promote his craft, Gerry contended that "there is no positive proof whatever of any spiritual agency, only evidence that certain persons *believe* it exists." This was the defense's entire case, that the photographs were evidence of belief, not fraud, and Gerry was drawing a line in the sand.

Suppose instead of spirit pictures this was a case of spirit-guided murder, he offered. In such a case, the only exculpable defense would be if the one who committed the crime suffered from a suspension of moral and mental faculties. Mumler could claim no such exemption since he had all along claimed knowledge of his actions and their results. It was a calculated if preposterous analogy, clearly intended to align the present case with criminal conduct and, in his own language, "insanity." The previous week he had intended to call an "expert in insanity, and the chief physician of the Lunatic Asylum, Blackwell's Island," who would "state the effect of these spiritual delusions," up to and including "disordered imaginations and incurable mental disease." Townsend had objected on the grounds that "it was a most outrageous thing for a prosecuting officer to suggest to prove insanity on persons . . . merely because they believed in a certain form of religion." Upon hearing the prosecution's intent, Dowling had "suggest[ed] that the witness not be called." In his closing argument, Gerry had found a way to paint the picture on his own.[74]

Having suggested that those who believed in the picture were, at best, suffering from "disordered imaginations," Gerry turned to his rival's attempt to locate the origins of modern Spiritualism in the Bible. In what must have been an effort to deflate Townsend's closing statement, Gerry in effect awkwardly accepted its premise. "The truths of the Christian religion, as asserted in the Bible," he began, "have always been acknowledged by the people of this Nation. That religion is the basis of all human law, and constitutes the vital essence of our legal system." Spiritualism, "this theory," he snapped, "is directly antagonistic to the Christian religion." Reading from Andrew Jackson Davis's 1857 autobiography, *The Magic Staff*, Gerry argued in court that the belief system was based on "a denial" of the "authenticity of the Holy Scriptures," "the faith of Christ crucified, and the efficacy of the atonement," the "doctrine of a general resurrection and final judgment to come," and a total "repudiation" of the doctrine of original sin. In effect, a case in support of Spiritualism was a case against American law, which, for Gerry, was inseparable from Christian theology.[75] In the prosecution's final case, Spiritualism itself was criminal, and Mumler, regardless of the sincerity of his belief, violated the law through exercising and promoting those beliefs through his photographs.

As for Townsend's argument that modern Spiritualism was echoing biblical instances of spiritual manifestations, Gerry would have none of it. Rebutting the example of Balaam's ass, for instance, he retorted that Townsend "seems to concede that an ass would be more likely than an ordinary man to perceive a spirit, and I believe with him in this view." Ribbing aside, this case was no laughing matter. Spiritualists' use of scripture invoked the "enemy of mankind, who, centuries ago, both quoted and perverted Scripture in his arguments with the Savior." Whereas Townsend had focused the court's attention first onto the legal parameters of the case and then on the continuity between scriptural episodes and modern instances of spiritual manifestation, Gerry concluded his defense by returning to the photographs themselves. He reminded the court that witnesses had detailed nine possible techniques for manufacturing spirit photographs — Bogardus had intimated there were hundreds of methods — using mechanical means. Gerry then went through the catalogue of twenty-four photographs entered as evidence by the defense, exposing each one as evidence not of spirits but of the "bogus" techniques of manipulation. One need not have caught him in the act to know the trick, Gerry implied. Too much was at stake. His final appeal was to re-

 Agents of a Fuller Revelation

mind the court of the magnitude of the charge. "This is no private prosecution," he intoned. Mumler was a menace to the bereaved and grief-stricken people of New York, a cheat "in the common habit of deceiving the *public*."[76] This case was not about belief, it was about truth. And the photographs were nothing if not true.

Was William Mumler guilty of a crime? Did his photographs convey the truth of the immortality of the soul or the truth of an orchestrated swindle? Were the mothers, fathers, widows, and children of deceased persons to be believed when they said they recognized their beloved in the spirit photographs, or should the court instead place confidence in the professional experts who could themselves deliver similar results through no agency but their own? Was the measure of truth in the Bible or in the photograph? What role had the court in determining the distance between belief and truth? "However I may be morally convinced that there may have been trick and deception practiced by the prisoner," Judge Dowling allowed in his decision, "yet as I sit as a Magistrate to determine from the evidence given by the witnesses, according to law, I am compelled to decide that I would not be justified in sending this complaint to the Grand Jury." Mumler was acquitted, but little had been decided. "The phenomena of Spiritualism may or may not be genuine," the *New-York Tribune* reported the day after the conclusion of the trial, "spirit photography may or may not be a delusion, for all Justice Dowling has decided. . . . The prosecution undertook to prove that the shadowy figure which Mumler produced in the background of a photograph was *not* the portrait of a spirit. It failed to prove it to the satisfaction of Justice Dowling."[77]

170 West Springfield Street, Boston

Although he had essentially won his case in the court of law, in the long days before the summer of 1869, William Mumler had by other measures lost in the court of public opinion. On the Saturday following the examination's conclusion, *Harper's Weekly* devoted the entire front page to the "swindle." In addition to broadcasting the proceedings to its readership — "remarkable and without precedent in the annals of criminal jurisprudence" — *Harper's* published engravings based on the spirit photographs that had appeared in court. Much had been said about Mumler's pictures in the press, but few people beyond his patrons, critics, and those fortunate to have a seat in the courtroom gallery had actually seen examples. "We devote this page to illustrations bearing upon [the case of the people against William H. Mumler]," the article began, and indeed the pictures dominated the page (fig. 26). It was still not possible to reproduce photographs in the press in 1869, and the engravings convey the paper's solution to the problem of showing its readers what had riled the hullabaloo of the previous month. While not photographs, on the published page the engravings accomplished visually what Gerry and the prosecution had failed to do in court: here, the pictures condemned Mumler as a fraud. There was a portrait of Mumler (sans ghosts), six spirit pictures produced by the Boston medium, and two, virtually indistinguishable in the published engravings, by the New York photographer George Gardner Rockwood. Like Bogardus and others who had demonstrated their own talents in creating bogus spirit pictures in an effort to debunk Mumler's claims, Rockwood's pictures had made little difference in the courtroom. But on the pages of *Harper's* they painted him an experienced huckster who got away with the store.

On April 21, a writer for *Harper's*, James R. Gilmore, had been called as a reluctant witness by the defense. He testified that the periodical had commissioned him in March "to investigate this spiritual photography affair and write an article regarding it." Before visiting Mumler, he had gone to another photographer to learn "where can this humbug come in." He knew there to be trickery afoot and wanted to know where to look. Armed with this knowledge, Gilmore observed Mumler make three pictures. The photograph shown in court "was a fair likeness of Mr. Gilmore," the *Tribune* reported, "but the spiritual accompaniment was much more dim and indistinct than on most of the others shown." Gilmore did not recognize the likeness, though observed from the stand that it resembled Dowling, "being only . . . a little better looking." Two more pictures were made, and still he did not recognize "a departed relative" (here he observed that the second picture "greatly resembled a gentleman now in Court," but the defense stepped in before he could point this person out). Still, he "could detect nothing unusual in Mumler's operations." Defeated, Gilmore enlisted Rockwood to make "spiritual figures by natural means" so as to test his powers of observation. Rockwood had begun his trade as a daguerreotypist in St. Louis in the 1850s before moving to New York in 1859, where he purchased the studio at 839 Broadway, about nine blocks north of where Mumler would set up shop a decade later.[78] Rockwood tried various methods, Gilmore testified, "but I always detected some trickery."[79] (Years later, Rockwood touted the uses of "photography as a detective" to his photographic brethren, particularly in "legal cases, for the identification of forgeries in documents, etc." By the 1890s, Rockwood claimed, he had "for many years made a speciality out of

                              Agents of a Fuller Revelation

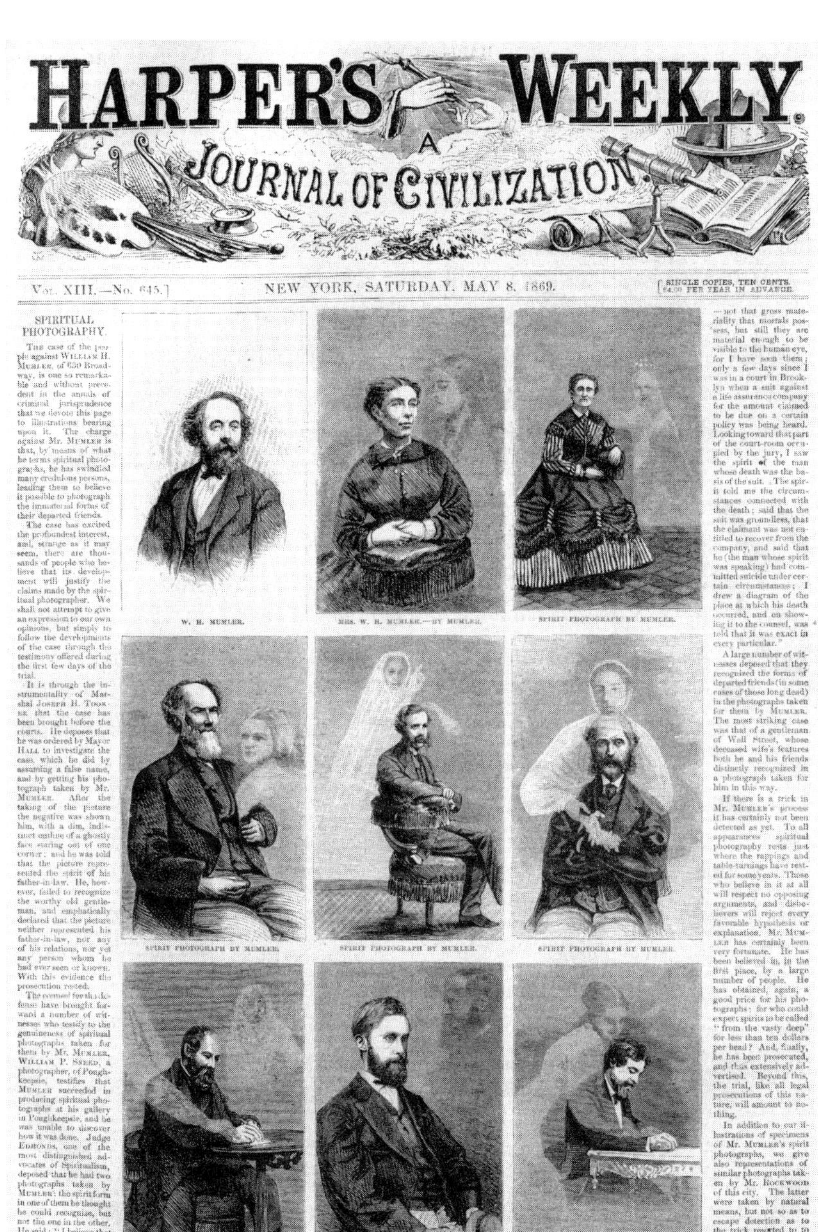

HARPER'S WEEKLY.

A JOURNAL OF CIVILIZATION.

VOL. XIII.—No. 645.] NEW YORK, SATURDAY, MAY 8, 1869. [SINGLE COPIES, TEN CENTS.
[$4.00 PER YEAR IN ADVANCE.

SPIRITUAL PHOTOGRAPHY.

The case of the people against WILLIAM H. MUMLER, of 630 Broadway, is one so remarkable and without precedent in the annals of criminal jurisprudence that we devote this page to illustrations bearing upon it. The charge against Mr. MUMLER is that, by means of what he terms spiritual photographs, he has swindled many credulous persons, leading them to believe it possible to photograph the immaterial forms of their departed friends.

The case has excited the profoundest interest, and, strange as it may seem, there are thousands of people who believe that its development will justify the claims made by the spiritual photographer. We shall not attempt to give an expression to our own opinions, but simply to follow the developments of the case through the testimony offered during the first few days of the trial.

It is through the instrumentality of Marshal JOSEPH H. TOOKER that the case has been brought before the courts. He deposes that he was ordered by Mayor HALL to investigate the case, which he did by assuming a false name, and by getting his photograph taken by Mr. MUMLER. After the taking of the picture the negative was shown him, with a dim, indistinct outline of a ghostly face staring out of one corner; and he was told that the picture represented the spirit of his father-in-law. He, however, failed to recognize the worthy old gentleman, and emphatically declared that the picture neither represented his father-in-law, nor any of his relations, nor yet any person whom he had ever seen or known. With this evidence the prosecution rested.

The counsel for the defense have brought forward a number of witnesses who testify to the genuineness of spiritual photographs taken for them by Mr. MUMLER. WILLIAM P. SLEED, a photographer, of Poughkeepsie, testifies that MUMLER succeeded in producing spiritual photographs at his gallery in Poughkeepsie, and he was unable to discover how it was done. Judge EDMONDS, one of the most distinguished advocates of Spiritualism, deposed that he had two photographs taken by MUMLER; the spirit form in one of them he thought he could recognize, but not the one in the other. He said: "I believe that the camera can take a photograph of a spirit, and I believe also that spirits have materiality

—not that gross materiality that mortals possess, but still they are material enough to be visible to the human eye; for I have seen them; only a few days since I was in a court in Brooklyn when a suit against a life assurance company for the amount claimed to be due on a certain policy was being heard. Looking toward that part of the court-room occupied by the jury, I saw the spirit of the man whose death was the basis of the suit. The spirit told me the circumstances connected with the death; said that the suit was groundless, that the claimant was not entitled to recover from the company, and said that he (the man whose spirit was speaking) had committed suicide under certain circumstances; I drew a diagram of the place at which his death occurred, and on showing it to the counsel, was told that it was exact in every particular."

A large number of witnesses deposed that they recognized the forms of departed friends (in some cases of those long dead) in the photographs taken for them by MUMLER. The most striking case was that of a gentleman of Wall Street, whose deceased wife's features both he and his friends distinctly recognized in a photograph taken for him in this way.

If there is a trick in Mr. MUMLER's process it has certainly not been detected as yet. To all appearances spiritual photography rests just where the rappings and table-turnings have rested for some years. Those who believe in it at all will respect no opposing arguments, and disbelievers will reject every favorable hypothesis or explanation. Mr. MUMLER has certainly been very fortunate. He has been believed in, in the first place, by a large number of people. He has obtained, again, a good price for his photographs; for who could expect spirits to be called "from the vasty deep" for less than ten dollars per head? And, finally, he has been prosecuted, and thus extensively advertised. Beyond this, the trial, like all legal prosecutions of this nature, will amount to nothing.

In addition to our illustrations of specimens of Mr. MUMLER's spirit photographs, we give also representations of similar photographs taken by Mr. ROCKWOOD of this city. The latter were taken by natural means, but not so as to escape detection as to the trick resorted to to secure the result. Mr. MUMLER has certainly the advantage of a longer experience in the business.

Figure 26. Front page, *Harper's Weekly*, May 8, 1869. Modern Graphic History Library, Washington University in St. Louis. Used with permission.

this peculiar branch of work."[80]) *Harper's* grew reluctant to publish the story, coming belatedly to the "conclusion that if it was a humbug it would come out, and if not, that it would not do any good by putting it in the *Weekly*."[81] By the conclusion of the trial, *Harper's* had again changed course and ran the story, complete with the illustrations Gilmore had acquired in his investigation. News of the sensation and the acquittal spread throughout the country over the next several weeks, but the press would soon lose interest in Mumler and his pictures. And yet even if Mumler's fame was a flash in the pan, his notoriety is linked not only to the birth of spirit photography but also to habits of beholding that cut across American society. The fraught space between what the camera recorded and what beholders saw was quite literally on trial in 1869, but it would continue to haunt the communion of shadows through the end of the century.

After the hearing, William and Hannah returned to Boston, where they took up shop at 170 West Springfield Street. They slowly built a clientele, he leaning more on her until their separation several years later. They remained known in Spiritualist circles, but the popular press had lost interest. The trial had severely undercut Mumler's trade—he had, after all, been the subject of a lengthy and well-documented fraud investigation—and had left him deeply in debt with little promise of remuneration. Within weeks of the resolution of his hearing, Hunter & Co. of Hinsdale, New Hampshire, placed an ad for "copies of the celebrated $10 Spiritual Photographs. Made by Mumler . . . The greatest wonder of the age," now for the bargain price of "25 cents each, 3 for 50 cents, 8 for $1, or $10 for a hundred."[82] Photographs that had once commanded high prices were now being sold wholesale. More of his clients now were self-affirmed Spiritualists rather than a cross-section of the bereaved. And yet even as Mumler rather precipitously became a whispered memory, not unlike the shadowy outlines in his pictures, the field of spirit photography continued into the twentieth century and remained a subject of private interest and public scrutiny. By the 1890s, at least one photographer had figured out how to turn the probity of suspicion into cash. R. L. Green charged $2 for personal sittings (a small premium was added for sittings by mail) and $10 for "test sittings"—if they were unsuccessful, however, there would be "no charge." "If the above conditions don't suit you," he taunted would-be investigators, "DON'T SIT, and save my time and yours."[83]

Still, even as his notoriety evaporated into oddity, tales of William Mumler's remarkable talents occasionally surfaced. In late 1871, Emma Hardinge Britten, one of the earliest chroniclers of modern Spiritualism, called upon Mumler. She had elected not to include him in her compendium of Ameri-

    Agents of a Fuller Revelation

can Spiritualism a few years earlier but found herself "impelled" to visit him now "by the remarkable accounts of tests furnished to me by reliable persons who had obtained . . . proofs of their spirit friends' presence and identity." After an unsuccessful attempt—it bore "some resemblance to a dearly departed friend, [though] not sufficiently obvious to constitute a likeness"—Britten was delighted when Beethoven appeared at her side. She had not disclosed to Mumler or "anyone in America," she explained, that prior to calling upon the photographer she had been "writing musical criticism" during a recent residence in England. "Whilst engaged in these writings," she continued, "I have the best reasons for believing that the spirit of the noble German was frequently with me." Upon receiving the likeness of the noble German, Britten offered her "unsought-for testimony" in defense of the "virulently assailed and publicly prosecuted" photographer to anyone who would listen to or, better, print her tale. She also touted the remarkable success of sittings by mail. Wherever one lived, the bereaved or inquisitive need only send their own likenesses to Mumler as a kind of proxy and, complying with "the conditions announced in the enclosed circular," would receive portraits "just as true and faithful to life as those who have attended the sittings in person."[84] The oil merchant Mr. Chapin availed himself of this service and received his "spirit wife & babe recognized." Even as new photographic techniques developed that, for many, called into question the sincerity of spiritual likenesses—composite photography, for instance, as well as dry-plate techniques that no longer required photographers to sensitize plates in their studios—Green continued this practice of giving sittings "by mail" into the 1890s. Connecting photography to previous corporeal proxies, patrons could also send him a "lock of hair (your own preferred)." Julia C. Vanders of Richmond, Virginia, received such a "picture (from lock of hair)" in December 1891. It "*is more* than I expected," she wrote. "The man's face at the top of photo is my husband, and the little girl, my child." It was truly a gift, she continued, that she "appreciate[d] . . . very dearly, AS WE HAVE NO PICTURE OF MY LITTLE GIRL IN LIFE."[85]

The material record of Mumler's practice in many cases survived where memory faded. Two months before William Howard Mumler died in May 1884, a grizzled company of faculty from the University of Pennsylvania assembled in the dimly lit rooms of Mrs. S. E. Patterson at 508 S. 16th Street. Twenty-nine-year-old George S. Fullerton had been appointed professor of philosophy in 1883 when Henry Seybert, son of the distinguished Penn medical school alum and Pennsylvania congressman Adam Seybert, endowed a chair in his father's name. As a condition of the gift, the university was to appoint a commission "to investigate 'all systems of Morals, Religion, or Philosophy which assume to represent the Truth, and particularly of Modern Spiritualism.'" So it was that Fullerton and his colleagues, among them Presbyterian minister and professor of history and literature Robert Ellis Thompson, the renowned anatomist Joseph Leidy, and Provost William Pepper, called on Mrs. Patterson, Spiritualistic medium.[86] With the enthusiasm of a conditional commission, charged to "men whose days are already filled with duties which cannot be laid aside, and who are able, therefore, to devote but a small portion of their time to these investigations," the preliminary report published in 1887 assured readers that despite the burden, "from the outset your Commission have been deeply impressed with the seriousness of their undertaking" and "that the farther our investigations extend the more imperative appears the demand for these investigations." At the outset, furthermore, the commission noted that "the belief in so-called Spiritualism is certainly not decreasing" in these modern times and asked, in sympathy with those, like Seybert, who so believed, "who can fail to stand aside in tender reverence when crushed and bleeding hearts are seen to seek it for consolation and for hope?" As such, the men of the committee "beg that nothing which they may say may be interpreted as indicating indifference or levity." Formalities and assurances aside, the report was a scathing indictment of the physical manifestations of modern Spiritualism. "I have been forced to the conclusion," Fullerton wrote in his capacity as commission secretary, "that Spiritualism, as far at least as it has shown itself before me . . . , presents the melancholy spectacle of gross fraud, perpetrated upon an uncritical portion of the community." In their investigations of slate writing, rapping, spectral caressing, and other physical manifestations of the spirits, the Seybert Commission had "not been cheered in our investigations by the discovery of a single novel fact" and had, alas, preserved evidence of such conclusions "in our sad museum of specimens of misdirected ingenuity."[87]

Spirit photographs occasionally appeared in the commission's investigations, as when, at a subsequent visit to Mrs. Patterson, she "exhibited" two such specimens. "In one the Spirit was her own mother," Fullerton had noted, and hinting at Mumler's technique, the "Spirit in each appeared as a white apparition behind a person seated in the foreground." Patterson's spirit pictures prompted no further report from Fullerton or speculation on their provenance. By contrast, the commission's report spared no ink in their assessment of William M. Keeler, a spirit photographer from Washington, D.C., who had also practiced in Boston. Keeler was visiting Philadelphia in late 1885 when Shakespearean scholar and commission member Horace

   Agents of a Fuller Revelation

Howard Furness requested "in writing a statement of his terms and conditions under which an investigation by this Commission could be held." Ever the showman, the self-styled Dr. Keeler obliged Professor Furness's request. "In regard to giving the Photographic Séances," he wrote on November 6, 1885, with a list of conditions. He would give three séances for a payment of $300, to be paid in full "whether my efforts prove satisfactory or not," and he noted that such an arrangement was required "as I cannot guard against the influences which others may bring." Only "regularly appointed members of the Commission" were to attend, furthermore, and Keeler would be able to invite "an equal number of persons, if necessary, to harmonize the antagonistic element which might be produced by those persons not in perfect sympathy with the cause."[88]

The commission might have assented to these conditions, in pursuit of their worthy investigations—although the fee of $300 (roughly equivalent to $8,000 in 2015 money) was an outrageous sum to the committee—had Keeler not also required "the exclusive use of the dark room and my own instrument."[89] Confident that Keeler intended with these conditions to deter the commission's investigation, Furness was composed in his response to the demands, careful "to give him no loop to hang a charge of discourteous or illiberal treatment on." Calling the photographer's bluff, Furness called on Keeler in his rooms on Green Street, asserting that he "must know how very simple a process this 'composite photography' is" and, as there "being no mystery whatever in it," that "the conditions he demanded were such as to render any investigation simply silly." There may have been no mystery in composite photography, but there was certainly wonder. At an 1884 meeting of the National Academy of Sciences in Newport, Rhode Island, the geologist Raphael Pumpelly had delivered a paper on "an experimental composite photograph of members of the academy," becoming one of the first Americans to experiment with this new arena of photographic manipulation. Thirty-one photographs of academy members had been acquired at a meeting earlier in the year, and "three composites had been made from the full-face views," all of which "had a far more youthful appearance than any of the pictures from which they were taken."[90] George Rockwood, the Broadway photographer whose hoax spirit pictures were printed in *Harper's Weekly*, described composite photographs as "a succession of photographic impressions imposed one upon the other in the same plate, so as to produce in a single picture the combined likenesses of various persons."[91] The application of this new trick, another member of the academy wrote a year later, was to ascertain "a type representing *par excellence* the peculiar characteristic for which the originals were grouped together." "In combining the portraits of criminals," he explained, "the object is to get a type of criminality; in combing the portraits of national academicians, one of recognized scientific ability."[92] Furness may have had this new technique to "reduce the art of type-getting to a mechanical one" in mind when he chided Keeler for his "silly" terms. (William James would apply this meaning to his notion of "saintliness" in *The Varieties of Religious Experience*. "The saintly character is the character for which spiritual emotions are the habitual center of the personal energy," he wrote, "and there is a certain composite photograph of universal saintliness, the same in all religions, of which the features can easily be traced."[93]) More likely, however, Furness was referring to another kind of composite portraiture in which multiple likenesses from different plates were combined into a single print. Mumler's ghosts had appeared as diaphanous specters, often embracing the sitter or, in the case of sittings by mail, appearing as half- to full-length figures. Keeler's spirits were, by contrast, described as faces encircling the sitter, not unlike this one (fig. 27) from the turn of the twentieth century of the Chicago medium John K. Hallowell by S. W. Fallis. Here fourteen faces encircle the entranced medium, among them Sitting Bull, Henry Ward Beecher, Swami Vivekananda, Daniel Webster, and Annie Besant. Furness's description suggests that Keeler's ghosts were more like Hallowell's company than Pumpelly's scholars. (After signing his report, Furness could not help himself from adding that he showed Keeler a composite taken by one of his sons, "wherein a Spirit quite as ethereal as any of Mr. Keeler's, appears in the background." Keeler looked at the photograph and "returned it to me without remark.")[94]

Ever protective of the commission's reputation, Furness "repeated my reply to his wife" before leaving Keeler's room. "We were ready to investigate," the professor minded, "if we could be allowed to watch the very points where material agency cease and spiritual begins, but these very points Mr. Keeler forbade us to examine, and that the failure rested with him." Even if Hannah had kept a tight rein on William soon after his discovery, Mumler had quite early invited, even taunted, critics to investigate his method to prove that the spirits appeared by something other than mechanical technique. This was in keeping with the broader investigative culture of American Spiritualism. Keeler, by contrast, had stymied investigation by closing the darkroom to observation. This stonewalling flummoxed Furness, who later concluded with an obvious wink that the darkroom "could have nothing to do with Spiritual forces, for the Spirits had already done their work in

   Agents of a Fuller Revelation

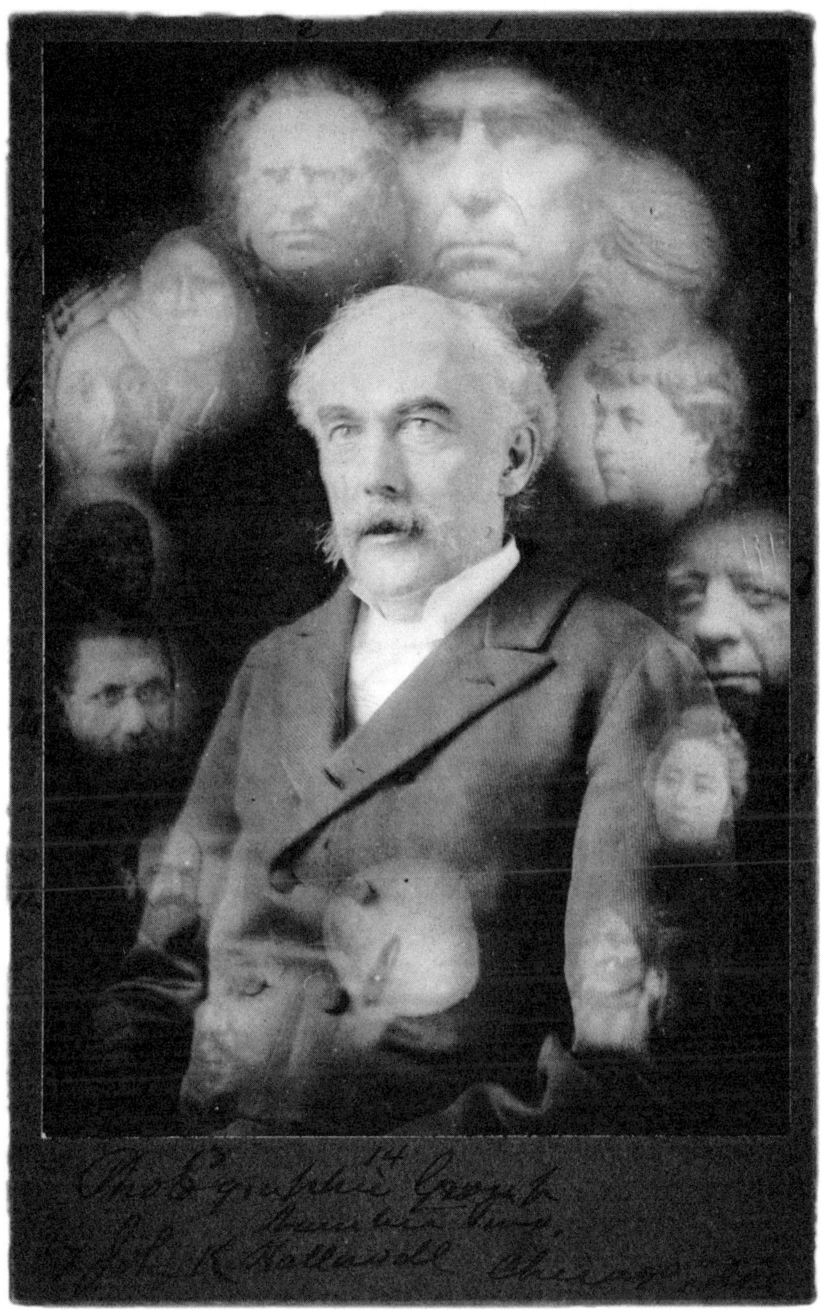

Figure 27. Spirit photograph showing half-length portrait of John K. Hallowell, facing left, surrounded by superimposed faces of fourteen deceased people. S.W. Fallis, photographer. Chicago, Ill., 1901. Library of Congress.

the Camera." As he left the visiting showman empty handed, the professor turned to Keeler and asked him to arrange a sitting, in his private capacity, declaring "that I should not be satisfied with less than a cherub on my head, one on each shoulder, and a full-blown angel on my breast. He laughingly assented."[95]

Keeler's obstinacy aside, the commission compiled specimens of spirit photographs for its files. Among the handful that survive, many appear to be artistic experimentation and professional spoofs rather than spiritual communion. The portrait submitted by C. D. Mosher of Chicago features a fully "opaque" bearded spirit showing a scandalous amount of leg, and the print bearing the mark of one of Philadelphia's finest portraitists, J. W. Hurn, appears to be (like Bogardus's photograph of Barnum) an intentional hoax of a faceless woman appearing over the left shoulder of a sitting chap. Also in the commission's sad museum is a Mumler photograph of Fanny Conant, medium of the Boston spiritualist paper the *Banner of Light*. On the back of the card, the commission scribbled that Conant's spiritual guide was "a little Mexican Indian girl." Conant had called on Mumler after his return to Boston; her visit, he later recalled, "was without any prearrangement, and entirely unexpected." As he was preparing to expose the plate, Conant turned to the side where, she said, there was a spirit. "On developing the negative," Mumler recorded in his memoir, "there appeared the form of a young girl, bearing the features of a white person, but dressed in Indian costume, with feathers on her head, large rings in her ears, while encircling her neck was a chain, to which was attached a charm of crescent shape."[96] What the Commission had recognized as a "little Mexican Indian girl," Conant knew as Vashti, who had first controlled her in 1870 as she was recovering from a severe illness. In life, "Vooshti" was the daughter of "Big Buffalo" and his wife, of the northern plains Piegan nation. Before her birth, Mumler narrated, the Piegans had taken a white woman captive and, because her mother had "continued thought of her pale-faced rival during the gestative period," the babe "resembled a white child in a strongly-marked degree." Vooshti (Piegan for "the captive") was slain along with her father by the army of General Philip Henry Sheridan in December 1869, at the age of seven years. Soon after her bodily demise, Vashti (her given name "being comparatively difficult of pronunciation by white lips") began to "entrance" Conant and quickly became a steadfast companion.[97] There had been a long tradition of so-called Indian guides in American Spiritualism, dating to at least the early 1850s and frequently manifesting, as had Vashti, as healers of white bodies. Several historians have argued that such understandings of heightened Native American spirituality

                                                    Agents of a Fuller Revelation

"amounted to an extension of the colonial project" that posited through appropriation (and relative neglect of political and social plight) that Indians were "better off as spirit guides than as living beings."[98] Photographs of native peoples had not always been vehicles of cultural imperialism. There is much evidence that daguerreotypes of Native Americans were, like nearly all portraits, made to tell the stories of their sitters, not their makers. This had a lot to do with the limited commercial reach of individual daguerreotype portraits. Wet-plate photography changed the politics of representing Indians. Glass plate negatives, and their ostensibly endless reach of reproducibility, as Sandweiss argues, transformed artifacts of "private remembrance" into "piece[s] of a public story." Even though spirits of indigenous persons had been visiting Spiritualists for nearly twenty years before Mumler captured Vashti on his plate, his medium subsumed these controls into the "overarching narrative" that replaced private mementos of remembrance with "the determinist tale of a 'vanishing race.'" On Mumler's plates, the vanishing act was dramatically visualized.[99]

Conclusion

In April 1872, the *Religio-Philosophical Journal* of Chicago, a Spiritualist newspaper, informed readers of a spirit photograph "kindly sent" by "Brother W. H. Mumler." "The likenesses are quite plain and perfect," the paper assured, and "indeed, it is a piece of work that must silence skeptics upon the subject of spirit photography."[100] Mumler had been spared a legal conviction of fraud three years earlier, but the rift his pictures had exposed in the communion of shadows between revelation and deception was as wide as ever. When the veiled woman walked into his Boston studio in early 1872, the crepe "so thick it was impossible to distinguish a single feature of her face," she had given the name Mrs. Lindall and insisted on covering her face until the instant Mumler was ready to expose the plate. Three days later, the widow returned to collect her likeness. Hannah was "engaged in conversation with a lady-friend when the doorbell rang," Mumler recalled in his autobiography, when Mrs. Lindall arrived and requested her prints. "Do you recognize the likeness?" the women asked. Yes, the widow "hesitatingly" replied. "My wife was almost instantly entranced," Mumler reported, saying, "Mother, if you cannot recognize father, show the picture to Robert; he will recognize it." The widow again repeated that she did recognize the likeness in the picture, "but who is now speaking?" "The control replied: 'Thaddeus!' A long conversation ensued. Mr. Lincoln afterward controlled and talked

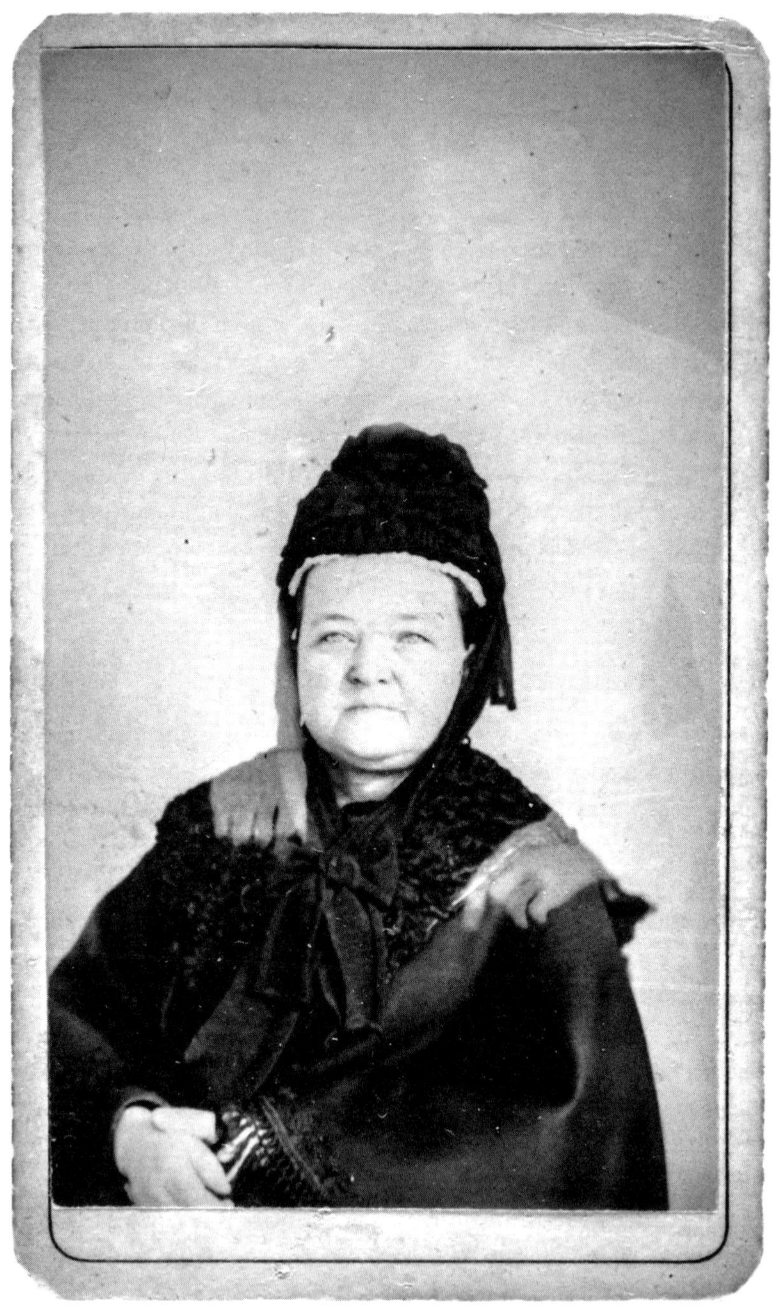

Figure 28. Mary Todd Lincoln (1818–82) (untitled spirit photograph with Abraham Lincoln's shadow). William H. Mumler. Albumen silver print, ca. 1872. Harvard Art Museums/Fogg Museum, Transfer from Special Collections, Fine Arts Library, Harvard College Library. Bequest of Evert Jansen Wendell.

with her. . . . When my wife resumed her normal condition, she found Mrs. L weeping tears of joy that she had again found her loved ones, and apparently anxious to learn, if possible, how long before she could join them in their spirit home."[101]

While at his studio on Washington Street in 1865, Mumler had printed a celebrity carte de visite of Mary Todd Lincoln from an illustration, so despite his claims to the contrary, he likely recognized the grieving widow when she stepped into his studio in 1872, heavy crepes and pseudonym notwithstanding.[102] What is more, the spirit photograph of the late lamented president did not revive Mumler's business to any substantial degree. But the intimacy of the exchange between the grieving widow and mother, on one side of the glass, and her deceased beloved, on the other, registers a tension between the sensationalism of spirit photography—played out in the court and press alike—and the deeply personal experiences that the technology promised for the bereaved. The divisive debates surrounding what Mumler's camera had recorded—imperceptible truth or impossible hokum—carried far into the communion of shadows. In the next two chapters, we follow these debates and the habits of beholding within them from the fuzzy margins of memory and into the footsteps of a particularly notable ancient Galilean.

FOUR

By Pencil and Camera

In October 1893, sixteen-year-old Ivy Ledbetter Lee stood among the crowd gathered on the elevated rail platform in Chicago. The weather was mild for mid-October — the morning *Tribune* had forecast a comfortable sixty degrees — but Ivy still had a tingle run down his spine as he thought about what the day had in store. Four days earlier he had left Atlanta with fifty dollars in his pocket and a brown cloth memorandum pad. To pass time on the rail passage through Chattanooga, Cincinnati, Indianapolis, and Lafayette, Ivy had come up with a list of "terms of interest in Chicago." Throngs of tourists had taken similar routes to the "phenomenal city, so gigantic, so young, so rich, strong and powerful," earlier in the summer to witness the World's Columbian Exposition.[1] And while the sweltering summer crowds had dissipated, there was still much to behold as autumn's long shadows crept into the city. Ivy's father, a Methodist minister, had been in Chicago a few weeks earlier when he delivered a paper at the World's Parliament of Religions, an auxiliary congress to the exposition that testified both to the triumphalist sensibilities of such Protestant ministers as James Wideman Lee and to the cosmopolitan aspirations of many other participants. But Ivy made no mention of his father other than the forty-five dollars "Rec'd from Papa" on October 13. He had other things to think about. Miss Pearl Mozley, a family friend, had insisted that Ivy see the "Special Pictures in [the] Art Gallery," so he made a list of sculptures and oil paintings by nationality — the United States, France, Germany, Belgium, Denmark, England, Norway, Russia, Spain, and Italy. Julian Hawthorne had directed him to the "portrait of Lady Macbeth" — a study of the British stage actress Ellen Terry by the American artist John Singer Sargent — gushing that it was "first picture in the Exposition." He also scribbled that he must "see Tiffany Diamon[d] Exhibit and Stain Glass in M. & L. A. Fine"—the Manufactures and Liberal Arts Building located on the Grand Basin, America's leviathan answer to Mr. Eiffel's towering pièce de résistance of the Paris Exposition four years earlier.[2]

In addition to these exhibits of fine arts from Europe and the United States, the exposition had other attractions that would have drawn the attention of a teenage boy striking out on his own. Having purchased his guidebook (twenty-five cents) and fair admission (a dime), Ivy quaffed a glass of orange cider and ambled his way over to the "Anthropological—Ethnological" attractions on the Midway Plaisance. He flipped open the memo book. "Go: Streets of Cairo." A wedding procession complete with "gaily caparisoned camels" and a "half-stripped Egyptian who danced with his shoulders, after the Asiatic, African, and Muscovite manner" was a "typical scene in Cairo Street" according to one souvenir book of the fair.[3] Within earshot of the "tom-tom beaters" he may also have seen bangle-clad performers of the *danse du ventre* at the Egyptian Theatre, an attraction that had stirred up quite the media sensation over the summer.[4] From Cairo Street, Ivy cocked his head up to gauge the towering Ferris wheel but "did not go on." He also went to the Javanese and South Sea Islanders Villages and Old Vienna. He witnessed the "mon-poy" at the Chinese Theatre but missed the Moorish Palace. At the Algerian Village he bought a coin for a nickel, one of several purchases he made that afternoon: a wooden waiter inlaid with pearl for Mrs. Mozley, a glass souvenir, a Japanese coin, two spoons, and an unspecified assortment of "Souvenirs (aluminum)." Ivy spent a week in the Dream City of the West, the enthusiastic moniker bestowed on Chicago, where he spent a good deal of time exploring the city beyond the fair. Although certainly enjoying the privilege his father's rising status in the Methodist Church afforded, Ivy's story is not unlike thousands of others who visited Chicago in the summer and early fall of 1893. What does make his story remarkable is the connection it exposes between growing interest in the "ethnographic" uses of photography and biblical imagination at the turn of the twentieth century.

The Columbian Exposition's cacophonous orchestration of fine art and ethnographic spectacle anticipated the visual habits of elision and recognition that Ivy Lee's father would help facilitate for Americans over the course of the next decade by bringing them to the pages of the Bible. In the same way that patrons beheld gyrating Egyptians and joss houses and Japanese coins but saw them to signal something else—heathenry, greed, frivolity—so did photographs of "the Holy Land" in the coming years cloak underlying hermeneutics of elision that denied the contemporary circumstances of Palestinian subjects.[5] On Cairo Street in Chicago and on a Cairo street in Egypt, the camera was used at once to document events—the ethnographic—and to disclose higher orders—be they political, racial, or religious—by asking beholders to look beyond what had been recorded. In its simultaneous conditioning of aesthetic contemplation, wide-eyed wonderment, and religioracial hierarchies, the Chicago World's Fair modeled in microcosm the visual habits of an era of increased colonial engagement and immigration, both of which sorted out a multitude of anxieties and aspirations through visual strategies of representation that frequently obscured far more than they revealed. Hundreds of thousands of visitors ambled their way through the fair's labyrinth of exhibits and spectacles. For those who could not attend, dailies and weeklies provided countless sketches of interest for the curious and the intrigued. And during the 1880s, technical advances in the field of photomechanical reproduction enabled publishers to print photographs directly into manuscripts. These "halftone" techniques profoundly influenced the visual habits of Americans in the last decade of the nineteenth century by bringing photographic representations of racially and religiously coded populations to the fingerprints of millions of Americans—Midway "others" from the World's Fair, urban tenement dwellers in Jacob Riis's *How the Other Half Lives* (1890), Filipinos in periodicals during the Spanish-American and Philippine-American Wars, indigenous populations the world over in the pages of *National Geographic*, and inhabitants of the Holy Land in a seemingly endless sea of publications.[6] The halftone's integration of photographs with printed text drastically augmented the market for photographic media. These publications were tremendously popular in part because, like older photographic techniques, they advertised *presence*. Can't get to Chicago? Buy our book. Can't stomach the stench of the tenement? Look at these photographs. Can't afford a trip to the Holy Land? We will bring it to you. The discourse of Holy Land presence—and vicarious access—was arguably as old as the medium of photography. But halftone publications economized space, time, expense, and, most significant, narrative instruction. Halftone images' intimate commingling with text commanded explicit consideration of the relationship between photography and the word.

Using this newly popular technique to print photographs within published text, James Wilson Pierce authored a "profusely illustrated" *Photographic History of the World's Fair* that included "a minute account of the GREAT EXPOSITION" alongside scores of photographic "illustrations."[7] Pierce was not alone. At least 600 souvenir photographic albums were avail-

                    By Pencil and Camera

able to visitors to the fair and patrons of sundry publications.[8] In April 1894, for instance, new subscribers to the *Southern Cultivator* received "50 photographic views of the World's Fair" as a free gift, "$25.00 Worth of Instantaneous Photographic Views."[9] Similarly, the *Religious Herald* of Hartford, Connecticut, issued the "profusely illustrated" *Picturesque Chicago* that included a guide to the fair, and the *Chicago Times* serialized halftone photographs of "midway types" by the Canadian portrait photographer James J. Gibson.[10] While Gibson's portraits have been credited for resisting contemporary caricatures of the groups found along the Midway, his portrayals were the exception to the rule when it came to the cultural legacies of photographic representations of the performers and artisans found at the fair.[11] Cultural theorist and historian Fatimah Tobing Rony has defined the late nineteenth-century hunger for images of natives as "fascinating cannibalism," by which she means to draw attention to "the consumers of the images of the bodies — as well as actual bodies on display — of native peoples offered up by popular media and science."[12] According to Rony, the category of the ethnographic was implicated in the construction of racialized categories it portended merely to demonstrate through empirical and, often enough, visual technologies. But her analytics of spectacle leaves little room for the sense of manifest presence that photographs of the Holy Land were intended to convey — these were designed to draw beholders into a landscape, simultaneously historical and biblical — even as they participated in the "pervasive form of objectification of indigenous peoples" that Rony labels "ethnographic."[13] The Columbian Exposition's visual campaign, nurtured by decades of photography's association with imperialist projects, of expecting blindness to what was within the compositional frame *and* promising to clarify what the image actually disclosed helps us understand the role of photography in an increasingly visually sophisticated biblical imaginary among American Protestants. In both souvenir tours of the fair and in portfolios of the Holy Land, halftone prints became material disclosures of an unfixed past.

The publishing firm of N. D. Thompson of St. Louis was directly involved in publishing photographic records of both the fair and the Holy Land. And Ivy Lee's father, James Lee, was instrumental in making the connections explicit. In 1893, Thompson published *The Dream City: A Portfolio of Photographic Views of the World's Columbian Exposition* and, a few months later, *Oriental and Occidental, Northern and Southern: Portrait Types of the Midway Plaisance*, a collection of eighty halftones of "all the queer people you gazed at 'down on the Midway'" comprised in large part from the negatives of the

Chicago photographers Place and Coover.[14] If there was any doubt that the prints in *Dream City* were tokens of a cosmic design, the biblical reference on the title page put it to rest: "And they shall bring the glory and honor of the nations into it. — Rev. 21:26." This photographic journey through monuments to American civilization and "Anthropological — Ethnological" attractions on the Midway was at once ethnographic evidence of American progress and the fulfillment of biblical promise. In March 1894, Thompson asked James Lee if he would be "disposed to make the trip outlined on the map of Palestine showing the journeys of Christ and the Apostles" with a photographer he would hire "in that country or in Egypt." As a gesture of his "sincere regard" for Lee, Thompson enclosed in his correspondence a "Worlds Fair Series of Views."[15] The visual strategy of the fair was going biblical.

By the time the United States hosted the international exposition in St. Louis a decade later, the connections between the ethnographic gaze and Holy Land topographies would be manifest in the orchestration of the fair itself. The wildly popular Jerusalem Exhibit at the Louisiana Purchase Exposition in 1904 was, as historian Burke O. Long has noted, situated strategically between the magnificent Fine Arts building and the hubbub of the Pike, St. Louis's boisterous echo of Chicago's Midway Plaisance. James Lee both advised its construction and authored the exhibit's official guidebook.[16] Long suggests that the exhibit's position demonstrated ambivalence about the cultural location of Jerusalem. By 1904, however, Americans had long been policing the boundary between the sublime and the subjected through photographic artifacts that teetered between visual habits of emulation and elision. As contemporary inhabitants of "the Orient," the peoples of Palestine and Egypt, especially, were subjected to a dismissive colonialist gaze. At the same time, when rendered as types — icons — rather than individuals, these same figures were understood to disclose the hidden truths of the Bible. Through the camera, inhabitants of the Holy Land were simultaneously configured as ethnographic icon and biblical relic. It was not a matter of ambiguity but of duality. It was a messy affair, to be sure, but there was little confusion, little ambivalence, about the place that Jerusalem and its attendant Holy Land locales occupied in the religious imagination of turn-of-the-twentieth-century America.

There was no causal sequence between the Midway Plaisance, photographs of the Holy Land, and the Jerusalem Exhibit. But these events do help place the photographs within a cultural milieu that was electrified with practices of representation that influenced the visual habits of beholding the Holy Land. James Lee had at least a cameo appearance in all three acts. But

   By Pencil and Camera

as much as this is a story about the visual habits of an imperialist gaze that linked the racialized renditions of the midway with representations of colonized subjects and both with a biblical imaginary, it is also, and more directly, a story of migrating photographs. As such, it considers relationships between "the pencil and camera," between text and image, as these photographs moved from souvenir book to the pages of the Bible. The book project that Thompson pitched to Lee was for a tour of the Holy Land in which Lee would lead with "the pencil" alongside a photographer who wielded a camera.[17] In the end, Lee agreed to Thompson's terms. But the photographer who accompanied him through the Holy Land—a designation derived, according to Lee, "from the fact that God's chosen people lived in it"—was not an operator hired in Egypt but rather the American landscape artist, Robert Edward Mather Bain. Lee and Bain were in the Holy Land for only a few months, but the legacy of the journey is profound. Bain's photographs were published in at least three documents over the course of the next decade: the originally commissioned plates, which were later published under the uniform title *Earthly Footsteps of the Man of Galilee*; a photographically illustrated New Testament; and a photographically illustrated edition of the Bible, published under the telling title *The Self-Interpreting Bible*. In all these volumes, the visual habits of erasure and disclosure that animated interest in Chicago—of overlooking what the camera had recorded to see what was *really* there—were mirrored in the Holy Land. And despite Thompson's earliest inclinations, Bain's photographs would have a longer shadow on biblical interpretation than Lee's learned commentary.[18]

Earthly Footsteps: The Man of Galilee and the "Worldly St. Louisan"

In January 1894, three months before Lee and Bain would set sail, the *Freeman* of Indianapolis, a weekly "national illustrated colored newspaper," printed "coupons" redeemable for the first installment of *The Holy Land Photographed*, "a photographic panorama of sacred history" published in "seven royal parts." Designed in part by the weekly's editor, George L. Knox, to boost sales by coupling the one-dollar price tag with a six-month subscription to the *Freeman*, each part of the "elegant and tastefully bound" series included "sixteen photographs printed on heavy ivory [. . .] paper," totaling 112 photographs of "everything of any special interest in the Holy Land." Knox's ballyhoo that the volume represented "the first effort ever made to hold before the eyes of the reader the very spot where Jesus and his disciples walked and lived" was, by 1894, entirely wrong. Photographs of the Holy Land had been popularized early in the medium's history and had reached a level of artistic import through the works of the English Quaker Francis Firth and the Belgian Felix Bonfils in the 1850s and 1860s, and reaching wider audiences, stereographs of the Holy Land had been in circulation for decades by the 1890s. The discourse of Holy Land presence and vicarious access, in other words, was nearly as old as the medium of photography. But the seven-issue series was nevertheless important for, in Knox's words, placing the "photographic panorama of sacred history" into the "hands of every man, woman and child of the race." This "indispensible [*sic*] companion of the Christian home," Knox further boasted, was to "delineate graphically the scenes portrayed, and to connect them with the familiar and important events of Bible history." The editor spared no words in his endorsement of the volume: "it makes the Bible a new book."[19]

The *Freeman's* "elegantly and tastefully bound" volumes were likely similar to (if not the same as) those advertised the same week, at discount, in the Methodist book concern *Zion's Herald* as "Neil's Photographs of the Holy Land," a series of 112 views "of the exact scenes of the great events of the Bible and a panoramic view of Jerusalem on the day of the crucifixion."[20] Indeed, while his confidence in the transforming power of the photographs was no doubt in part a calculated effort by the successful editor to boost his paper's sales, *The Holy Land Photographed* was one of many series of photographs of the Holy Land sold by subscription at the end of the century. In addition to the entrepreneurial aspect of the photographs, for nineteenth-century Americans, such pictures not only illustrated religious narratives but also actually shaped how such narratives were interpreted among contemporary audiences. During this last decade of the nineteenth century, claims would increasingly be made that photographs had a unique ability among the visual arts to "make the Bible real," an ability that was located in a presumed collaboration between photographs and texts, between photographs of the Holy Land and the pages of the Bible. Although this collaboration was particularly poignant in stereographs, with their prominent captions, biblical references, and flipside descriptive analyses, similar conventions were also utilized in a number of techniques that conditioned the mutual significance of photographs and texts in matters of biblical interpretation. In other words, despite claims — both implicit and direct — that photographs, particularly within the pages of Bibles, were interpretive supplements, they often enough yielded interpretive cues beyond those of the surrounding scriptural context.

                                          By Pencil and Camera

Three months after the *Freeman* advertised its series of *The Holy Land Photographed*, James Lee and Robert Bain set out from St. Louis, via New York, to Egypt, freighted with nine boxes of glass plates from the Cramer Dry Plate Company of St. Louis, an impressive cargo of more than six hundred pounds. Dry plates were a relatively recent development that freed photographers from carrying cumbersome sensitizing equipment into the field—a young banker from Rochester named George Eastman was instrumental in popularizing dry plates in the United States. Whereas less than a decade earlier Bain would have had to carry a veritable cabinet of chemicals with him, sensitize each plate with a wet emulsion, and make an exposure before the emulsion dried, the Cramer plates came presensitized. This not only reduced their cargo load—six hundred pounds was still no feather to bear—but also enabled Bain more latitude in selecting his camera positions and, thus, it was presumed, greater accuracy in treading the footsteps of the Man of Galilee. (It also freed his time, as the *Post-Dispatch* reported upon their return in July, to procure "a number of very interesting relics of the journey.") [21]

The pairing of Lee and Bain was itself something of a comic episode according to contemporary accounts. "Nobody would ever suspect the young, fat, good-natured and very worldly St. Louisan, Mr. Robert E. M. Bain, of having traveled all over Palestine in company with a distinguished Methodist minister," chortled the *St. Louis Post-Dispatch* a year after their return, "but that is precisely what he did." [22] Lee was now pastor of St. John's Methodist Episcopal Church in St. Louis, and Bain, on his passport application filed March 19, had claimed for his occupation "European Steamship Agent." [23] Although Thompson and later publishers would defer to Bain's expertise as a photographer in their promotional materials, throughout the decade Bain identified as an "amateur," which explains his occupational status on official documentation. Nevertheless, "by amateur photographer," he explained in an article published in the trade journal *Photographic Times and American Photographer* in 1891, "I mean one with a complete outfit—tripod, camera, focusing cloth, and all. The fiend with the alleged detective camera is at best a base imitation." [24] Bain had no tolerance for what he called "the button-pusher," that rising class of tourists and hobbyists who preferred film over glass and who would not know their way through a darkroom or around a box of plates. [25] The underlying visual claims to transparency among the button pushers were, however, also at work in Bain's photographs as well as in the developing arena of news photography, itself a direct product of the visual technology of the halftone. In fact, Bain's younger brother, George Grantham Bain, would in 1898 establish the first commercial bank of news photographs — Bain News Service — and through it transform journalism in the twentieth century. Although a journalist himself, George was never a photographer and did not, despite some early claims to the contrary, pioneer photojournalism.[26] What is more, Robert's pictures never made their way into his brother's News Service files. Even if Robert assiduously policed the boundaries between his own amateur project and the button pushers, the underlying visual claim in the new field of news photography — that the picture recorded fact — mirrored the ethnographic claims of Bain's pictures. This was the birth of a visual regime that would shape habits of beholding well into the twentieth century. Historians have long noted the role that news photographers and photojournalists played in the rising cultural influence of the daily press during the Spanish-American War — pictures certainly helped sell more papers. But we can see the visual habits of the new regime being worked out in the Holy Land well before the campaigns of 1898.[27]

Pocketing their "letters of introduction" to foreign dignitaries — this was indeed a great commission — Lee "carried the pencil" and Bain "manipulated the camera" from April through late June as the men roughed the sacred terrain with a caravan of "four tents, five mules, four horses and eight men, including dragoman, cook and waiter."[28] The team followed a route familiar to many Americans, whether from their own travels or those facilitated by book or brush. From New York the minister and the photographer had crossed the Atlantic to Egypt, where they visited the Heliopolis, Memphis, Cairo, and Alexandria, jotting down descriptions of each place "with pen and camera" while making sure to relate each place to its biblical significance. Even recently unearthed mummies were poised to illuminate the pages of scripture. Describing Bain's photograph of Ramses II, John Heyl Vincent — who collaborated with Lee in writing commentaries for Bain's photographs, although he did not travel with the pair in the spring of 1894 — reminded his readers how the pharaoh had reigned during the time that the Israelites were exiled in Egypt. "Rameses II. was . . . great, but egotistical and vain. . . . He vaunted himself as a god. He introduced polygamy into Egypt. He was brave, but boasted excessively of his bravery. With it all he was a selfish tyrant. Look at him."[29]

From Egypt, Bain and Lee sailed north to Palestine, where they arrived at the port of Joppa on Sunday morning, April 22, 1894. From the port city, they traveled through the country and into Turkey, Greece, Italy, and "the Archipelago Islands" — in short, "all Biblical points of interest" — for two months, their precious cargo of brittle glass plates miraculously surviving the harrowing journey "over the road traveled by our Savior and his Apostles" as

 By Pencil and Camera

well as "the footsteps of St. Paul in his missionary journeys" and into "the city of Plato and Aristotle and the home of the Caesars." Especially telling of the plates' divine protection was that their journey was often not in the careful stewardship of Lee and Bain's personal entourage. "From place to place by railway cars, by express wagons, by carriages, by steamboats, by row-boats, by porters," the plates exchanged many hands but never escaped God's protective eye before arriving back in St. Louis in early July "without the loss of a single box."[30]

Beginning in December 1894, six months after their return to St. Louis, a selection of the prints—the *Post-Dispatch* cited at least fifteen hundred negatives in Bain's collection, although Thompson had originally commissioned only a third of that sum—were serialized in twenty-four parts, each consisting of sixteen photographs, and sold by subscription under the uniform title *Earthly Footsteps of the Man of Galilee*.[31] The *Congregationalist* of Boston advised against having "the Series . . . permanently bound," since, in their loose form, the photographs "are convenient for reference, can be easily handled, carried into the Sunday School class, or kept at one's elbow for use at a moment's notice." Five months later, the same periodical had changed its tune, at least enough to cater to subscribers who "would prefer to have their Footsteps in a more solid form." Eventually, the complete set included the original twenty-four parts as well as "an extra number" that was "issued in obedience to the call for a general alphabetical index and also to round out the work in other important particulars." Each part, including the extra number, was ten cents. For those who "wish[ed] them bound," the price of a full-cloth binding, embossed in gold, was $1.50 for subscribers who made arrangements through the *Congregationalist* office, and the more elegant Half Morocco was $2.00.[32]

Not everyone opted to bind these *Footsteps*. In July 1895, the *Southern Cultivator* gave special notice to its readers that "*A Handsome and Durable Portfolio Holder* in rich English cloth stamped in gold will be given to EVERY ONE completing the entire series of 24 parts."[33] The *Congregationalist* similarly pledged that a "Portfolio to hold the 25 Parts will be furnished *free* to all who have paid for the entire series, if delivered at our office."[34] To the *Congregationalist's* credit, the bound volume was particularly cumbersome, making it less likely to be handled frequently or carted to Sunday school, which contributed to different modes of interaction with Bain's photographs. The bound "art folio" was an impressive volume of full-plate halftone prints, a feat of technological no less than devotional importance, made possible by the patented "chemigraph process" utilized by Cramer Dry Plate Works.[35]

Throughout the century a variety of photographic technologies had made halting, inconsistent, yet vociferous claims to representational authority based on discourses of empirical exactitude, claims that were echoed in *Footsteps of the Man of Galilee*. Although by the 1890s photography was understood as an artistic no less than a scientific or commercial endeavor, these domains were hardly exclusive. In fact, the incorporation of photographic mediums and methods into the rising fields of biblical history relied on both artistic and scientific claims to authority in their "exact" reproductions of "picturesque" Palestine—and tethered both to consumer demand. The folio of "delightful pictures, so handsomely taken," promised the *Post-Dispatch*, "give one the impression that he is there and gazing upon the reality."[36] Lee affirmed the assessment when he described how they had "stood amid the scenes of [Jesus's] prayers, tears, sermons and wonderful works, and transferred them, with the blush and bloom of Palestine, to the delicate, sensitive surface of our glass plates."[37]

Promotional material often noted Bain's recognition as an award-winning "landscape artist" to bolster his authority as a photographer and thus the integrity of the photographs deemed not merely to represent but to reproduce the Holy Land for American beholders. An advertisement in the *Atlanta Constitution* quoted James Lee in an "explanatory" intended to bolster public confidence in the pictures. "We simply secured the best pictures that ever came from the East," the minister boasted. Such a claim, moreover, came "without any seeming surplus of overconfidence, for the National Photographers' Convention, held this year in St. Louis, awarded Mr. Bain a medal on all the twelve views he entered—being the first he developed."[38] In the same way that Marcus Aurelius Root had praised heliographers as "artists" who were gifted with the ability to manifest subtle, even imperceptible, qualities in portraits, Lee credited his companion with manifesting something greater than technical skill: "to the function of the photographer he unites the genius of the artist." By combining the technical aptitude of the medium with the technique of the artist, Lee promised subscribers that "an opportunity is here given of making a delightful tour of Palestine and the countries adjacent to it without leaving home."[39] Pilgrims who followed in Lee and Bain's footsteps could rest assured that the photographs were not merely adequate representations but also, by all standards, good pictures.

Of course, Bain himself had not always been a part of the picture. Robert Bain's changing role in the retellings of the initial journey demonstrates changing attitudes to the role of photographs in American Protestant biblical interpretation. Although photographic techniques had long been used

 By Pencil and Camera

to illustrate Holy Land topographies in an effort to "make the Bible real," placing these images within the Bible itself required both the development of appropriate methods of photomechanical reproduction *and* theological wiggle room. In short, one had to be certain that what readers saw in the photographs was not contemporary Palestine or Egypt or Greece but flesh and blood—and brick and mortar—representatives of the "ancient orient."[40] In his introduction to *Earthly Footsteps*, Bishop John Heyl Vincent of the Methodist Episcopal Church underscored this mindset: "The manners and customs of this Eastern country have not been changed. People dress and eat and sleep and live and labor as they did two thousand years ago. *The scenes of the Bible are reproduced with startling fidelity to the old record. . . .* The old customs and costumes remain."[41] Such a rendering of Ottoman culture is easy to critique. But such claims to continuity were necessary for photographs to become relics of the biblical past in spite of glaring visual evidence to the contrary.[42]

Recall from Thompson's original correspondence to James Lee that he expected a photographer would be "procured in that country [Palestine] or Egypt." In this initial pitch, the photographer was incidental to the project; it was the narrative of the journey and the commentary that carried the project's instructional promise.[43] By the time Thompson published the *New Testament Illustrated and Explained* in 1895, however, it was Bain's "direction" of "a corps of assistants, interpreters and guides" that yielded the "novel but forceful and instructive plan of illustration" provided in the edition.[44] Indeed, in the "Map of Bible Lands" that unfolded from inside the front cover of this edition—maps were included in all published iterations of the journey—James Lee is all but erased from the story. "Showing in red line the journeys of Christ and the Apostles while on earth," the map also shows "the journey of Photographic Artist Robert E. M. Bain, in the year 1894."[45] The map formalized the footsteps of Jesus such that they could be followed by a photographer who, it was implied, stood in for all beholders. It was this conflation, combined with the presumptive timelessness of the region, that made the halftone prints of contemporary Palestine, Egypt, Greece, and Italy relevant to biblical interpretation. The publishers' confidence in the edition's "acceptability, desirability and absolute helpfulness" in biblical instruction, in other words, extended from their conviction that the "superb engravings" they selected from Bain's portfolio "represent[ed] authentically the places made famous in those earthly journeys."[46] In both the map and the explanatory material, the eye of the beholder was synchronized with the eye of the photographer. Such an interpretation, however, masks variations in seeing that contributed to the many different circumstances of beholding. In particular, while editors and commentators worked to situate Bain's photographs first as a journey through the Holy Land and subsequently as biblical illustration, the pictures simultaneously bled beyond such interpretive frameworks.

A year after Thompson published *The New Testament Illustrated and Explained* and *Earthly Footsteps of the Man of Galilee*, Bain's photographs and Lee's commentary were published by R. S. Peal — Thompson's former associate — and J. A. Hill in the *Self-Interpreting Bible*. Sold in four folio volumes, the *Self-Interpreting Bible* was an Authorized translation that included detailed references, explanatory notes, tabulated statistics, geographic, historical, and explanatory illustrations, expository notes, dissertations, sidelights, reflections — in short, "all the helps, tables, commentaries, dictionaries, illustrations and side lights necessary to enable any one to understand it" — and, not the least among this impressive catalogue, were halftone prints from the photographs by R. E. M. Bain. Chief editor of the project was James Lee, and notably, his introduction to the volumes includes a defense of the use of photographs within its pages.[47] Whereas Thompson had staunchly claimed that his "illustrated edition of the New Testament . . . is in no sense experimental," Lee chose to capitalize on the novelty of the mode of illustration in the Peale and Hill edition. "The Publishers of the Photographic Edition of the Holy Bible," Lee erroneously reported, were the "first to carry out the unique idea of specifically showing by means of PHOTOGRAPHY the actual places mentioned in the Bible, thus securing pictorial results of the very highest order." The use by previous Bibles of "sacred pictures of a general nature, such as portraits, copies of well-known paintings, representing scenes and incidents of more or less importance," he explained, was not only imperfect but actually detrimental to the tasks of spiritual growth and historical knowledge, being "in the main wholly imaginary and hence untrue." The present edition, however, "by means of the absolutely perfect record of the camera, and also in immediate connection with the text" was to be, Lee anticipated, "stimulating and satisfying to Christians everywhere" for giving them the "privilege of beholding, through the medium of a wonderful art, those sacred places which they have heretofore been able to see in imagination only."

The decades before publication of the *Self-Interpreting Bible* abounded with intense debates around the historical authority of the Bible. In response to the historical scrutiny of "higher criticism" in the 1860s and 1870s, a Revised New Testament was published in May 1881 that sought to defend the

  By Pencil and Camera

scriptures against modern "scientific" knowledge. Rather than cooling debates, however, the publication of the revised Testament further enflamed debates between liberal Protestants' sympathy to principles of higher criticism and evangelical defenses of the Authorized (King James) Version, first printed in the seventeenth century. One result of these debates was an increased attention within Bibles to archaeological and geographic "proofs" of scriptural claims.[48] Against this background, photographs played a significant role in mediating the truth claims of scientific empiricism—an engine of higher criticism—and habits of beholding informed by biblical imagination. In a guidebook for a stereographic tour of the Holy Land at the turn of the twentieth century, Lee's fellow Methodist minister Jesse Lyman Hurlbut praised photographs' "power to give us a vivid realization of actuality in the Bible narrative" by *stimulating* the imagination.[49] For Lee, however, the intended effect of "the absolutely perfect record of the camera" was to control such fancies, although he later concluded that "the imagination, as informed by the eye, is helped to interpret [biblical events], and we believe that with these helps the Bible itself will become a more tangible and interesting book than ever before."[50] In both cases, the truth claim of the photograph was not in its compositional referent but in the imaginative act of beholding. Thus, however they approached the tricky topic of imagination, both volumes considered photographs of the Holy Land indispensable to the task of biblical interpretation, largely through strategic positioning of image and text. This kind of spiritual sight required a good deal of overlooking what the camera had recorded—a hermeneutics of elision—and, by the same token, deciphering what had passed before its lens.

Bain's prints did not, of course, displace scripture. Rather, all three publications featuring Bain's photographs cultivated a sense of direct correspondence—"immediate connection," in Lee's words—between the prints and accompanying text. In *Earthly Footsteps of the Man of Galilee*, the collaboration between the perfect record of the camera in Bain's photographs and the perfect truth of the Holy Writ was given graphic representation in the frontispiece to the volume. Below the vignettes of "Our Tourists"—which included Bishop John Heyl Vincent, although he did not accompany Lee and Bain—is a medallion of an ancient stone dwelling flanked by books and quill on the right and camera on the left (fig. 29). Both *The New Testament Illustrated and Explained* and the *Self-Interpreting Bible* identified the prints as "illustrations," a designation that signals how the photographs were intended to illuminate the text rather than supplement or augment scriptural interpretation. In both editions of the Bible, moreover, scriptural references were explicitly aligned with each print in the accompanying commentary, and in *Earthly Footsteps*, the "descriptions" centered primarily on biblical figures.

Yet claims to the perfect collaboration of image and text were challenged as no direct correspondence existed between the photographs and the scriptures they were intended to "illustrate." Among the most glaring evidence of this in the *Self-Interpreting Bible* is the frequent use of New Testament events to explain Old Testament prophecies, an interpretive approach common enough to many nineteenth-century American Christians, but one that also points to the interpretive work of visual material. The Photographic Bible underscores how photographs were used to accomplish this familiar biblical typology by freighting a discourse of empiricism — the "honest eye" of the camera — that collaborated with biblical hermeneutics. When Bain's photograph of the Via Dolorosa — a ritual site developed in early Christianity that is nowhere specifically mentioned in the Gospels — was placed opposite Psalms 35:7, the "gloomy street" became a visual reference for David's lament of the "pit, which without cause they have digged for my soul."[51] In this case, David prefigures Christ and a view of 1894 Jerusalem depicts the anguish of both. Many more photographs in the Old Testament volumes of the *Self-Interpreting Bible* were used to position Jesus firmly in the pages of the ancients. For instance, opposite Deuteronomy 6:4–10 (a passage that was cited in the commentary below the print), a view of "Mosque El-Akso, With Basin," depicted "Where Our Savior Held the Conversation with the Lawyer." According to the commentary, "Upon one occasion Christ was approached by a lawyer tempting him and enquiring of him concerning the law. . . . We give a picture of the Mosque el-Aksa which stands upon part of the grounds once occupied by the temple, and is doubtless near the spot where our Savior stood when he held the conversation with the lawyer."[52] Using a Muslim mosque to mark the space where "our Savior stood" in order to exegete a passage from the Pentateuch, photographs such as this one facilitated not only illustrative but also theological work within the pages of the *Self-Interpreting Bible*.

Using visual cues to inscribe Jesus literally into the pages of the Old Testament was one of the ways in which photographs influenced biblical interpretation. But in addition to this hermeneutics of presence, the photographs also required beholders to overlook the faces who on occasion stared back. The rest of this chapter focuses on the analytics of absence and its relation to ideologies of imperialism that characterized popular representations of "foreign" peoples both within and beyond the nation's borders.

    By Pencil and Camera

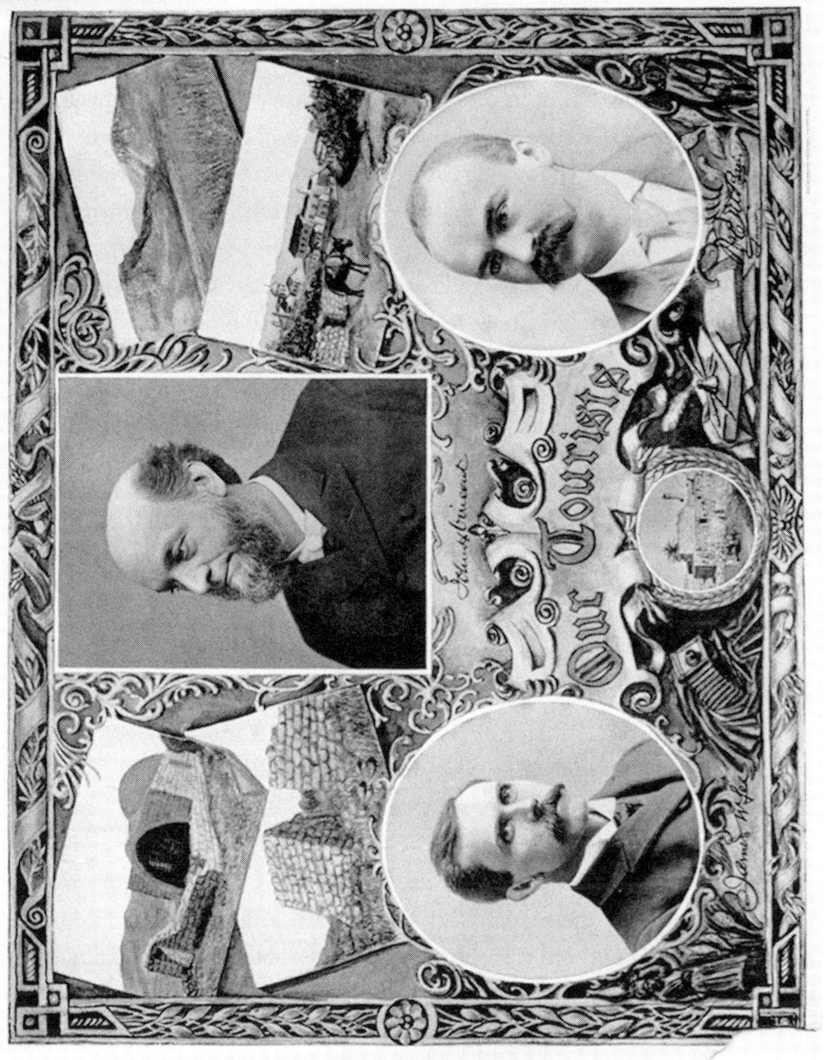

Figure 29. Frontispiece from *Earthly Footsteps of the Man of Galilee* (New York: N. B. Thompson, 1894).

Palestine and other regions of the Holy Land were never American colonies, but through such cultural mechanisms as the camera they were nevertheless wrapped up in colonialist ideologies of appropriation, representation, and domination. Unlike other modes of contemporary American imperialism in the 1890s, Americans had little interest in changing the peoples, practices, or landscapes of the Holy Land. In other contexts "the savage became a signifier of an earlier period," writes David Brody, and it was "the responsibility of colonialism to rescue the [native] artist from his modern-day anachronistic life." Galilee and Matariyeh, however, were more useful as anachronisms — indeed, as relics — than as evidence of American progressive intervention.[53] Just as surely as minarets, bicycles, and parasols were evident in Bain's photographs, let alone the people who wore and used them, they were seldom acknowledged as evidence of cultural change.[54]

Indeed, a constant refrain throughout *Earthly Footsteps* and the commentaries on Bain's photographs in Bibles is the glacial passage of time. People still practice "very ancient" methods of agriculture and other industry, and descriptions slip easily between travels in 1894 and 1863 and "Joseph's day."[55] Matthew Frye Jacobson has noted how "timelessness" was a "staple of travel reportage" at the turn of the century and how ethnographic icons facilitated "a timeless present tense."[56] This colonialist operation of timelessness was surely at work in Bain's photographs and other contemporary views of the Holy Land beheld by Americans. But the perpetual present tense also had theological implications. Describing Bain's photograph of the "Jewish Wailing Place," taken in the spring of 1894, Bishop Vincent told readers how "on Friday afternoon, March 13, 1863, the writer visited this sacred spot" and "found between one and two hundred Jews of both sexes and of all ages, standing or sitting, and bowing as they read, chanted and recited, moving themselves backward and forward, the tears rolling down many a face."[57] By overlooking the significant changes in the political, religious, and social landscape of Jerusalem that came with an influx of Jewish migrants and refugees in the 1880s, Vincent presents Jews as ethnographic subjects that were, at best, not affected by such changes and, at worst, inured to changes. In fact, throughout the various iterations of Bain's photographs, this print was positioned as evidence of Jewish resistance to change. "All the years of change and war and bloodshed and fire and persecution," read the caption to Bain's photograph of the "Jewish Wailing Place" in the *Self-Interpreting Bible* (fig. 30), "have not been able to destroy the affection which this ancient people of God have for their Holy City."[58] For Christians who analyzed the photograph alongside the scripture it was designated to illustrate — Luke 13:35 — the image was not

                                    By Pencil and Camera

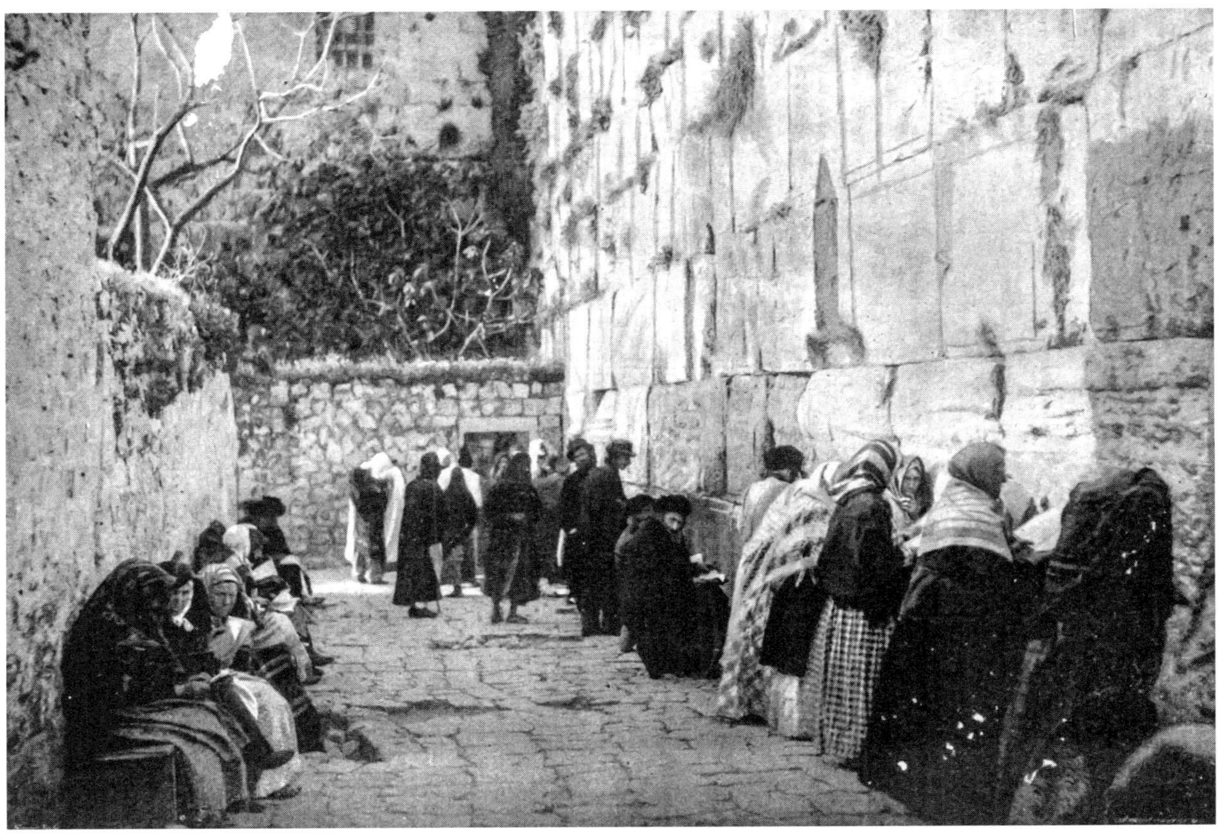

Figure 30. Robert Edward Mather Bain, "Jewish Wailing Place." From *The Self-Interpreting Bible.*

one of laudable perseverance but rather condemnable obstinacy: "Behold, your house is left unto you desolate: and verily I say unto you, Ye shall not see me, until *the time* come when ye shall say, Blessed *is* he that cometh in the name of the Lord." If there was any doubt of the intended interpretation that the juxtaposition between the verse and the photograph suggested, the "reflections" on the chapter—authored by the eighteenth-century British theologian John Brown—put it to rest: "With great care should we guard against uncharitable censures of those whom God hath sorely afflicted, remembering that his strokes on them are warnings to us, and that nothing short of evangelical repentance can prevent our eternal ruin. . . . The most unfruitful sinners may be renewed and turned to God by the gospel; but the obstinate abuse of this will at last issue in men's just and inexpressible ruin. Cries for mercy will then become vain, hopes and pleas from external privileges will be defeated, and there will be none to intercede for the sinner."[59] There is nothing in the chapter or in Brown's reflection that directly identifies Jesus's injunction with a specific population. But by the end of the nineteenth century, the American Protestant icon of recalcitrance to the gospel was the wailing Jew.

In addition to this interpretive operation of rendering the people in Bain's photographs as ahistorical icons of theological mandates, the theologically inflected present tense also enabled beholders of his photographs to position themselves within the biblical narratives. "The Son of Man is on his way to Jerusalem," begins Lee in his commentary for a photograph entitled "Ahab's Well in Jezreel." Compositionally speaking, the photograph was nothing to boast of. Six figures stand around what we are told is a well. One person looks quizzically at the camera. But the picture plopped viewers onto the road that Jesus trod on his "final departure from Galilee" some nineteen centuries earlier just the same. This ability to transcend the passage of time through embodied visual practices was especially important in the 1880s and 1890s. During the last decades of the century, practices of biblical interpretation had spurned a number of new translations which in turn popularized theretofore academic debates about the presumed timelessness of scripture. Although Bain's photographs were never designated with the authority of scripture, when they were positioned within editions of the Bible they were charged, according to Thompson, with the purpose of "throwing light on Scriptural facts, and fixing more indelibly in the mind scriptural incident."[60] The accompanying commentary did not always keep the grammatical present tense, but both Lee and Vincent consistently associated Bain's photographs with specific biblical events, a representational

     By Pencil and Camera

strategy that bolstered the claim that the views exceeded illustration in their reproduction of the Holy Land. They were, in short, relics to behold just as surely as they were icons to interpret. Whereas the scriptures were becoming increasingly challenged by evidence of canonical debates and scribal traditions, Bain's photographs provided direct evidence of the "very footsteps" of Jesus.

LIVING RELICS OF THE BIBLICAL PAST

In his introduction to *Earthly Footsteps of the Man of Galilee*, James Lee framed the pious project in the rhetoric of a military objective. It would be several years before tensions between the United States and Spain erupted into the flash of armed conflict, but the cultural ethos of nation building, couched in the language of civilization and Christianity, was already in the air, as the events on the Midway Plaisance and in the World's Parliament of Religions had made abundantly clear. Describing the book's conception, Lee related how Thompson and Peale had "proposed to capture the countries about the Mediterranean Sea and transport them to America without destroying their cities or disturbing their people." The instruments of this ostensibly benevolent enterprise were Bain's camera and Lee's pencil. "No bombardment was to be inaugurated, except such as passed through the lens of the camera, and no missile was to be projected deadlier than the thought that passed through a pencil to the pages of a note-book."[61] Bain, too, commented on the militaristic similitude of their holy errand. "The picture-making outfit was, I must confess, rather formidable in appearance," he wrote in the *Photographic Times and American Photographer*, "and must have impressed each custom-house guardian with the idea that our mission was the destruction of the country, and the contents of our cases dynamite."[62] But more than Bain's musings on customs agents' perceptions of the picture-making outfit, Lee's use of militaristic language fit within the prevailing colonialist ethos of late nineteenth-century America. As many scholars have noted, colonialism was a duplicitous visual enterprise that promised freedom yet delivered violent appropriations of land and charged racializations of native peoples through exaggerated imagery.[63] In Brody's telling, for instance, both supporters of and antagonists to American presence in the Philippines resorted to "racially loaded representations in the expanding popular press" to shore up their ideological stance and, just as important, "sell more newsprint."[64] While there are important distinctions between official colonialist projects and unofficial visual campaigns of suasion, Bain's photographs of the Holy

Land nevertheless created ethnographic iconographies that both denied the individuality of persons depicted — a visual habit at odds with contemporary domestic portraiture — and relied on racially charged imagery to regulate the cultural distance between Anglo-Protestant American beholders (a crafted subjectivity in its own right) and living relics of the biblical past. Indeed, Bain's photographs demonstrate how Bibles were complex cultural artifacts that archived both individual likenesses and imperialist stereotypes.

The chemigraph halftone technique used in *Earthly Footsteps* allowed less room for the stylized racial stereotypes common in lithographs and newsprint drawings. Or rather, photography required different approaches to the visual coding of race. The front cover of *Earthly Footsteps* features an embossed engraving of the group "as we journeyed from Jerusalem to Damascus." Three figures are on horses — presumably Lee and Bain and possibly their guide. Four additional figures ride mules. One figure, however, stands in the center of the composition and, unlike the rest of the group, stares directly out at the reader. It is unclear who the shrouded figure was intended to represent, and no corresponding photograph was included in the book. The racial codes, however, are unquestionable. The most obvious signs of racial difference are on the face, which is represented with a broad nose, full lips, and deeper hatching to indicate dark skin. Juxtaposed to the two mustachioed Americans in modern dress — including dapper riding caps — the figure's sartorial cues were intended to signify difference. The androgyny of the figure is also telling. Bain and Lee, sitting perfectly erect astride well-groomed horses, are represented as paragons of American manhood and thus a stark contrast to an effeminized native masculinity. But the figure's androgyny also invokes a common ethnographic icon of the "savage beauty," who, according to Jacobson, was made "to *stand for* an entire people and their land."[65] Whatever insurgency the native figure may signal through his or her stare, it was effectively subdued through the visual habits of an imperialist gaze. The concept of an imperialist gaze by no means adequately describes the range of visual habits that were brought to bear upon or that were facilitated through Bain's photographs. Recall, for instance, that similar series were issued through African American periodicals during the 1890s and that Bain's series was issued through both northern and southern offices. Variations across region and race no doubt influenced the valences of racial representations for beholders of Holy Land prints. Yet it is difficult to assess the juxtaposition of text and image in these photographs without accounting for a cultivated sense of superiority that straddled national, racial, and religious discourses without ever settling firmly into any one category.

    By Pencil and Camera

A view printed early in *Earthly Footsteps of the Man of Galilee* established a number of the viewing strategies expected of beholders. As Bain and Lee were making their way across the "Plains of Jezreel" in central Palestine on May 4, 1894, they came across a group of men plowing their fields with teams of oxen. Because the plains evoked so many biblical events—Deborah and Barak conquering Jabin's army, Josiah's defeat by Pharaoh Necho, the battle between Gideon and the Midianites, the travels of Mary and Joseph, the Philistines encampment during their conflict with Saul—the outfit decided to stop for a picture. "Our dragoman asked the people . . . if they would stop long enough for us to take a photograph," Lee related in his commentary in *Earthly Footsteps*. "For the usual 'Baksheesh' they granted his request."[66] First, the print works to establish Bain and Lee as self-guided pilgrims and to circumvent the thorny issue of Ottoman control, which required a native escort, by obscuring the identity of their translator and guide. Although the "dragoman" is mentioned frequently in the volume and appears in a number of photographs, he is never named. An article in the *St. Louis Post-Dispatch* identified the guide as Abraham Lyons, "a native of Jerusalem, but a Hungarian by descent" and "a member of the English church" who had guided tourists through the Holy Land for three decades.[67] Second, the photograph indicates that the Americans were not above staging their views. Many of the photographs in *Earthly Footsteps* include people who appear to have been positioned—if not hired—by Bain or Lee. People did not appear in all of Bain's photographs. Many of the views were landscapes, and others were long shots that only circumstantially included passersby. Occasionally he would stage his camera to include people as compositional cues, such as for scale. But many of the views appear to have been deliberately composed around specific figures, even if the commentary neglected to mention them. A print entitled "The King's Chamber" demonstrates the last category (fig. 31). The focal point of this interior view of "the pyramid of Cheops—the great pyramid" at Giza is a man crouched against a wall near the center of the print. Another man stands behind him, back also against the wall. Despite the prominent position of both men in the print, the closest that Lee came to acknowledging them was when he wrote that "the ascent [into the chamber] is difficult and requires the assistance of two or three Arabs who pull and push and prop as the exigencies of the ascent demand."[68] The fact that a photograph was staged did not necessarily undermine its authority or integrity. But the difference between conventions of studio portraiture that relied on staged apparatus to convey cultural and religious meaning, on the one hand, and staged "Arabs" to convey continuities with a biblical past is

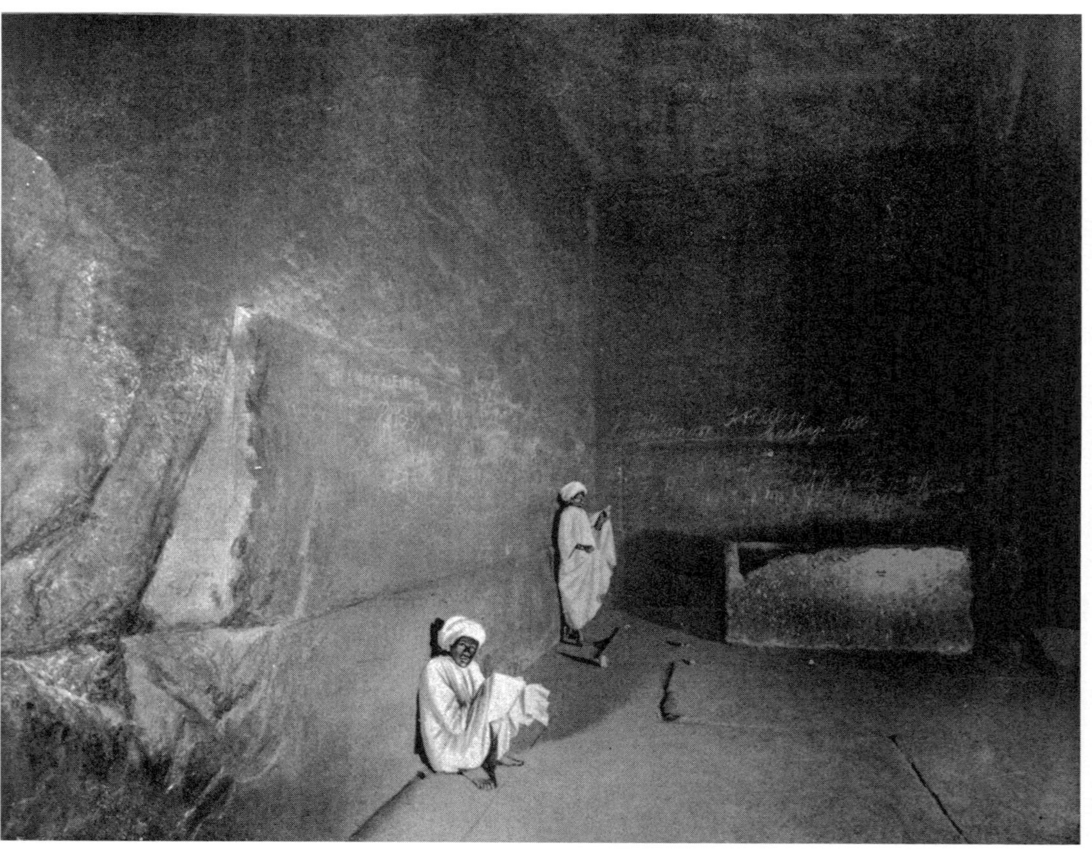

Figure 31. Robert Edward Mather Bain, "The King's Chamber." From *Earthly Footsteps of the Man of Galilee*. St. Louis Mercantile Library, University of Missouri–St. Louis. Used with permission.

significant. In Bain's views, the staged composition of the photographs and the deliberate gloss of the Arabs' presence in Lee's descriptions evinces the cultivation of a hermeneutics of elision that situated the biblical imaginary within the visual politics of colonial encounter.

Another example of this elision is in Bain's photograph of the tomb of Lazarus (fig. 32). The print in *Earthly Footsteps* is one of only a handful that were positioned in portrait orientation, which required the viewer to turn the heavy volume lengthwise to see the image and read the commentary comfortably. The print features seven figures posed around the opening to an ancient stone structure. Lee's commentary challenges the site's biblical accuracy — "it is, of course, nothing but a tradition" — and speculates that the real sepulchre was surely "within the sound of our voices" before recounting the story of Lazarus's miraculous resurrection. Not once does Lee mention the figures who so deliberately look at the camera. Not once does he acknowledge the woman nursing her child. His muted commentary on the figures' presence is a pregnant void. Perhaps her presence is unremarkable. And yet this is a photograph of an empty tomb, and their presence is no doubt intentional. Whatever else they are doing, for whatever reason they were staged in the composition, the suckling babe and the exposed breast signaled an inherent tension for contemporary beholders. On the one hand, the figures invoked "the native" that had come to populate early photographically illustrated periodicals — from souvenir folios of the World's Fair to missionary organs to popular scientific journals. This framework distanced the photographic subjects from American beholders through a visual vocabulary that transformed a maternal bond into a signal of cultural inferiority. On the other hand, however, the image hints at a photographic tradition that elevated the maternal bond into religious iconography. Since the daguerrean period, the photographic convention of the mother and child had been a common motif in American studio portraiture. Visually invoking the Pietà, this motif included both nursing infants and postmortems. In this framework, the nursing mother encoded a biblical promise of redemption. In both the colonialist and the redemptive frameworks, however, the woman is a relic or an icon but never a historical contemporary.

As much as these seemingly deliberate photographs of people invite the assumption of compositional staging, Lee and Bain were also quick to emphasize the spontaneity — which, for them, operated as a kind of authenticating device — of some of the views. In a print entitled "A Woman of Samaria," for instance, Lee recounted how Bain was "taking pictures in Shechem" when a woman and a little boy "appeared upon the scene, and showed much

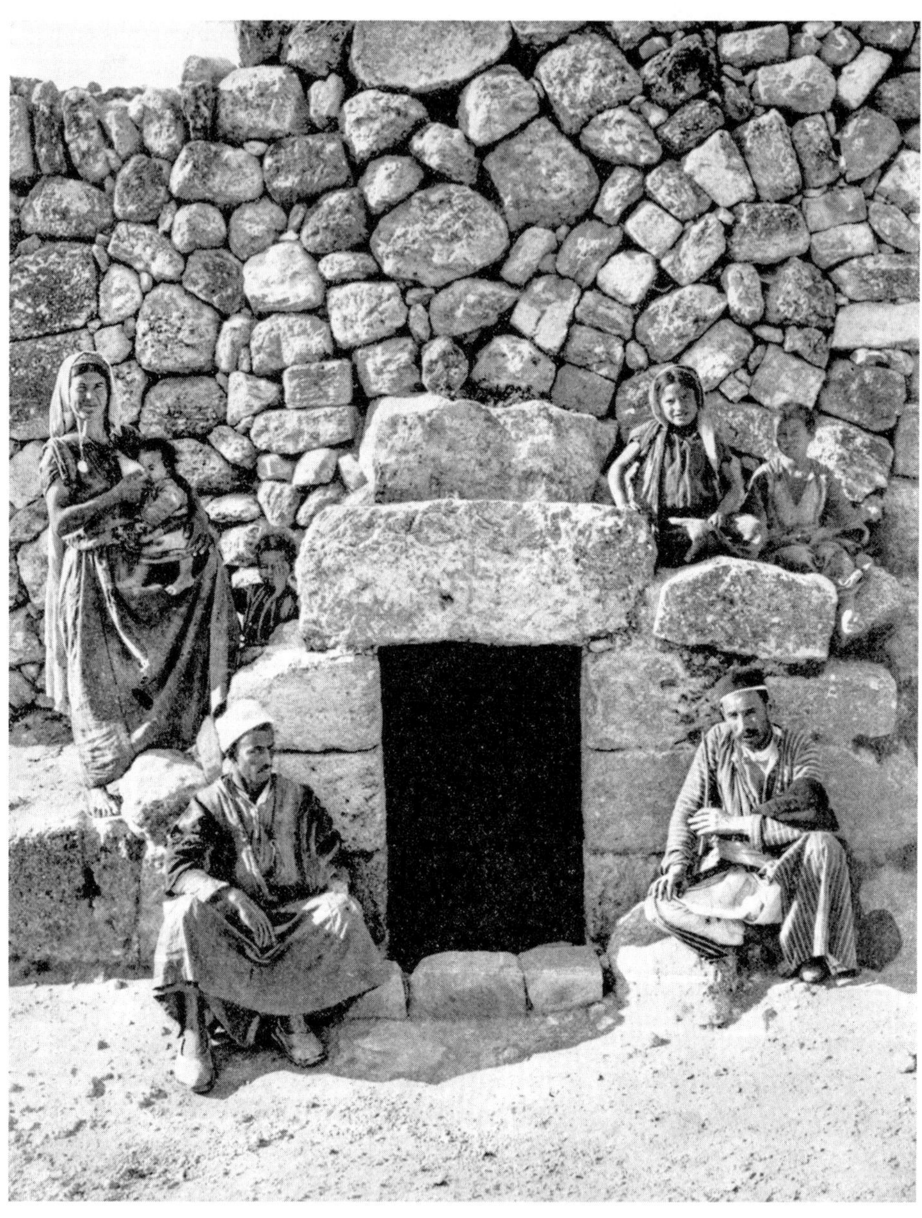

Figure 32. Robert Edward Mather Bain, "Tomb of Lazarus." From *Earthly Footsteps of the Man of Galilee*. St. Louis Mercantile Library, University of Missouri–St. Louis. Used with permission.

anxiety to know exactly what we were about" (fig. 34). His condescending tone suggests that the woman and child were unfamiliar with the contraptions and culture of photography — "wherever we stopped [the natives] gathered about us, and it was sometimes very difficult to keep them from standing directly in front of the lens" — when, in truth, it would have been difficult to find anyone in the region without some familiarity with camera-toting Westerners. In any case, as Lee continued in his narration, he demonstrated just what he meant by the camera's "bombardment" of the Holy Land. "The artist, having taken a picture of the city, quietly turned his camera upon the tripod and took a photograph of this woman before she knew what he was doing." Such blatant acknowledgment of the photographer's stealth worked in favor of Lee's larger point. For him, the woman represented "the naïve and unsophisticated manners" of a people — "her people" — who had "forgotten the moral and spiritual teaching of the Lord who lived and taught among them." In short, in spite of the technological savvy of contemporary inhabitants of Palestine, for Lee, the woman in the picture did not represent nineteenth-century Samarians but rather her biblical antecedent: "There is still among these natives the same work to do — the work of reproof and conviction, instruction and salvation which Christ performed when He was here."[69]

The likelihood that Bain's photograph of "A Woman of Samaria" transpired as spontaneously as Lee recounted is debatable. Even given the latest equipment, the operation would have taken long enough — at least a minute or so — and the figures are relatively in focus (although the woman appears to have been retouched). Several years later, in fact, Bain wrote about his experience photographing Palestine for the photographic guild. "The trip is intensely interesting except from a photographic standpoint," he lamented, "for the country is of the 'dead and buried' description, and there is but little to attract the cameraist outside of the cities, and they are few and far between." Contradicting Lee's narrative of spontaneity, moreover, Bain bemoaned the difficulty of "securing figures to liven up a scene," musing that their resistance extended from "seeing something diabolical in the appearance of the camera, with its cannon of brass and glass projecting from its front." Indeed, he confessed to having traipsed "for a mile or more" around the Mount of Beatitudes "to endeavor to make an attractive photograph."[70] Shortly after returning from the journey, he had described the "distinct understanding" with the group's dragoman that "he could and would secure me native subjects for camera use." Describing a scene in Cairo, Bain wrote that upon arriving he had "hired a carriage and sallied forth" into the "na-

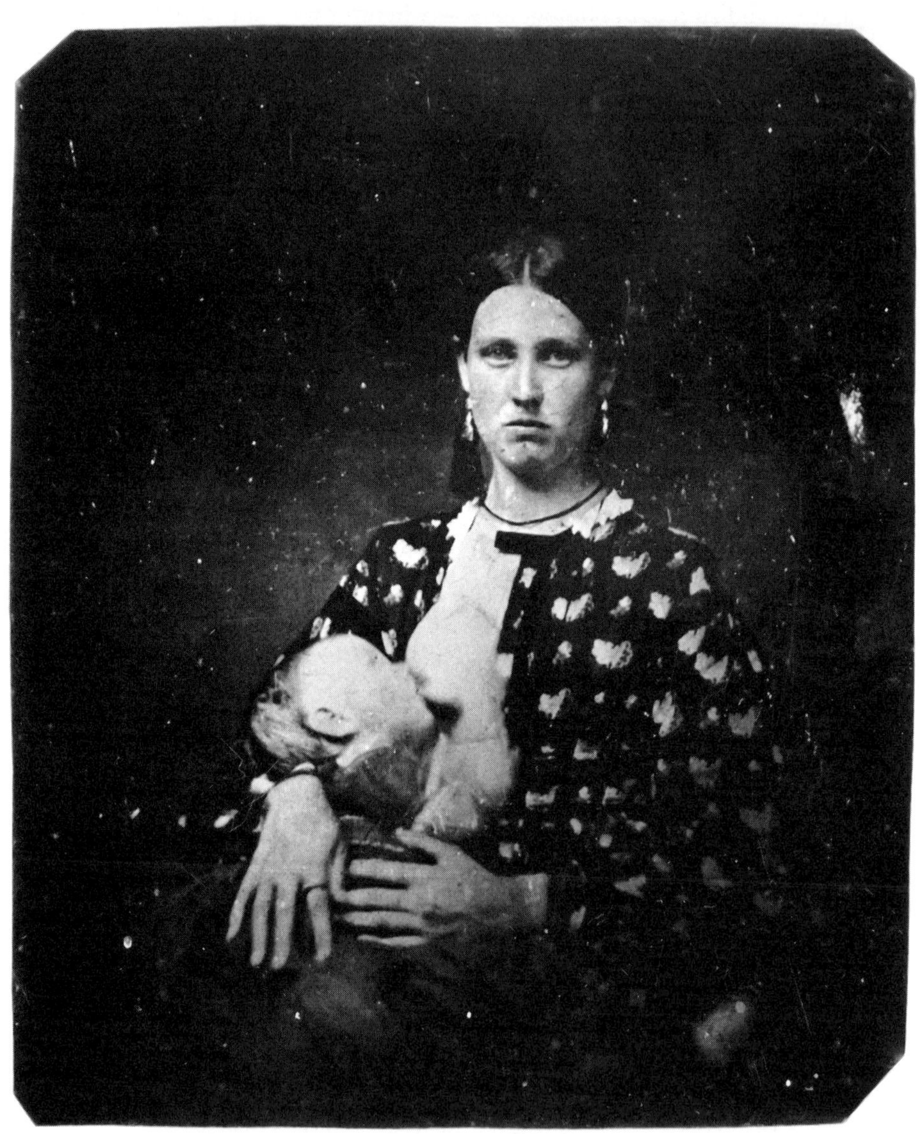

Figures 33a and 33b. Nursing mother "Pietà" motif. Quarter-plate tintype ca. 1860 (*above*). Sixth-plate daguerreotype ca. 1860 (*opposite*). Schlesinger Library, Radcliffe Institute, Harvard University.

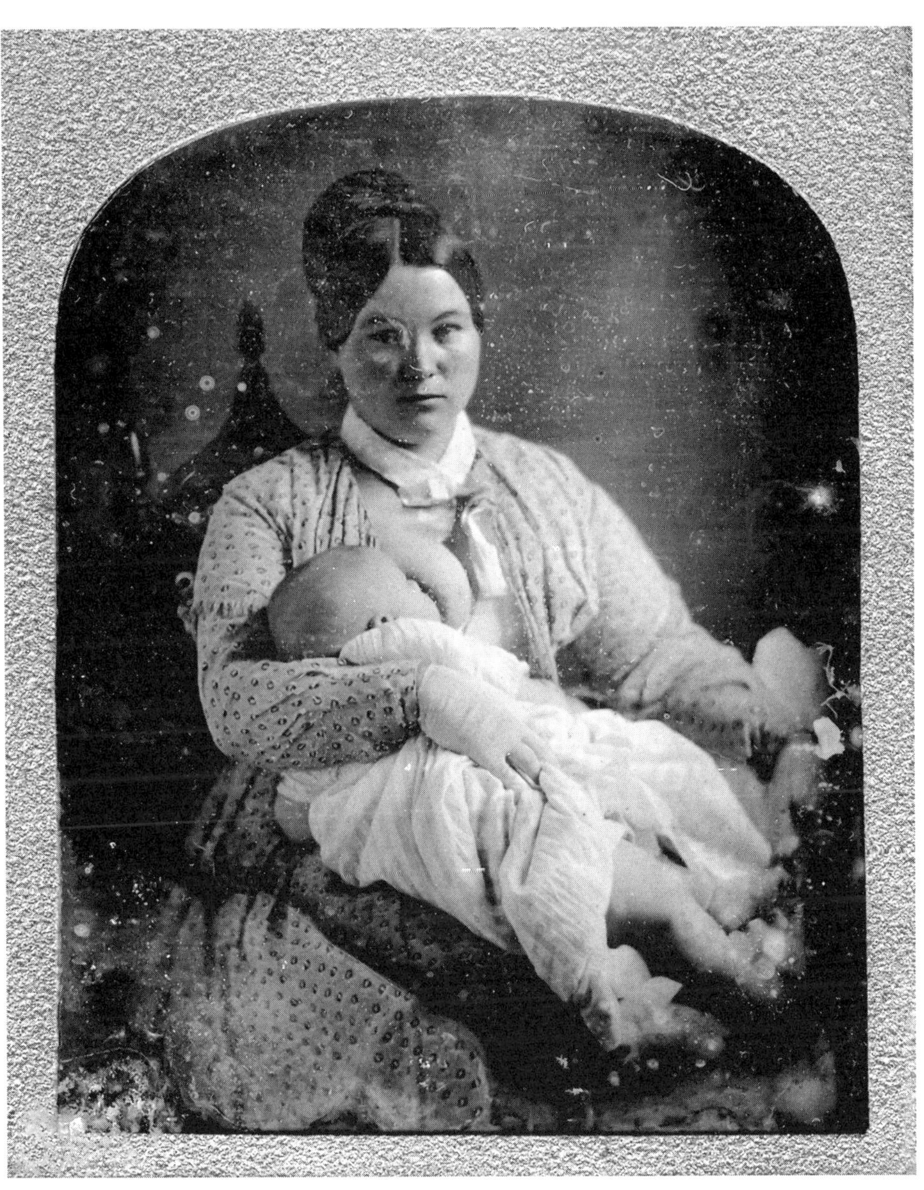

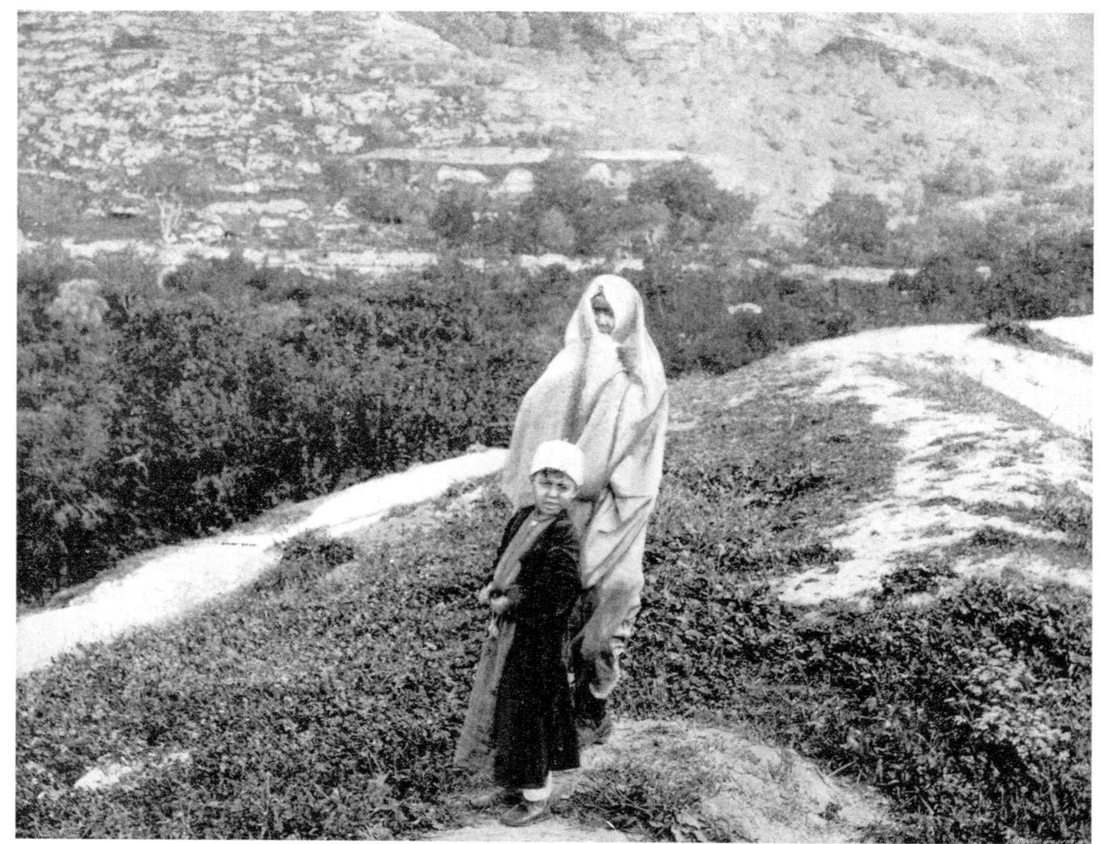

Figure 34. Robert Edward Mather Bain, "A Woman of Samaria." From *Earthly Footsteps of the Man of Galilee*. St. Louis Mercantile Library, University of Missouri–St. Louis. Used with permission.

tive quarter" where he "erected my 8 x 10 camera and prepared for victims." "After some argument," his subject "was induced to pose." Unlike Lee's descriptions of passive "natives," Bain's descriptions in the photographic press presented subjects who were curious about the process and even playful with the strange American and his clunky gizmo. "The neighbors, having proverbially more time than anything else," Bain condescended, "would insist on getting in the way, looking into the lens, etc."[71] Lee and Bain were writing to two different audiences. Holy Land pilgrims would want nothing of this messiness behind photographic production. Indeed, the narrative device of spontaneity provided a kind of authenticating measure for Lee, assuring beholders that the camera was a transparent lens to the world of the Bible. More than the circumstances in which they were positioned, the mere presence of the woman and the young boy did the work that Lee needed. However Bain's victims were "induced to pose," the people in his pictures demonstrated the continuity with biblical times necessary to underwrite the theological utility of photographs. If the medium of photography worked to disclose the Holy Land to middling Americans, contemporary inhabitants of the region — whether Jews, Muslims, or Christians — provided the evidence the camera needed to stake its claim. Bain's photograph entitled "Traveling in Galilee" was printed in both *Earthly Footsteps* and *The New Testament Illustrated and Explained*. Under the title "Traveling in Galilee [Mark, iii:7–8]" in *The New Testament*, the commentary collapses scriptural incident within contemporary practice: "Jesus Christ was brought up in Galilee and often traveled through it. This scene is common to the country. Every day one is likely to meet families traveling just as is here shown. Things never change in Palestine. As they travel today, they have always traveled."[72] Never mind the parasol.

"GIFTED WITH THE KNOWLEDGE OF THE NINETEENTH-CENTURY MAN": BEHOLDING PANORAMAS AND BIBLICAL PAGEANTRY

Robert Edward Mather Bain's ethnographic photographs of the biblical relics living in Jerusalem and its environs were beheld within a wider tradition of visualizing the Holy Land and Christian pageantry of salvation. One of the more remarkable effects of the communion of shadows was its ability to encapsulate other visual techniques within its embrace, to anoint nonphotographic traditions of visual representation with the solvents of photographic autonomy. In the next chapter I hone in on habits of behold-

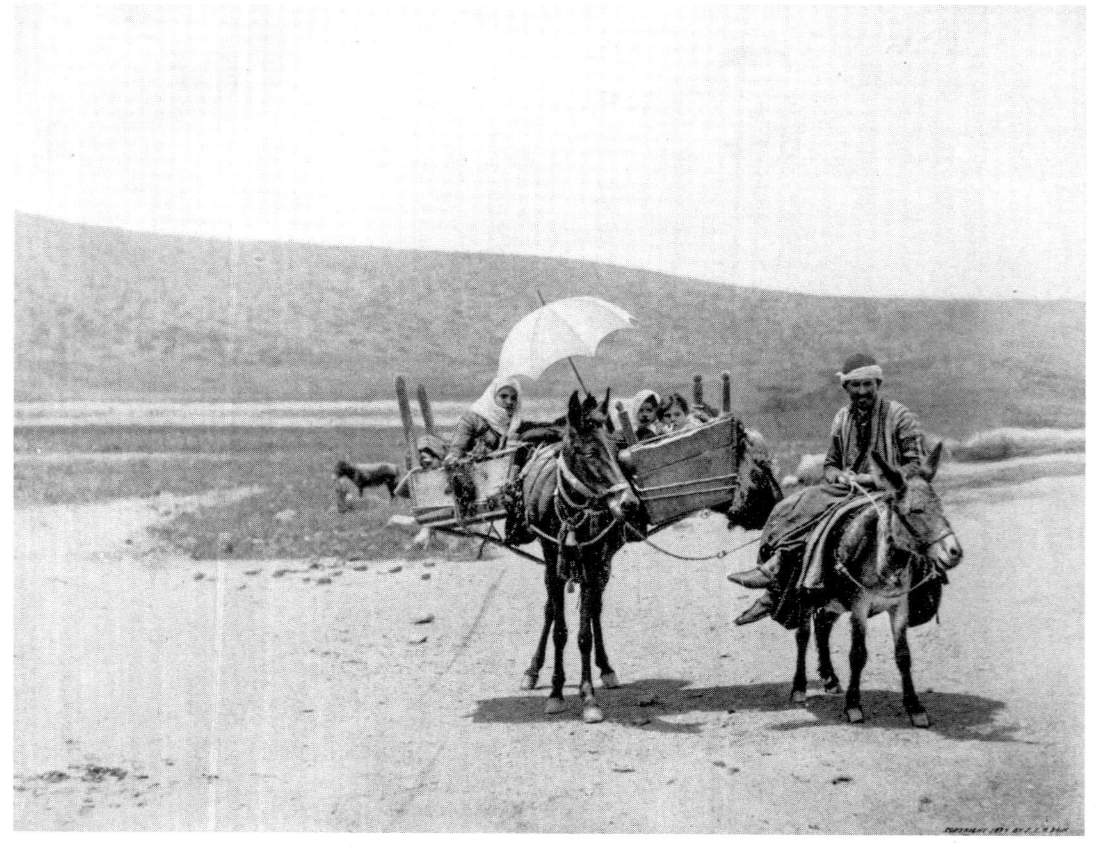

Figure 35. Robert Edward Mather Bain, "Family Traveling in Galilee." From *Earthly Footsteps of the Man of Galilee*. St. Louis Mercantile Library, University of Missouri–St. Louis. Used with permission.

ing facilitated by stereographs, but here it is helpful to think across the visual conventions of the communion of shadows in at least one regard: Bain's Holy Land views were among a number of refracted visual techniques used to produce devotional narratives for late nineteenth-century American beholders. Alongside photographic pilgrimages to the Holy Land, popular series of biblical tableaux from the New Testament gospels, especially the events leading up to and following Jesus's crucifixion, were distributed in various visual formats — stereographs, halftones, panoramas, and magic lantern slides — throughout the century and especially in the decades following the Civil War. These "Life of Christ" series differed from Holy Land tours in important ways; among the most obvious was that the former used figurines and paintings as compositional subjects instead of live actors or geographic vistas. Makers and distributors of Life of Christ visual narratives in the late nineteenth century had reason for caution against using live actors. As Kristin Schwain has noted in her study of F. Holland Day's *The Seven Last Words of Christ*, there was "extensive debate" at the turn of the century about the theological implications of representing Christ in human form, a debate that was not limited to the visual arts.[73] But even as they differed, at times, in compositional referents, each of these series drew upon "iconographic traditions and protocols of spectatorship," in Schwain's helpful phrasing, to elicit viewing experiences that positioned Life of Christ panoramas, stereographs, and photographic plates not only as visual tableaux but also as relics of a biblical past.[74] Unlike Holy Land stereographs that, as discussed in the next chapter, promised to pluck beholders from their armchairs and drop them into biblical Israel, Life of Christ views were more closely tied to established devotional practices such as the Stations of the Cross that were replicated in panoramas and other visual media. Painted panoramas and Life of Christ stereograph series were each folded into the visual habits of ethnographic beholding and into Bain's own photographic sensibilities.

A popular series of twenty-four stereographs reproduced under numerous imprimaturs throughout much of the latter half of the century featured what appears to be stylized wax miniatures arranged into biblical tableaux against painted backgrounds. Beginning with the adoration of the shepherds and the wise men at the Nativity, the first six views are of Jesus's birth and boyhood, the wedding at Cana, and the Sermon on the Mount. In the seventh view, Jesus is shown entering Jerusalem astride a colt as the crowd prepares his way with branches and garments, as the accompanying biblical reference to the Gospel of Mark explains.[75] This view commences the trajectory of Jesus's final hours and the remainder of the series carries the beholder from Judas's betrayal in the Garden of Gethsemane (view 8) through the remaining Stations of the Cross (views 9–22) on to the Resurrection (view 23) and the Ascension (view 24). In the 1890s, the stereograph agency of Underwood and Underwood distributed the entire twenty-four-view series, complete with corresponding biblical verse, explanatory commentary, and caption in six languages (English, French, German, Spanish, Swedish, Russian). Although this series bears the telling marks of the Underwood stereograph format, the views are identical to the series published by Strohmeyer & Wyman of New York. The paucity of identifying information on large numbers of views in circulation during the late nineteenth century makes precise dating, distribution, and circulation seemingly impossible in many instances. Nevertheless, the same negatives used by Underwood and Underwood (or new negatives acquired surreptitiously from previously published stereographs) were used by the International Stereoscopic View Company of New York to produce much poorer quality views at the turn of the century. Two more views from the same series printed earlier in the century bear markings of French origins.[76] The Life of Christ stereographs demonstrate how biblical narrative was transformed into a truncated series of visual events, commercially available and steeped within a communion of shadows that associated visual technologies of the camera with tangible relics of a biblical past.

The Philadelphia establishment of William and Frederick Langenheim had been the first to produce stereoscopic plates in the United States in the mid-1850s, but many views in circulation through the 1870s were still imported from Europe, particularly England and France. In 1875, for instance, Benerman and Wilson of Philadelphia profited handsomely by issuing in English a catalogue of "transparencies for the stereoscope" manufactured by J. Levy and Company of Paris, of which were included 92 views from their "New Travels in the Holy Land" tour.[77] The Passion views reproduced here evince such borrowing. Rather than mounting two prints, the distributor has acquired a single reproduction of the previous stereograph, including the decorative divider bisecting the two prints on the original mount. In the first, published as "French, Stereo, Publisher" out of Lawrence, Kansas, as one of the "Scenes in the Life of Christ," not only is there clear evidence of borrowing in the faint markings along the interior space between the two views, but the title on the face of the card, within the photographic print, is in French, "*La Nativité. Adoration des Bergers.*" All other markings on the view are in English. A similar view, apparently taken from the same original series and published by the same Kansas firm—they have the same series title in

 By Pencil and Camera

the same typeface—has been mounted on to the telltale bright orange card of the 1870s. In this view, moreover, the medallion at the top of the print is clearly labeled "Paris," although any other identifying information was lost in the reproduction. In all other respects—sequence, title, verse, caption—the view is the same as that printed by Underwood and Underwood in the 1890s.

The focus of the series on the Passion narrative might initially suggest, in the words of one recent historian, "a dominantly Catholic clientele." However, during the heyday of stereographs in the 1870s to early twentieth century, the Passion was a familiar visual sequence to a broad swath of American Christians, Protestant no less than Catholic, in part owing to the immense popularity of Passion plays and the even greater popularity of biblical panoramas.[78] Between 1885 and 1892, cities from New York to Los Angeles, Boston to Milwaukee, St. Louis, and Chicago boasted panoramas and cycloramas of the Holy Land, elaborate paintings in specially constructed buildings that encircled patrons as narrators explained the scenes that unfolded before their eyes, often complete with visual effects. A frequent focal point in these Holy Land excursions was an elaborate vignette of the crucifixion, as in the long-awaited "Jerusalem the Day of the Crucifixion" that opened for admission at the rotunda on Chicago's Wabash Avenue in September 1887. As a contemporary newspaper recounted, the "central feature" of the painting was "the sixth hour," from the Via Dolorosa to the reed of hyssop at the foot of the cross.[79] The next summer a "just completed" panorama of "Jerusalem and the Crucifixion" opened at a theater "made cool artificially" on Madison Avenue and 59th Street in New York, thus enabling patrons to attend at their leisure "day and night."[80]

Although travel narratives of pilgrims' journeys had been popular since the seventeenth century and had become standardized in the new genre of the nonfictional travelogue in the eighteenth century, it was the moving painted panorama of the early nineteenth century that most immediately prepared photographic beholders for their vicarious voyages.[81] Dating to late eighteenth-century Edinburgh, the term "panorama" was coined by the Irish-born artist Robert Baker to describe an enormous painting exhibited in a custom-built rotunda to provide a seemingly exhaustive eye-level visual sweep from a fixed vantage point. By the 1840s when a so-called panoramania swept across Europe and the United States, providing picture-viewing publics with an array of cosmoramas, cycloramas, georamas, and pantascopes of cities, river routes, and overland trails, the custom-built rotunda had in some cases been exchanged for a stage, which enabled the ticket holder to remain stationary while the narrated scenes were unfurled before

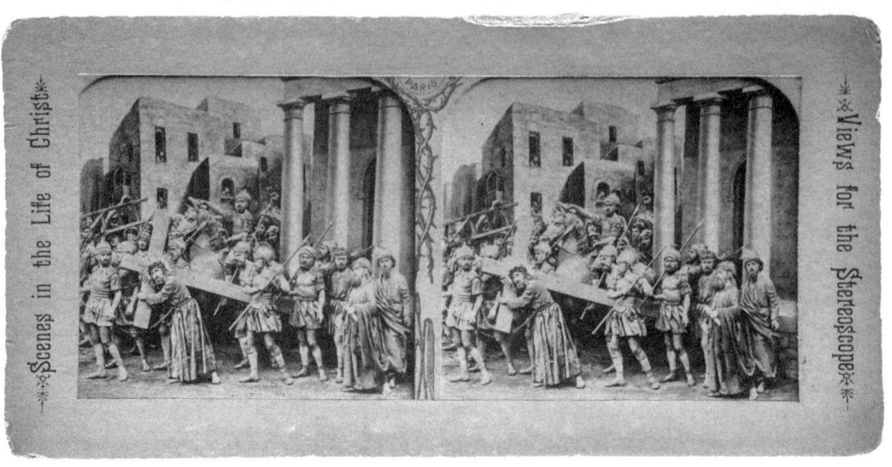

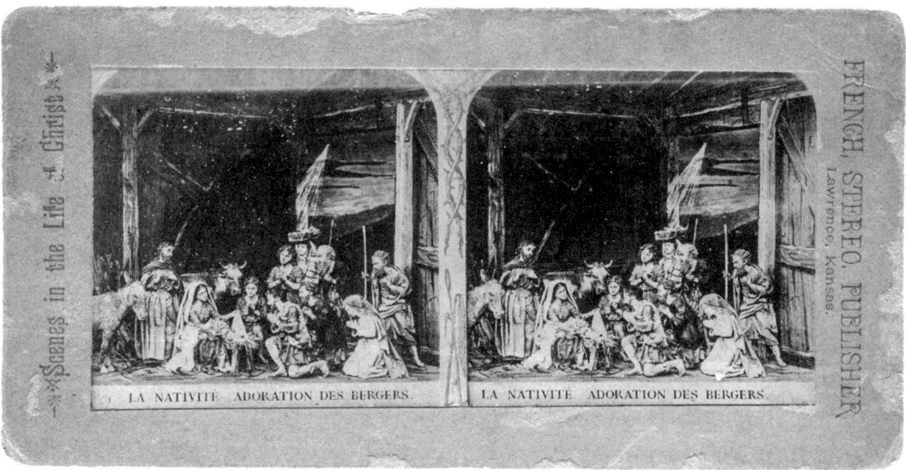

Figure 36. Life of Christ stereographs, ca. 1875–80. Top: "No. 10." "Jesus Bearing the Cross," "Scenes in the Life of Christ, views for the Stereoscope." Bottom: "La Nativité. Adoration des Bergers." "Scenes in the Life of Christ, French, Stereo, Publisher, Lawrence, Kansas." Author's collection.

her eyes. In addition to lively narration—which could take the travelers in either direction along the Mississippi or across the West, depending on which side of the stage the previous journey had left the painting—the long journey across the painted canvas (in some cases it would take three hours to unfurl the entire journey) was often accompanied by live music, while more enterprising stagers included elaborate special effects. Beholders of the *Bombardment of Vera Cruz* in New York, for instance, were awed by thundering fireworks, while steam and smoke wafted about travelers on Leon Pomarede's canvas of the Mississippi River.[82]

Panoramas of cities, rivers, and westward migration were perhaps most popular among midcentury American audiences, but there were also several early moving canvases of the Holy Land. In 1846, just before introducing his immensely popular panorama of the Mississippi River at Amory Hall in Boston, John Banvard advertised his "Great Panorama of the Holy Land" at the Lower Music Hall on Winter Street. Set to "music suited to the scenes represented" on the organ harmonium and the piano forte, the "very original, interesting, and instructive" painting, which was "explained" every evening at eight o'clock as well as on Wednesday and Saturday afternoons at three, featured "hundreds of figures, of life size," arranged in narrative sequence to "illustrate the manners, customs, and religious ceremonies of the inhabitants, who are Christians, Mohammadans and Jews," as well as "all the important" topographical features "mentioned in the Bible, or in the History of the Crusades." By far the most exciting part of the demonstration, however, was the "great mechanical picture" of the destruction of Jerusalem, in which Banvard "has so combined painting, music and acoustic effects, as to produce a striking and life-like representation of this most terrific and memorable siege." Unlike the moving panorama, the "mechanical picture" of the siege of Jerusalem was a diorama, a stationary image that manipulated light to give the illusion of movement. In "The Destruction," the scene was "represented under the shades of night, the better to produce the striking effect of the terrible conflagration." Beholders would stand in wonderment as the moon struggled through "intervals of smoke and flame," its pale face conspicuous against the "lurid glare of the burning city."[83]

Panoramas of the Holy Land provided an important context in the history of photographic biblical narration, in both landscape series such as *Earthly Footsteps* and in stereographic tours. Many of the earliest photographic expeditions across the American West, for instance, were valued *more* for their assistance to panoramic paintings, which could follow conventional narrative lines, than as works of intrinsic value in their own right, an attitude reflected by the disappearance of daguerreotype plates from these journeys within years of their manufacture. Similarly, the American biblical archaeologist James Barclay was among the first from his country to show biblical images in panorama, although the plates he made from his excursions in the early 1850s also disappeared shortly after his return.[84] Even after photographs took hold as narrative devices, however, panoramas continued to provide important visual strategies whereby familiar events were placed into meaningful sequence. As the *Daily Tribune* reported at the opening of the Jerusalem panorama in Chicago in 1887, "that wonderful country, that wonderful people, that wonderful atmosphere, that mystic semi-darkness of a great past . . . are not only reproduced, but revived, brought face to face with the beholder, who may now pursue the study and investigation of the greatest event in human history with almost the same advantages as he would have enjoyed had he been an eye-witness, gifted with the knowledge of the nineteenth-century man."[85] As Life of Christ stereograph series had done with the pageantry of the cross, panoramas of the Holy Land and biblical narratives had thus made the sacred routes conventionally associated with specific devotional practices familiar to various audiences by the time Lee and Bain set out from St. Louis.

There were also more direct associations between panoramas and photographs. The American stereographer Benjamin West Kilburn had started his "work of the camera" in 1855 while working with his father as a machinist and founder in Littleton, New Hampshire. Two decades later he was running a stereoscopic firm with his brother Edward. Kilburn Brothers made a number of significant views with Benjamin as chief photographer and developer until the partnership dissolved in 1875. Benjamin then struck out on his own until hiring his son-in-law, D. C. Remich, at which time the company grew to international repute. Using a camera "specially constructed . . . by The American Optical Co." for his tripod work and a Henry Clay stereoscopic camera for handwork, in 1893 Kilburn was selected from a prestigious battery of photographers to be the official stereoscopic photographer at the World's Columbian Exposition in Chicago, where he created such enduring scenes from the fair as the "Surging Sea of Humanity."[86] Two years before he and his general agent, James M. Davis, made the "Surging Sea" an icon of the Columbian Exposition, Kilburn issued a series of stereographs depicting biblical tableaux. The third view (fig. 37), is entitled "Father into Thy hands I commend my Spirit" and has the beholder looking across a deep gorge to the cliffs of Golgotha, upon which three crosses are erected. This view was sold individually (see the catalogue number to the left of the caption, "6483") but

   By Pencil and Camera

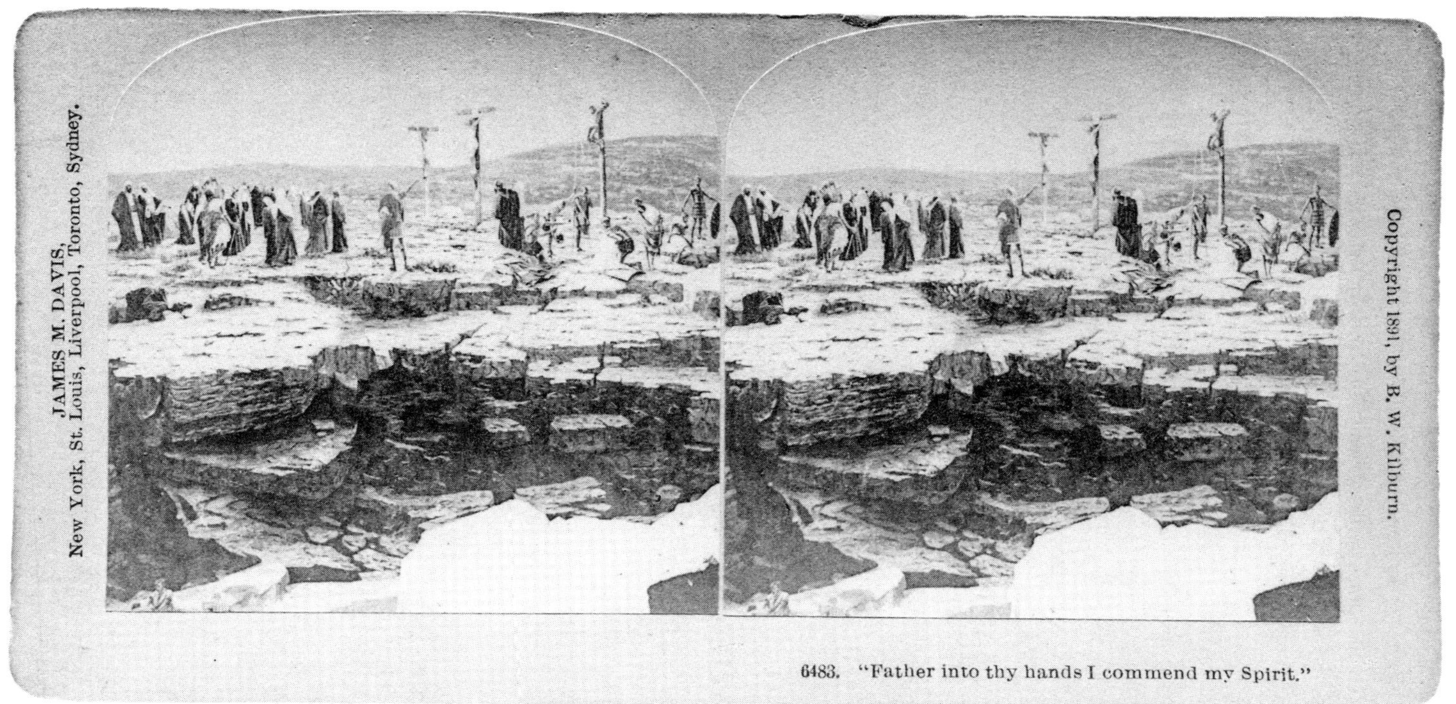

Figure 37. "Father into thy hands I commend my Spirit," copyright 1891, by B. W. Kilburn. Author's collection.

was also part of an intended series, as the sequencing on the back of the card indicates ("No. 3"). The stereograph, distributed by Davis, has the beholder looking across the gorge onto Jesus's "last moments of earthly torture," as the narration on the back of the card indicates. Although the view clearly consists of two separate prints mounted onto faded orange stock, the two prints are identical, thus diminishing the effect of solidity the technique was intended to provide.

The stereograph bears a striking similarity to the souvenir foldout from the exhibition brochure for Bruno Piglhein's panorama "Jerusalem on the Day of the Crucifixion," which was completed in Munich in 1886 and toured Europe until it was destroyed by fire in 1892. Piglhein and his team had gone to Palestine in 1885 to sketch the views they would re-create in the painting. They also took photographs. The completed painting was 50 feet high and 390 feet long. But despite strong similarities in composition and scale, Kilburn's stereograph is not an exact reproduction from the brochure representation. Piglhein was bound by contract not to replicate his painting of Jerusalem. But his partners were bound by neither contract nor scruple, and panoramas based on Piglhein's painting were re-created in the United States, London, and elsewhere, including the one displayed in Chicago in September 1887. The Munich panorama also inspired the chromolithograph "Jerusalem on the Day of the Crucifixion" in Thomas DeWitt Talmage's 1890 bestselling *From Manger to Throne*, one of many Life of Christ books published in the latter half of the nineteenth century. As the celebrated Brooklyn preacher explained in his description of the "panoramic view of the world's greatest tragedy," the "Grand Panorama" in *From Manger to Throne* was "a perfect reproduction of the famous cyclorama of Munich."[87] Both Kilburn and Talmage likely missed Piglhein's original in Munich. Talmage was in Europe and "the Christ-Land" in 1889 to research his book, but he did not arrive until October. Kilburn traveled frequently to Europe, but his most recent venture had him returning to Boston from England, via Ireland, in July 1890.[88] Either Talmage or Kilburn could also have visited the panorama of "Jerusalem and the Crucifixion" on Madison and 59th in New York or "Jerusalem the Day of the Crucifixion" on Wabash in Chicago — each of which was inspired by the Munich marvel.[89] The "Grand Panorama" in *From Manger to Throne* is in effect a tinted replication of the Munich exhibition brochure foldout, but in a rich example of photographs influencing painting influencing photography, Kilburn's stereograph also visually quoted the Munich panorama.[90]

Panoramas were a tradition of graphic representation that influenced the visual habits of photographic beholding. They also provided a visual ar-

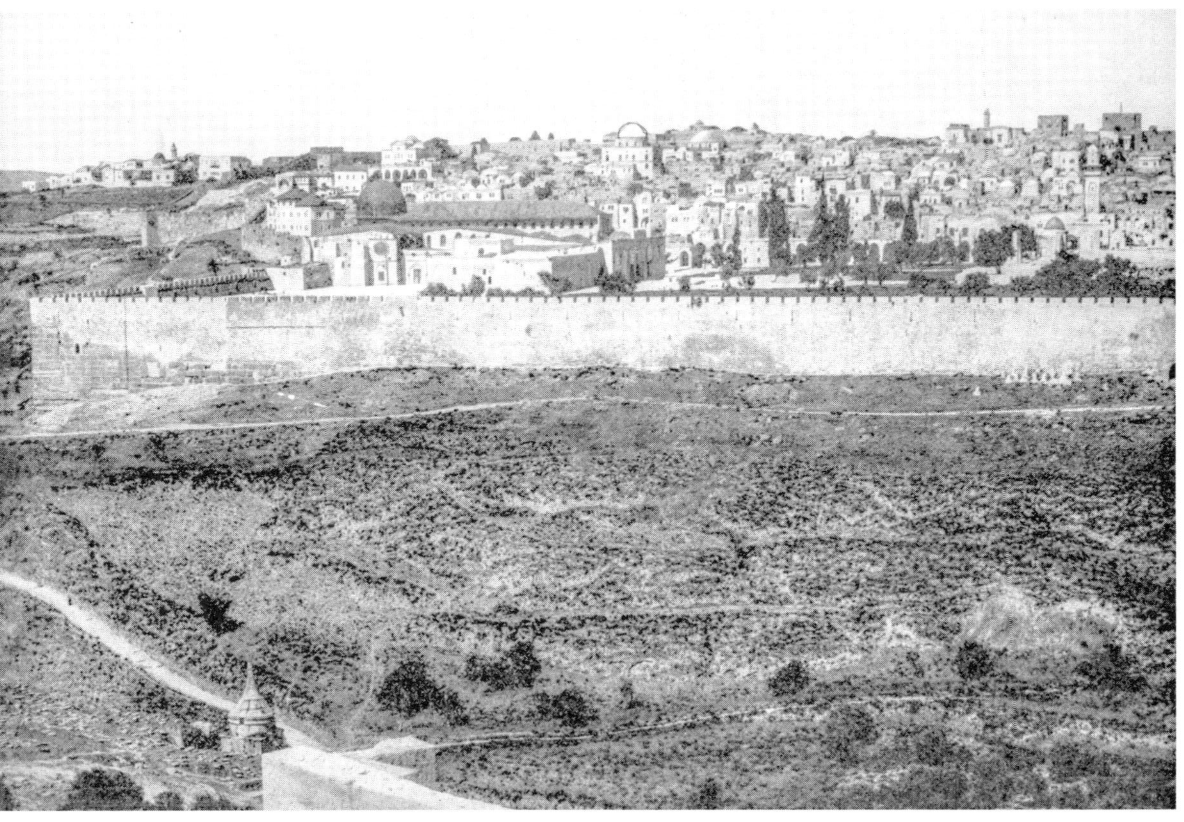

Figure 38. Robert Edward Mather Bain, "Panorama of Jerusalem—as Seen from the Top of the Mount of Olives," 1894. Printed in *Earthly Footsteps of the Man of Galilee*. Lenkin Family Photography of the Holy Lands Collection at the University of Pennsylvania Libraries, Library at the Herbert D. Katz Center for Advanced Judaic Studies, University of Pennsylvania.

chitecture for those behind the camera. "Panorama of Jerusalem—As Seen from the Top of the Mount of Olives" was printed toward the beginning of *Earthly Footsteps*. Bain's camera could not yet replicate the magnitude or the physical experience of the painted panorama, but in an important sense his prints replaced the visual sweep the paintings had provided previous generations. The first painted panoramas preceded the invention of photography by almost half a century, but the communion of shadows stitched these two visual technologies into a common visual legacy. Inverting the earlier processes, wherein daguerreotypes were made for artists to consult in their paintings, in later years the visual conventions of panoramas, ingrained in the consciousness of the visual pilgrim, would instruct photographers where to position their cameras and what to prioritize in their compositions. Bain's camera could not capture the endless horizon of Piglhein's painting, but this view of the Holy City gestured far beyond the edge of the frame. "Between where we stand and Jerusalem," Lee wrote, "is the valley of Jehoshaphat. To the extreme left is a cluster of minarets with a small dome. This is the tomb of David on Mount Zion. To the north of it is Zion's gate. Coming eastward nearer to our point of view, almost at the bottom of the valley, you see the pillar of Absalom. The road passing it leads to Bethany. . . . To the west of the extreme right of the picture is the tower of David near the Jaffa Gate." Gifted with the knowledge of the nineteenth-century man, panoramas and stereograph series of clay figurines, through the communion of shadows, made Americans eyewitnesses to the greatest event in human history.

"Jerusalem (By No Means the Golden)"

When James M. Buckley described his recent visit to the Jerusalem Exhibit at the Louisiana Purchase Exposition in an editorial for the *Christian Advocate* in November 1904, he related that, "so far as its external scenery is concerned," the organizers had accomplished an "accurate reproduction" of the city. Sitting on eleven acres, Jerusalem "displayed 22 streets; 700 people, including Mohammedans, Jews, and Christians, reside in it, and there are more than 200 houses." There were also some unfortunately "divers incongruities" with the real thing. Camel rides were evidently not allowed in Jerusalem, although they were freely available at the Exhibit, and the Arabian wedding "performed by a sheik . . . in the square of the Church of the Holy Sepulchre" would never have transpired beyond the perimeters of the Pike. "But the scenery well repays the visit," Buckley insisted. James Lee had authored a "pamphlet history" of the city that served "as a handbook which

                                                  By Pencil and Camera

those who have not mastered the history of that wonderful people will do well to carry with them" as they ambled up "the steep, narrow streets" and "visited chapels, temples, the tower of David, and the wailing-place of the Jews." On the banks of the mighty river, fairgoers could, with the assistance of Rev. James Lee, walk in the footsteps of the man of Galilee.

But "the Walled City of Jerusalem — in St. Louis," John Brisben Walker jested in his 1904 guide, could be as deceptive as it was illustrative. Chatting with one of the "native attendants" in the exhibit, Walker had soon learned that despite an initial claim to have hailed from Palestine, he actually had "a push-cart in New York, and live[d] in Hoboken."[91] As picture books came alive before fairgoers' eyes, this was an oft-repeated disjuncture. True relics were harder to come by outside the carefully policed boundaries of the communion of shadows. One exhibit found a solution in tinctures. In addition to the scaled replica of the Holy City, the Jerusalem Exhibit Company sponsored a cyclorama of the Crucifixion of Christ and Jerusalem. Locating visitors in an ethnographic space, the entrance to the building, a souvenir pamphlet assured, "is an exact reproduction of the Portal to the Church of the Holy Virgin in Jerusalem." The painting itself measured 350 feet in length and towered to a height of forty feet. The painting bore some resemblance to Piglhein's 1886 panorama, but it was not an exact replica. But no mind. "The picture of the Crucifixion," the cyclorama pamphlet assured, "tells better than words the culmination of the life of Jesus."[92] The painting, a copy of a copy of a picture based on photographs of nineteenth-century Palestine, became an invitation to bear witness, yet again, to the greatest event in human history.

Bain's photographs of the Holy Land were beheld as relics of a biblical imaginary that was anchored in visual habits of an imperial age, wherein Americans looked beyond the photographic contemporary to see what was really there. These efforts to make the Bible a new book, as several commentators alleged, were echoed in another corner of the communion of shadows. But whereas halftone travel guides and panoramas of biblical tableaux positioned Palestine and its inhabitants as relics of the biblical past, the visual technology of the stereoscope transported beholders themselves into the midst of unfolding biblical drama.

FIVE

Beyond the Sense Horizon

On Easter Sunday 1896, wearied from months of travel, the American entrepreneur Elmer Underwood sat down at the desk in his room of the Howard's Hotel in Jerusalem to write a note to his wife. "My Dear Jennie," he wrote on the sheet of hotel stationary, "Bert and I are having a grand and interesting time here. I arrived on Good Friday morning and have been seeing and photographing the grand parades and ceremonies." Upon arriving in Jerusalem, the mustachioed thirty-six-year-old Elmer wrote to his wife that he and his brother Bert had witnessed a spectacle of "Catholic Franciscan pilgrims follow[ing] the Via Dolorosa" and the "great sight" of the Holy Sepulchre. "The Christians (Roman Catholic), the Armenians, the Greeks, and various pilgrim churches took their turn in the ceremonies," he wrote, "which mostly were anything but sacred. Pomp and form was the order of the evening." Underwood's strained gentlemanly detachment in his descriptions of these "grand and interesting" scenes buckled when he reported to Jennie the "blasphemous ceremony" at the Church of the Holy Sepulchre and the solemn practice of "passing by and kissing the great stone slab which is claimed to be the stone upon which the Lord's body was anointed." "Much of all this," he wrote with an almost audible huff, "is the grossest humbug, of course." But one site quieted Elmer's sardonic criticisms of the city and its Holy Week observances. "There is a sacred spot outside of the city which I have faith in as the identical place (or at least probable place where Christ was Crucified and buried)." "I really believe that we have looked into the *very tomb* where Christ's body was laid, the new and unfinished tomb of Joseph of Arimathea," Elmer gushed. "We shall photograph it."[1]

Bert and Elmer Underwood were in the Holy Land to take pictures.

Drawing on a reservoir of photographic beholding that wed empirical conceit with biblical imaginary, Elmer's letter to Jennie intimated that his photograph of the "empty tomb" would facilitate access to the sacred site without physical travel. Like many of his contemporaries, he was confident in the power of photography not merely to represent but to reproduce the experiential conditions of the *real* Holy Land—the sites and scenes of the biblical narrative absent later accretions of "pomp and form."[2] But while this can be said of photographs of many varieties, Elmer and Bert were makers of no ordinary pictures. As founders of one of the largest stereograph companies in the United States, Elmer and Bert were in the business of transforming the Bible from a text that was read into a space that was inhabited through the optical marvel of the stereoscope.

The stereoscope was a handheld contraption, devised early in the nineteenth century, that created the effect of three-dimensional relief when the elongated, slightly differentiated prints were positioned at the appropriate distance in the beholder's gaze. Look again inside the tomb. Here, the photograph (fig. 39) is reproduced as a stereograph. When beheld through a stereoscope—as the view would have been by the Underwoods' contemporaries—the shadows become cavernous, the tomb appears to plummet to an unknown depth, the kneeling figure descends backward, and, as Elmer later wrote, the Holy Land appears "to you in a more life-like aspect than it has ever before been reproduced."[3] For many beholders and producers of "sacred subjects"—one of many classifying schema used throughout the end of the nineteenth century—the technology was far more than an optical trick. The stereoscope was a mechanism of revelation, a contraption that revealed what previous interpretive traditions of biblical narrative had obscured. The Underwoods' pictures, among the entire catalogue of biblical views, mimicked the convention of travel views popularized from the 1870s forward, but they also made further claims to what was beheld. In Elmer's description of "the Jews' wailing place," for instance, he addresses the hinge between the pursuit of representational exactitude and biblical beholding that his pictures opened. Describing the "interesting spot" where the city's Jews "congregate on Fridays especially, and where they face the wall with their Hebrew Old Testament and weep and wail," Elmer boasted to Jennie that he had "splendid photographs" of the sight but lamented in the next breath that the pictures "lack the wailing." Despite his own sense of thwarted replication, Elmer's pause at the percussive void between Holy Land pilgrimage and its photographic representation was by and large missed by contemporary audiences, who, echoing a Sunday school lesson commentary, gushed that

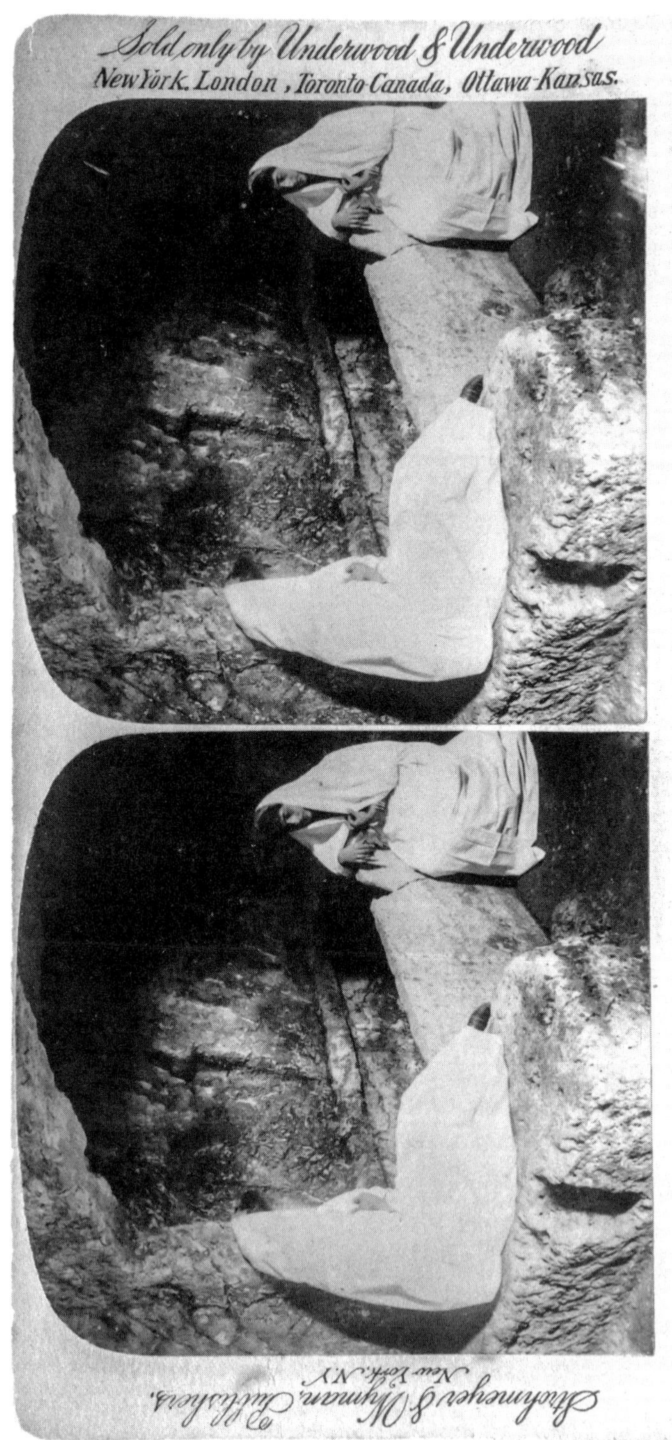

Figure 39. "The Tomb of Our Lord,' 'New Calvary,' outside of Jerusalem, Palestine." Copyright 1897 by Underwood & Underwood. Author's collection.

looking at the Underwoods' photographs "is almost the same as if we were actually traveling in the Holy Land."[4] Indeed Elmer and Bert themselves would later write that with their photographs, the beholder "may feel that [she] is actually visiting the places" before her eyes.[5] And when the Methodist minister Jesse Lyman Hurlbut wrote the companion travel book to the Underwoods' Holy Land series of views, he marveled more robustly at their ability "to make the Bible *real* to us."[6] In these photographs, the communion of shadows positioned beholders not in contemporary Jerusalem but in the very midst of biblical drama.

In their coordination of the senses of sight and touch, as well as their ability to fray the constraints of time and space, stereographs were similar to other types of nineteenth-century commonplace photographs. And yet, whereas portraits, memorial photographs, and spirit pictures promised the continued presence of the beheld despite corporeal absence, stereographs offered beholders themselves an embodied technology of corporeal displacement, a device specially configured, according to contemporaries, to unhinge the senses from their corporeal frame. This thoroughly tactile experience of temporal and spatial drift was regulated viewing through specific, body-centered instructions that promised, without a hint of irony, to wing students "far beyond the sense horizon that shuts them in."[7] Even if Elmer and Bert Underwood borrowed existing conventions of representing the Holy Land for American Protestants and Catholics from painterly and other visual practices, the stereographic format changed the experience of beholding by magnifying the beholder's own sense of corporeal drift. Pressing one's face into a well-fitted stereoscope and adjusting the position of the card while training one's eyes on a distant point until the ancient port of Joppa sprung into life beyond the bow of the vessel was a very different entrance to the Holy Land than sitting in a darkened room as the gaslight of the magic lantern slowly focused onto the suspended sheet, bringing the city into view, or thumbing through Bain's photographs in *Earthly Footsteps* and, later, *The Self-Interpreting Bible*.

At the same time, emphasis on the photographs as a conduit of biblical experience, was, as with Bain's prints, a discourse that masked an orchestrated correspondence between the photographic contemporary and the biblical imaginary. In this sense, by using present-day inhabitants of Palestine to evoke biblical figures, Bert and Elmer relied on existing Protestant conventions of photographic representation. In the photograph "Tomb of Our Lord," for instance, the brothers arranged "two young Syrian girls from the English Protestant school," "dressed in the costumes of their people," to demonstrate how the resurrection scene might have appeared, with "one [angel] at the head and the other at the feet, where the body of Jesus had lain."[8] Such staging was not to deceive viewers, a later commentator explained, but was a technique to correct beholders' fanciful imaginings of biblical pageantry through the honest eye of the camera. This same principle was at work elsewhere in the Easter morning letter when Elmer recalled that at the house in Jaffa "claimed to be" that of Simon the Tanner, where heaven opened to the apostle Peter, "of course we took the picture, and we went up on top to see the place where Peter's vision was, and tried to imagine a great deal." Standing on the rooftop at Jaffa and "imagining a great deal," on the one hand, and positioning contemporary inhabitants of Ottoman Palestine within the compositional frame of their prints, on the other, were different ways of accomplishing the same interpretive feat, namely, conscripting the present into the biblical past through the authorizing mechanisms of photographic technology. Here, the communion of shadows worked less to produce relics of the biblical past for contemporary beholders than to transport beholders themselves into biblical narratives so long presumed to be confined to an inaccessible past.

Stereographs and Religion

By the time Elmer Underwood boarded the steamship *Majestic* in September 1895 to ferry his young family from New York to Liverpool, the stereograph had become a national passion on the brink of obsession.[9] Stereographs were first introduced to the American market in 1850 by the Philadelphia establishment of Frederick and William Langenheim upon Frederick's return from studying with Daguerre in Paris.[10] Despite early improvements, the expense and experience of daguerreotype and glass-plate slides were not optimal for mass production. In 1859, Oliver Wendell Holmes, who Elmer Underwood later described as "an enthusiastic prophet as to the development of the stereoscope as a means of visual instruction," waxed on the "brilliancy in a glass picture" that outshone prints upon paper, but then quickly added that "twenty-five glass slides, well inspected in a strong light, are *good* for one headache."[11] Indeed these early apparatuses were often bulky, heavy, and very costly, although that hardly deterred fascination among the well-heeled and those with access to respected photographic firms that provided full-plate stereoscopic entertainment to draw patrons into their salons. Southworth and Hawes of Boston, for instance, installed an elaborate, piano-size "grand parlor stereoscope" that revolved daguerreotype plates by the turn of a crank

Beyond the Sense Horizon

in their gallery for the benefit of their patrons, at a cost of twenty-five cents per visit, or a "season ticket" for half a dollar.[12] Not all early stereoscopes were as grandiose as the grand parlor. In 1855 J. F. Mascher of Philadelphia advertised a "stereoscopic medallion" in *Humphrey's Journal*, "the first photographic journal in the world."[13] "The article, when closed, looks so like the ordinary locket, that no one can distinguish one from the other, when worn," the journal assured, and "the difference in expense is more than counterbalanced by the beauty of the results."[14] The promise to make the visage of one's dearest evermore present in absence would certainly have drawn potential clients, but it seems that the medallion was never put into production.

The stereoscope that attained broadest cultural influence was neither jewelry nor grand parlor. In the 1860s, Oliver Wendell Holmes designed a prototype of a handheld device for views on paper, rather than glass, that was made of wood and featured multiple slots for viewers to adjust the position of the card. Holmes referred to his "very convenient" viewer in an 1861 *Atlantic Monthly* article, but did not advertise it until after the Civil War.[15] Significantly, the convenience and relative affordability of what came to be known as the "Holmes Scope" was an important development in shaping the stereograph market in the last decades of the nineteenth century. As Elmer Underwood wrote to historian Robert Taft in the late 1920s, by the turn of the century his firm alone — one of a handful of operations with comparable output — was printing "25,000 stereoscopic photographs per day, or 7,500,000 per year," along with the "approximately 250,000 to 300,000" stereoscopes they manufactured each year.[16] Historians and collectors have furthermore estimated that between three and four million stereoscopic *negatives* were produced in the United States between 1854 and 1920.[17] Even if only a fraction of these views featured religious subjects or were marketed to religious populations, it is nevertheless difficult to deny their prominence in the communion of shadows.

While definite sales figures of religious stereographs during the nineteenth century are difficult to nail down, their sale was lucrative enough for swindle. In the late winter of 1876, advertisements ran in several religious newspapers for "100 different views of the Holy Land" from the firm of J. C. Henry and Company of Glen Falls, New York. The same advertisement was later signed by the firm of C. W. Whitney and Company of Chester and placed in the *Sunday-School Times* of Philadelphia and the *Methodist, Episcopal Journal* of New York. By April, Clarence W. Miller of Saratoga County was before United States commissioner Aubrey H. Smith, charged with the crime of "using the mails for the purpose of fraud." The "great scope of his operations" ranged from Maine to Virginia and west to Indiana and had spanned several years. At the time of his arrest, Miller was found with "some 300 letters and postcards addressed to the bogus firm" along with evidence of payments received, although he testified to Special Agent C. B. Barrett of the U.S. Post Office that he "had no photographs, and gave no return for the money sent to him."[18] With so many of the "religiously inclined" having been "mulcted" by Miller's duplicity, there is evidence that trade in sacred subjects was robust.

We have more affirmative evidence as well. Take, for example, the abundant catalogue of stereoscopic views available for the "religiously inclined" consumer. In addition to Holy Land tours—of which there were several—one could purchase serials of the Life of Christ, innumerable views of church and cathedral interiors and exteriors from around the world, reproductions of master paintings—which, according to one historian, "had absolutely no dimensional effect"—views of Shakers, Mormons, and camp meetings, Bibles, ministers, magnificent organs, memorials of religious figures, priests, Bible verses in elaborate typographical displays, bishops, a "pilgrimage to see the Holy Father," monks praying in the catacombs of Rome, and penitent Hindu devotees.[19] The *production* of these views, however, and many more that feature religious subjects, whether in sincerity or in levity, does not demonstrate how they were used. William Culp Darrah, a historian and collector of stereoscopic views, has argued that despite their immense popularity, views of the Holy Land, as well as Rome and Egypt, "are properly to be considered as travel, archaeology, or history, rather than religious."[20] This would seem to be the case for early views of Mormons, which were frequently sold as views from the railcar of the Union Pacific, "West from Omaha," or other familiar rail routes.[21] Based on contemporary catalogue descriptions, views of the Holy Land were consistently placed within the genre of travelogue. An 1865 catalogue for E. & H. T. Anthony and Company's Emporium of American and Foreign Stereoscopic Views, for instance, one of the leading manufacturers of stereographs in the 1850s and 1860s, listed its views of "Egypt and the Holy Land" in the section on foreign tours, and the Philadelphia firm of Benerman and Wilson explicitly catalogued its views of Palestine as "New Travels in the Holy Land."[22] But the typical cataloguing of these views of the Holy Land as "travel, archaeology, [and] history" did not preclude them from also being religious. In fact, it was the narrative mechanism of the travelogue that legitimized views of the Holy Land for Protestant beholders, in particular, as collaborators of scriptural interpretation rather than potentially disruptive icons.[23]

Stereographs of "sacred subjects" in general drew on a variety of different viewing practices and narrative genres — travelogue, biblical iconography, devotional imagery, comic series, landscapes, and so forth — none of which necessarily denied religious interpretation or significance. For instance, several landscape views from the Holy Land series, such as one entitled "A Barley Harvest, near Bethlehem of Judea, Palestine," copyrighted in 1899, invoked not only the agrarian subsistence intended to suggest an immediate link to "Bible times" but also the popular genre of stereographs of African American sharecropping in the United States, depicted in the view "Cotton Field," a "characteristic Southern scene," by the South Carolina photographer J. A. Palmer, likely from the late 1860s or early 1870s as indicated by the square corners and yellow mount. Indeed, whether the subject matter of a stereograph was explicitly "religious" — as designated by producers — did not determine how the artifact was viewed, nor was the category of "sacred subjects" unaffected by the entire catalogue of views available to beholders. Just exactly what the relevant interpretive visual archive for any particular view was for specific beholders is impossible to identify with certainty. Nevertheless, despite the paucity of personal accounts of the use of stereoscopic views in the domestic and devotional lives of religious Americans, close readings of the sources do provide occasional glimpses, however oblique, of the visual habits at work in stereographic beholding.

As with the firms of Anthony and Benerman and Wilson before them, the "photographs" that Bert and Elmer Underwood made in the April 1896 became part of their firm's first stereoscopic "tour" of the Holy Land, issued in 1897 as *Journeys in the Holy Land through the Perfecscope*, a boxed set of "seventy-two original stereoscopic photographs" to be viewed through the firm's patented scope.[24] Although the popularity of this first set of Holy Land views was a whisper in comparison with the clamor surrounding their set of one hundred views, *Traveling in the Holy Land through the Stereoscope*, first issued three years later, the Perfecscope series was among the first tours the firm had issued from their own negatives, having to this point been exclusively distributors of views created from the negatives of other photographic establishments, including Jarvis, Bierstadt, and the Littleton View Company, as well as Messrs. Strohmeyer & Wyman of New York City.[25] The companion text to *Journeys in the Holy Land*, moreover, was written by the brothers themselves and drew largely from their travel diaries scribbled in moonlight along the "rocky trails" and "rugged ravines" of their own Holy Land pilgrimage. For the companion volume to *Traveling in the Holy Land*, the firm hired the Methodist minister Jesse Lyman Hurlbut to compose the text, which was

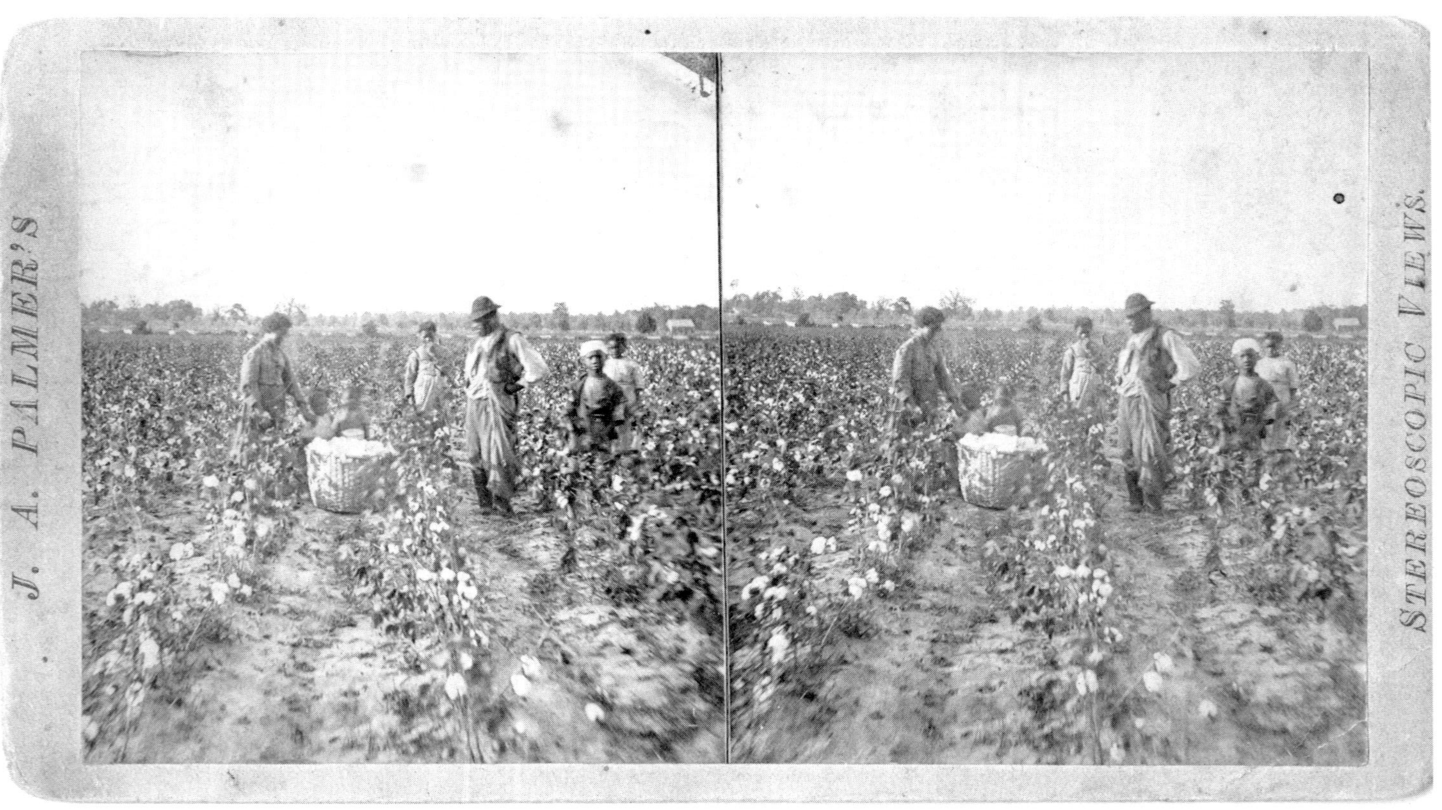

Figure 40. "Characteristic Southern Scenes. Cotton Field." J. A. Palmer, Aiken, South Carolina, ca. 1870. Black History Collection, History Museum on the Square, Springfield, Missouri. Used with permission.

published in three editions between 1900 and 1909 before changing the name to *Traveling in Palestine*. Hurlbut also narrated a tour of Jerusalem, "taken bodily" from the Underwood tours of Palestine, while the Underwood series *Travel Lessons on the Life of Christ* and *Travel Lessons on the Old Testament* were authored by Presbyterian minister William Byron Forbush. All these tours could be purchased "in neat Volume cases" resembling bound books or, for a prettier penny, in an "Underwood Extension Cabinet," which would hold up to "2,000 stereographed places, or more," and was recommended "when two or more of the '100' tours are wanted." The firm's decision to market its travel series in "volume cases" reflects a deeper ambivalence about the role that the stereographs played in relation to conventional instruction, namely, through books, and raises even more interesting questions when considered within the context of biblical subjects. Although Forbush was quick to concede that "seeing Bible lands [through the stereoscope] does not take the place of the Bible," the discourse of authenticity draping the marketing and use of the views, the meticulous system of biblical references on both the cards and in the guidebooks, as well as the deliberate bibliophilia of the packaging, indicates a more complicated culture of image/text correspondence than vocabularies of "illustration" convey.[26]

In addition to being available for purchase through catalogue subscription, these tours could also be purchased by way of the company's "Bible Study Department," a correspondence department at the firm's New York office, "to which any teacher may freely apply in any perplexity."[27] Teachers heeded the call. As early as 1875, "photographs of the Holy Land, with the stereoscope," were "recommended in the line of apparatus" befitting a "well appointed Sunday-school" by Lyman Abbot's *Christian Union*.[28] Twenty-five years later, stereoscopic entertainments punctuated the "strain of solid study in midsummer" for Methodists at Ocean Grove — a group which later in the week "witnessed the marvelous powers of the vitagraph," Thomas Edison's recently patented motion picture projector and augur of the technological displacement of stereographs by the middle of the century.[29] A 1903 review in the *Congregationalist and Christian World* indicated something more of the devotional use of stereoscopic images of the Holy Land in the course of biblical study: the "value [of a stereograph] is not exhausted in a single view, but it becomes more helpful with frequent reference. When the life of our Lord or the history of Israel is being studied these pictures will illuminate every lesson."[30] To this effect, the Reverend J. W. Raine of Riverhead, New York, "conduct[ed a] class in mission study, also a Sunday school class, using Forbush's Life of Christ, with stereoscopes," and Mrs. J. Woodridge Barnes demonstrated "manual methods in Sunday school work, including the use of sand tables, notebooks, stereoscopic pictures, map drawing and coloring" at the Broadway Tabernacle in New York.[31]

If Underwood and Underwood had invited teachers "in any perplexity" to send for materials and advice, their stereographs were also an important part of home instruction. In 1908 Mrs. W. W. Stark of Jackson County, Georgia, wrote to Underwood, extolling that "I don't see how any parents with children could afford to be without Traveling in the Holy Land through the Stereoscope." "We are perfectly delighted with it," she continued, adding, "I expect to know more Bible history than in all my life before I bought the stereographs."[32] Stereographs were thus an important component of biblical instruction among American Protestants at the turn of the twentieth century, both in the home and in the church. Such testimony, moreover, demonstrates how the popularity of stereographs was as much rooted in its ability to entertain as in its capacity to instruct. Drawing on contemporary theories (rifled with ambiguity, to be sure) of race and progress, utilizing the narrative genre of travelogue, and sincerely seeking to root biblical interpretation in an empirical record, the Underwoods and their patrons envisioned within a flawed photographic contemporary a biblical past that could be experienced from anywhere, simply by leaving their "outward frames" and letting their "spirits" soar.

From Relic to "Reality"

For James Lee, as with many of his contemporaries, the principal benefit of the camera was in its capacity to make readers "see the events and histories and battles which are recorded in [the Bible] placed side by side with the very scenes where they took place. In this way the land is made to explain and interpret the book." Here, Lee sounds much like Jesse Lyman Hurlbut, both of whom were Methodist ministers affiliated with Chautauqua and who had working associations, if not personal endearments, with Bishop John Heyl Vincent. More difficult to suss about both ministers, however, were their claims that, in Lee's words, through "the aid of these representations of the lands of the Bible," the Old and New Testaments "become real books." Hurlbut would later write that the Underwoods' stereographs, through their ability to bring Americans into biblical Palestine, work "to make the Bible *real* to us."[33] Even if photographs did not displace the authority of the Bible, the ministers' agreement that the prints and stereographs were effective means of "making the Bible real to us" nevertheless elevated their

Beyond the Sense Horizon

influence beyond that of "illustration" to a more profound level of scriptural interpretation. Because of their archival placement, Bain's photographs in the *Self-Interpreting Bible* present different questions about the relationship between photographic images and biblical text from the stereographs in the Underwood tour. In his guidebook, for instance, Hurlbut identified the stereographs as "the real text" of his book, rather than "merely as an embellishment or supplement," a configuration that inverted Lee's stated subordination of image to text.[34] It mattered that Bain's photographs were in the Bible, of course, and that biblical text was of a different order than Hurlbut's guidebook. But while both series of Holy Land photographs claimed that their views were important contributions to biblical interpretation, they ultimately mounted different defenses of the common claim.

At first blush it might be argued that what the ministers *really* meant was that the land—which Hurlbut called the "Fifth Gospel"—was the authenticating mechanism in question and photography was just a convenient medium for its transmission. Such analysis, however, overlooks both the physical properties of the photograph itself as well as the ways in which photography was deemed capable of reproducing not only the physical likeness of a geographic terrain but the experience of standing in its "very presence." And here is where the two modes of presentation are most clearly differentiated. While both Lee and Hurlbut claimed that the photographic prints in their tours facilitated an experience of the Holy Land, Hurlbut was convinced that stereographs were much more effective in this regard than an "ordinary single photograph," using the word "real" or a variant ("realities," "realistic," "reality") more than twenty times in ten pages to drive his point home.[35] That stereographs facilitated a more "real" experience of the Holy Land than "ordinary" photographs, he argued, "could not be possible except for several reasons." First, the stereographs "are infinitely accurate in detail and proportion, and therefore marvelously realistic." Second, "and it is an absolutely indispensible [*sic*] condition," he assured, one that differentiated the medium from other photographic techniques, the stereographs "are not looked at in the hand, but with the eyes within the hood of the stereoscope, our immediate surroundings being entirely shut out." His language here invokes that of Jennie Pullen, an instructor at Cleveland Normal School, in her claim that stereographs were uniquely equipped to take her geography students "beyond the sense horizon that shuts them in." Whereas Bain's photographs had created relics of the biblical past for Americans to behold, through the stereoscope, the bodies of beholders were themselves lifted from their corporeal frame and planted in the land of the Bible.[36]

And every traveler needs a map. Writing the "instructions" for the tour in 1900, Hurlbut first oriented his fellow travelers to the "specially devised maps" folded into the binding at the back of the guidebook. "Constant reference should be made to the maps," he insisted, "first to the general map at the end of this book, and then to the detail maps of special sections when given." Each of the 100 positions were marked on the general map with red ink and the vantage point indicated by two intersecting red lines, wherein the "apex . . . indicates the place from which the view was taken" and the "branching lines . . . the limits of the stereographed scene, viz., the limits of our vision on the right and left when looking at the stereograph." This initial attempt to situate beholders in a physical environment—a practice that was also more subtly at work in editions of Bain's photographs—was followed by five additional instructions detailing correct use of the stereographs themselves. "Move the slide or carrier . . . to the point on the shaft of the stereoscope where the view can be seen most distinctly" and "see that the best light available falls on the face of the photograph," he advised. Then, "hold the stereoscope firmly against the forehead, excluding all surrounding light from the eyes." These instructions were important not only for shedding light, so to speak, on the physical conditions that beholders of stereographs were expected to manipulate to see correctly but also for suggesting how other forms of photographic viewing were assumed not to need instruction. Lee and Bain, for instance, never instructed their readers *how* to look at their prints. At the very least, then, through his instructions Hurlbut acknowledged that the stereographs were a very different viewing experience from "ordinary" photographs.[37]

Before disembarking at the "compact, solid-looking town" of Joffa— "the Joppa of the Bible!"—Hurlbut made one last defense of the use of stereographs, this time explicitly positing that *"your experiences of being in the presence of the land"* was of more instructional value than "the material Palestine," which "you do not . . . bring away with you on your return." Such a claim echoed a tradition reaching at least as far back as Benjamin Disraeli's 1848 novel, *Tancred; or, the New Crusade,* wherein the protagonist discovers, according to Annabel Jane Wharton, that "the representation of the Holy City is more deeply spiritual than its reality."[38] For his own part, Hurlbut contended that even if one were to fund the tremendous expense of travel to Palestine, ultimately "the places, buildings, people" one would encounter were "only means of giving us [the] experiences" of reality that would be freighted home. "So now, coming back to the stereoscope, . . . there is indeed an infinite difference between the picture and the place itself as objective

          Beyond the Sense Horizon

realities," the goodly minister concluded, "but there need be no essential difference between the ideas and emotions which the picture and the place can produce within us. We are dealing with realities in the stereoscope, but they are real *experiences* of seeing Palestine, not the material earth and water and air of Palestine."[39] Ostensibly this "subjective experience" could be acquired through other means, such as the scaled replicas of the Holy Land popularized throughout the century, a cultural phenomenon in which American Methodists played a particularly active role.[40] For Hurlbut, however, who was active in Chautauqua for nearly half a century, not even these replicas approached the level of "experience" that stereographs facilitated: "One hundred life-size models of stone and dirt of these same parts of Palestine, so rich in historical memories," Hurlbut penned in 1900, "could not be more definite and solid to the eyes — moreover, they would be vastly less accurate and not at all serviceable for use."[41] Just as photographic portraits drew on previous traditions of representation and commemoration — painted miniatures and hairwork, for instance — and yet generated novel experiences of presence, so too were stereoscopes able to facilitate "*real* experiences" through new technics of corporeality.

Like Bain's landscapes, stereographs of the Holy Land replicated in large measure the visual habits of an imperialist gaze that rendered contemporary inhabitants of Palestine, Samaria, and Egypt, especially, as relics of a biblical imaginary. But the culture of stereography was also particularly attentive to the corporeality of the beholder, whether in terms of strategic denials of the senses that enabled a kind of telegraphing of the body through the pulsations of sight or in instructional material that explicitly addressed the beholder's embodied relation to the views. It was this attentiveness to the beholder that facilitated an interpretive transition from relic to experience. For Hurlbut, photography was the medium best suited for facilitating experiences of the Holy Land — even better than physical travel to the Orient — experiences that were vital to comprehension of biblical events. And yet, not all photographs were created equal. The stereograph, with its seemingly miraculous duplication of physical space, was, in Hurlbut's estimation, the best vehicle for transmitting the "realities" of sacred terrain. But even this technology was grounded in interpretive traditions that animated habits of beholding. As panoramas had lent a visual architecture of devotional beholding to Bain's plates as they migrated from souvenir portfolios to the pages of the Bible, magic lantern demonstrations positioned stereograph tours within the authorizing tradition of travelogue.

In 1872, Presbyterian minister Robert Patton of the Jefferson Park Presbyterian Church in Chicago gave a public lecture "illustrated by stereoscopic views" of the Holy Land.[42] Despite the *Daily Tribune*'s copy, the lecture was likely not illustrated by stereoscopes and stereographs but rather by a "magic lantern," which was a device used to project views onto a white sheet at the front of the room by means of a gas lamp. Magic lanterns preceded stereoscopes by more than a century, but it was not until the latter half of the nineteenth century that they were embraced by religious Americans as a popular mode of entertainment and instruction. Among earlier generations, magic lanterns were associated primarily with scientific and philosophical instruction, on the one hand, and bewitching devilry, on the other. Simultaneously earning a reputation as a "wonderful aid to pretenders" and an "optical and philosophical instrument," until the middle of the nineteenth century magic lanterns used painted lantern slides in all manner of exhibitions.[43]

The first technique to enable photographic lanternslides was developed at around the same time that magic lanterns began to gain a foothold as an acceptable mode of religious instruction. Among the earliest evidence of an emerging market of magic lantern views for religious instruction was in an advertisement in the *Episcopal Recorder* in October 1850 for McAllister and Company of Philadelphia. "Prepared to furnish Sabbath Schools and public Lecturers with MAGIC LANTERNS," McAllister listed "scripture subjects in sets packed in neat boxes" as well as in "separate views" and "views of the Holy Land, Palestine, etc." among a catalogue of other subjects, from temperance to natural history to "Comic Slides in almost an endless variety." McAllister was an agent of William and Frederick Langenheim, who just that year had devised a method of securing "views . . . taken from Nature on glass, by the Camera Obscura"—they called it a "yalotype"—by modifying William Henry Fox Talbot's calotype to produce a positive image on glass. The Langenheim process made it possible, for the first time, to produce photographic magic lantern slides.[44]

Associations between magic lantern slides and stereographic prints were nurtured in trade catalogues and in visual practices. But whereas magic lanterns had the advantage of corporate viewing—which was better suited for public lectures, whether religious, civic, or academic—the projected view nevertheless conditioned a quite different viewing experience for its beholders in terms not only of collectivity but also in removing the depth that was yielded through the scope. Still, stereograph manufacturers could use the same negatives for both magic lantern slides and stereoscopic prints. In the 1850s, for instance, the Langenheims of Philadelphia used half-stereos in their lantern work, and a decade later, advertising their extensive selection of "pictures on glass," E. & H. T. Anthony made them available "for either the LANTERN or the STEREOSCOPE."[45] Even if images shared visual content, the respective technologies conditioned different viewing experiences and visual subjectivities. Beholders' experiences of photographs were, in other words, not limited to the positive image itself, whether a paper print mounted on a piece of stock or a glass negative that produced a positive image when projected onto a white sheet. They were also shaped by the conditions in which such images were encountered.

How were magic lantern slides used as religious instruction? Jesse Lyman Hurlbut, who narrated the Underwood and Underwood Holy Land tour in 1900, had been giving popular illuminated sermons since at least 1893. His earlier lectures featured "slides" of well-known paintings—those of Félix-Joseph Barrias, Louis-Édouard Dubufe, Leonardo da Vinci, Heinrich Hoffman, and others—arranged into narratives such as "The Last Week" (his Easter sermon) and "The Holy Child" (his Christmas sermon), both of which were interspersed with selected hymns from the Methodist hymnal. For instance, notes for his "Illustrated Bible Reading and Song Service" on the Holy Child, which was given at least eighteen times between 1892 and 1916, enumerate thirty-five slides that illuminated the young Messiah's life from "The Sistine Madonna" to the "The Boy Jesus with the Commandments." Five songs peppered the lesson—such as when the Methodist anthem "How Firm a Foundation" was sung between slides of Raphael's *Madonna of the Chair* (1514) and William Charles Thomas Dobson's rendition of the return of the Holy Family to Nazareth (1857).[46]

Hurlbut was not alone. In the 1890s the Riley Brothers of England, whose American headquarters were in New York, fashioned what was perhaps the most lucrative trade in religious slides and embarked a campaign to win American churches' approval. A partial list of their "general lectures" on "Bible Lands and Bible Themes" for the magic lantern included series on "Wanderings in Bible Lands" (54 slides); Stories of Ruth, David, Solomon, Esther, and Moses, among others, ranging from a handful of slides to a couple dozen; "Manners and Customs of the East in the Times of Christ" (50 slides); "How We Got Our Bible," parts I, II, and III; "Women of the Bible" (18 slides); and a number of lectures centered on the Life of Christ and the Crucifixion, including "Ben-Hur" (72 slides), "The Life of Christ" (50 slides), "The Passion of Christ and the Acts of the Apostles" (44 slides), "The Passion of Our Lord" (34 slides), "The Stations of the Cross" (14 views), and "Christ on Calvary" (12 slides). Riley also provided slides of "words and pictures" for scores of "illustrated hymns," which consisted of three to ten slides per hymn. Large-type hymns and Roman Catholic hymns could be "hired separately."[47]

The Riley Brothers were by no means exclusive dealers in sacred subjects. Their catalogue listed hundreds of other series, from tours of Asia and Europe, to illustrated songs and stories, to "Educational, Historical, Scientific Lives, Etc.," to comic slides and "war sets." But in 1895 the firm issued a sixty-five-page booklet entitled *Solved; or, the Sunday Evening Problem*, which included nearly a dozen glowing essays by Protestant ministers across the country—Congregationalist, Methodist, Lutheran, Baptist, and Presbyterian—who had begun to incorporate lantern lectures into their Sunday evening services, as well as "specimen Sunday evening lantern services" complete with illustrated hymns and sermons "illustrated by . . . magnificent hand paints."[48] The hire list distributed a few years later indicated that subscribers could rent not only the slides and elaborate equipment but also lantern operators and, if circumstance demanded, an "experienced lecturer."[49] Churches seem to have foregone the latter in favor of the expertise of ministers and pastors who drew, as did Hurlbut in his Christmas sermon, upon the authority of verses cut and pasted from the pages of the New Testament into his notes to explain and interpret the slides.

Well before the 1890s, however, magic lanterns had been used in religious instruction, as Patton's 1872 lecture and McAllister's 1850 advertisement indicate. In addition to the shared visual content of stereographs and magic lanterns, each of these popular visual technologies was sanctioned through the narrative convention of travel. As media historian Charles Musser has argued, in the late nineteenth century, Passion plays, particularly that of Oberammergau, were accepted as public demonstrations through the authorizing mechanisms of travelogue. At a time when stage performances of sacred drama were under intense scrutiny and public censure—a correlative to the representational dilemmas in stereographs of Jesus—popular lecturers such as John Lawson Stoddard were able to present photographic lantern slides of live actors with great public support, including the adulation of the very clergy who so vociferously opposed the slides' theatrical counterparts. This support was extended at least as long as the performances were firmly established as medieval survivals, in Stoddard's estimation, akin to "the last sacred fire kindled on a neglected shrine by the ardent breath of simple piety."[50]

In December 1880, within a week of having successfully prevented the

   Beyond the Sense Horizon

New York premiere of Salmi Morse's *The Passion*—a "miracle play in 10 acts" that had enjoyed a brief run in San Francisco before it too succumbed to public outrage, with lead actor James O'Neill charged a heavy fine "for personating Christ"—"a fair-sized and very select audience" ambled over to Chickering Hall to hear Stoddard's account of the Bavarian miracle play, "still performed with all the simplicity and reverence of ancient days" and "abundantly illustrated" by fifty lantern slides "delineating the principle [*sic*] scenes of the drama."[51] Unlike the wares advertised by Riley, these slides were photographic. Although the actors were Catholic, including Joseph Maier, who played the part of Christ for several of the decennial performances at Oberammergau in the late nineteenth century, Stoddard was careful to situate the performance as a historical legacy that preceded the Protestant Reformation in order to quell the fever of contemporary anti-Catholic sentiment. Anticipating the discomfiture of his largely Protestant readers, for instance, in his written account Stoddard prefaced this episode, in a remarkably ecumenical tenor, by writing that "if our souls are responsive to all that is divinely great and pure in every form of faith, we can easily find ourselves in sympathy with those who see in this sacred drama a form of their religion, cherished through generations as a precious privilege, and hallowed by centuries of historical associations."[52] In addition to amplifying the play's historical connotations, Stoddard was also careful to distance the festivities at Oberammergau from the New York stage, writing that Morse's "so-called 'Passion Play' . . . has nothing whatever to do with this Play at Ober-Ammergau. That was a purely modern drama written by Mr. Salmi Morse, and possessing neither the music nor the text of the Bavarian play, nor even the arrangement of its parts, while it was of course wholly lacking in its remarkable religious traditions and historical association."[53] If the Passion play at Oberammergau was legitimized in part by its "remarkable religious traditions and historical associations," Stoddard's lantern exhibition was legitimized by his mode of presentation, namely, photographs and travelogue.

Beginning the lecture from the railway station in Munich, Stoddard took his audience by rail and carriage to the Bavarian hamlet of Oberammergau and then proceeded to give a tour of the "little village itself" before arriving at the play proper nearly a third of the way through the hour and a half demonstration. The travelogue genre was invoked in other ways as well. A month after his lectures in New York, Stoddard announced "a series of his illustrated souvenirs of foreign travel" at Central Music Hall in Chicago. "His plan . . . to make European tourists for the evening of his audiences" during the week-long series began in southern France and continued on to northern Italy,

Oberammergau, and "various interesting places in the German Fatherland," before jaunting to "the Orient" on Friday and Spain on Saturday.[54] Positioning the events at Oberammergau within a narrative of European and world travel was also at work in published editions of Stoddard's lectures. In his 1883 illustrated book *Red-Letter Days Abroad*, for instance, his account of the 1880 play, from which his earlier lectures were also drawn, comes between "Travels in Sunny Spain" and "The Cities of the Czar." By approaching the play as part of a longer travel experience rather than a self-contained moment, Stoddard was able to circumvent some of the charges leveled against stage performances even as he was able to draw on the cultural authority of photographic representation of live actors dramatizing the gospel narrative. In this way, even if Stoddard's use of photographs of Oberammergau was not quite the same as the Underwoods' stereographs of the Holy Land, both explicitly drew on the narrative convention of travelogue to introduce audiences to their photographs, rendering them participants in, rather than voyeurs of, sacred drama and sacred space.

Stoddard's lectures were also significant in that they were the first time photographs of actors representing Jesus were accepted by the American public. As Charles Musser writes, Stoddard's "bold step in showing a photographic representation of a man playing Christ" constituted "a notable and potentially hazardous departure from earlier lantern shows of the Passion that relied on paintings." But his success was limited, as the fracas around F. Holland Day's photographs twenty years later amply demonstrates. For Musser, it was the genre of travelogue, wherein Stoddard became not an author of the drama, as Morse had been for his ill-fated play, but an observer "that allowed him to claim objectivity" and thus secure public approval rather than opprobrium. Of course, Stoddard's lectures *were* crafted, and his status as an "observer" was just as charged as that of an "author." Despite the strategy of staging the lantern exhibit, with its cultural ties to education and religious instruction, combined with the narrative convention of the travelogue, "as a documentary account of this single sacred performance" at Oberammergau, Stoddard employed the empirical conceit of the camera to deflect from his narrative craft.[55] With the lecture's narrative driven by photographic slides carefully interpreted by Stoddard's lively commentary, moreover, the charges leveled against stage performances, namely, that of scriptural embellishment, were greatly circumscribed, despite the fact that it was still a commercial enterprise performed in public space. In short, the narrative and visual conventions of Stoddard's lantern exhibition animated a

Beyond the Sense Horizon

particular mode of viewing habits that legitimized his lecture and the photographs despite precedent to the contrary.

The connection between Stoddard's magic lantern exhibit and stereograph tours that cover similar terrain was further evinced by Stoddard's contemporary, Edward L. Wilson, editor of the *Philadelphia Photographer*. In 1880, the same year that Stoddard published his lantern lectures, Wilson published the sixth edition of his three-volume *Wilson's Lantern Journeys*, "a series of descriptions of journeys at home and abroad . . . for use with views in the magic lantern or stereoscope." The impetus behind his collection of "descriptions" was sparked by a conviction that "the magic lantern and the stereoscope would be much more enjoyable and instructive in their way if, when we are looking upon the lovely pictures which blessed photography produces for such instruments, we could also have at hand some little bits of information concerning the places and things we are viewing." Anticipating Hurlbut's comparison of stereographs and physical travel, moreover, Wilson confessed to having jotted down his commentaries during "the many long hours waiting for trains, and for . . . dinners at restaurants, and for servants to come after [he rang] the bell, and for things to move generally," inconveniences of physical travel that could now be avoided through the "lovely pictures which blessed photography produces." Thanks to these pictures, Palestine was toured in thirty slides, numbers 19 to 49 in Journey E, between Egypt and Constantinople.[56]

Wilson's strategy of complementing his photographs with instructive and situational commentary was repeated in stereographic tours, such as those authored by the Underwoods and by Jesse Lyman Hurlbut, and the practice reached a new level of collaboration between images and texts when Underwood and Underwood began to print excerpts from their commentaries on the reverse side of the stereographic cards in the early twentieth century. Beyond this practice of commentary, moreover, Wilson's lantern tour evinced important visual strategies of touring the Holy Land that were based on conventional overland routes and that were repeated in later, more popular stereographic series. Even if Wilson's views were made for both "instruments"—the stereoscope and the magic lantern—it is important here to underscore that the later stereographic tours were based on established visual conventions of the Holy Land no less than customary travel routes. Not all travelogues of the period followed the same route from the port at Jaffa in the south to Baalbek with its colossal ruins at the northern border. Mark Twain's journey in *The Innocents Abroad*, for instance, followed a reverse route from Baalbek to the port city, where his party of "strong, healthy men, accustomed somewhat to fatigue and rough life in the open air," were re-united with their less robust, seafaring companions.[57] And yet, the route from Jaffa through Jerusalem, Bethany, Bethlehem, and Nazareth, on north to Baalbek, was familiar enough, either in practice or in pictures, to become the dominant visual passage through the Holy Land in both lantern slides and stereographs. Take, for example, some of the numerous shared views, at least in name if not in vantage, between Wilson's lantern slides and later Underwood tours: Jaffa, "the Joppa of Bible Times"; Lydda; the Garden of Gethsemane and its grove of olive trees; the Mosque of Omar; the Church of the Holy Sepulchre; "The Wall of Solomon, or The Jews' Wailing-Place"; the Tomb of Rachel; Bethany; Bethlehem; Hebron; the Jordan, "where Christ was baptized"; Nazareth; the village of Tiberias on the Sea of Galilee; and Baalbek, "by many supposed to be the house of the forest of Lebanon, which Solomon built for his Egyptian wife."[58] Thus auditors of Hurlbut's lantern lectures on the life of Christ and the holy city of Jerusalem were likely to have had a sense of the established visual conventions of travel routes through the Holy Land, as well as the narrative convention of travelogue, each of which had been part of religious instruction for decades.

Of course, magic lantern lectures were not only delivered but also heard. No contemporary description of Hurlbut's lectures appears to have survived, but an *Independent* correspondent's eyewitness account of the "Georgian Oberammergau" he witnessed in October 1899 at the "negro settlement" in Ocalita, Georgia, gives some insight into the pageantry that unfolded. Writ-ten in a jocular tone from the vantage of a curious, nearly dismissive, north-ern white male onlooker, Edward Irenaeus Prime-Stevenson's plucky de-scription nevertheless describes a scene that wove aural and ocular, sacred and profane, reverent and comical, within a singular space and moment in time.[59] Here, we bear witness to ways in which magic lantern demonstrations conditioned distinct modes of viewing and beholding that were related to the visual practices at work in stereographs.

"Goliath Whistle's 'Celebrated Unique Biblical Perspective'" was held at St. Philip's AME Church, crowded and dim, with the light of a dozen oil lamps casting long shadows on the walls and the "familiar strong smell of lamp and soot" lingering in the close air. When the program began, Goliath Whistle's "deep voice boomed out of the darkness" and invited the audience to sing the National Anthem. As they sang the lights dimmed further until the only light in the room was the "round white disk on the screen" before them. And then the Perspective began. The first pictures were photographic

     Beyond the Sense Horizon

slides of President McKinley "and his amiable wife," who, incidentally, was also the subject of more than one Underwood and Underwood series.[60] Next followed more "portraits of our Chief Executives" from Washington through Lincoln, the "martyr President." Then came a series of "mechanical slides," which gave the illusion of movement through deft maneuvering of successive plates, a method similar to the "great mechanical picture" of the destruction of Jerusalem in Banvard's panorama half a century earlier. "And now the show grows biblical apace."

From Adam and Eve in the garden to the drowning of Pharaoh in the Red Sea to Daniel and Jonah, David and Saul, each of the thirty or more pictures of, in Prime-Stevenson's words, "the Old Testament's great actors and figures" were accompanied by "the familiar lyric of the plantations." As with panoramas, photobooks, and stereographs, Goliath Whistle's Celebrated Unique Biblical Perspective arranged visual cues to narrate biblical interpretation, using a familiar story to naturalize its sequence, all of which was performed to what are assumed to be variations of black spirituals in the highly sensorial theater of the darkened sanctuary. After an hour or more of this viewing and singing, Mr. Whistle intoned from behind the screen that "the last hour of our Biblical Perspective will be devoted to the blessed story of the life and death of Jesus Christ, our Divine Redeemer." When the pictures for this dispensation began, Prime-Stevenson noticed something different about the slides: "instead of the crude or commonplace representations by unskilled mechanics" exhibited earlier in the program, one was now seeing "faithful" reproductions "from the masterpieces of classic and modern religious art." "The effect was complete and profound," Prime-Stevenson wrote. "Sighs and sobs began to rise all over the dark building when Da Vinci's Cenacola and August Geiger's 'Betrayal,' and Munkaesy's [*sic*] spectacular 'Christ Before Pilate' appeared. There were low moans of 'O dear Lord!' 'O, the Precious Blood!' 'The Blessed Jesus!' as the Flagellation, by Sedoma, the Crucifixion according to Van Dyk's appalling work, and the Descent from the Cross, after Rubens, each appeared." "From first to last," Prime-Stevenson concluded, the Perspective's "religious power over that humble audience . . . and ourselves was sustained. It was plain that wherever it might go, it would be a kind of Oberammergau . . . with influences of grace and beautiful import."[61]

Comparing Goliath Whistle's magic lantern entertainment to the most famous Passion play in the nineteenth century, if hyperbole, nevertheless demonstrated the narrative power that such visual spectacles could wield in their beholder's devotional practices. Hurlbut's illustrated lectures most likely resembled the scene described by Prime-Stevenson in some key regards, even if we allow for the difference in mood that the selections of images, hymns, and commentaries would condition. Where it is likely that Hurlbut interspersed photographic views into earlier lectures, his later sermon on "Jerusalem, the Holy City," so closely resembles the text and sequence of *Traveling in the Holy Land through the Stereoscope* that it was almost certainly exclusively comprised of Underwood views. By the time of this lecture, Hurlbut's Underwood text had gone through three editions (1900, 1905, and 1909), and his notes closely correspond with the published volume. In his notes, however, we get a feel for how his lectures were adapted for different audiences over the next decade. Changes in sequence, for instance, are indicated by arrows and the instruction to "omit" in different shades of ink. In his notes, Hurlbut does not specify *how* he illustrated his sermons, but we can assume that he utilized the magic lantern instead of acquiring scopes for his entire audience, perhaps assuming that they were already familiar with the stereographs or ribbing them to go purchase the views after his lecture.[62]

Beholders of stereographs and magic lantern slides both experienced images as artifacts in particular circumstances of encounter that elicited different meanings and conditioned different relationships to biblical texts and scriptural knowledge. But the fact that each medium could be produced from common negatives points to the social biography of images, to the multiple terrains a single image could navigate across the cultural landscape of the turn of the twentieth century. And yet, the written word of the commentary and caption, the spoken word of the sermon, and the sung word of hymns each elicited different dynamics of image and text that informed the experiences of photographic encounters, which could vary from pew to pew as much as from church to church or parlor to parlor. In the final section of this chapter, I return to a closer examination of the interaction between images and texts in stereographs, keeping in mind that both the visual and the narrative content were informed by traditions of representation and interpretation.

Visual Archives of "the Word"

If the idea of the Holy Land was conditioned by a complex matrix of archaeological, historical, devotional, and theological imaginings, so too was the visual practice of stereography. Historian Shirley Wajda has argued that beholders of stereographs were equipped with a host of "situational cues" that provided them "with evidence to reconstruct the story line—the totality

Beyond the Sense Horizon

of assumptions and actions of the actors—encapsulated within one stereo-graphic frame."[63] Although it is difficult to parse the "totality of assumptions" in sacred series that deliberately aimed to displace the photographic contemporary in an effort to enter a sacred history that had been previously, in the words of Jesse Lyman Hurlbut, "unreal to us," stereographs of sacred series were nevertheless presented as complex artifacts containing visual cues of their intended interpretation.[64] The most apparent "situational cues" on the cards, even before extended commentary was printed on the reverse at the turn of the century, were the inclusion of biblical references, often printed on both the front and the back of the stereograph. The Underwoods' first guide-book did not include the kind of extensive scriptural cross-references that were included in later series volumes by Hurlbut and Forbush. On the sur-face these references suggest that the text was intended to determine what was beheld in the stereoscope and that there was a direct correspondence between text and image. On a second look, this visual archive of the Word reveals complexity within the communion of shadows.

In the introduction to the Perfecscope series, the Underwoods had writ-ten that "Bible references are freely given in [the] descriptions," but there was no uniformity in the citations, and many views were absent any specific biblical reference.[65] By the time *Travel Lessons on the Life of Christ* was pub-lished, however, both Hurlbut and Forbush had asked their would-be tour-ists to *first* identify and familiarize themselves with the corresponding bibli-cal reference either printed on the face of the stereograph, on the back of the stereograph, in the guidebook, or in a specified Bible lesson. "A most impor-tant point," Forbush declared, was "never [to] show a stereographed scene, seldom even distribute copies of it, until after you have told what it is." His reason was both pedagogical and theological. In the first instance, premature circulation of the cards ran the risk that "the scholar will get so interested in its details that he will forget what it is about."[66] But the effect of this "special hint" was indeed theological in at least two interrelated ways. First, related to Forbush's pedagogy, proper interpretation of the stereographs required that the visual field first be delimited by a scriptural proof. To be sure, the details of the composition were important for maximizing the visual effect of relief and solidity, but they were often considered by the guides (and, it seems, Sunday school teachers and Bible professors) to be incidental to the theological work the views were intended to perform. In other words, the pedagogical underpinning of Forbush's statement was linked to its theologi-cal potential—the views were indeed marvelous, but they required a studied gaze to be truly instructive. Second, and tantamount to the first, Forbush's caution against the lure of details suggests an interest by the Bible Department at Underwood and Underwood in establishing a veneer of perfect correspondence between photograph and biblical text in which the latter always explained the former and neatly circumscribed its interpretive possibility. The stereographs themselves, however, like Bain's photographs, often tell a different story. First, biblical references, perhaps to the consternation of churchly schoolmarms and ministers, did not *determine* interpretation even if they did work to situate the view within a beholder's theological paradigm. Second, in addition to this explicit verbal situational cue, there were more subtle interactions between the biblical text and the photographic image, wherein the latter was not merely a visual translation of the former but a constitutive component of its very substance.

Even as he wrote of being "very sad and solemn" as they stood in the footprints of Adam sunk into the red clay of "the Cave at Hebron where Adam and Eve hid themselves"—and mused that they "didn't see any rib laying round anywhere to represent Eve"—Elmer Underwood also indicated that the holiness of the Holy Land was to be created through the photographs themselves and not just something to be recorded through the lens, that the photographic contemporary was readily manipulated to more accurately disclose the biblical past. "We photographed Lazarus coming out of his tomb at Bethany," Elmer wrote of one of the "more impressive scenes" the brothers had taken during their month in Palestine. "Martha and Mary were there," and "we took Mary's baby away from her in order to have her pose in the picture." "Martha was not a very shapely woman," he continued, "but it won't show in the photograph."[67] Writing three years after Bain and Lee returned from their travels, Elmer may have been making a subtle jab at the suckling infant in Bain's photograph of Lazarus's tomb (see fig. 32).

Elmer Underwood's veiled critique of his own photographic project frames the practice of viewing stereographs as an imaginative process that posited an immediate link with the Holy Land—itself an indefinite place in an imaginative space—even as it obscured the range of visual, conceptual, and theological habits that invested the view with meaning. Certainly it is important to recognize the correspondence between image and text that these views assumed through such situational cues as biblical references and extended commentary. And yet there was nevertheless a superabundance of visual information—often in the form of "Arab" figures—that suggests a more complicated form of visual piety than direct correspondence between photographic image and biblical text.[68] Stereographs of the Holy Land surfaced a convergence of photographic realism, scriptural authority, and biblical geography in the seven-inch-by-three-inch card, a matrix of signification that eludes simple parsing or causal analysis. What is more, this interdependence of words and images began before the view was ever placed in the scope.

In the view entitled "Unclean! Unclean!"—taken by Elmer and Bert in April 1896 and included as part of their tours for more than two decades—we see this negotiation between photographic images and biblical text at work in the lifting of "wretched people" from their present circumstance into a devotional context that resignified them as indices of the beholders' piety. The view would call to the mind's eye of some beholders Bain's photograph "Dervish Beggars" which came a little more than halfway through *Earthly Footsteps* and which was used to illustrate 1 Chronicles 28:9 in *The Self-Interpreting Bible*. In the first text, the photograph was used specifically to mount a critique of the "Mohammedans" who "have reduced begging to a science." In his caption, Lee wrote that the "two sad-looking creatures . . . represent a large class of Moslems who account it a thing of merit to renounce earthly comfort," adding that "it is an easy thing to lose the first impulses and convictions which the truth inspires, and to allow selfishness and avarice to use the outward signs of the good for the accomplishment of evil."[69] In the Photographic Bible, the image now titled "Dervish Beggars—Such as Stand and Beg in the Holy City Where Solomon Lived and Reigned," the critique is more cautionary than indicting. "We give a view of Dervish beggars such as are found to-day in Jerusalem," the caption reads, "and they serve to illustrate what comes to people when they violate the laws of God. The most wretched and inhuman looking creatures we have ever seen are found among the beggars of Palestine. They are diseased, degraded, and as miserable as humanity with the dregs of generations of sin can make them." Although there was some recognition that their "degradation . . . is perhaps due in some respect to the tyrannical, remorseless and outrageous Turkish civilization under which they live," the unfortunate state of the dervish beggars was less a matter of accident than Providence.[70]

The Underwood counterpart to Bain's beggars was published in at least three series between 1897 and 1914. In the view, three figures, two young and one old, sit on rocky earth against a stone wall, their knees bent up toward their chests and their hands out with palms facing upward. In the Perfecscope view of the "wretched lepers outside Jerusalem," the Underwoods described with a disdainful curiosity the "deformed and decaying creatures . . . suffering the torture of an untold hopeless misery which is finally to be relieved only by the merciful hand of death." After describing the biblical sig-

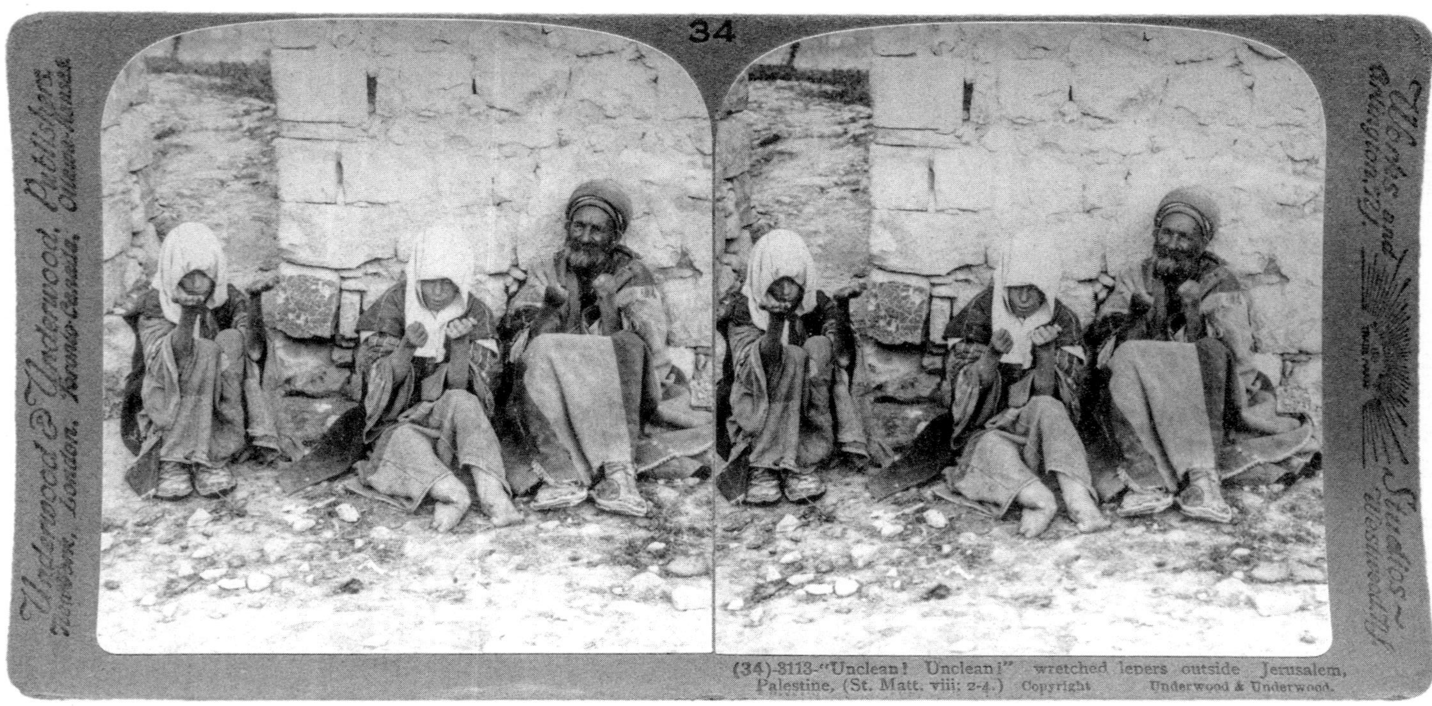

Figure 41. "'Unclean! Unclean!' wretched lepers outside Jerusalem, Palestine (St. Matt. viii: 2–4)." Copyright 1897 by Underwood and Underwood. Author's collection.

nificance of the disease in the laws of Moses as well as the prognosis of those afflicted, they conclude that it is "incurable except by the divine hand" and, moreover, "is verily typical of the sin of the world." They then pointed their readers to the seventeenth chapter of Luke for scriptural corroboration.[71] The view was subsequently also issued as part of the Holy Land tour conducted by Jesse Lyman Hurlbut and in William Byron Forbush's *Travel Lessons on the Life of Christ*, a Bible study system designed by Forbush "to enable the student to get close to Jesus, to see Him" through stereographic helps.[72]

In the case of "Unclean! Unclean!" the situational cue of the biblical reference, which by the reed of St. Matthew told of a leper who was healed by his faith and instructed to "tell no man; but go thy way, shew thyself to the priest . . . for a testimony unto them," was accompanied by further interpretive work in the commentary. In *Traveling in the Holy Land*, Hurlbut jumped from a command to "look at the stumps of hands from which the fingers have dropped off! See those twisted and deformed feet!" to an analysis of leprosy substantiated by further biblical reference. Why had lepers been "shut out of the cities," and why do they "live by themselves in loathsome communities"? Look at 2 Kings. Echoing both James Lee and Underwood in his appropriation of the afflicted Muslim bodies as salves for Catholic and Protestant souls, he announced that "there is no more cure now than there was in Naaman's day," although he reassured that the infected "never attempt to touch the passer," in effect soothing the anxieties of potential pilgrims through a buffer of physical distance.

In Forbush's commentary, we learn that these lepers are actually sitting outside the wall at Gethsemane, physically in close proximity and yet metaphorically, through their somatic condition, at great distance from the pageantry of redemption enacted within the wall. As with his predecessors, Forbush too instructs his pupils that "we need this horrible sight to make plain to us the awfulness of misery and sin to which Jesus ministered." But Forbush complicated the matter further when he added that "the disobedience and ingratitude of the leper mark his disfigurement as one of soul as well as of body." Such a statement raises doubts about whom the figures in the view are made to represent. Are they metaphors, visible signs, of the beholder's own sin? Do they refer to the "heathen" occupying the Holy Land, disfigured in body and soul by their disbelief and banned beyond the wall of redemption? Can they refer to both? In demonstrating the effects of this rendering in the Philippines, David Brody recounts the sensationalist story of William Lapeer, a soldier who was reputedly injected with a "leper's blood" as he lay unconscious. The story ran in an 1899 issue of the *World* entitled "The Revenge of the Filipino," and Brody uses it to address nationalist anxieties that pivoted on threats of blood contamination, an issue that was evidently on the front of Hurlbut's mind as well when he allayed readers' fears of the touch of lepers.[73] Thus, whereas vernacular photographs such as stereographs often suggest a collaboration between image and text that hints at direct correspondence, the deceptive clarity of situational cues masked an underlying thicket of entangled visual messages.[74]

Holy Land tours and stereographic Bible study lessons offered one context for situating the issue of correspondence between biblical text and photographic image in late nineteenth-century America. Another genre of stereograph that was first published in the late 1860s constituted a more explicit framework for exploring these associations. Whereas stereographs shared representational strategies and narrative conventions of panoramas, volumes of photomechanical prints, and magic lantern slides, none of these other techniques made the physical artifact of the Bible itself the compositional subject of their views. After the Civil War, as northern Americans began to reinvent a national heritage through regional histories, W. S. Robbins of Plymouth, Massachusetts, began issuing an irregular series of *Plymouth Views* consisting predominately of seventeenth-century Separatist artifacts, including a "Pot and Platter which belonged to Miles Standish" and "the gun-barrel with which King Phillip was killed," as well as gravesites of early New England magistrates and ministers. Among the views for purchase was one featuring a "Mug and Wallet which belonged to Thos. Clarke and a Bible brought over in the Mayflower" (fig. 42). Another stereograph in the series identifies Clarke himself as a "mate of the Mayflower," which would indicate that the Bible, too, belonged to Clarke. But at the time the stereograph was produced, there was considerable debate about Clarke's passage on that blessed vessel.[75]

The earliest known record of Thomas Clarke in Plymouth is July 1623 — three years after the *Mayflower* weighed anchor—when the twenty-four-year-old arrived on board the *Anne*. Clarke's impressive lifespan, ninety-eight years at a time when most never saw the hither side of sixty, no doubt encouraged his association with the *Mayflower* amid the political, mercantile, and religious tumults of the turn of the eighteenth century.[76] The stereograph produced nearly two centuries after Clarke's death, however, raises different questions about the claims to historical narratives that such material artifacts could make through their visual reproduction. In an 1869 genealogy, Thomas's descendant Samuel C. Clarke noted that among "the collection of relics at Forefathers' Hall, Plymouth, is a china mug and leather

   Beyond the Sense Horizon

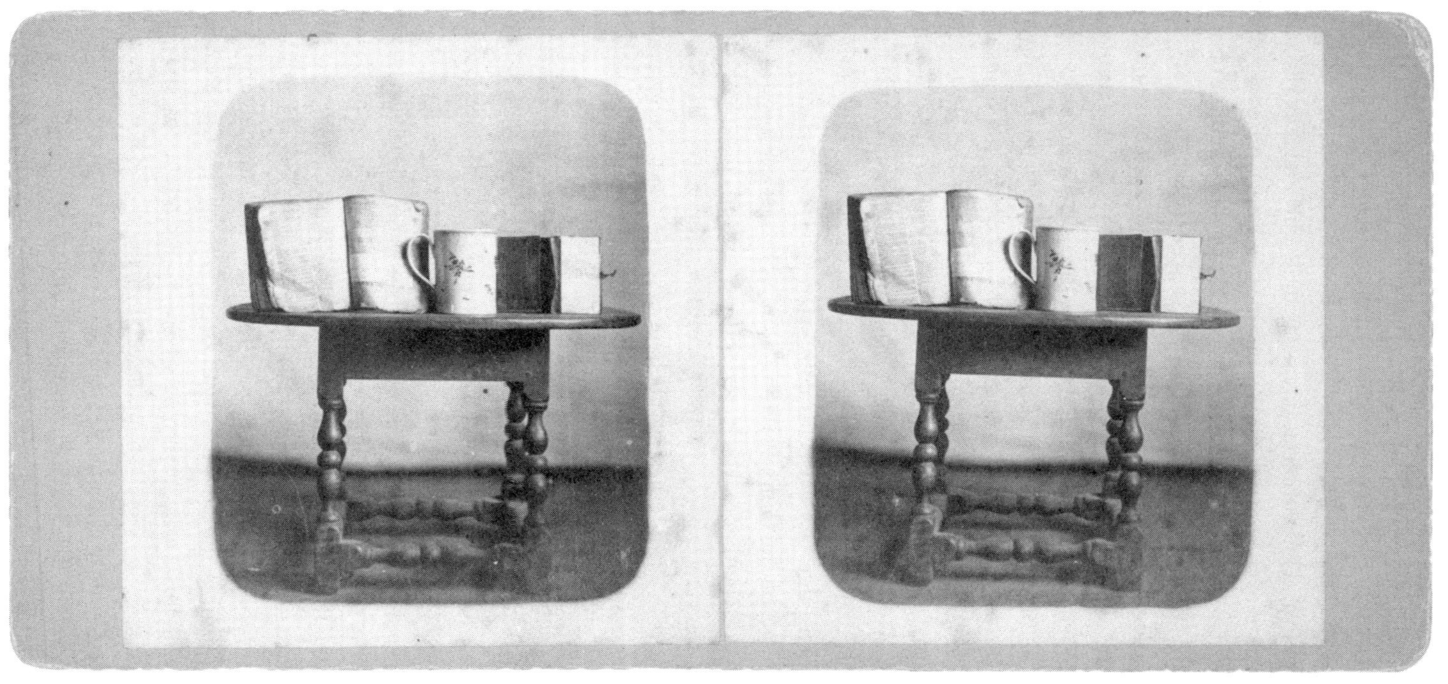

Figure 42. "Mug & wallet which belonged to Thos. Clark and a Bible brought over in the Mayflower." The Miriam and Ira D. Wallach Division of Art, Prints and Photographs. Photography Collection, New York Public Library.

wallet bearing the name of Thomas Clarke."[77] Adding a Bible to these "relics" enabled him to affirm Clarke's legacy as a "mate of the *Mayflower.*" It also spoke to a larger cultural effort to generate new regional identities grounded in the imaginative spaces of "Old New England" at a time when immigration, urbanization, and industrialization changed the cultural, religious, and political landscapes of the post–Civil War decades. Indeed, without uttering a word, rather than subordinating the view to textual illustration, Robbins used the stereographed Bible as a proof text to Yankee legacy.[78]

Robbins's stereograph of the *Mayflower* Bible was used to make historical claims about New England piety and culture. But it was an exception. Most views of opened Bibles — in this genre, the Bibles are seldom closed — are presented as timeless artifacts, carefully adorned, perhaps, but absent any specified historical identity.[79] A number of views from the 1860s and 1870s feature ornamented Bibles opened to the Psalms or the New Testament gospels. In one view from the prominent New York establishment of Edward and Henry T. Anthony entitled "Open Bible," the Holy Writ became an object of deliberate inspection and display. An 1865 catalogue of Anthony views lists "Open Bible" as "Miscellaneous" view No. 1470, between "The Suspension Bridge, on the Ohio, at Wilmington" (No. 1415) and "The Good Friends" (No. 1526), neither of which appear to be categorically related, thus indicating that the view was not part of a narrative sequence.[80] The stereograph below bears the same title and label but is sequenced as No. 7023, indicating a later circulation than the catalogue listing, although it is possible that the later view came from the same negative. A pair of spectacles drapes over the verso page — a prop used in a number of Bible views — which has been opened to Psalms 144 through 146. A decorated placard with the phrase "Search the Scriptures" (a silent nod to the Gospel of John) ensconced in a scroll loosely encircling the vertical arm of a cruciform covers the recto page of the opened Bible. These props effectively obscure the biblical text.[81] Two candles, with flames flickering from their wicks, sit in their holders in the foreground of the view, one in front of each page of the opened text. The entire assemblage sits on a two-tone floral spread, and patterned fabric hangs behind. When placed in the stereoscope, the relief between the curtain in back, the upright Bible, the candles, and the front edge of the table becomes distinctly discernible. By using textured patterns, contrastive tones, and multiple vertical planes, this view exhibits several of the tactics used by producers of stereographs to enhance the optical effects of depth and solidity.

But why a Bible? The text is not legible through the scope, and it is doubtful that Anthony intended beholding the view to be an equal substitute

    Beyond the Sense Horizon

for Bible study. At first blush, it seems as though the view could be a visual affirmation of the cultural role Bibles played in fomenting bourgeois American identities over the course of the nineteenth century. At least one historian of American photography early noticed the parallel cultural space—if not final significance—that Bibles and stereoscopes played in American domestic spheres.[82] But such a functionalist interpretation does not explain the obvious instruction to "search the Scriptures," an injunction that points less to middle-class aesthetics than to personal piety. A view published by L. E. Walker of Warsaw, New York, entitled "The Bible Lesson," affirms the instructive impetus of stereographed Bibles. As part of their series *Pleasing Studies for Our Young Folks*, the Bible in this view stands vertically on a Moresque tablecloth, propped against a horizontal text with a cross, wreathed in ivy, rising from behind. As with the Anthony view, the pages are opened to a specific page, the cloth page marker draping the left margin of the verso page suggesting a deliberate selection of Luke chapter 11, the first four verses of which are the Lord's Prayer.

Curiously, the prayer itself, which is recited by Jesus in Luke and in Matthew, was also the compositional subject of stereographs in the 1870s, such as Kilburn Brothers' view No. 222, "The Lord's Prayer" (fig. 44). In this rather uninteresting view, the longer prayer from the Gospel of Matthew has been printed onto a plain white placard and propped against a bed of White Mountain snow. The visual relief is apparent, but the subtlety of the monochromatic composition warrants consideration of the view not for its visual effects but for its textual content. Thus it would seem, in this instance at least, that the stereograph of the Word—taken verbatim from the pages of Matthew—is directed toward a particular viewing practice rather than the dimensional effects of stereoscopy. In other words, stereographs of Bibles and their words were used to different effects by different producers. But each instance was nevertheless calculated to the visual habits that stereographic viewing conditioned—to positioning beholders within the biblical event. Rather than facilitating a correspondence between photographic image and biblical text, such images used the power of the photograph to encompass beholders within the pages of the Bible itself.

Stereographs of Bibles and Bible verses, in short, gesture to the mutual operation of icon and relic in the communion of shadows. One example is the Kilburn Brothers view "One Hundred and Thirty-Third Psalm," from the 1870s. In this view the Bible is surrounded by ice—one of Benjamin Kilburn's favorite optical effects—and seems to be held open by a square and compasses. When viewed through the scope, however, it becomes clear

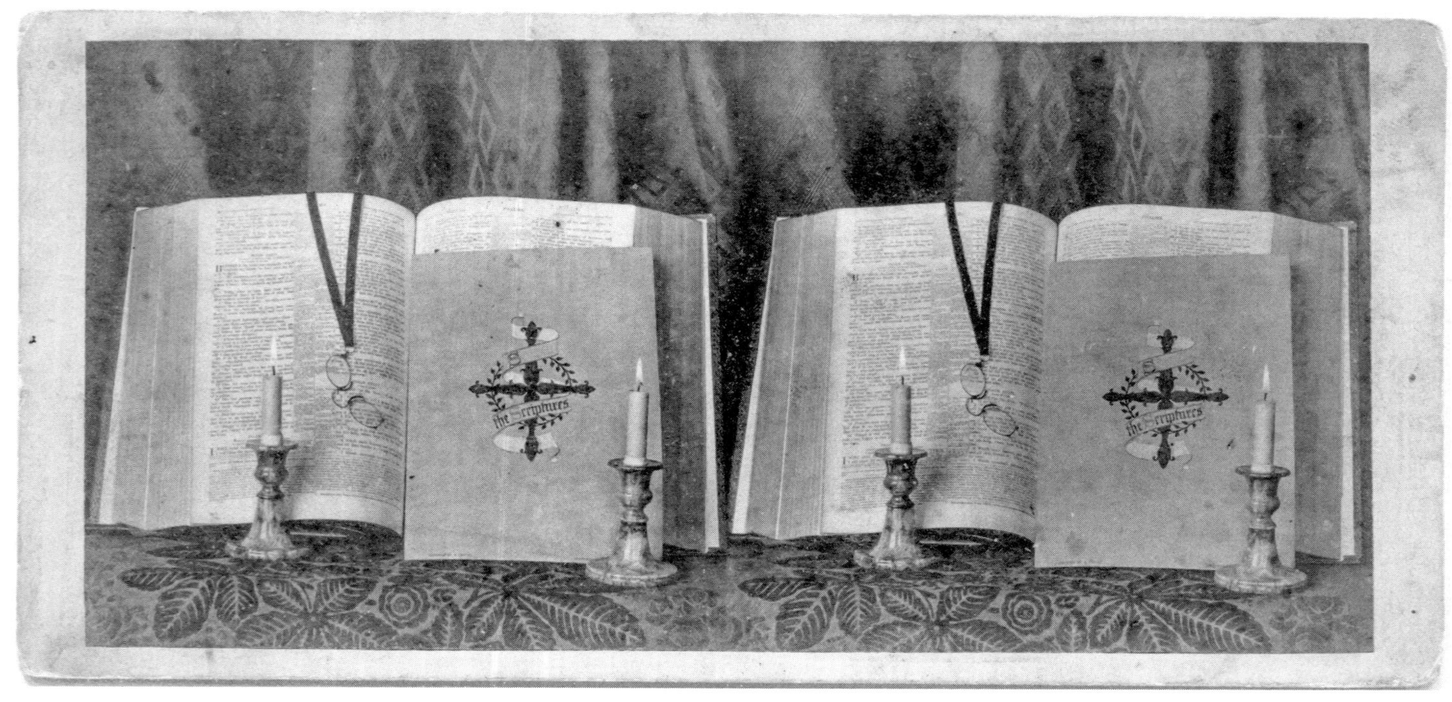

Figure 43. "Open Bible." Anthony's Stereoscopic Views No. 7023, E. & H. T. Anthony and Co., ca. 1865. Author's collection.

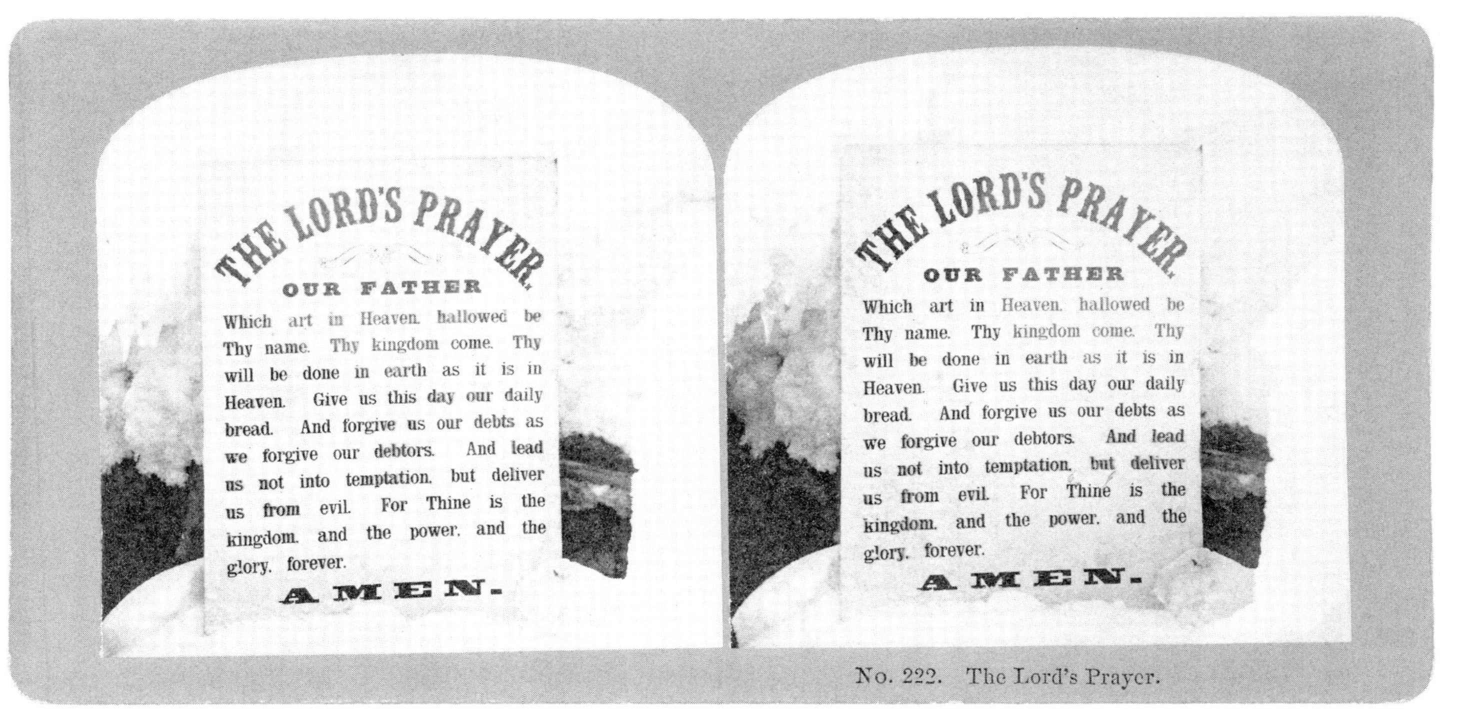

Figure 44. Kilburn Brothers, "No. 222. The Lord's Prayer," n.d. (ca. 1875). Graphic Arts Collection, Princeton University Library. Used with permission.

that the square and compasses are in fact suspended in front of the opened Bible. The stereograph is a photographic quotation of Masonic "hieroglyphs" printed in earlier Masonic charts—it is, in short, a catalogue of icons. The three objects—Bible, square, and compasses—constituted the "Great Lights by which a [Freemason] must walk and work," according to the *Morals and Dogma*, first published by Grand Commander Albert Pike in 1871.[83] As with "so many oath-bound men" at the turn of the century, Benjamin Kilburn had joined more than one fraternal society: in addition to being a member of the Ancient Free and Accepted Masons, he was also a member of the Independent Order of Odd Fellows and of Post No. 48 of the Grand Army of the Republic, a society established for Union veterans of the American Civil War that, like its contemporary organizations, departed from earlier and later veterans' societies in its emphasis on ritual, including "elaborate successions of initiatory degrees."[84] Among both Odd Fellows and Freemasons, the Holy Bible played an important ritual role. "No Lodge can transact its business," wrote J. F. Newton for the Masonic Service Association in 1924, "much less initiate candidates into its mysteries, unless the Book of the Holy Law lies open upon its altar." Although Newton was ambiguous about the origins of the Bible in Masonry, he wrote that "students have traced about seventy-five references to the Bible in the Ritual of the Craft" and noted that, more important than the "direct references," was "the fact that the spirit of the Bible, its faith, its attitude toward life, pervades Masonry."[85]

Newton was writing well into the twentieth century, but the "direct references" to which he referred are evident much earlier. In *The True Masonic Chart, or Hieroglyphic Monitor*, published by A. S. Barnes and Company in 1854, a line drawing under the "Section Third" of the Entered Apprentice Degree depicts an opened text with an inverted square intersecting opened compasses. Along the uppermost margin of the book is "Psalm CXXXIII."[86] Flipping past the hieroglyphs to the text, Right Worthy Jeremy Cross explained that "the third section" of the Entered Apprentice Degree of the American Rite "explains the nature and principles of our Constitution" and departs "instructions relative to the *form, supports, covering, furniture, ornaments, lights,* and *jewels* of the Lodge." Agreeing with Pike's account of the Ancient and Accepted Rite, the order in which Kilburn had been initiated, Cross wrote that "every well-governed Lodge is furnished with the *Holy Bible,* the *Square,* and the *Compasses*" and further explained that "the Holy Bible is dedicated to God; the Square, to the Master; and the Compasses, to the Craft."[87]

Nothing in Cross's "lecture," however, or in the "CHARGE at Initiation

                                                        Beyond the Sense Horizon

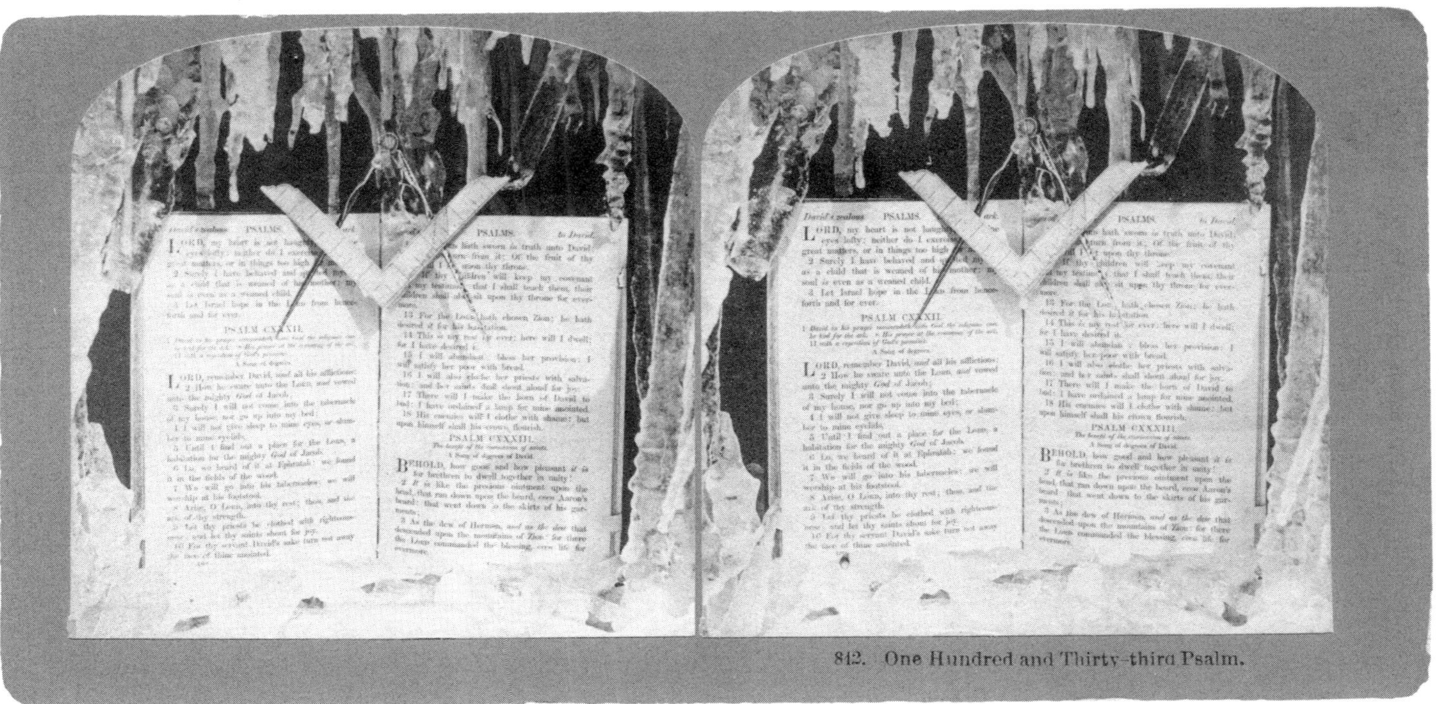

Figure 45. Kilburn Brothers, "842. One Hundred and Thirty-third Psalm," n.d. (ca. 1875). Author's collection.

into the First Degree" mentioned the significance of Psalm 133. On one level, the association is obvious. The first verse of this "Song of degrees of David" reads, "Behold, how good and how pleasant *it is* for brethren to dwell together in unity!" and appears to have been used in sermons directed toward fraternal audiences, as when Edward Abraham Foggo, rector of Christ Church in Philadelphia, chose the verse in his sermon on "the value of organization, and the true method to preserve it in perfection," which he delivered to the "members and officers" of the Right Worthy Grand Lodge of the Independent Order of the Odd Fellows on September 17, 1876.[88] But as all brethren would have known, the true meaning of the verse was hidden from view—Foggo was not an Odd Fellow—and to assume such a transparent interpretation was either folly or hubris. While not all views of open Bibles fell into the same analytic paradigms as the fraternal orders, the practices of deliberate selection of a scriptural passage and adornment are found in a number of views that have no obvious connection to Masons or the Odd Fellows. As an image that referred to something beyond itself, for photographers such as Benjamin West Kilburn and Edward and Henry Anthony, stereographs of Bibles encapsulated a sort of iconicity in the visual landscape of nineteenth-century America.

But these stereographs also beckoned beholders to look beyond what they were *of* and to pay attention to what they were. In a word, these stereographs were not only pictures of Bibles. *They were Bibles.* Stereographs of Bibles lacked the twists of human hair, pressed flowers, mourning badges, and other mementos that were folded into their three-dimensional counterparts. But these artifacts nevertheless prompted meditations on materiality and presence in such a way that reinforced the materiality of Bibles and photographs. The stereographs were not meant to be read but to be seen and touched. They were not to be studied as scripture but inspected as objects. Through their physical encounter, beholders were confronted with the sensorial experiences of perception even as they calibrated these experiences to registers of corporeal transcendence. In other words, they invited meditation on the artifact's position in time and space, as a fragment of something thought to be absent, despite competing interpretive cues that rendered the photograph as a transparent void. When they are recognized as relics no less than icons of religious practice, stereographs of Bibles become less curious and more emblematic of the complexity within the communion of shadows.

Turn-of-the-twentieth-century celebrations of photography, and especially stereography, as a medium charged with making the Bible real reveal a culture of disclosure that rendered physical objects, available to the senses,

Beyond the Sense Horizon

as fragments of a biblical imaginary that had been, according to Jesse Lyman Hurlbut, critically displaced both temporally and geographically. The visual archives of "the Word" refer to the strategies of narrativization that incorporated visual and verbal into a single, if multivalent and unstable, artifact and can be seen in different modes in stereographs of the Holy Land, the Life of Christ, and the Bible as a physical artifact. The circumstances of beholding and claims to interpretive authority varied from medium to medium — stereographs, magic lanterns, and panoramas each boasted different stakes — that were in no small part related to the corporeal experiences of spectatorship. And yet each evinced a relationship to words, and to the Word in particular, that bound them into a common archive. Far from being auxiliary to bibliocentric reading practices, the communion of shadows enabled Americans to enter the biblical text and walk among the apostles.

How Mr. Eastman Changed the Face of American Religion

On Tuesday, March 20, 1900, the *Los Angeles Times* ran an inconspicuous advertisement on a crowded page for S. G. Marshutz, an optician and supplier of photographic materials on Spring Street. "We Place on Sale Today a New Eastman Kodak, 'The Brownie,' at $1.00 Each."[1] It had been more than a decade since George Eastman, the tinkering banker from Rochester, New York, had "perfected" the "little rollholder breast camera" that substituted paper negative film for glass plates and paved the way for a generation of picture *takers* by distinguishing them from picture *makers*.[2] The age of the button pusher had arrived. By providing a product that enabled consumers to take pictures and then mail the exposed film to Rochester for development, Eastman effectively bifurcated the production of photographs into ostensibly distinct processes to great commercial success. Despite meteoric success and the launch of an international distribution market, however, Kodak sales during the first decade were largely limited to an affluent clientele. The Brownie changed that. "So simple they can be operated by any school boy or girl," as a widely printed advertisement promised, the Brownie was also very affordable. Earlier Kodaks had been loaded with film for 100 exposures, which, when completed, were sent back to Rochester, camera and all, for development, printing, and reloading. These were the "detective cameras" that Robert E. M. Bain had deplored as "base imitation" ten years earlier.[3] The Brownie was loaded for six exposures measuring 2¼ by 2¼ inches—for an additional fifteen cents—and marketers were quick to clarify that, despite its diminutive size and simple operation, the camera "takes perfect pictures . . . and is no toy."[4]

The history of vernacular photography in the nineteenth century is not a prehistory to the Kodak. The decades that preceded were rich with innovation and adaptation, and as this book has shown, the communion of shadows was a diffuse traffic more than a direct route from one point to another. But the introduction of a simple-to-operate, affordably priced camera did profoundly influence the cultural practices of photography in the United States. As the new face of vernacular photography, Kodak culture continued in a long tradition of visual habits in the communion of shadows. It was also a turning point in the history of photography that warrants a new page.

The commercial success of Kodak marks a moment when, for the first time, the ability to *take* pictures was attainable for a wide range of socioeconomic, regional, and ethnic populations. Curators and scholars have been tempted to associate this technological development with unprecedented documentation of Americans' quotidian experiences. The association between the snapshot, spontaneity, and the instantaneous record of American life was articulated as early as 1944 by Willard D. Morgan, then director of photography at the Museum of Modern Art, in the catalogue for a "folk art" exhibit on "the American snapshot": "For some fifty years now the hand-held camera, with its instantaneous shutter, has been recording the American scene in infinite, spontaneous detail—the new baby, the family group, the home, friends, small and large adventures, discoveries. . . . Today it is possible for everyone to know what it means to see, to enjoy, and to capture for re-enjoyment the outward essence of a moment."[5] Morgan's effort to reevaluate snapshots as folk art was matched by contemporary efforts, including those within his own institution, to embrace street photography, social photography, and the larger catalogue of "documentary" photography as indices of experience and prompts for political action. Government-commissioned documentary projects in the 1930s and early 1940s were launched to document areas in need of relief but quickly turned into political projects that exceeded their commission. Drawing on a tradition of social photography that reached back to the 1880s with Jacob Riis's negatives of tenement life among New York's immigrant populations and the early 1900s with Lewis Hine's portraits of child labor, "photo leagues" from New York to San Francisco were created that wed a documentary photopolitics with an aesthetic of the everyday. Instead of signaling a rupture from the communion of shadows, these twentieth-century efforts were consanguine with habits of beholding that had been tendered through devotional and theological no less than social and political channels. The moral framework of twentieth- and twenty-first-century documentary photography, in its many instantiations, is heir to the nineteenth-century communion of shadows.

That history is another book, but it is instructive here to consider how these threads also contribute to curatorial and scholarly efforts to bridge the presumed spontaneity of snapshots with their "highly significant form of self expression."[6] Stephanie Snyder, for instance, has written that the "origin and genius of the vernacular American photo album," an artifact generated by "everyday photographers," coincided with the marketization of Kodak in 1888—an assessment that denies the possibility of vernacular albums prior to the introduction of the technologies of the 1880s. More to the point, Terry Toedtemeier has claimed that "the Kodak camera marked the beginning of a new era in photography: that of the snapshot," and Douglas Nickel affirmed similar interpretive correlations in a late twentieth-century exhibit at the San Francisco Museum of Modern Art.[7] By positing connections between spontaneity, transparency, and authenticity, this curatorial model both exaggerates the probability of spontaneity—the briefest encounter with turn-of-the-twentieth-century snapshots betrays awareness of the camera's presence—and reinforces the interpretive assumption of immediacy that obscures the thingness of photographic artifacts. Even as these snapshots have been carefully exhibited in museum displays, their material existence has often been subordinated to the images they convey—"a bridal couple dashing through a rain of rice" and "an English bulldog giving the Bronx cheer from the doorway."[8] And to the extent that the thingness of the image is a shadow of its beholder, the singular concern with the subject matter of images collapses the history of beholding into the sensibilities of the modern museumgoer.

For Americans at the turn of the twentieth century, the possibility that their whimsical Kodaks would ever be displayed in a New York museum likely crossed few minds. While snapshots could be archived in or affixed to any variety of artifacts, from serving trays to wine cabinets, the snapshot album became the most ubiquitous place to encounter amateur photographs in the years leading up to the Great War. Photograph albums had, of course, been around since the early 1860s. Albums, moreover, were modeled after commonplace books, souvenir albums, and even quilting and other varieties of domestic handicraft that had been around since the mid-thirteenth century.[9] What changed was the degree to which photographs were now archived as narrative cues. Still thoroughly tactile sensorial artifacts, snapshots nevertheless became more closely identified with what David Morgan has defined as the "token" operation of material culture. "A token . . . occludes, shapes, or highlights memories that the owner of the token wants to remember," he explains, and as such, the token "constructs any number of visual fields—occlusive, aversive, or devotional—depending on what story

Epilogue

the owner wishes to tell."[10] Unlike a relic that purports to disclose the past through its very existence, the token is fully dependent on a narrative structure to convey its meaning. All modes of commonplace photography in the communion of shadows promoted narratives, from ancestral pedigree to the drama of redemption. But the physical arrangement of snapshot albums, in particular, transformed the visual politics of photographic beholding. A loose page from an early twentieth-century album demonstrates the shift (fig. 46). Four snapshots are carefully arranged on a black paper page, and unlike previous albums, someone has captioned the images in white crayon. The arrangement of photographs and script tells the story of a trip to Leavenworth, Kansas, in 1921. The narrative is integral to the arrangement rather than imputed through conditioned acts of beholding.

Ironically, at the same moment that the premier authorizing mechanism in American culture shifted from the autograph to the photograph—consider, for instance, how Anthony's National Daguerreotype Gallery had required signatures to authenticate the "counterfeit presentments" of Congress in the early 1840s against the increasingly common practice of using photographs to authenticate identification in the 1890s—Americans were ever more conscious of the orchestrated semiotics of identity at work in photographic likenesses.[11] In other words, even as photographs came to authorize identity, they were simultaneously recognized for their ability to confuse identity. The bottom right photograph on the album page (fig. 46) demonstrates the ambiguity that the reputedly spontaneous and transparent snapshot often nurtured. Below the photograph of a person in a black suit and hat holding a shotgun, the compiler scribbled a question: "Can you guess he or she?"[12]

Mr. Eastman changed the face of American religion by extending the communion of shadows into new horizons of photographic production. His invention neither broke from nor categorically replaced previous modes of photographic beholding, but it did contribute to a broader visual politics that took root in a variety of new photographic interests, from news photography to documentary projects to household cameras. In the twentieth century, missionaries packed cameras and documented their toils in foreign lands; families catalogued baptisms and holidays; the faithful captured apparitions of saints and ghosts as they appeared in the course of their daily lives. Document. Catalogue. Capture. These are the verbs of a visual order confident in the empirical conceit of the camera. It is tempting to argue that the photographic technologies of the twentieth century introduced a new politics of visual agency. On the one hand, photographs of people, in particular, were

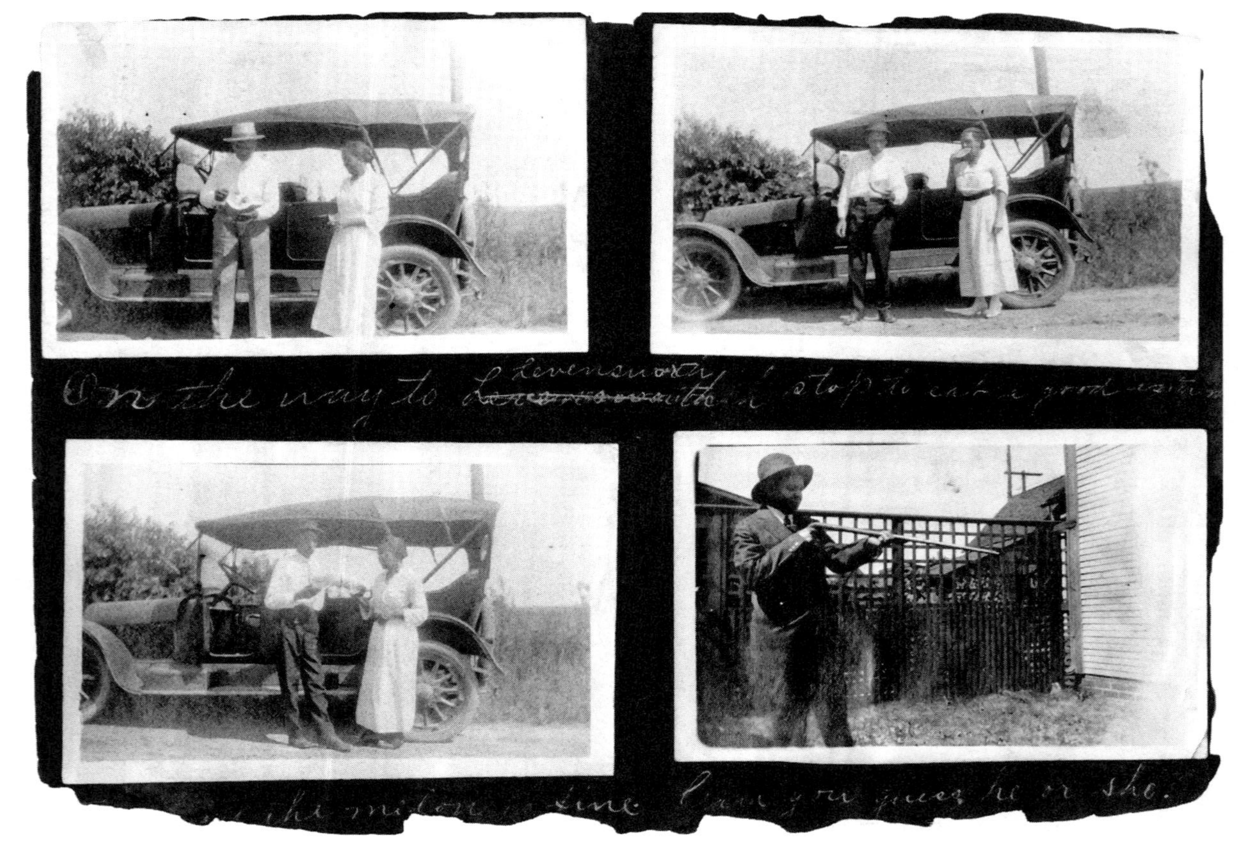

Figure 46. Loose page from album, ca. 1921. Katherine G. Lederer Ozarks African American History Collection, Special Collections and Archives, Missouri State University. Used with permission.

increasingly identified as authenticating mechanisms of truth, an interpretive dynamic that had been coursing through the medium for decades. But on the other, photographic techniques were becoming recognized and celebrated as artistic processes that disrupted the empirical calculus of observation and reportage. Kodak culture thrived at this mercurial impasse. These photographs reported *and* orchestrated. They documented *and* they devised. They were at once heirs of generations of vernacular photographic viewing habits and rebellious offspring who held aspirations unimaginable to their forebears. Amateur photography created the conditions necessary for quotidian circumstances to become common subject material. Yet the truly banal was rarely photographed unless it was framed to suggest something beyond itself. Eating a meal signified conviviality rather than daily sustenance; baby pictures spoke to the fecundity of one's lineage or the nostalgia of youth rather than to the daily toils of childrearing. Whereas the quotidian in earlier photographic modes was largely defined by circumstances of encounter, after 1900 the quotidian itself was often on display—and defined through these compositional frames—in ways that previously orchestrated domestic scenes anticipated but never accomplished on the scale that snapshots enabled.

A Communion of Shadows has worked to identify a place in our studies of American religious history to approach nineteenth-century vernacular photographs as historical artifacts that not only signified but also worked to disclose. It has asked historians to approach photographs in the way that nineteenth-century Americans did—as complicated and often contradictory material artifacts that navigated between imagined pasts and anticipated futures, that simultaneously affirmed the sensorial conditions of perception and subordinated the senses to truths coded in photographic referents, that traversed contexts of display and encounter as deftly as they conditioned sophisticated habits of beholding. But even as it has advocated for historians to recognize photographs as relics no less than icons, this book has also interrogated the relationship between material culture, analytics of the quotidian, and religious experience. In this regard, recognizing the materiality of photographs is not only necessary for scholars interested in photography, technology, or visual cultures of American religion. If we are going to continue to use photographs and other modes of material culture as registers of religious experience, we desperately need to be sensitive to the epistemological assumptions trafficked through these approaches. If definitive answers remain elusive—they do—my sincere hope is that the book has nevertheless succeeded on the primary level of articulating the problem in a way that resonates beyond the particular narrative it weaves.

Notes

A NOTE ON THE IMAGES

1. Albert Sands Southworth, "Suggestions to Ladies Who Sit for Dageurreotypes [*sic*]," in *The Lady's Almanac for 1854* (Boston: John P. Jewett; Cleveland, Ohio: Jewett, Proctor and Worthington, 1854), 102–3.

2. "Disgusting Quackery," *Spiritual Telegraph*, May 18, 1855.

3. Sontag, *On Photography*, 97.

INTRODUCTION

1. "Photograph of Walter G. Jones, Pvt., 8th New York Cavalry, Co. C., U.S.A., half-length, facing front and his New Testament with bullet holes, and the two bullets which lodged in the book," *Library of Congress, Prints and Photographs Online Catalog*, http://www.loc.gov/pictures/item/2005695741/; "8th Cavalry Regiment New York," *American Civil War Regiments*, ancestry.com (accessed June 30, 2009); "His Bullet-Proof Bible," *Philadelphia North American*, September 12, 1899, 12; Carlebach, *Working Stiffs*, 5; *New York Civil War Muster Roll Abstracts, 1861–1900*, New York State Archives, digital access through ancestry.com (accessed July 13, 2014).

2. "Testament (A)," *Catalogue of Title Entries of Books and Other Articles Entered in the Office of Register of Copyrights, Library of Congress*, vol. 21, fourth quarter (Washington, D.C.: Government Printing Office, 1899), 778; "Ordinations and Installations," *American Baptist Magazine* 14 (January 1, 1834): 47; New York State Census, 1855; "Aaron B. Jones," United States Federal Census, Chenango County, New York, 1860; "Walter Jones," United States Federal Census 1860, Broome County, New York, ancestry.com.

3. The "communion of saints" was, and remains, a theological concept rich in history and interpretation. Dating to the first centuries of Christianity, and emerging in credal statements formulated during an intensely polemical period in the formation of Christian orthodoxy, my intent is not to wash over this history but instead to use this fraught and cherished tradition to draw attention to the theological work of photographs in the nineteenth century. For an excellent study of another cultural site

of the communion of saints in early nineteenth-century America, see Schmidt, *Holy Fairs*, 101–3.

4. "The Communion of Saints . . . ," *New York Observer and Chronicle (1833–1912)*, September 30, 1858.

5. Edwards, Gosden, and Phillips, *Sensible Objects*, 3.

6. Douglass, "Pictures and Progress," reprinted in Stauffer et al., *Picturing Frederick Douglass*, 167.

7. In her analysis of government photographs produced in the 1930s and 1940s with the Farm Security Administration and the Office of War Information, Colleen McDannell asserts that these images "give us an unprecedented glimpse into the religious world of everyday people" in spite of a visual record often marshaled in defense of the period's secularization. Rather than a visual record of American religion—as if such a thing were possible to produce—she contends that the government files document a politics of representation, a particular framing of what religion means in the story of the American people, regardless of the belief or unbelief of individual Americans. See McDannell, *Picturing Faith*, 4.

8. In addition to McDannell's invitation to see government pictures within the "documentary impulse" of the period, and the visual politics of representation that such official campaigns freighted, Laura Wexler focuses attention on nineteenth-century photographs within longer theological traditions of visual representation and practice. Writing of a later period in the history of photography, Daniel Wojcik positions Catholic pilgrims' Polaroid pictures from a Marian apparition site in Queens within histories of miraculous images. More recently, Paul Christopher Johnson has explored photography as a "technology of memory work" that paralleled spirit possession— that other nineteenth-century "art of revelation"—and Kati Curts argues that the new marvel of composite photography late in the century exposed the "misty margins of religion and the secular." Other studies of nineteenth-century American visual culture have addressed photography as one of many new visual technologies adopted by religious Americans, most notably David Morgan's early study of the shift from didactic instruction to devotional material in American Protestantism over the course of the century. See McDannell, *Picturing Faith*; Wexler, "The Puritan in the Photograph"; Wojcik, "'Polaroids from Heaven'"; Johnson, "Objects of Possession: Photography, Spirits, and the Entangled Arts of Appearance"; and Curts, "Shadowy Relations and Shades of Devotion: Production and Possession of the 1886 Smith College Composite Photograph," in Promey, *Sensational Religion*, 25–46 and 113–34, respectively; Morgan, *Protestants and Pictures*; and Schwain, *Signs of Grace*.

9. For more on the cultural and political acts of beholding, see Edwards, Gosden, and Phillips, *Sensible Objects*; Houtman and Meyer, *Things*; Pinney, *Photos of the Gods*; and Jay and Ramaswamy, *Empires of Vision*.

10. Catholic historian Julie Byrne models the approach I take here. Despite the fact that scholars have become increasingly attentive to "popular sources and lay subjects," she writes, "we still tend to look for piety in traditionally religious phenomena, such as household devotions, missionary travels, or sacred artifacts. Even when this approach is embedded in social history, it implicitly isolates religion from the rest of life, bringing light to what people did when they practiced their faith but not the many everyday

experiences that overlaid, surrounded, supported, and challenged formal observance." Byrne, *O God of Players*, 10–11.

11. An excellent study demonstrating the usefulness of the alternate approach is Lerone A. Martin's history of "phonograph religion" in the early twentieth century. See Martin, *Preaching on Wax*.

12. Bynum, *Christian Materiality*, 28–29, 35, 41.

13. Barnett, *Sacred Relics*; Smith, *American Archives*.

14. Kirshenblatt-Gimblett, "Objects of Ethnography," in Lavine, *Exhibiting Cultures*, 387. Religious studies theorist Jonathan Z. Smith has made similar arguments about religion being the object of scholarly production. See Smith, "Religion, Religions, Religious," in *Relating Religion*, 179–96.

15. *Westfield Republican*, May 28, 1902; "His Bullet-Proof Bible," *Philadelphia North American*, September 12, 1899.

16. Kirshenblatt-Gimblett, "Objects of Ethnography," 387–88.

17. For a model of how art history has approached this question, see Edwards and Hart, *Photographs Objects Histories*.

18. On the origins of "lived religion," see Hall, *Lived Religion*. See also Maffly-Kipp, Schmidt, and Valeri, *Practicing Protestants*, which makes a strong case for critical engagement with practice theory, along the two "intellectual lineages" of social theory and contemporary theology (2).

19. Batchen, *Each Wild Idea*, 57.

20. Braive, *Photograph*; Frizot, *A New History of Photography*; Nickel, *Snapshots*; Taft, *Photography and the American Scene*.

21. Batchen, *Each Wild Idea*, 59.

22. The following discussion is based on close readings of Primiano ("Vernacular Religion") and fellow folklorist Marion Bowman (Bowman and Valk, *Vernacular Religion in Everyday Life*). In his pivotal article, Primiano identified historiographical and sociological biases in the category of "folk" and advanced "vernacular" as a concept that better approximated "religion as it is lived: as human beings encounter, understand, interpret, and practice it." As the primary register of "the experiential," belief figures prominently in Primiano's discussion of vernacular religion. "Vernacular religious theory," he wrote, "involves . . . special attention to the process of religious belief, the verbal, behavioral, and material expressions of religious belief, and the ultimate object of religious belief." Critiquing a disciplinary preoccupation with hierarchies and artificial cultural schematics, Primiano posited that the critical orientation of vernacular religion nevertheless "emphasizes the study of the belief systems of religious people." See "Vernacular Religion," 44–51.

The British folklorist and religious studies scholar Marion Bowman draws heavily from Primiano in her own advancement of the interpretive potential of vernacular religion. Echoing the Bhaktinian privileging of individual linguistic acts above structural hegemony, Bowman defines vernacular religion as "the study of articulated beliefs," as determined by what individual actors "do, think and say in relation to what they believe" rather than "abstract belief systems, world religions or other forms of a priori knowledge." Along with narratives and practices, Bowman identifies material culture as an iteration of the "expressions of belief" that define her approach. Coming out of a union of folklore and religious studies, it is not surprising that vernacular religion so defined prioritizes the generative and consequential cultural work of individual actors engaged in creative acts of "belief in action." "The vernacular religious approach," Bowman asserts, "anticipates heterogeneity and individual creativity and therefore does not dismiss it as methodologically inconvenient or deviant." Bowman and Valk, *Vernacular Religion in Everyday Life*, 7.

23. Keane, "Evidence of the Senses," S124.

24. Edwards, Gosden, and Phillips, *Sensible Objects*, 10.

25. For a catalogue of hidden mother techniques, see Nagler, *The Hidden Mother*.

26. Levine, *The Unpredictable Past*, 280.

27. See, for instance, Fusco and Wallis, *Only Skin Deep*.

28. Ulrich, *The Age of Homespun*, 8.

29. The possibility for the existence of subjectivities existing apart from material practices that constitute ideological apparatus is addressed most directly by Louis Althusser in "Ideology and Ideological State Apparatuses."

CHAPTER 1

1. "Note to Agents," *Specimen Pages of the New Devotional and Practical Pictorial Family Bible* (Philadelphia: National Publishing Company, n.d.), Michael Zinman Collection of Canvassing Books, University of Pennsylvania. See also the advertisement in *Friends' Intelligencer*, October 5, 1872, and Gutjahr, *An American Bible*, 77. An advertisement for the Nashes' edition of the *Polyglot Family Bible* in another National Publishing Company publication includes the following pitch to potential agents: "Bibles are always in demand, and you can often sell a *really valuable, handsome,* and *cheap* one to persons who will buy no other book." See James D. McCabe Jr., *Paris by Sunlight and Gaslight* (Philadelphia: National Publishing Company, 1869), unpaginated.

2. Advertisement at end of McCabe, *Paris by Sunlight and Gaslight*, n.p.; "Price List, June, 1872," *Annual Report of the American Bible Society* (New York: American Bible Society, 1872), 13. Gutjahr indicates that an 1880 edition of a National Publishing Company Bible cost between $6.50 and $15.00 (*An American Bible*, 79).

3. *New Illustrated Devotional Practical and Polyglot Family Bible* (Philadelphia: National Publishing Company, 1870), 763, Rare Books and Special Collections, Princeton University. What is fascinating about this table is that it exceeds the biblical prohibition of incest by including a number of relations created through marriage, such as "Brother's Wife" and "Husband's Brother's Son," thus charting family through nonbiological relations.

4. For more about family Bibles in the nineteenth century, see McDannell, *Material Christianity*, 67–102, and Gutjahr, *An American Bible*. For an excellent archive of family Bible registries, see "North Carolina Family Records Online: A Project of the State Library and State Archives of North Carolina," accessible through the North Carolina Digital Collections database, http://statelibrary.ncdcr.gov/dimp/digital/ncfamily records/.

5. On the carte de visite, see McCauley, *A. A. E. Disdéri and the Carte de Visite Portrait Photograph*.

6. Ellis, *The Life of an Ordinary Woman*, 104–6.

7. S. B., "The Best Album," *Little Gleaner: A Monthly Magazine for the Young*, vol. 1 (London, 1879), 55–56.

8. Taft, *Photography and the American Scene*, 138; Langford, *Suspended Conversations*, 24–25. In her study of nineteenth-century portrait photographs, Shirley Wajda writes that "the parlor album may have served as a social register, not solely as a family record—a function fulfilled by the family Bibles in which family history was recorded and mementos, like locks of hair, letters, and dried flowers, were stored." Wajda, "'Social Currency,'" 520, 543.

9. Gutjahr, *An American Bible*, 79, 81, graphic on page 86; McDannell, *Material Christianity*, 90.

10. My thanks to Rob and Jacoba VandeWeghe for graciously allowing me use of their historical family Bibles for this book. See also Margaret Hills's 1961 bibliography of Bible editions published in the United States through 1957 in *The English Bible in America*.

11. Portrait galleries of studio photographs were not the only form of photography incorporated into American Bibles during the nineteenth century. *The Self-Interpreting Bible*, published by R. S. Peale and J. A. Hill of New York, included dozens of halftone prints of photographs of the Holy Land taken by St. Louis photographer Robert E. M. Bain and originally published in Lee, Bain, and Vincent, *Earthly Footsteps of the Man of Galilee*. Other Bible publishers in this later period also incorporated the new halftone printing process into their copious visual records, including the Philadelphia firm of A. J. Holman, arguably the most successful Bible publisher of the last two decades of the nineteenth century.

12. For an early account of the introduction of cabinet portraiture, see Taft, *Photography and the American Scene*, 321–24.

13. Pegler-Gordon, *In Sight of America*, 11. Pegler-Gordon problematizes this distinction in her study of Chinese immigration identity documents, writing that "the rupture between these two traditions and their visual conventions is not nearly as complete as . . . critics suggest. In fact, immigration identity documentation offers an example of repressive, racialized, state-based photographic identification that challenges this photographic history" through immigrants' strategies of self-representation (42).

14. Smith, *Photography on the Color Line*, 7.

15. McCandless, "The Portrait Studio and the Celebrity: Promoting the Art," 49. At least one historian of photography has identified Anthony's gallery as the premier "collection of celebrities" in the United States. For McCandless, however, it was Mathew Brady who first made a deliberate attempt to identify portraits of "illustrious Americans" with instruction in the virtues of citizenship, particularly through the publication of twenty-four lithographs drawn from daguerreotype originals. Although costly to the point that only twelve of the original twenty-four were actually published in his folio volume *Gallery of Illustrious Americans*, the fact of publication ostensibly rendered these likenesses to a broader audience than did Anthony's gallery, which demanded a visit to the corner of Broadway and Murray-street. See Trachtenberg, *Reading American Photographs*, 33–52, and Newhall, *Daguerreotype in America*, 80–81.

16. Sandweiss, *Print the Legend*, 330.

17. "Introduction to the Portrait Album," no date (ca. 1859–80) (emphasis added). The

address on the placard indicates that it was printed in Brighton, United Kingdom, but it eventually made its way to a West Virginia attic before being auctioned on eBay.

18. Newhall, *Daguerreotype in America*, 24.

19. Taft, *Photography and the American Scene*, 17; Newhall, *Daguerreotype in America*, 22; Burrows and Wallace, *Gotham*, 532. For an intriguing discussion of windows in early photography, see McCauley, "Talbot's Rouen Window."

20. Samuel F. B. Morse to M. A. Root, "Who Made the First Daguerreotype in This Country?," *Photographic and Fine Art Journal*, September 1, 1855, 280.

21. Bogardus, "Thirty-Seven Years behind a Camera," *Photographic Times and American Photographer*, February 1, 1884, 73; *Charivari*, August 30, 1839, quoted in Newhall, *Daguerreotype in America*, 27; Newhall, *Daguerreotype in America*, 23–25. Newhall notes that despite Americans' frequent claims to the contrary, portraits had been made by Daguerre's process in France before his technique crossed the Atlantic and were "probably no better—nor worse—than the corpse-like images Morse produced of his daughter and her friends, with whitened faces and closed eyes." See Newhall, *Daguerreotype in America*, 26.

On the introduction of daguerreotypes to the United States, see Taft, *Photography and the American Scene*; Rudisill, *Mirror Image*; Newhall, *Daguerreotype in America*; and Trachtenberg, *Reading American Photographs*.

22. McCandless, "The Portrait Studio and the Celebrity," 52; Newhall, *Daguerreotype in America*, 24–25, 38–41.

23. "Superb Daguerreotypes," *Spirit of the Times: A Chronicle of the Turf, Agriculture, Field Sports, Literature*, March 8, 1845. The article "adopt[ed] . . . with pleasure" the sentiments "so much better expressed by the 'Review.'" *Knickerbocker; or, New York Monthly Magazine*, June 1846.

24. The 1880 census records identify Munger as a white male "Artist photog." living at home in Oconomowoc with his wife, four young children, servant and two boarders. See also "Douglas G. Munger," *Portrait and Biographical Record of Waukesha County, Wisconsin* (Chicago: Excelsior, 1894), 419–20.

25. Bogardus, "Thirty-Seven Years behind a Camera," 73.

26. McDannell, *Material Christianity*, 79.

27. See, for instance, Severa, *My Likeness Taken*, and Romer and Wallis, *Young America*.

28. Root, *The Camera and the Pencil*, 106.

29. Louisa Fisher Hawes, *Memoir of Mrs. Mary E. Van Lennep* (Hartford, Conn., 1850), 134–35.

30. On the first printing by Bowles and Dearborn of Boston, see "Quarterly List of New Publications," *North American Review* 19 (January 1829).

31. Channing, "Likeness to God: Discourse at the Ordination of the Rev. F. A. Farley," in *The Works of William E. Channing, D.D.* (Boston, 1849), 3:228, 233, 239–41.

32. See Trachtenberg, *Reading American Photographs*, 45, and Newhall, *Daguerreotype in America*, 81. Significantly, Channing's was the only lithograph in the collection that was based on a daguerreotype of a painted portrait.

33. Jackson, *Suffering Here—Glory Hereafter*, 109, 111, 114. Jackson's sermons were first published posthumously in 1872. The phrase "hid with Christ in God" comes from Colossians 3:3 in the New Testament.

34. Henry Read, *Memoirs and Sermons of Rev. Wm. J. Armstrong, D.D.* (New York: M. W. Dodd, 1853), 210–11, 220.

35. Ibid., 215.

36. See, for instance, Crary, *Techniques of the Observer.*

37. Alfred Lee, *A Life Hid with Christ in God. Being a Memoir of Susan Allibone. Chiefly Compiled from Her Diary and Letters* (Philadelphia: J. B. Lippincott, 1867 [1855]), iii–v, 447.

38. *Journal of the Life and Religious Labors of Sarah Hunt* (Philadelphia: Friends' Book Association, 1892), 153, 156.

39. Deborah H. Cushing Porter, March 29, 1839, in Anne T. Drinkwater, *Memoir of Mrs. Deborah H. Porter, Wife of Rev. C. G. Porter of Bangor* (Portland, Me., 1848), 156.

40. See Lindsey, "'Mirror of All Perfection.'"

41. Griffith, *Born Again Bodies*; Finch, *Dissenting Bodies.*

42. McCandless, "The Portrait Studio and the Celebrity," 55.

43. Rembrandt Peale, "Portraiture," *Crayon*, February 1, 1857.

44. Root, *The Camera and the Pencil*, 44, 121, 144–46.

45. Rogers, *Delia's Tears*, 123.

46. I use the neologism "agnotology" here instead of the more prevalent "pseudo-science" to accentuate the cultural repercussions of circulating erroneous scientific data. See Proctor and Shiebinger, *Agnotology.*

47. Root, *The Camera and the Pencil*, 84.

48. Ibid., 84–89. Historians Shawn Michelle Smith and Alan Trachtenberg further delineate the relationships between ideologies of race and character. See Smith, *American Archives* and *Photography on the Color Line*, and Trachtenberg, *Reading American Photographs.* Molly Rogers's excellent study of the daguerreotypes of seven slaves from South Carolina plantations in 1850 is an especially poignant discussion of race, photography, and science at the dawn of photographic discourse. See Rogers, *Delia's Tears.*

49. Rogers, *Delia's Tears*, 12–13. In her theorization of the "interpretive moment" of photographic beholding, Rogers writes that "the photographic image comes to have meaning only when it is viewed, and viewing is an act of the imagination" (16).

50. Griffith, *Born Again Bodies*, 58–61.

51. The census data also indicate that the Nashes had a "domestic" living with them, Neomi Jones, age thirty-five. It is not impossible that the Nashes could have afforded the extra expenses that hired labor would have demanded, although it is possible that Jones, who was also of Welsh nativity, was related to their neighbor, Jerry Jones, who was also a miner and was born in Wales.

52. Biographical information culled from census records, digitized through ancestry .com, and the family records pages of the Nash Family Bible, Rare Books and Special Collections, Princeton University.

53. "News Items," *Saturday Evening Post*, November 29, 1862.

54. "Christmas Goods," classified advertisement, *Sun*, December 19, 1864.

55. "For the Holidays," classified advertisement, *Sun*, December 19, 1865.

56. "Something New and Appropriate," classified advertisement, *Sun*, June 7, 1864.

57. The authority on canvassing books in the nineteenth century is Keith Arbour,

Canvassing Books. See also the Michael Zinman Collection of Canvassing Books, Rare Book and Manuscript Library Collections, University of Pennsylvania.

58. Gutjahr, *An American Bible*, 81.

59. *The Holy Bible, Translated from the Latin Vulgate* (Philadelphia: John Kelly, 1872); *The Holy Bible, Translated from the Latin Vulgate* (New York: D. & J. Sadlier, 1876); *The Holy Bible* (Philadelphia: John E. Potter, 1879); *The Holy Bible: Containing the Entire Canonical Scriptures: According to the Decree of the Council of Trent* (Philadelphia: John E. Potter, 1883). Of the seventy-three Bibles that included pages for family portraits that I have catalogued in this study, eighteen have been Douay-Rheims translation.

60. My thanks to Joe Azure for kindly lending me the Droney Family Bible and to Judith Weisenfeld and Stephen Ferguson, Curator of Rare Books, Princeton University Library, for coordinating the loan.

61. In the 1880s, for instance, the New York publisher John Williams & Co. included such studies in its Douay-Rheims family Bible. David Morgan has argued that Warner Sallman's immensely popular *Head of Christ* (1940) "conform[ed] to the standards of popular commercial portrait photography" and that a significant shift occurred in Protestant iconography at the end of the nineteenth century when Protestant devotional art began to emphasize personality and individual character rather than biblical narrative. And yet he seems not to have noted in any of his extensive writings on Sallman and turn-of-the-twentieth-century religious art how Catholic portraiture participated in this shift. See Morgan, "Warner Sallman," 31. See also Morgan, *Protestants and Pictures*.

62. I do not want to read too much into Enoch's absence, as there is no way of knowing for certain whether, at some point, his portrait was also included in the gallery.

63. Lindley, "National Society of N.E. Women," *New England Magazine: An Illustrated Monthly* (September 1905–February 1906), 491. On the National Society of New England Women, see also Zieber, *Ancestry*, 19, and Hood and Young, *American Orders and Societies and Their Decorations*, 35.

64. Lindley, "National Society of N.E. Women," 491.

65. Lindley, "New England Women," *New England Magazine: An Illustrated Monthly* (September 1905–February 1906), 334. See, for instance, Smith, *American Archives*, 136–56.

66. For a broader discussion of religion, race, and nation, see Goldschmidt and McAlister, *Race, Nation, and Religion in the Americas*.

67. "Books! Books! Books!," classified advertisement, *San Francisco Chronicle*, December 21, 1870.

68. Specimen book for Boyd's *Wonders of the Heavens, Earth, and Ocean*, no. 180, Zinman Collection of Canvassing Books, University of Pennsylvania.

69. *American Publishers' Circular and Literary Gazette*, December 5, 1861.

70. The metonymic association of pen and camera would become a popular representational device in Holy Land literature at the end of the century.

71. Kathleen Collins, "Portraits of Slave Children," *History of Photography* (July–September 1985), 189.

72. Reprinted in ibid., 197.

73. Mirzoeff, "The Shadow and the Substance," 117.

74. McCandless, "The Portrait and the Celebrity."

75. "Photographalbumanie," *Vanity Fair*, November 29, 1862.

76. Smith, *American Archives*, 115–16, 125.

77. Galton, *Inquiries into Human Faculty*, 25. In this volume, it should be noted, Galton makes use of "specimens of composite portraiture," a method that he "contrived" to avoid "the difficulty of procuring really representative faces" (8). For a definition and his process, see *Inquiries into Human Faculty*, 8–11, 339–63. For the claim that Galton was not popularized in the United States until *Hereditary Genius* was reprinted in 1892, see Smith, *American Archives*, 129.

78. Galton, *Hereditary Genius*, v; Root, *The Camera and the Pencil*, 87. Recall that Root described all heliographers as "physiognomists in practice, if not in theory" (89).

79. Galton, *Life History Album*, 5. Galton even provided specific dimensional instructions for those who obtained photographs "especially taken for this purpose," to wit, "reductions to one-seventh the size of the original face" so that, in the full-face portrait, "between the line of the pupils of the eyes and that passing between the lips would then be four-tenths of an inch" (ibid.).

80. Psalm 133 was also an important text in Masonic stereographs of open Bibles. I have found no association of this particular Bible with Freemasonry, although to date I have not been able to locate an extant copy.

81. Isaias 60:20 (D-R).

CHAPTER 2

1. Lincoln signed the Emancipation Proclamation, which would go into effect at the start of the new year, just days after Antietam. "Emancipation Proclamation," *Brooklyn Circular*, September 25, 1862.

2. William Stilwell to Molly Stilwell, September 18, 1862, reprinted in Lane, *"Dear Mother,"* 184–86. See also Faust, *This Republic of Suffering*.

3. Richard Cecil, *A Friendly Visit to the House of Mourning* (Charlestown, Mass., 1803), 57–60. The first identified edition in the United States was in Charlestown, Massachusetts, in 1796 and was printed by a number of independent publishers until 1830, when it was published by the American Tract Society (ATS). The latest known ATS publication is 1848.

4. Ibid., 60.

5. Greeley, "Death of Children," 65.

6. Cecil, *A Friendly Visit*, 61.

7. For postmortem photography and its painterly precedents, see, for instance, Ruby, *Secure the Shadow*; Linkman, *Photography and Death*; Burns, *Sleeping Beauty*; and Burns, *Sleeping Beauty II*.

8. Logan, manuscript diary, 3:28, Historical Society of Pennsylvania, Philadelphia. Reprinted in Stabile, *Memory's Daughters*, 191.

9. Audrey Linkman has recently argued that postmortem photographs "may have offered a form of proxy admission to the theatre of death and so provided some measure of consolation" for those who, because of contingencies of time or place, were "denied the 'privilege' of the deathbed." See Linkman, *Photography and Death*, 16.

10. Batchen, *Forget Me Not*, 47. The daguerreotype of Christ is in Batchen's private

collection. In his study of photography and memory, moreover, Batchen notes that the doggerel—"The grass is green The rose is red / Here is my name when I am dead"—was also inscribed in at least two Bibles later in the nineteenth century.

11. "Brady's Photographs," *New York Times*, October 20, 1862. See Trachtenberg, *Reading American Photographs*, and Frassanito, *Antietam*.

12. W. R. Stilwell, Pension Applications of Confederate Soldiers and Widows, *Georgia, Confederate Pension Applications, 1879–1960*, ancestry.com.

13. Copies were made of the original ambrotype and sold, "together with a beautiful piece of music . . . composed upon the incident," to benefit Humiston's widow and children. "The Soldier Identified," *New York Observer and Chronicle*," December 3, 1863; "The Dead Soldier and His Children," *Zion's Herald and Wesleyan Journal*, November 2, 1864. See also Morris, *Believing Is Seeing*.

14. "Wilbraham Is Mourning," ca. 1830–40 (Springfield, Mass.). American Antiquarian Society copy, American Broadsides and Ephemera, series 1, no. 3992.

15. On textiles in New England at the turn of the nineteenth century, see Ulrich, *The Age of Homespun*. While the poem itself was circulated in the mid-nineteenth century, the tragic drowning occurred in 1799, as the following section discusses.

16. *Connecticut Courant*, May 6, 1799.

17. Laderman, *The Sacred Remains*; Prothero, *Purified by Fire*; Steiner, *A Study of the Intellectual and Material Culture of Death*. According to Laderman's antebellum mortality statistics for northern states, in the late eighteenth century, 80 percent of Americans died before the age of seventy, females in Massachusetts in 1849 could expect to live to the age of thirty-six, provided they survived childhood illness, which claimed between a fifth and a third of children younger than ten, and 8 to 10 percent of persons between age one and age twenty-one died. "No significant decline in mortality figures emerged until after the Civil War" (*The Sacred Remains*, 24–25).

18. Beecher, *Autobiography*, 178. See also White, *The Beecher Sisters*, 4.

19. Cuyler, *The Empty Crib*, 11.

20. Ibid., 10.

21. In the early twentieth century, Freud would articulate a distinction between "mourning" and "melancholia" that demonstrated how, a century later, the gendered qualities of these purportedly related states were still eluding clinical precision. To a degree, Freud's distinction echoed those of ministers and consolationists writing centuries before who also defined appropriate displays of sorrow in relation to unbridled, frequently effeminized grief. See Freud, "Mourning and Melancholia," 243–58.

22. Richard Allestree, *The Whole Duty of Mourning* (London, 1695), 2, 153–57.

23. John Dunton, *The Mourning Ring, in Memory of Departed Friends*, 2nd ed. (1692), 121.

24. John Flavel, *A Token for Mourners: or, The Advice of Christ to a Distressed Mother, Bewailing the Death of Her Dear and Only Son* (London, 1674).

25. See Stabile, *Memory's Daughters*, 208, and Winner, *A Cheerful and Comfortable Faith*, 141–77.

26. Cotton Mather, *The Cure of Sorrow* (Boston, 1709), n.p.

27. DeLorme, *Mourning Art and Jewelry*, 26.

28. Nehemiah Adams, *Agnes and the Key to Her Little Coffin* (Boston, 1857), 15–16, 56,

65. Subsequent editions were titled *Agnes and the Little Key*, indicating a shift in emphasis from the coffin to the key as the locus of significance.

29. See Stabile, *Memory's Daughters*, 218, and Allestree, *The Whole Duty of Mourning*, 21.

30. Stabile, *Memory's Daughters*, 210. For a brief study of sumptuary laws' relation to dress practices in early colonial America, see Finch, "'Fashions of Worldly Dames.'"

31. Charles Winslow, no. 7, Cornhill, Boston, trade card. American Antiquarian Society copy, American Broadsides and Ephemera, series 1, no. 20311.

32. Chapin, M.D., Mrs. City Bonnet Warehouse, trade card. American Antiquarian Society copy, American Broadsides and Ephemera, series 1, no. 19700.

33. Besson & Son, 1851 spring and summer circular of the Philadelphia Mourning Store, American Antiquarian Society copy, American Broadsides and Ephemera, series 1, no. 22183.

34. DeLorme, *Mourning Art and Jewelry*, 52.

35. Thanks to Nicole Kirk for suggesting I probe the patriotic dimensions of mourning attire.

36. Linkman, *Photography and Death*, 54–62.

37. Linkman, for instance, asserts that women who chose to be photographed in mourning attire "were not only demonstrating their virtue in honouring the dead in the prescribed manner, but they were also asserting or upholding their own and their family's claim to a position within society." Similarly, Ruby contends that, as visual records of garbs that signaled mourners' "propriety" to "society," "having your picture painted or photograph taken provided a record of your status not unlike the soldier in uniform." Such analyses leave little room for grief as a motive for being photographed and also stymie widows' agency in mourning ritual. See ibid., 127, and Ruby, *Secure the Shadow*, 110.

38. Stabile, *Memory's Daughters*, 203.

39. Ibid., 188.

40. MacDonald, *Monuments*, 3–4.

41. Stebbins, *Our Departed Friends*, 222.

42. Mount Auburn, incidentally, was the subject of a "rather dull set" of Southworth and Hawes whole-plate daguerreotype stereoviews in the 1850s. Newhall, *Daguerreotype in America*, 45; McDannell, *Material Christianity*, 106.

43. Stebbins, *Our Departed Friends*, 222–23.

44. MacDonald, *Monuments*, 7–8.

45. Bell, *Essays on the Anatomy of Expression in Painting*, vi–vii.

46. "New York Daguerreian Convention," *Daguerreian Journal*, July 15, 1851.

47. Quoted in Stabile, *Memory's Daughters*, 193.

48. Advertisement reprinted in Julius F. Sachse, "The Dawn of Photography. Early Daguerreotype Days," *American Journal of Photography*, March 1, 1897, 103.

49. Sampler, made by Martha Taylor, Lancaster, Pennsylvania, 1797, silk embroidered on linen, 1995.1, gift of Elizabeth Oat Rockwell in memory of Martha Elizabeth Taylor Oat, Winterthur Museum. Reproduced in Stabile, *Memory's Daughters*, 215.

50. "The Gazette Museum," *National Police Gazette*, May 8, 1880.

51. Jolly, *Faces of the Living Dead*; Chéroux et al., *The Perfect Medium*; Ferris, *The*

Disembodied Spirit; Harvey, *Photography and Spirit*; Kaplan, *The Strange Case of William Mumler*. Spirit photography is the subject of the next chapter.

52. MacDonald, *Monuments*, 7–8.

53. Green, "My Still-Born Babe." The giftbook was reprinted in 1848.

54. Mildred Mifflin, *Out of Darkness into Light; From the Journal of a Bereaved Mother* (Shelbyville, Ill.: Our Best Words, 1888), 3.

55. In the 1840s, it would still be decades before embalming would even begin to become a practical recourse in the disposal of dead bodies, let alone socially or theologically acceptable.

56. James M. MacDonald, *My Father's House; or, the Heaven of the Bible* (New York: Charles Scribner, 1855), 247, 254.

57. McDannell and Lang, *Heaven*, 181–227.

58. See, for instance, Herbert Broughton, *The Spirit Disembodied*, 3rd ed. (Edinburgh, 1867), 201–7; John Redman Coxe, *Considerations Respecting the Recognition of Friends in Another World* (Philadelphia, 1845), 1–33; Catherine Sinclair, *The Journey of Life* (London, 1845), 148–55; Rufus Wilmot Griswold, *The Cyprus Wreath: A Book of Consolation for Those Who Mourn* (Boston, 1844), 35–36; William Branks, *Heaven Our Home* (Boston, 1864), 149–215; Daniel Sharp, *Recognition of Friends in Heaven* (Boston, 1857); and Benjamin Dorr, *Recognition of Friends in Another World* (Philadelphia, 1840).

59. Adams, *Agnes and the Key to Her Little Coffin*, 185.

60. Stebbins, *Our Departed Friends*, 465–66.

61. Ibid., 473.

62. For a more detailed examination of commercial memorial photography in the late nineteenth century, see Linkman, *Photography and Death*, 134–44.

63. Advertisement, *Christian Advocate*, June 18, 1868; advertisement, *Maine Farmer*, January 22, 1870; advertisement, *Cincinnati Daily Gazette*, May 10, 1870.

64. Jane Eliza Stebbins was the daughter of Cyrus Stebbins and Mary Ann Harris.

65. Stebbins, *Our Departed Friends*, vi.

66. Ibid., 520.

67. See also Barnett, *Sacred Relics*.

68. Daniel Clarke Eddy, *The Young Woman's Friend, or, The Duties, Trials, Loves, and Hopes of Woman* (Boston: Wentworth and Company, 1857); James Grant Wilson and John Fiske, eds., *Appleton's Cyclopaedia of American Biography*, vol. 2 (New York: D. Appleton and Company, 1887), 299; *The American Dictionary* (1830), s.v. "relic"; *A Critical Pronouncing Dictionary and Expositor of the English Language* (London, 1823), s.v. "relick."

69. DeLorme, *Mourning Art and Jewelry*, 65.

70. Joseph Anthony tradecard (10 by 17 cm), Philadelphia, ca. 1780–90, American Antiquarian Society copy, American Broadsides and Ephemera, series 1, no. 19575.

71. West and Abbott, *Tokens of Affection and Regard*, 35. The fifteen categories include bracelets, buttons, "charm bracelet" pieces, earrings, hair bands, mourning pins/badges, necklaces, pendants, pins, rings, stickpins, viewers, watch lockets, watch fobs, and watch keys. They subsequently classify these articles into decorative, functional, and commemorative pieces.

72. "Lost and Found," *Baltimore Sun*, May 3, 1853.

73. Ibid., October 25, 1856.

74. "Lost and Found," *New York Times*, September 27, 1858.

75. The most recent and most thorough study of hairwork in American history is Sheumaker's *Love Entwined*.

76. "Arm-Chair," *Godey's Lady's Book and Magazine*, September 1863.

77. "Hair Work," *Godey's Lady's Book*, December 1850, 377.

78. See Sheumaker, *Love Entwined*.

79. DeLorme, *Mourning Art and Jewelry*, 66.

80. *Catalogue of Artistic Hair Work for Mementoes and Souvenirs* (Chicago, 1886). Library of Congress online catalog, https://lccn.loc.gov/ca10002593 (accessed November 22, 2016).

81. For further analysis of hair and photography, see Batchen, "Ere the Substance Fade." Despite Batchen's helpful contribution, however, the scholarship is extremely thin. See also Sheumaker, *Love Entwined*.

82. West and Abbott identify open-faced photo pins as the most commonly preserved format of photographic jewelry, followed by watch lockets. West and Abbott, *Tokens of Affection and Regard*, 40.

83. In her history of hairwork, Helen Sheumaker argues quite the opposite of my analysis, that hair and photographs "served quite different purposes of self-representation." (*Love Entwined*, 49). She makes her case by arguing that, unlike worked hair, "photographic likenesses simply presented an image of one's true appearance, and thus marked a return to the eighteenth-century ideal of the sincere self." While it is true that daguerreotypes were early criticized for their unforgiving harshness in recording imperfections of the face—tales abound of patrons demanding additional exposures until the operator secured the "real" likeness—photographs were no less unmediated than other forms of self-representation. Hair and photographic likenesses, moreover, were each considered relics of the dearly departed and were the two tokens most frequently tucked into family Bibles. In short, the fact that hair and likenesses were so commonly associated in jewelry, in daguerreotype and ambrotype cases, and in albums clearly demonstrates their shared cultural history if not a singular ideological purpose. See Sheumaker, *Love Entwined*.

84. Advertisement from 1844 for W. and F. Langenheim reprinted in Sachse, "The Dawn of Photography"; see also the classified ad for Jones' Daguerrian Gallery, *Baltimore Sun*, May 4, 1848.

85. "Daguerreotypes," *Youth's Companion*, December 11, 1851.

86. "Fashions in Jewelry Forty Years Ago," *Jewelers Circular and Horological Review*, February 3, 1892. Reprinted in West and Abbott, *Tokens of Affection and Regard*, 232–34.

87. Laderman, *Sacred Remains*, 49.

CHAPTER 3

1. "Pictures of Dead Men," *Daily Evening Bulletin*, January 1, 1863. The same copy was printed in the *Polynesian* (Honolulu, Hawaii) on the last day of the month, among perhaps others, and it is unclear what city sent the delegation to investigate. See "Pictures of Dead Men," *Polynesian*, January 31, 1863.

2. Mumler, *The Personal Experiences of William H. Mumler*, reprinted in Kaplan, *The Strange Case of William Mumler*, 69, 87.

3. *Boston Investigator*, March 18, 1863.

4. Ibid., March 11, 1863.

5. "Spirit Photographs," *Photographic News*, January 2, 1863; ibid., February 13, 1863.

6. Guay had been commissioned by Andrew Jackson Davis, one of the leaders of modern Spiritualism, to "make a strict investigation into the process." *Tribune*, April 22, 1869.

7. Bernard Valeur and Mário N. Berberan-Santos, "A Brief History of Fluorescence and Phosphorescence before the Emergence of Quantum Theory," *Journal of Chemical Education* 88, no. 6 (June 1, 2011): 735.

8. Kaplan, *The Strange Case of William Mumler*, 70.

9. For histories that extend to consideration of "fluid" photography, see Gunning, *Fugitive Images*, 42–71; Chéroux et al., *The Perfect Medium*; and Jolly, *Faces of the Living Dead*.

10. Theodore Parker (Spirit) and John W. Day, *Biography of Mrs. J. H. Conant, the World's Medium of the Nineteenth Century* (Boston, Mass.: William White and Company, 1873), 99.

11. Green, *Some Questions and Answers in Regard to Spirit Photography*, undated pamphlet, Seybert Commission for Investigating Modern Spiritualism records, Rare Book and Manuscript Library, University of Pennsylvania.

12. *New York World*, May 4, 1869.

13. "Spirit Photographs — A New and Interesting Development," *Photographic Journal*, January 15, 1863. See also "The Evidence Is Irresistable," *Religio-Philosophical Journal*, May 15, 1869; "A Wonderful Mystery," *New York Sun*, February 26, 1869; and "Spiritual Photographs: Close of the Mumler Investigation — Summing Up of Counsel — Justice Downling's Decision — Discharge of the Accused. Science and Spiritual Photographs," *New York Times*, May 4, 1869.

14. As Ann Braude has shown, Spiritualists were prolific publishers of periodicals, almost all of them vanishing within a few years of their founding but collectively paving networks in print that transcended local happenstance and created a national movement. Braude, "News from the Spirit World."

15. *Philadelphia North American and United States Gazette*, February 10, 1863.

16. "Original Communications," *Boston Investigator*, November 9, 1862.

17. Braude, *Radical Spirits*.

18. *Daily Cleveland Herald*, December 19, 1870.

19. Carroll, *Spiritualism in Antebellum America*, 8.

20. Parker (Spirit) and Day, *Biography of Mrs. J. H. Conant*, 99.

21. Kaplan, *The Strange Case of William Mumler*, 87.

22. Ibid., 88.

23. Ibid., 141.

24. "The London Anti-Slavery Demon-Stration," *Manchester Guardian*, January 31, 1863; "Pictures of Dead Men," *Daily Evening Bulletin*, January 31, 1863.

25. "Ghosts Photographed Gratis," *Spectator*, February 28, 1863.

26. "Spirit Photographs — A New and Interesting Development."

27. "Spirit Photographs," *Boston Investigator*, March 11, 1863.

28. "Let's Have Fair Play!," *Boston Investigator*, March 25, 1863.

29. Braude, *Radical Spirits*, 19.

30. A. B. C., "Spirit Photographs — More Details from Boston," *Liberator*, November 21, 1863.

31. "Spirit Photographs — A New and Interesting Development." The account was first published in the *Herald of Progress* in late 1862 and was reprinted in spiritualist, popular, and trade periodicals over the next several months.

32. Georgiana Houghton, *Chronicles of the Photographs of Spiritual Beings* (London: E. W. Allen, 1882), viii.

33. A. B. C., "Spirit Photographs."

34. Green, *Questions and Answers*, n.p.

35. A. B. C., "Spirit Photographs."

36. William Lloyd Garrison to Oliver Johnson, May 25, 1874, in Merrill and Ruchames, *Letters of William Lloyd Garrison*, 323.

37. "John Jenkins," *Boston Investigator*, June 24, 1868.

38. The quoted deposition recounts a conversation with Mumler's alleged partner, William Silver.

39. Kaplan, *The Strange Case of William Mumler*, 79.

40. "A Wonderful Mystery."

41. Gerry and Devine, *The Mumler "Spirit" Photograph Case*, 5.

42. "Spiritual Photography," *Harper's Weekly*, May 8, 1869.

43. For the two most complete scholarly accounts of the trial, see Kaplan, *The Strange Case of William Mumler*, and Cloutier, "Mumler's Ghosts." On the legal aspects of the case, see Mnookin, "Image of Truth."

44. "Ghosts in Photography," *New York Sun*, April 13, 1869.

45. "Spiritual Photography: Continuation of the Mumler Investigation — Interesting Testimony — Goblins of All Sorts," *New York Times*, April 24, 1869.

46. "A Stupendous Fraud: Pretended Spiritualistic Portraits of Deceased Persons Taken by a Broadway Photographer — Arrest of the Proprietor and His Operator — Examination in the Case by Justice Dowling," *New York Times*, April 13, 1869.

47. John D. Townsend, *New York in Bondage* (New York, 1901), xiii.

48. "A Stupendous Fraud."

49. "Spirit Photographs," *Boston Investigator*, March 11, 1863.

50. "A Stupendous Fraud."

51. Carroll, *Spiritualism in Antebellum America*, 118.

52. "The Courts," *New-York Daily Tribune*, April 17, 1869.

53. W. D. L., "Can a Spirit Be Photographed?," *Spiritual Magazine*, June 1869.

54. Gerry and Devine, *The Mumler "Spirit" Photograph Case*, 22.

55. Mnookin, "Image of Truth," 9.

56. Kaplan, *The Strange Case of William Mumler*, 87.

57. Brewster, *The Stereoscope*, 205–6.

58. "Spiritualism in Court," *New-York Daily Tribune*, April 22, 1869.

59. Coverage of the case is fairly consistent with the number of photographs introduced as evidence, but is not an official record. The New York papers covered the

proceedings from April through May under various uniform titles, including "Spiritual Photographs" (*New York Times*); "The Spirit Photographs" (*New York Sun*); and "Spiritualism in Court" (*New-York Tribune*). In addition to these recurring reports, for a partial sampling of coverage of the Mumler trial reprinted in various Spiritualist journals in both the United States and Britain, see "A Stupendous Fraud: Pretended Spiritualistic Portraits of the Deceased," *New York Times*, April 13, 1869; "Law Reports," *New York Times*, April 14, 1869; "The Spiritualists and the Spirit Photographs," *New York Times*, April 14, 1869; "Spiritual Photographs: The Mumler Fraud Case—Large Gathering of Spiritualists at the Tombs—Interesting Proceedings," *New York Times*, April 17, 1869; "Spiritual Photography," *New York Times*, April 24, 1869; "New Yorkisms," *Philadelphia Evening Telegraph*, May 4, 1869; "The Spirit Photographer," *Memphis Daily Appeal*, May 9, 1869; "The Evidence Is Irresistable"; W. D. L., "Can a Spirit Be Photographed?," *The Spiritual Magazine*, June 1869;

60. "Spirit Photographs," *British Journal of Photography*, May 28, 1869.

61. "Spiritualism in Court," *New-York Daily Tribune*, April 24, 1869; "Spiritual Photography," *New York Times*, April 24, 1869.

62. Barnum, *Humbugs of the World*, 112–13.

63. Ibid., 11. For more on Barnum's religious theory of humbug in nineteenth-century America, see Walker, "The Humbug in American Religion."

64. Barnum, *Humbugs of the World*, 21.

65. "The Spirit Photographing Case—Amusing Testimony of P. T. Barnum," *Daily National Intelligencer* (Washington, D.C.), May 1, 1869.

66. Barnum, *Life of P. T. Barnum*, 349–51.

67. "Spiritualism in Court," *New-York Daily Tribune*, April 29, 1869; "The Spirit Photographs," *New York Sun*, April 29, 1869.

68. "Spiritualism in Court," *New-York Daily Tribune*, April 29, 1869.

69. Matthew 17:1–7 (KJV). Court records do not indicate what English translation Townsend was reading from. I presume it was the King James Version.

70. "Spiritualism in Court," *New-York Daily Tribune*, April 29, 1869.

71. "Spiritual Photographs," *New York Times*, May 4, 1869.

72. "Spiritual Photographs: Close of the Mumler Trial," *New York Times*, May 4, 1869.

73. "Mumler's Speech at the Close of His Trial," *Religio-Philosophical Journal* (Chicago), May 29, 1869; "Spiritualism in Court," *New-York Daily Tribune*, May 4, 1869.

74. "Spiritualism in Court," *New-York Daily Tribune*, April 24, 1869.

75. Gerry argued that "our law interferes with and constrains no man in the exercise of his religious belief." Reynolds v. United States (1879) was the first time the Supreme Court defined the constitutional right of religious freedom as limited to beliefs and not actions. Even then, however, religious freedom remained a federal issue until it was incorporated to the states in the 1940s. See Gordon, *The Mormon Question*. At the time of Mumler's trial, federal rights of religious freedom were neither clearly defined in law nor applicable under New York statute.

76. Gerry and Devine, *The Mumler "Spirit" Photograph Case*, 5.

77. "Spiritualism in Court," *New-York Daily Tribune*, May 4, 1869. Mumler was discharged, but the debate around spirit photography had hardly begun. Mumler had

exhausted his resources on his defense and would never fully recover. He died penniless in 1884.

78. Palmquist and Kailbourn, *Pioneer Photographers from the Mississippi to the Continental Divide*, 518.

79. "Spiritualism in Court," *New-York Daily Tribune*, April 22, 1869; "Spiritual Photography," *Harper's Weekly*, May 8, 1869.

80. *Wilson's Photographic Magazine*, November 1893.

81. "The Spirit Photograph Case," *Daily Cleveland Herald*, April 24, 1869.

82. *Frank Leslie's Illustrated Newspaper*, May 22, 1869.

83. Green, *Questions and Answers*, n.p.

84. Emma Hardinge Britten, "Spirit-Photographs and Other Wonderful Phenomena," *Religio-Philosophical Journal*, January 20, 1872.

85. Green, *Questions and Answers*, n.p.

86. "Spiritualism in Court," *New-York Daily Tribune*, April 29, 1869.

87. Pepper et al., *Preliminary Report of the Commission*, 3–4, 18, 26, 29.

88. Ibid., 29, 91. See also Arthur Twining Hadley, *Commemorative Tributes to Horace Howard Furness, Henry Charles Lea, Donald Grant Mitchell, Daniel Coit Gilman* (New York: American Academy of Arts and Letters, 1922).

89. "Consumer Price Index (Estimate)," *Federal Reserve Bank of Minneapolis*, www .minneapolisfed.org (accessed February 10, 2016).

90. "The October Meeting of the National Academy of Sciences," *Science* 4, no. 90 (1884): 396.

91. George G. Rockwood, "Amateur Photography," *Art Amateur* 17, no. 1 (1887): 13.

92. Joseph Jastrow, "Composite Portraiture," *Science* 6, no. 134 (1885): 165.

93. William James, *The Varieties of Religious Experience* (London, 1902), 271. For an incisive reading of James's epistemic borrowing of composite photography, see Curts, "Shadowy Relations and Shades of Devotion: Production and Possession of the 1886 Smith College Composite Photograph," in Promey, *Sensational Religion*, 113–34.

94. Jastrow, "Composite Portraiture," 166; Pepper et al., *Preliminary Report of the Commission*, 91.

95. Pepper et al., *Preliminary Report of the Commission*, 91.

96. Mumler, *The Personal Experiences of William H. Mumler*, reprinted in Kaplan, *The Strange Case of William Mumler*, 110.

97. Parker (Spirit) and Day, *Biography of Mrs. J. H. Conant*, 188–90.

98. McGarry, *Ghosts of Futures Past*, 67, 93.

99. Sandweiss, *Print the Legend*, 216.

100. "Spirit Likenesses," *Religio-Philosophical Journal*, April 20, 1872.

101. Mumler, *The Personal Experiences of William H. Mumler*, 97–98.

102. See the digitized earlier carte de visite of "Mrs. Lincoln [Mary Todd Lincoln (1818–1882)] (from illustration)," Special Collections, Fine Arts Library, Harvard College Library, www.via.lib.harvard.edu (accessed December 9, 2016).

CHAPTER 4

1. Col. George R. Davis, introduction to *The World's Columbian Exposition, Chicago, 1893*, by Trumbull White and William Iglehart (Boston: John K. Hastings, 1893), 11. For a brief overview of the history and legacy of world's fairs in the United States, see Rydell, *All the World's a Fair*. For an excellent study of the role of photography at the 1893 Columbian Exposition, see Brown, *Contesting Images*.

2. "Memorandum," Ivy Lee Papers, 1881–1989, MC085, box 15, Mudd Manuscript Library, Princeton University; "Official Weather Forecast," *Chicago Daily Tribune*, October 17, 1893. A program for the papers delivered on September 18 was printed in the *Chicago Daily Tribune*. Lee's paper was entitled "Christ the Reason of the Universe." See "Last Edition. Idea of Theosophy . . . Religious Parliament Papers," *Chicago Daily Tribune*, September 18, 1893. There is no indication in Ivy's ledger that his father accompanied him on his trip a month later.

3. Ives, *The Dream City*.

4. For a lively discussion of the *danse du ventre*, see Schmidt, *Heaven's Bride*, 9–32.

5. "Memorandum," Ivy Lee Papers.

6. Riis's book originally included fifteen halftone prints; see Marien, *Photography*, 208. On "ethnographic" illustrations of Filipinos, see Brody, *Visualizing American Empire*.

7. Pierce, *Photographic History of the World's Fair*, xiv.

8. Marien, *Photography*, 208.

9. Display ad, *Southern Cultivator*, April 1894.

10. *Picturesque Chicago and Guide to the World's Fair* (Hartford, Conn.: D. S. Moseley, 1893); *Chicago Times Portfolio of Midway Types* (Chicago: American Engraving Company, 1893).

11. Brown, *Contesting Images*, 82–83, 150 n. 63.

12. Rony, *The Third Eye*, 10–12.

13. Ibid., 5.

14. Display ad, *Washington Post*, March 18, 1894. See also Brown, *Contesting Images*, 83, 150 n. 66.

15. N. D. Thompson to J. W. Lee, March 3, 1894, Ivy Lee Papers, box 19, folder 5, Mudd Manuscript Library, Princeton University.

16. Long, *Imagining the Holy Land*, 53–54.

17. Thompson also suggested that he expected Lee's "work will be perfected in collaboration with another author whom we are to select and arrange with." Thompson's partner, R. S. Peale, had a few leading lights in mind, including John Hall, pastor of Fifth Avenue Presbyterian Church in New York; David Swing, the celebrated and scandalized pastor of Central Church in Chicago; and General Lewis "Lew" Wallace, the former Union general and author of the immensely popular 1880 novel *Ben-Hur: A Tale of the Christ*. In the end, Lee's collaborator would be fellow Methodist clergyman John Heyl Vincent. Thompson to Lee, March 3, 1894, Ivy Lee Papers.

18. Lee, Bain, and Vincent, *Earthly Footsteps of the Man of Galilee*, 79.

19. "The Holy Land Photographed," *Indianapolis Freeman*, January 27, 1894, 4–5.

20. "New England Methodist Book Depository," *Zion's Herald*, January 24, 1894. See the next chapter for further discussion of panorama of the day of the crucifixion.

21. "Back from the Holy Land," *St. Louis Post-Dispatch*, July 4, 1894.

22. "St. Louisa[n]s in the Holy Land: Rev. Dr. Lee and R. E. M. Bain Tramped Over Palestine," *St. Louis Post-Dispatch*, July 21, 1895.

23. Robert E. M. Bain, March 19, 1894, U.S. Passport Applications, 1795–1925, ancestry.com (accessed May 18, 2014). In April 1893 Bain was among a "committee of five" from St. Louis to petition the International Navigation Company in Philadelphia to name a steamer for the American Line after their city. Moreover, on the 1900 census table, his occupation is listed as "Rep. White Star Line" and in 1910 as a "Steamship Agent." See "Want the Vessel Named St. Louis," *Washington Post*, April 23, 1893; "St. Louis Wants a Namesake," Special Dispatch to the *Baltimore Sun*," *Baltimore Sun*, April 25, 1893; and "Robert Bain, St. Louis, b. 1859," United States Federal Census records, AncestryLibrary.

24. R. E. M. Bain, "An Amateur Photographer in Paris," *Photographic Times and American Photographer*, October 16, 1891, 513. The "detective camera" was a period term for the newly introduced box cameras which consisted of a shutter and lens and which, without a viewfinder, could only estimate the resulting image. George Eastman's Kodak was by far the most commercially successful after it entered the market in June 1888. See Colin Harding, "Kodak," in Hannavy, *The Encyclopedia of Nineteenth-Century Photography*, 1:803.

25. Robert E. M. Bain, "Hints to Those Who Wish to Photograph Abroad," *American Annual of Photography*, 1898, 128+.

26. Carlebach, *Bain's New York*, vii.

27. See, for instance, Wexler, *Tender Violence*; Jacobson, *Barbarian Virtues*; and Brody, *Visualizing American Empire*.

28. James W. Lee, introduction to Lee, Bain, and Vincent, *Earthly Footsteps of the Man of Galilee*, [2]; "Back from the Holy Land," *St. Louis Post-Dispatch*, July 4, 1894. For a personal account of Lee's return voyage through the eyes of his teenage son, Ivy, see "Diary," Ivy Lee Papers, 1881–1989, MC085, box 15, Mudd Manuscript Library, Princeton University.

29. John Heyl Vincent, "Rameses II., or Rameses the Great," in Lee, Bain, and Vincent, *Earthly Footsteps of the Man of Galilee*, 61. It seems possible, though not confirmed, that Vincent's mention of polygamy was a nod to contemporary deliberations regarding the statehood of Utah, which was ratified in 1896. Vincent, of course, was not on the 1894 trip but had been to Cairo in 1887, before the Church of Jesus Christ of Latter-day Saints had officially ruled against polygamy (ibid.).

30. Display ad, *Atlanta Constitution*, December 6, 1894; Lee, introduction, [2].

31. "Palestine in Pictures!," *Congregationalist*, November 29, 1894, APSO; display advertisement, *Atlanta Constitution*, December 7, 1894; Thompson to Lee, Ivy Lee Papers.

32. "Palestine in Pictures!," *Congregationalist*, November 29, 1894; "Palestine in Pictures Now Complete," *Congregationalist*, May 16, 1895.

33. Lee, introduction, [2]; advertisement, *Southern Cultivator*, July 1895; "Palestine in Pictures," *Congregationalist*, May 16, 1895.

34. "Palestine in Pictures Now Complete," *Congregationalist*, May 16, 1895.

35. "Chemigraph" reproduction was patented by the National Chemigraph Company of St. Louis and seems to have been used by Cramer's Dry Plate Works on numerous

occasions. See "The Chemigraph," *American Bookmaker: A Journal of Technical Art and Information* 20 (January 1895): 54–56.

36. "St. Louisa[n]s in the Holy Land."

37. Ibid.

38. "Earthly Footsteps of the Man of Galilee," *Atlanta Constitution*, December 7, 1894.

39. Lee, introduction, [2].

40. John Heyl Vincent, "Approach to the Nile Bridge," in Lee, Bain, and Vincent, *Earthly Footsteps of the Man of Galilee*, 48.

41. John Heyl Vincent, introduction to Lee, Bain, and Vincent, *Earthly Footsteps of the Man of Galilee*, [3] (emphasis added).

42. I have found no evidence that such claims were made with the intent to deceive. Rather, the sentiment—broadly shared by late nineteenth-century Americans (as I discuss later in the chapter)—demonstrates how biblical interpretation was enmeshed with the cultural politics of colonial power, in both its explicit and its subtle manifestations.

43. Travel narratives remained an important interpretive context for photographic tours of the Holy Land. In chapter 5 I am especially attentive to the trope of the travelogue in stereographic tours of the Holy Land and series of the life of Christ.

44. *The New Testament . . . Illustrated and Explained by Over One Hundred Photographs* (St. Louis: N. D. Thompson Publishing Company, 1895), v.

45. "Map of Bible Lands," in ibid., n.p.

46. "Publisher's Preface," in ibid., v.

47. James W. Lee, *Self-Interpreting Bible*, 4 vols. (New York: R. S. Peal and J. A. Hill, 1896), 1:5. *The New Testament . . . Illustrated and Explained* also included a thicket of "notes, explanations, references, commentaries and other aids and helps," including "historical, biographical, chronological and tabular features" so as to provide "a most valuable and satisfying adjunct to daily Bible reading" (vi).

48. On higher criticism and "biblical criticism," see Marsden, *Fundamentalism and American Culture*, and Kern, *Mrs. Stanton's Bible*. My thanks to Darren Dochuk for prompting these associations with the Photographic Bible.

49. Hurlbut, *Traveling in the Holy Land*, 14.

50. Lee, *Self-Interpreting Bible*, 1:7.

51. Ibid., 2:1007.

52. Ibid., 1:385.

53. Brody, *Visualizing American Empire*, 60.

54. A bicycle is rather conspicuous in the photograph of "Arch of Constantine" (opposite page 391), as is a parasol in "Traveling in Galilee [Mark, iii:7–8]" (opposite page 114). A number of views of Jerusalem in Bain's photographs feature minarets.

55. See, for instance, "Drawing Water" (46) and "Grain Boats on the Nile" (47) in Lee, Bain, and Vincent, *Earthly Footsteps of the Man of Galilee*.

56. Jacobson, *Barbarian Virtues*, 115.

57. John Heyl Vincent, "Jewish Wailing Place," in Lee, Bain, and Vincent, *Earthly Footsteps of the Man of Galilee*, 147.

58. "Jewish Wailing Place," in Lee, *Self-Interpreting Bible*, 4:183.

59. "Reflections [on Acts 13]," in Lee, *Self-Interpreting Bible*, 4:181.

60. Publisher's preface, *The New Testament . . . Illustrated and Explained*, v.

61. Lee, introduction, [2].

62. Bain, "Picture Making in the Orient," *Photographic Times and American Photographer* 28, no. 2 (February 1896): 86.

63. See, for instance, Pinney, *Photos of the Gods*; Edwards, Gosden, and Phillips, *Sensible Objects*; and Jay and Ramaswamy, *Empires of Vision*.

64. Brody, *Visualizing American Empire*.

65. Jacobson, *Barbarian Virtues*, 112.

66. "Plowing in the Plains of Jezreel," in Lee, Bain, and Vincent, *Earthly Footsteps of the Man of Galilee*, 16.

67. "St. Louisa[n]s in the Holy Land."

68. James Wideman Lee, "The King's Chamber," in Lee, Bain, and Vincent, *Earthly Footsteps of the Man of Galilee*, 54.

69. James Wideman Lee, "A Woman of Samaria," in Lee, Bain, and Vincent, *Earthly Footsteps of the Man of Galilee*, 164.

70. Robert E. M. Bain, "Palestine Photographically Considered (in Brief). By Robert E. M. Bain," *Photographic Times and American Photographer* 30, no. 3 (March 1898): 108.

71. Robert E. M. Bain, "Photographing in the Streets of Cairo," *Photographic Times and American Photographer* 26, no. 1 (January 1895): 14+.

72. James Wideman Lee, "Traveling in Galilee," in *New Testament . . . Illustrated and Explained*, 115.

73. In addition to the emerging popularity of the "life of Christ" genre, spurred largely by Ernst Renan's 1863 *Vie de Jésus*, in which greater attention was given to biographical narrative as a means of historical criticism, many commentators designated within the historiographical embrace of "muscular Christianity" offer insight into the theological stakes of recognizing Jesus's human form across a denominational spectrum. On muscular Christianity, see Putney, *Muscular Christianity*. For a contemporary "life of Christ" that designated more than one hundred pages to "Jesus of Nazareth as Art Reveals Him," see William E. Barton, *Jesus of Nazareth: The Story of His Life and the Scenes of His Ministry* (Boston: Pilgrim Press, 1903). Importantly, Barton made ample use of the new photogravure technology and included scores of halftones throughout his 558-page tome. On photography and muscular Christianity, see Lindsey, "Mirror of All Perfection."

74. Schwain, *Signs of Grace*, 71–76.

75. Mark 11:8, 11:9. As with other chapters in this book, all biblical references are to the King James Version of the Bible, which was the most common translation used by Protestant Americans during the nineteenth century, despite the introduction of alternative translations by the American Revising Committee in the 1880s and 1890s.

76. Underwood & Underwood bought out the New York establishment in the early 1890s. Darrah, *Stereo Views*, 109.

77. *Classified Catalogue of Magic Lantern Slides and Transparencies for the Stereoscope*, 78–79. Microfilmed from the George Eastman House Photography Collection.

78. Morgan, *Protestants and Pictures*, 302.

79. "Amusements," *Chicago Daily Tribune*, September 7, 1887.

80. Classified advertisement, *New-York Tribune*, June 18, 1888.

81. See Batten, *Pleasurable Instruction*. For a history of the illustrated travelogue, see Stafford, *Voyage into Substance*.

82. Sandweiss, *Print the Legend*, 52–56.

83. "Banvard's Great Panorama of the Holy Land" (Boston, ca. 1846), *American Broadsides and Ephemera*, series 1, no. 22859, Graduate School research files, Princeton University primary source collection database (accessed June 2010).

84. Hallote, "Photography and the American Contribution to Early 'Biblical' Archaeology," 28.

85. "Jerusalem and the Crucifixion," *Chicago Daily Tribune*, September 3, 1887.

86. "Benjamin West Kilburn," *Photographic Times* 23 (May 19, 1893), 257; "Notes and News," *Photographic Times* 23 (May 19, 1893), 266.

87. Talmage, *From Manger to Throne*, 653. The volume was sold by subscription only and ranged in price from $3.75 to $10.00, depending on the binding, according to an advertisement at the end of James William Buel's *Heroes of the Dark Continent* (Philadelphia: Historical Publication Company, 1889). The advertisement claimed that the publishers were able to offer such low prices because "415,000 COPIES were placed . . . before the first [subscription] form was printed" and estimated that "not less than ONE MILLION copies will be sold the first year." Although the title page to *From Manger to Throne* boasts that the panorama is "ten feet in length," the chromolithographs are actually presented in nine segments, and each is bound into the volume.

88. Talmage, *From Manger to Throne*, 17; "B. W. Kilburn," U.S. Passport Applications, 1795–1925, 14 April 1890, AncestryLibrary; "B. W. Kilburn," Boston Passenger and Crew Lists, 1820–1943, 21 July 1890, AncestryLibrary.

89. Comment mentions that Piglhein's associate, Karl Frosch, replicated the Munich panorama in an effort to skirt Piglhein's contractual obligations. He specifically mentions "three different versions" that Frosch personally oversaw, although he proceeds only to cite the exhibition at Niagara Hall in London, which opened in December 1890. It is possible that the New York panorama was one of Frosch's replicas, just as it is possible that Kilburn and Talmage saw a different version attributed to Piglhein. See Comment, *The Painted Panorama*, 69.

90. Ibid., 69–70; Wharton, *Selling Jerusalem*, 169–72.

91. James M. Buckley, "Editorial Letter: The World's Fair, III," *Christian Advocate*, November 10, 1904; John Walker "The Walled City of Jerusalem — In St. Louis," *World's Fair*, special issue of *Cosmopolitan*, September 1904, 575–76.

92. *Souvenir Crucifixion of Christ and Jerusalem* (St. Louis, 1904), Missouri History Museum Library and Research Center, St. Louis.

CHAPTER 5

1. Elmer Underwood to Jennie Underwood, April 5, 1896, California Museum of Photography, University of California, Riverside.

2. Elmer and Bert were both enrolled at Ottowa University in Ottowa, Kansas, a Baptist missionary school, in 1879–80. Their father was Reverend Elias Underwood (b. 1828, New York).

3. *Journeys in the Holy Land through the Perfecscope*, 3.

4. F. N. Peloubet and M. A. Peloubet, *Select Notes: A Commentary on the International Lessons for 1904* (Boston: W. A. Wilde, 1904), ix.

5. *Journeys in the Holy Land through the Perfecscope*, 3.

6. Hurlbut, *Traveling in the Holy Land*, 12 (emphasis in original); James W. Lee, *Self-Interpreting Bible*, 4 vols. (New York: R. S. Peal and J. A. Hill, 1896), 1:6–8.

7. Jennie D. Pullen, instructor in geography at the Cleveland Normal School, in Osborne, *The Stereograph and the Stereoscope*; advertisement for "The Underwood Stereographs in the Schools" (New York: Underwood and Underwood, 1909), n.p.

8. *Journeys in the Holy Land through the Perfecscope*, 34; Hurlbut, *Traveling in the Holy Land*, 76.

9. Underwood, "Copy of an Outline Re. the Firm of Underwood and Underwood," MSS 172, box 12, Robert Taft Collection, Kansas State Historical Society, Topeka; Elmer Underwood, UK Incoming Passenger List, Liverpool, England, September, 28, 1895, National Archives, London, England, ancestry.com (accessed March 12, 2012).

10. Brewster, *The Stereoscope*; Taft, *Photography and the American Scene*, 167–85; Darrah, *Stereo Views*; Darrah, *The World of Stereographs*; Earle, *Points of View*; Crary, *Techniques of the Observer*; Paul Wing, *Stereoscopes*.

11. Holmes, "The Stereoscope and the Stereograph," 747; Underwood to Robert Taft, January 27, 1936, Robert Taft Collection, Kansas State Historical Society, Topeka.

12. Newhall, *Daguerreotype in America*, 46.

13. Taft, *Photography and the American Scene*, 84.

14. Reprinted in Wing, *Stereoscopes*, 82.

15. Holmes, "Sun-Painting and Sun-Sculpture," *Atlantic Monthly*, July 1861; Wing, *Stereoscopes*, 85–86.

16. Underwood to Taft, January 27, 1936.

17. Scholars and collectors have estimated that between 3 and 4 million stereoscopic negatives were made between 1854 and 1920. See Wajda, "A Room with a Viewer," 112, and Darrah, *The World of Stereographs*, 6.

18. Advertisements, *Friends' Review; a Religious, Literary and Miscellaneous Journal*, February 19, 1876, 434; "Swindling on a Large Scale," *New York Times*, April 11, 1876.

19. Jenkins, *Two Points of View*, 14; John Talbot Smith, *A Pilgrimage to See the Holy Father, Pope Pius X and Members of His Household in the Vatican and St. Peter's* (New York: Underwood and Underwood, 1904).

20. Darrah, *Stereo Views*, 77.

21. See, for instance, "Brigham Young's House, Salt Lake City," Union Pacific R.R. Stereoscopic Views. Across the Continent West from Omaha, view No. 12. Utah Series Continued, Dennis Collection, New York Public Library. Many of these "railway" series were distributed by East Coast establishments, such as Charles Bierstadt of Niagara Falls, New York, E. & H. T. Anthony of New York City, and C. L. Pond of Buffalo, although many photographers were long-time residents of Salt Lake and its environs. On Utah photographer Charles L. Carter, see Darrah, *The World of Stereographs*, 88–90. For an excellent primer in Mormon vernacular photography, see Tobler and Wadsworth, *The History of the Mormons in Photographs and Text*.

22. *New Catalogue of Stereoscopes and Views, Manufactured and Published by E. & H. T.*

Anthony & Co., Emporium of American and Foreign Views (New York, 1865), 90; Benerman and Wilson, *Classified Catalogue of Magic Lantern Slides and Transparencies for the Stereoscope Manufactured by J. Levy & Co. Paris* (Philadelphia, 1876), 78–79.

23. Musser's argument is more attentive to theatrical and filmic productions, but the genre of travelogue as a legitimizing mechanism can also be seen in stereographs and other photographic collections of the Holy Land, in particular, which were nearly always presented as "tours" or "pilgrimages." See Musser, "Passions and the Passion Play."

24. *Journeys in the Holy Land through the Perfecscope*; Long, *Imagining the Holy Land*, 90.

25. As young men, Elmer and Bert Underwood had peddled stereographs supplied from three East Coast firms—Charles Bierstadt of Niagara Falls, New York; J. F. Jarvis of Washington, D.C.; and the Littleton View Company of Littleton, New Hampshire— door to door, in Kansas and Missouri. Darrah, *Stereo Views*. See *Wilson's Photographic Magazine*, February 1, 1894, 66.

26. Forbush, *Illuminated Lessons on the Life of Christ*, 26.

27. Forbush, *Travel Lessons on the Life of Jesus*, 13; Hurlbut, *Traveling in the Holy Land*, n.p. [backmatter].

28. "The Sunday-School," *Christian Union*, September 29, 1875, 260.

29. "Ocean Grove," *Christian Advocate*, July 26, 1900.

30. "A Journey through the Holy Land," *Congregationalist and Christian World*, March 14, 1903.

31. "Women in the Churches," *New-York Tribune*, April 28, 1906; "Church and Ministerial Record," *Congregationalist and Christian World*, May 13, 1905, 667.

32. Advertisement, *New York Times*, December 3, 1908.

33. Hurlbut, *Traveling in the Holy Land* (1900), 12 (emphasis in original); Lee, *Self-Interpreting Bible*, 1:6–8.

34. Hurlbut, *Traveling in the Holy Land* (1905), 15.

35. Ibid. (1909), 9–18. Hurlbut's introduction in both the 1905 and 1909 editions of his guidebook are signed "New York City, January, 1900" and are identical save variations in typeface. See also ibid. (1905), 9–19.

36. Ibid. (1909), 11.

37. Ibid. (1905), 15, "Palestine Tour, Map 1," n.p.

38. Wharton, *Selling Jerusalem*, 148.

39. Hurlbut, *Traveling in the Holy Land* (1905), 18.

40. Hurlbut, *Traveling in the Holy Land*, 12; Long, *Imagining the Holy Land*. It is also probable that stereographs of the Holy Land were more popular, in terms of raw numbers, than excursions to these models, which raises interesting methodological questions about comparison between the two modes of vicarious travel.

41. Hurlbut, *Traveling in the Holy Land*, 10.

42. "The City in Brief," *Chicago Daily Tribune*, December 19, 1872.

43. "Phrenology," *New-Hampshire Gazette*, June 22, 1841; "Optical and Philosophical Instruments," *Christian Register and Boston Observer*, December 15, 1838.

44. "Magic Lanterns," *Episcopal Recorder*, October 26, 1850; Robert Hunt, "On the Application of Science: To the Fine and Useful Arts Improvements," *Daguerreian Journal*, April 15, 1851.

45. Jenkins, *Two Points of View*, 5; *New Catalogue of Stereoscopes and Views*, n.p.

46. Frederic William Farrar described Dobson's as a "beautiful specimen of purist painting," even if it was criticized by Ruskin as "very tender in expression, if commonplace; and in general idea more or less false or improbable." Farrar, *The Life of Christ as Represented in Art*, 271.

47. Riley Brothers, *Hire List of Magic Lanterns, Stereopticons, Animated Picture Machines, Slides and All Accessories for Optical Lantern Work* (New York: Riley Brothers, ca. 1898), 8–9.

48. *Solved; or, the Sunday Evening Problem* (New York: Riley Brothers, 1895), 39. Riley Brothers had branches for the sale or loan of slides in Boston, Chicago, Kansas City, Minneapolis, Chattanooga, San Francisco, and Portland, Oregon.

49. Riley Brothers, *Hire List of Magic Lanterns*, 2.

50. Stoddard, *Red-Letter Days Abroad*, 62.

51. Musser, "Passions and the Passion Play," 424–28; "Ober-Ammergau's Passion Play," *New York Times*, December 12, 1880; "The Lecture Platform," *New-York Tribune*, December 12, 1880.

52. Stoddard, *Red-Letter Days Abroad*, 101.

53. Ibid., 62.

54. "The Stoddard Lectures," *Chicago Daily Tribune*, January 16, 1881.

55. Musser, "Passions and the Passion Play," 433.

56. Wilson, *Wilson's Lantern Journeys*. Quotes from unpaginated preface.

57. Twain, *The Innocents Abroad*, 422–23.

58. Wilson, *Wilson's Lantern Journeys*, 154, 157, 159; Hurlbut, *Traveling in the Holy Land* (1909), 20.

59. Sacred and secular, among other analytic polarities, are not intended as empirical referents but as helpful heuristics for mapping the visual and interpretive landscapes that the people I study were in the process of creating. On Prime-Stevenson, see John Lauritsen, "Edward Irenaeus Prime-Stevenson," in Dececco and Bullough, *Before Stonewall*, 35–40.

60. See advertisements for "President McKinley Tour No. 5" (60 views) and "President McKinley Tour No. 2" (24 views) in Hurlbut, *Traveling in the Holy Land* (1905), n.p.

61. Edward Irenaeus Prime-Stevenson, "A Georgian Oberammergau," *Independent*, October 19, 1899, Google Books digital scan (accessed December 9, 2016).

62. Jesse Lyman Hurlbut Papers, United Methodist Archive Center, Drew University, Madison, N.J.

63. Wajda, "A Room with a Viewer," 119, 122.

64. Hurlbut, *Traveling in the Holy Land* (1909), 13.

65. *Journeys in the Holy Land through the Perfecscope*, 3.

66. Forbush, *Travel Lessons on the Life of Jesus*, 28–29.

67. Elmer Underwood to Jennie Underwood, April 25, 1896, California Museum of Photography, University of California Riverside.

68. See Morgan, *Visual Piety*, 2–3, 140, 150; Crary, *Techniques of the Observer*; and McDannell, *Material Christianity*, 3–4.

69. Lee, Bain, and Vincent, *Earthly Footsteps of the Man of Galilee*, 239.

70. Lee, *Self-Interpreting Bible*, 2:841.

71. *Journeys in the Holy Land through the Perfecscope*, 41–42. See also Luke 17:11–19 for a gospel account of Jesus's encounter with lepers.

72. Forbush, *Travel Lessons on the Life of Jesus*, 7.

73. See Anderson, *Colonial Pathologies*; Brody, *Visualizing American Empire*; and "The Revenge of the Filipinos," *World*, January 22, 1899.

74. See Wajda, "A Room with a Viewer," 122.

75. "Plymouth Views," verso, *Mug and Wallet which belonged to Thos. Clark, "mate of the Mayflower,"* Robert N. Dennis Collection of Stereoscopic Views, Miriam and Ira D. Wallach Division of Art, Prints, and Photographs, MFY Dennis Coll 90-F279, box 79, NYPG90-F279.092, New York Public Library.

76. See, for instance, Heyrman, *Commerce and Culture*; Hall, *Worlds of Wonder, Days of Judgment*; Peterson, *The Price of Redemption*; and Valeri, *Heavenly Merchandize*.

77. Samuel C. Clarke, *Records of Some of the Descendants of Thomas Clarke, Plymouth, 1623–1697* (Boston, 1869), 7.

78. Joseph A. Conforti defines "Old New England" as a "geography of the imagination that dominated representations of regional identity into the twentieth century." See Conforti, *Imagining New England*, 204.

79. Historical context of the view can be parsed from certain cues, such as date of copyright or publication; the operator, photographer, or distributor; or the "props" used within the frame itself. Nevertheless, these views were by and large not intended to make historical claims in the way that Robbins's was.

80. *New Catalogue of Stereoscopes and Views*, 12.

81. John 5:39 reads, "Search the scriptures; for in them ye think ye have eternal life: and they are they which testify of me" (KJV).

82. Taft, *Photography and the American Scene*.

83. Pike, *Morals and Dogma of the Ancient and Accepted Scottish Rite of Freemasonry*, 10.

84. James R. Jackson, ed., *History of Littleton, New Hampshire*, rev. Ezra Stearns, 3 vols. (Cambridge, Mass., 1905 [1897]), 294–95, 718; Harwood, "Secret Societies in America," *North American Review* 164 (May 1897): 617; Carnes, *Secret Ritual and Manhood in Victorian America*, 8. By the turn of the twentieth century, the Independent Order of Odd Fellows was the largest fraternal organization in the United States, with more than 800,000 members. See ibid., 1, 171 n. 1.

85. J. F. Newton, *The Three Degrees and Great Symbols of Masonry* (Washington, D.C.: Masonic Service Association of the United States, 1924), 61.

86. Cross, *The True Masonic Chart*, 4.

87. *Ibid.*, 15–16. Pagination is noncontinuous.

88. Independent Order of Odd Fellows, Grand Lodge of the United States, *Journal of Proceedings of the Right Worthy Grand Lodge of the United States and the Sovereign Grand Lodge of the Independent Order of Odd Fellows . . .* , 9 vols. (Columbus, Ohio, 1888), 9:7097–100.

EPILOGUE

1. Display ad, *Los Angeles Times*, March 20, 1900.

2. This distinction was made by Colin Harding in John Hannavy, ed., *The Encyclopedia*

of Nineteenth-Century Photography, 2 vols. (New York: Taylor and Francis Group, 2008), 1:803.

3. Robert E. M. Bain, "An Amateur Photographer in Paris," *Photographic Times and American Photographer*, October 16, 1891, 513.

4. Advertisement, *Youth's Companion*, April 26, 1900; Advertisement, *Scientific American*, April 14, 1900; Display ad, *Los Angeles Times*, March 20, 1900.

5. A digital scan of the original press release includes excerpts from Morgan's catalog description and is available on the Museum of Modern Art's website. See "Snapshots Exhibited at Museum of Modern Art as an Important American Folkart," Museum of Modern Art, Press Release Archives, 1929–97, http://www.moma.org/docs/press _archives/923/releases/MOMA_1944_0009_1944-02-28_44228-8.pdf?2010 (accessed April 12, 2012).

6. Snyder, "The Vernacular Photo Album," 25.

7. Toedtemeier, "Photography's Love Child: Origins of the Snapshot," 183; Nickel, *Snapshots*. For an earlier association of snapshots with "everyday life," see Graves and Payne, *American Snapshots*. And for a more recent continuation of the theme, see Waggoner, Kennel, and Witkovsky, *The Art of the American Snapshot*.

8. "Snapshots Exhibited at Museum of Modern Art."

9. On these domestic precedents to the photograph album, see Curtis, "Page by Page: The Album as Object," in *Photographic Memory*, 7–8, and Snyder, "The Vernacular Photo Album," 25–26.

10. Morgan, *The Embodied Eye*, 87. Morgan discusses the token as one of two "common mediums of religious exchange" — the other being the amulet — that he uses to "frame consideration of the icon," which he defines as "the portrait image of a sacred person" that "create[s] a sense of presence" through a "reciprocal gaze." While his comparative analysis is helpful for parsing the various operations that material culture can facilitate in religious contexts, I am using his language here to chart an important distinction between the organization of photographs in CDV and cabinet card albums of the 1860s through the 1880s and early snapshot albums in the 1890s to 1920s.

11. Martha Langford similarly discusses how the album transitioned from a collection of autographs to a collection of photographs over the course of the nineteenth century. See Langford, *Suspended Conversations*, 23–24.

12. Katherine G. Lederer Ozarks African-American History Collection, Special Collections and Archives, Missouri State University, Springfield.

BIBLIOGRAPHY

Complete citations of primary sources are found in the Notes.

Abel, Elizabeth. *Signs of the Times: The Visual Politics of Jim Crow*. Berkeley: University of California Press, 2010.

Allestree, Richard. *The Whole Duty of Mourning*. London, 1695.

Althusser, Louis. "Ideology and Ideological State Apparatuses (Notes towards an Investigation)." In *Lenin and Philosophy and Other Essays*. Translated by Ben Brewster. New York: Monthly Review Press, 1977.

Ames, Kenneth. *Death in the Dining Room and Other Tales of Victorian Culture*. Philadelphia: Temple University Press, 1992.

Anderson, Warwick. *Colonial Pathologies: American Tropical Medicine, Race, and Hygiene in the Philippines*. Durham, N.C.: Duke University Press, 2006.

Arbour, Keith. *Canvassing Books, Sample Books, and Subscription Publishers' Ephemera, 1833–1951, in the Collection of Michael Zinman*. Ardsley, N.Y.: Haydn Foundation for the Cultural Arts, 1996.

Asad, Talal. *Genealogies of Religion: Discipline and Reasons of Power in Christianity and Islam*. Baltimore, Md.: Johns Hopkins University Press, 1993.

Barnett, Teresa. *Sacred Relics: Pieces of the Past in Nineteenth-Century America*. Chicago: University of Chicago Press, 2013.

Barnum, Phineas Taylor. *The Humbugs of the World: An Account of Humbugs, Delusions, Impositions, Quackeries, Deceits and Deceivers Generally, in All Ages*. Carleton, 1866.

———. *Life of P. T. Barnum*. Sampson Low, 1855.

Barthes, Roland. *Camera Lucida: Reflections on Photography*. 1980. New York: Hill and Wang, 2010.

Batchen, Geoffrey. *Each Wild Idea: Writing, Photography, History*. Cambridge, Mass.: MIT Press, 2002.

———. "Ere the Substance Fade: Photography and Hair Jewellery." In *Photographs Objects Histories: On the Materiality of Images*, edited by Elizabeth Edwards and Janice Hart, 32–46. New York: Routledge, 2004.

―――. *Forget Me Not: Photography and Remembrance.* Amsterdam: Van Gogh
Museum; New York: Princeton Architectural Press, 2004.

―――. "Vernacular Photographies." *History of Photography* 24 (Autumn 2000): 262–72.

Batten, Charles. *Pleasurable Instruction: Form and Convention in Eighteenth-Century Travel Literature.* Berkeley: University of California Press, 1978.

Bederman, Gail. *Manliness and Civilization: A Cultural History of Gender and Race in the United States, 1880–1917.* Chicago: University of Chicago Press, 1995.

Beecher, Lyman. *Autobiography, Correspondence, &c. of Lyman Beecher, D. D.* Edited by Charles Beecher. 2 vols. New York: Harper and Brothers, 1865.

Bell, Charles. *Essays on the Anatomy of Expression in Painting.* London, 1806.

Belting, Hans. *Likeness and Presence: The History of the Image before the Era of Art.* Translated by Edmund Jephcott. Chicago: University of Chicago Press, 1994.

Benjamin, Walter. "The Work of Art in the Age of Mechanical Reproduction." In *Illuminations: Essays and Reflections*, edited by Hannah Arendt, 219–53. New York: Harcourt, Brace and World, 1968.

Bogdan, Robert, and Todd Weseloh. *Real Photo Postcard Guide: The People's Photography.* Syracuse, N.Y.: Syracuse University Press, 2006.

Bordieu, Pierre, Luc Boltanski, Robert Castel, Jean-Claude Chamboredon, and Dominique Schnapper. *Photography: A Middle-Brow Art.* Translated by Shaun Whiteside. Stanford, Calif.: Stanford University Press, 1990.

Bowman, Marion, and Ü. Valk, eds. *Vernacular Religion in Everyday Life: Expressions of Belief.* Bristol, Conn.: Equinox Publishing, 2012.

Braive, Michel. *The Photograph: A Social History.* New York: McGraw-Hill, 1966.

Braude, Ann. "News from the Spirit World: A Checklist of American Spiritualist Periodicals, 1847–1900." *Proceedings of the American Antiquarian Society* 99 (1989): 399–462.

―――. *Radical Spirits: Spiritualism and Women's Rights in Nineteenth-Century America.* 2nd ed. Bloomington: Indiana University Press, 2001.

Brewster, Sir David. *The Stereoscope: Its History, Theory, and Construction.* London, 1856.

Britten, Emma Hardinge. *Modern American Spiritualism: A Twenty Years' Record of the Communion between Earth and the World of Spirits.* New York: By the author, 1870.

Brody, David. *Visualizing American Empire: Imperialism and Orientalism in the Philippines.* Chicago: University of Chicago Press, 2010.

Brown, Julie K. *Contesting Images: Photography and the World's Columbian Exposition.* Tucson: University of Arizona Press, 1994.

―――. *Making Culture Visible: The Public Display of Photography at Fairs, Expositions, and Exhibitions in the United States, 1847–1900.* Amsterdam: Harwood Academic Publishers, 2001.

Burns, Stanley B. *Sleeping Beauty: Memorial Photography in America.* Altadena, Calif.: Twelvetrees Press, 1990.

―――. *Sleeping Beauty II: Grief, Bereavement and the Family in Memorial Photography, American & European Traditions.* New York: Burns Archive Press, 2002.

Burrows, Edwin G., and Mike Wallace. *Gotham: A History of New York City to 1898.* New York: Oxford University Press, 1999.

Bynum, Carolyn Walker. *Christian Materiality: An Essay on Religion in Late Medieval Europe*. New York: Zone Books, 2011.

Byrne, Julie K. *O God of Players: The Story of the Immaculata Mighty Macs*. New York: Columbia University Press, 2003.

Carlebach, Michael L. *Bain's New York: The City in News Pictures, 1900–1925*. New York: Dover Publications, 2012.

———. *Working Stiffs: Occupational Portraits in the Age of Tintypes*. Washington, D.C.: Smithsonian Institution Press, 2002.

Carnes, Mark C. *Secret Ritual and Manhood in Victorian America*. New Haven, Conn.: Yale University Press, 1989.

Carnes, Mark C., and Clyde Griffen, eds. *Meanings for Manhood: Constructions of Masculinity in Victorian America*. Chicago: University of Chicago Press, 1990.

Carroll, Bret E. *Spiritualism in Antebellum America*. Bloomington: Indiana University Press, 1997.

Cecil, Richard. *A Friendly Visit to the House of Mourning*. Charlestown, Mass., 1803.

Chéroux, Clément, Pierre Apraxine, Andreas Fischer, Denis Canguilhem, and Sophie Schmit. *The Perfect Medium: Photography and the Occult*. New Haven, Conn.: Yale University Press, 2005.

Chudacoff, Howard P. *The Age of the Bachelor: Creating an American Subculture*. Princeton, N.J.: Princeton University Press, 1999.

Classified Catalogue of Magic Lantern Slides and Transparencies for the Stereoscope, Manufactured by Messrs. J. Levy & Co., Paris. Translated and published by their American trade agents, Benerman and Wilson. Philadelphia, 1876.

Clifford, James. "Objects and Selves—An Afterword." In *Objects and Others: Essays on Museums and Material Culture*, edited by George W. Stocking Jr., 236–48. Madison: University of Wisconsin Press, 1985.

Cloutier, Crista. "Mumler's Ghosts: The Trial and Tribulations of Spirit Photography." M.A. thesis, Arizona State University, 1998.

Cobb, Jasmine Nichole. *Picture Freedom: Remaking Black Visuality in the Early Nineteenth Century*. New York: New York University Press, 2015.

Collins, Kathleen. "Portraits of Slave Children." *History of Photography*, July–September 1985, 187–88.

Comment, Bernard. *The Painted Panorama*. Translated by Anne-Marie Glasheen. New York: Harry N. Abrams, 2000.

Conforti, Joseph A. *Imagining New England: Explorations of Regional Identity from the Pilgrims to the Mid-Twentieth Century*. Chapel Hill: University of North Carolina Press, 2001.

Crary, Jonathan. *Techniques of the Observer: On Vision and Modernity in the Nineteenth Century*. Cambridge, Mass.: MIT Press, 1992.

Cross, Jeremy L. *The True Masonic Chart, or Hieroglyphic Monitor. . . .* New York: A. S. Barnes and Company, 1854.

Curtis, Verna Posever, ed. *Photographic Memory: The Album in the Age of Photography*. New York: Aperture/Library of Congress, 2011.

Cuyler, Theodore Ledyard. *The Empty Crib: A Memorial of Little Georgie*. New York, 1868.

Daguerre, L. J. M. *An Historical and Descriptive Account of the Various Processes of the Daguerréotype and the Diorama*. New York: Kraus Reprint Company, 1969.

Darrah, William Culp. *Cartes de Visite in Nineteenth Century Photography*. Gettysburg, Pa.: W. C. Darrah, 1981.

———. *Stereo Views: A History of Stereographs in America and Their Collection*. Gettysburg, Pa.: Times and News Publishing Company, 1964.

———. *The World of Stereographs*. Gettysburg, Pa.: W. C. Darrah, 1977.

Davis, Col. George R. Introduction to *The World's Columbian Exposition, Chicago, 1893*, by Trumbull White and William Iglehart. Boston: John K. Hastings, 1893.

Davis, Natalie Zemon. "'Women's History' in Transition: The European Case." *Feminist Studies* 3 (1976): 83–103.

Dececco, John, and Vern L. Bullough. *Before Stonewall: Activists for Gay and Lesbian Rights in Historical Context*. New York: Routledge, 2002.

DeLorme, Maureen. *Mourning Art and Jewelry*. Atglen, Pa.: Schiffer, 2004.

Dunton, John. *The Mourning-Ring, in Memory of Departed Friends*. 2nd ed. London, 1692.

Earle, Edward W., ed. *Points of View: Stereographs in America—A Cultural History*. Rochester, N.Y.: Visual Studies Workshop Press, 1979.

Edwards, Elizabeth. "Photographic Uncertainties: Between Evidence and Reassurance." *History & Anthropology* 25, no. 2 (March 2014): 171–88.

Edwards, Elizabeth, and Janice Hart, eds. *Photographs Objects Histories: On the Materiality of Images*. New York: Routledge, 2004.

Edwards, Elizabeth, Chris Gosden, and Ruth Bliss Phillips. *Sensible Objects: Colonialism, Museums and Material Culture*. New York: Berg, 2006.

Ellis, Anne. *The Life of an Ordinary Woman*. Introduction by Lucy Fitch Perkins. Boston: Houghton Mifflin, 1929.

Farrar, Frederic William. *The Life of Christ as Represented in Art*. New York: MacMillan, 1894.

Fauset, Arthur Huff. *Black Gods of the Metropolis: Negro Religious Cults of the Urban North*. 1944. Philadelphia: University of Pennsylvania Press, 2002.

Faust, Drew Gilpin. *This Republic of Suffering: Death and the American Civil War*. New York: Alfred A. Knopf, 2008.

Feher, Michel. *Fragments for a History of the Human Body*. Vol. 1. New York: Urzone, Inc.; Cambridge, Mass.: MIT Press, 1989.

Ferris, Alison, curator. *The Disembodied Spirit*. Brunswick, Me.: Bowdoin College Museum of Art, 2003.

Finch, Martha L. *Dissenting Bodies: Corporealities in Early New England*. New York: Columbia University Press, 2009.

———. "'Fashions of Worldly Dames': Separatist Discourses of Dress in Early Modern London, Amsterdam, and Plymouth Colony." *Church History* (2005): 494–533.

Flavel, John. *A Token for Mourners: or, The Advice of Christ to a Distressed Mother, Bewailing the Death of Her Dear and Only Son*. London, 1674.

Fogarty, Lori. Foreword to *Snapshots: The Photography of Everyday Life, 1888 to the Present*, edited by Douglas R. Nickel. San Francisco: San Francisco Museum of Modern Art, 1998.

    Bibliography

Forbush, William Byron. *Illuminated Lessons on the Life of Christ*. New York: Underwood and Underwood, 1903.

———. *Travel Lessons on the Life of Jesus*. New York: Underwood and Underwood, 1904.

Frassanito, William A. *Antietam: The Photographic Legacy of America's Bloodiest Day*. New York: Scribner, 1978.

Freedberg, David. *The Power of Images: Studies in the History and Theory of Response*. Chicago: University of Chicago Press, 1991.

Freud, Sigmund. "Mourning and Melancholia." In *On the History of the Psycho-Analytic Movement, Papers on Metapsychology, and Other Works*. Vol. 15 of *The Standard Edition of the Complete Psychological Works of Sigmund Freud*. Translated by James Strachey, Anna Freud, Alix Strachey, and Alan Tyson, 243–58. London: Hogarth, 1957.

Frizot, Michel, ed. *A New History of Photography*. Köln: Könemann, 1999.

Fusco, Coco, and Brian Wallis, eds. *Only Skin Deep: Changing Visions of the American Self*. New York: Harry N. Abrams, 2003.

Galton, Francis. *Hereditary Genius: An Inquiry into Its Laws and Consequences*. London: Macmillan, 1869.

———. *Inquiries into Human Faculty and Its Development*. London: Macmillan, 1883.

———. *Life History Album*. London: Macmillan, 1884.

Geertz, Clifford. *Interpretation of Cultures*. New York: Basic Books, 1977.

Gernsheim, Helmut. *The Rise of Photography, 1850–1880: The Age of Collodion*. London: Thames and Hudson, 1988.

Gerry, Elbridge T., and Andrew Devine. *The Mumler "Spirit" Photograph Case: Argument of Mr. Elbridge T. Gerry, of Counsel for the People, before Justice Dowling, in the Preliminary Examination of Wm. H. Mumler, Charged with Obtaining Money by Pretended "Spirit" Photographs, May 3d, 1869*. New York: Baker, Voorhis, 1869.

Gettings, Fred. *Ghosts in Photographs: The Extraordinary Story of Spirit Photography*. New York: Harmony Book, 1978.

Giggie, John M. *After Redemption: Jim Crow and the Transformation of African American Religion in the Delta, 1875–1915*. New York: Oxford University Press, 2008.

Gilbert, James. "Fixing the Image: Photography at the World's Columbian Exposition." In *Grand Illusions: Chicago's World's Fair of 1893*, edited by Neil Harris, 101–31. Chicago: Chicago Historical Society, 1993.

Goldschmidt, Henry, and Elizabeth McAlister, eds. *Race, Nation, and Religion in the Americas*. New York: Oxford University Press, 2004.

González, Jennifer. "Morphologies: Race as Visual Technology." In *Only Skin Deep: Changing Visions of the American Self*, 379–93. New York: International Center of Photography and Harry N. Abrams, 2003.

Gordon, Linda. *Dorothea Lange: A Life beyond Limits*. New York: W. W. Norton, 2009.

Gordon, Sarah Barringer. *The Mormon Question: Polygamy and Constitutional Conflict in Nineteenth-Century America*. Chapel Hill: University of North Carolina Press, 2003.

Graves, Ken, and Mitchell Payne. *American Snapshots*. Oakland, Calif.: Scrimshaw, 1977.

Greeley, Horace. "Death of Children." In *The Rose of Sharon: A Religious Souvenir*. Vol. 16. Edited by Mrs. C. M. Sawyer. Boston: A. Tompkins and B. B. Mussey, 1855.

Green, Frances H. W. "My Still-Born Babe." In *The Rainbow*, edited by A. J. McDonald, 167–69. Albany, N.Y.: A. L. Harrison; New-York: Bell and Gould, 1847.

Griffith, R. Marie. *Born Again Bodies: Flesh and Spirit in American Christianity.* Berkeley: University of California Press, 2004.

Griffiths, Alison. *Wondrous Difference: Cinema, Anthropology, and Turn-of-the-Century Visual Culture.* New York: Columbia University Press, 2001.

Gunning, Tom. *Fugitive Images: From Photography to Video.* Bloomington: Indiana University Press, 1995.

————. "Invisible Worlds, Visible Media." In *Brought to Light: Photography and the Invisible, 1840–1900,* edited by Corey Keller, 51–63. New Haven, Conn.: Yale University Press, 2008.

Gutjahr, Paul C. *An American Bible: A History of the Good Book in the United States, 1777–1880.* Stanford, Calif.: Stanford University Press, 1999.

Hales, Peter B. *Silver Cities: The Photography of American Urbanization, 1839–1915.* Philadelphia: Temple University Press, 1984.

Hall, David D. *Worlds of Wonder, Days of Judgment.* Cambridge, Mass.: Harvard University Press, 1989.

————, ed. *Lived Religion: Toward a History of Practice.* Princeton, N.J.: Princeton University Press, 1997.

Hallote, Rachel. "Photography and the American Contribution to Early 'Biblical' Archaeology, 1870–1920." *Near Eastern Archaeology* 70 (2007): 26–41.

Hannavy, John, ed. *The Encyclopedia of Nineteenth-Century Photography.* 2 vols. New York: Taylor and Francis Group, 2008.

Harvey, John. *Photography and Spirit.* London: Reaktion Books, 2007.

Henisch, Heinz K., and Bridgett Ann Henisch. *The Photographic Experience, 1839–1914.* University Park: Pennsylvania State University Press, 1994.

Heyrman, Christine. *Commerce and Culture: The Maritime Communities of Colonial Massachusetts, 1690–1750.* New York: W. W. Norton, 1986.

Higginbotham, Evelyn Brooks. "African-American Women's History and the Metalanguage of Race." *Signs* 17 (Winter 1992): 251–74.

Hills, Margaret T., ed. *The English Bible in America: A Bibliography of the Editions of the Bible and the New Testament Published in America, 1777–1957.* New York: American Bible Society and New York Public Library, 1961.

Holloway, Karla F. C. *Passed On: African American Mourning Stories.* Durham, N.C.: Duke University Press, 2002.

Holmes, Oliver Wendell. "The Stereoscope and the Stereograph." *Atlantic Monthly,* June 1859, 738–48.

Hood, Jennings, and Charles Young. *American Orders & Societies and Their Decorations: The Objects of the Military and Naval Orders, Commemorative and Patriotic Societies of the United States and the Requirements for Membership Therein, with Illustrations in Colored Relief.* Philadelphia: Bailey, Banks & Biddle, 1917.

Horowitz, Helen Lefkowitz. *Rereading Sex: Battles over Sexual Knowledge and Suppression in Nineteenth-Century America.* New York: Alfred A. Knopf, 2002.

Horton, James Oliver. "Freedom's Yoke: Gender Conventions among Antebellum Free Blacks." *Feminist Studies* 12 (Spring 1986): 51–76.

Houghton, Georgiana. *Chronicles of the Photographs of Spiritual Beings.* London: E. W. Allen, 1882.

Houtman, Dick, and Birgit Meyer, eds. *Things: Religion and the Question of Materiality.* New York: Fordham University Press, 2012.

Hurlbut, Jesse Lyman. *Traveling in the Holy Land through the Stereoscope.* New York: Underwood and Underwood, 1900.

————, ed. *Manual of Biblical Geography: A Text-Book on Bible History.* Chicago: Rand, McNally and Company, 1884.

Ibson, John. *Picturing Men: A Century of Male Relationships in Everyday American Photography.* Washington, D.C.: Smithsonian Institution Press, 2002.

Ives, Halsey C. *The Dream City: A Portfolio of Photographic Views of the World's Columbian Exposition.* St. Louis, Mo.: Thompson, 1893.

Jackson, Charles. *Suffering Here — Glory Hereafter, Sermons by the Rev. Charles D. Jackson, D.D.* New York: Anson D. F. Randolph and Company, 1888.

Jackson, Gregory S. *The Word and Its Witness: The Spiritualization of American Realism.* Chicago: University of Chicago Press, 2009.

Jacobson, Matthew Frye. *Barbarian Virtues: The United States Encounters Foreign Peoples at Home and Abroad, 1876–1917.* New York: Hill and Wang, 2001.

Jay, Martin, and Sumathi Ramaswamy, eds. *Empires of Vision: A Reader.* Durham, N.C.: Duke University Press, 2014.

Jenkins, Harold F. *Two Points of View: The History of the Parlor Stereoscope.* Elmira, N.Y.: World in Color Productions, 1957.

Jolly, Martin. *Faces of the Living Dead: The Belief in Spirit Photography.* London: British Library, 2006.

Journeys in the Holy Land through the Perfecscope: Describing a Series of Seventy-Two Original Stereoscopic Photographs. New York: Underwood and Underwood, 1897.

Jussim, Estelle. *Visual Communication and the Graphic Arts.* New York: R. R. Bowker, 1974.

Kaplan, Louis. *American Exposures: Photography and Community in the Twentieth Century.* Minneapolis: University of Minnesota Press, 2005.

————. *The Strange Case of William Mumler, Spirit Photographer.* Minneapolis: University of Minnesota Press, 2008.

Karabel, Jerome. *The Chosen: The Hidden History of Admission and Exclusion at Harvard, Yale, and Princeton.* Boston: Houghton Mifflin, 2005.

Keane, Webb. "The Evidence of the Senses and the Materiality of Religion." *Journal of the Royal Anthropological Institute* (2008): S110–27.

Kern, Kathi. *Mrs. Stanton's Bible.* Ithaca, N.Y.: Cornell University Press, 2001.

Kimmel, Michael S. *Manhood in America: A Cultural History.* 2nd ed. New York: Oxford University Press, 2006.

Kirshenblatt-Gimblett, Barbara. *Destination Culture: Tourism, Museums, and Heritage.* Berkeley: University of California Press, 1998.

Kouwenhoven, John. *Made in America: The Arts in Modern Civilization.* New York: Doubleday, 1948.

Krauss, Rosalind. "The Photographic Conditions of Surrealism." *October* 19 (Winter 1981): 3–34.

Laderman, Gary. *The Sacred Remains: American Attitudes toward Death, 1799–1883.* New Haven, Conn.: Yale University Press, 1999.

Lane, Mills, ed. *"Dear Mother: Don't grieve about me. If I get killed, I'll only be dead": Letters from Georgia Soldiers in the Civil War*. Savannah: Beehive Press, 1977.

Langford, Martha. *Suspended Conversations: The Afterlife of Memory in Photographic Albums*. Montreal: McGill-Queen's University Press, 2001.

Lavine, Steven D. *Exhibiting Cultures: The Poetics and Politics of Museum Display*. Later Printing edition. Washington, D.C.: Smithsonian Books, 1991.

Lears, T. J. Jackson. *No Place of Grace: Antimodernism and the Transformation of American Culture, 1880–1920*. Chicago: University of Chicago Press, 1994.

Lee, James Wideman, Robert E. M. Bain, and John Heyl Vincent. *Earthly Footsteps of the Man of Galilee*. St. Louis, Mo.: N. D. Thompson, 1895.

Levine, Barbara, curator. *Snapshot Chronicles: Inventing the American Photo Album*. New York: Princeton Architectural Press, 2006.

Levine, Lawrence W. *The Unpredictable Past: Explorations in American Cultural History*. New York: Oxford University Press, 1993.

Lindsey, Rachel McBride. "Mirror of All Perfection: Jesus and the Strongman in America, 1893–1920." *American Quarterly* 68, no. 1 (March 2016): 23–47.

Linkman, Audrey. *Photography and Death*. London: Reaktion Books, 2011.

Long, Burke O. *Imagining the Holy Land: Maps, Models, and Fantasy Travels*. Bloomington: Indiana University Press, 2003.

MacDonald, A. J. *Monuments, Grave Stones, Burying Grounds, Cemeteries, Temples, Etc.* Albany, 1848.

Mackay, Robert B. *America by the Yard: Cirkut Camera Images from the Early Twentieth Century*. New York: W. W. Norton, 2006.

Maffly-Kipp, Laurie F., Leigh Eric Schmidt, and Mark Valeri, eds. *Practicing Protestants: Histories of Christian Life and Practice in America, 1630–1965*. Baltimore, Md.: Johns Hopkins University Press, 2006.

Marien, Mary Warner. *Photography: A Cultural History*. 3rd ed. Upper Saddle River, N.J.: Pearson Prentice Hall, 2010.

Marsden, George M. *Fundamentalism and American Culture*. 2nd ed. New York: Oxford University Press, 2006.

Martin, Lerone A. *Preaching on Wax: The Phonograph and the Shaping of Modern African American Religion*. New York: New York University Press, 2014.

Martinez, Katharine A., and Kenneth L. Ames, eds. *Material Culture of Gender, the Gender of Material Culture*. Winterthur, Del.: Henry Francis du Pont Winterthur Museum, 1997.

Mavor, Carol. *Pleasures Taken: Performances of Sexuality and Loss in Victorian Photographs*. Durham, N.C.: Duke University Press, 1995.

McAlister, Melani. *Epic Encounters: Culture, Media, and U.S. Interests in the Middle East since 1945*. 2nd ed. Berkeley: University of California Press, 2005.

McCandless, Barbara. "The Portrait Studio and the Celebrity: Promoting the Art." In *Photography in Nineteenth-Century America*, edited by Martha Sandweiss, 48–75. New York: Harry N. Abrams, 1991.

McCauley, Elizabeth Anne. *A. A. E. Disdéri and the Carte de Visite Portrait Photograph*. New Haven, Conn.: Yale University Press, 1985.

———. *Industrial Madness: Commercial Photography in Paris, 1848–1871*. New Haven, Conn.: Yale University Press, 1994.

———. "Talbot's Rouen Window: Naturalism, *Naturphilosophie* and the Invention of Photography." *History of Photography* 26 (Summer 2002): 124–31.

McClintock, Anne. *Imperial Leather: Race, Gender and Sexuality in the Colonial Conquest*. New York: Routledge, 1995.

McCulloch, Lou W. *Card Photographs: A Guide to Their History and Value*. Exton, Pa.: Schiffer, 1981.

McDannell, Colleen. *Material Christianity: Religion and Popular Culture in America*. New Haven, Conn.: Yale University Press, 1995.

———. *Picturing Faith: Photography and the Great Depression*. New Haven, Conn.: Yale University Press, 2004.

McDannell, Colleen, and Bernard Lang. *Heaven: A History*. New Haven, Conn.: Yale University Press, 2001.

McGarry, Molly. *Ghosts of Futures Past: Spiritualism and the Cultural Politics of Nineteenth-Century America*. Berkeley: University of California Press, 2008.

McPherson, James. *Battle Cry of Freedom: The Civil War Era*. New York: Oxford University Press, 1988.

Merrill, Walter M., and Louis Ruchames, eds. *The Letters of William Lloyd Garrison*. Vol. 6, 1868–79. Cambridge, Mass.: Belknap Press of Harvard University Press, 1981.

Meyer, Birgit. "An Author Meets Her Critics around Birgit Meyer's 'Mediation and the Genesis of Presence': Toward a Material Approach to Religion." *Religion and Society* 1 (2014): 205–54.

Miller, Angela. *The Empire of the Eye: Landscape Representation and American Cultural Politics, 1825–1875*. Ithaca, N.Y.: Cornell University Press, 1993.

Mirzoeff, Nicholas. "The Shadow and the Substance: Race, Photography, and the Index." In *Only Skin Deep: Changing Visions of the American Self*, edited by Coco Fusco and Brian Wallis, 111–27. New York: International Center of Photography and Harry N. Abrams, 2003.

Mnookin, Jennifer L. "The Image of Truth: Photographic Evidence and the Power of Analogy." *Yale Journal of Law & the Humanities* 10 (1998): 1–74.

Morgan, David. *The Embodied Eye: Religious Visual Culture and the Social Life of Feeling*. Berkeley: University of California Press, 2012.

———. *Protestants and Pictures: Religion, Visual Culture, and the Age of American Mass Production*. New York: Oxford University Press, 1999.

———. *Religion and Material Culture: The Matter of Belief*. New York: Routledge, 2009.

———. *The Sacred Gaze: Religious Visual Culture in Theory and Practice*. Berkeley: University of California Press, 2005.

———. *Visual Piety: A History and Theory of Popular Religious Images*. Berkeley: University of California Press, 1998.

———. "Warner Sallman and the Visual Culture of American Protestantism." In *Icons of American Protestantism: The Art of Warner Sallman*, edited by David Morgan, 25–60. New Haven, Conn.: Yale University Press, 1996.

Morgan, David, and Sally M. Promey, eds. *The Visual Culture of American Religions*. Berkeley: University of California Press, 2001.

Morris, Errol. *Believing Is Seeing: Observations on the Mysteries of Photography.* New York: Penguin Press, 2011.

Musser, Charles. "Passions and the Passion Play: Theatre, Film and Religion in America, 1880–1900." *Film History* 5 (December 1993): 419–56.

Nagler, Linda Fregni. *The Hidden Mother.* London: MACK; Nouveau Musée National de Monaco, 2013.

Neal, Julia, and Elmer R. Pearson. *The Shaker Image.* Boston: New York Graphic Society; Hancock, Mass.: Shaker Community, 1974.

Newhall, Beaumont. *The Daguerreotype in America.* 1961. 3rd rev. ed. New York: Dover, 1975.

———. *Photography: A Short Critical History.* 2nd ed. New York: Museum of Modern Art, 1938.

Newhouse, Alana, ed. *A Living Lens: Photographs of Jewish Life from the Pages of the Forward.* New York: W. W. Norton, 2007.

Nickel, Douglas R., ed. *Snapshots: The Photography of Everyday Life, 1888 to the Present.* San Francisco: San Francisco Museum of Modern Art, 1998.

Nickel, Douglas R. "The Snapshot: Some Notes." In *Snapshots: The Photography of Everyday Life, 1888 to the Present,* edited by Douglas R. Nickel. San Francisco: San Francisco Museum of Modern Art, 1998.

Nir, Yeshayanu. *The Bible and the Image: The History of Photography in the Holy Land, 1839–1899.* Philadelphia: University of Pennsylvania Press, 1985.

Obenzinger, Hilton. *American Palestine: Melville, Twain, and the Holy Land Mania.* Princeton, N.J.: Princeton University Press, 1999.

Orsi, Robert A. "Everyday Miracles: The Study of Lived Religion." In *Lived Religion in America: Towards a History of Practice,* edited by David D. Hall, 3–21. Princeton, N.J.: Princeton University Press, 1997.

———. *Madonna of 115th Street: Faith and Community in Italian Harlem, 1880–1950.* 1985. 3rd ed. New Haven, Conn.: Yale University Press, 2010.

———. "When 2 + 2 = 5." *American Scholar* 76 (Spring 2007): 34–43.

Osborne, Albert E. *The Stereograph and the Stereoscope: With Special Maps and Books Forming a Travel System.* New York: Underwood and Underwood, 1909.

Painter, Nell Irvin. *Sojourner Truth: A Life, a Symbol.* New York: W. W. Norton, 1997.

———. "Ut Pictura Poesis; or, The Sisterhood of the Verbal and Visual Arts." In *Writing Biography: Historians and Their Craft,* edited by Lloyd E. Ambrosius, 103–31. Lincoln: University of Nebraska Press, 2004.

Palmquist, Peter E., and Thomas R. Kailbourn. *Pioneer Photographers from the Mississippi to the Continental Divide: A Biographical Dictionary, 1839–1865.* Stanford, Calif.: Stanford University Press, 2005.

Pegler-Gordon, Anna. *In Sight of America: Photography and the Development of U.S. Immigration Policy.* Berkeley: University of California Press, 2009.

Pepper, William, et al. *Preliminary Report of the Commission Appointed by the University of Pennsylvania to Investigate Modern Spiritualism in Accordance with the Request of the Late Henry Seybert.* Philadelphia: J. B. Lippencott and Company, 1887.

Peterson, Mark. *The Price of Redemption: The Spiritual Economy of Puritan New England.* Stanford, Calif.: Stanford University Press, 1997.

Petro, Patrice, ed. *Fugitive Images: From Photography to Video*. Bloomington: Indiana University Press, 1995.

Pierce, James Wilson. *Photographic History of the World's Fair and Sketch of the City of Chicago*. Baltimore, Md.: R. H. Woodward, 1893.

Pike, Albert. *Morals and Dogma of the Ancient and Accepted Scottish Rite of Freemasonry Prepared for the Supreme Council of the Thirty-Third Degree for the Southern Jurisdiction of the United States and Published by Its Authority*. Charleston, S.C., 1871. Reprint, Richmond, Va.: L. H. Jenkins, 1942.

Pinney, Christopher. *Photos of the Gods: The Printed Image and Political Struggle in India*. London: Reaktion Books, 2004.

Primiano, Leonard. "Vernacular Religion and the Search for Method in Religious Folklife." *Western Folklore* 54 (January 1995): 37–56.

Proctor, Robert N., and Londa Shiebinger, eds. *Agnotology: The Making and Unmaking of Ignorance*. Stanford, Calif.: Stanford University Press, 2008.

Promey, Sally M., ed. *Sensational Religion: Sensory Cultures in Material Practice*. New Haven, Conn.: Yale University Press, 2014.

Promey, Sally, and Shira Brisman. "Sensory Culture: Material and Visual Religion Reconsidered." In *Blackwell Companion to Religion in America*, edited by Philip Goff, 177–205. Malden, Mass.: Wiley-Blackwell, 2010.

Prothero, Stephen. *Purified by Fire: A History of Cremation in America*. Berkeley: University of California Press, 2002.

Prown, Jules David. *Art as Evidence: Writings on Art and Material Culture*. New Haven, Conn.: Yale University Press, 2002.

———. "Mind in Matter: An Introduction to Material Culture Theory and Method." In *Material Life in America, 1600–1860*, edited by Robert Blair St. George, 17–37. Boston: Northeastern University Press, 1988.

Prown, Jules David, and Kenneth Haltman, eds. *American Artifacts: Essays on Material Culture*. East Lansing: Michigan State University Press, 2000.

Putney, Clifford. *Muscular Christianity: Manhood and Sports in Protestant America, 1880–1920*. Cambridge, Mass.: Harvard University Press, 2001.

Raiford, Leigh. *Imprisoned in a Luminous Glare: Photography and the African American Freedom Struggle*. Chapel Hill: University of North Carolina Press, 2011.

Rockland, Michael Aaron. "The Masculine Bias of the Vernacular." In *The Material Culture of Gender, the Gender of Material Culture*, edited by Katharine Martinez and Kenneth Ames, 299–310. Winterthur, Del.: Henry Francis du Pont Winterthur Museum, 1997.

Rogers, Molly. *Delia's Tears: Race, Science, and Photography in Nineteenth-Century America*. New Haven, Conn.: Yale University Press, 2010.

Romer, Grant B., and Brian Wallis, eds. *Young America: The Daguerreotypes of Southworth and Hawes*. New York: International Center of Photography, 2005.

Rony, Fatimah Tobing. *The Third Eye: Race, Cinema, and Ethnographic Spectacle*. Durham, N.C.: Duke University Press, 1996.

Root, Marcus Aurelius. *The Camera and the Pencil; or, the Heliographic Art, Its Theory and Practice in All Its Various Branches*. Philadelphia, 1864.

Rotundo, E. Anthony. *American Manhood: Transformations in Masculinity from the Revolution to the Modern Era*. New York: Basic Books, 1993.

Rubel, Nora L. "'Chased Out of Palestine': Prophet Cherry's Church of God and Early Black Judaisms in the United States." In *New Black Gods: Arthur Huff Fauset and the Study of African American Religions*, edited by Edward E. Curtis IV and Danielle Brune Sigler, 49–69. Indianapolis: Indiana University Press, 2009.

Ruby, Jay. *Secure the Shadow: Death and Photography in America*. Cambridge, Mass.: MIT Press, 1999.

Rudisill, Richard. *Mirror Image: The Influence of the Daguerreotype on American Society*. Albuquerque: University of New Mexico Press, 1971.

Rydell, Robert. *All the World's a Fair: Visions of Empire at American International Expositions, 1876–1916*. Chicago: University of Chicago Press, 1987.

Sandweiss, Martha. *Print the Legend: Photography and the American West*. New Haven, Conn.: Yale University Press, 2002.

———, ed. *Photography in Nineteenth-Century America*. Fort Worth, Tex.: Amon Carter Museum; New York: Harry N. Abrams, 1991.

Schimmelman, Janice G. *The Tintype in America, 1856–1880*. Philadelphia: American Philosophical Society, 2007.

Schlereth, Thomas. *Artifacts and the American Past*. Nashville, Tenn.: American Association for State and Local History, 1980.

———. *Cultural History and Material Culture: Everyday Life, Landscapes, Museums*. Ann Arbor, Mich.: UMI Research Press, 1990.

———, ed. *Material Culture: A Research Guide*. Lawrence: University Press of Kansas, 1985.

Schmidt, Leigh Eric. *Hearing Things: Religion, Illusion, and the American Enlightenment*. Cambridge, Mass.: Harvard University Press, 2000.

———. *Heaven's Bride: The Unprintable Life of Ida C. Craddock, American Mystic, Scholar, Sexologist, Martyr, and Madwoman*. New York: Basic Books, 2010.

———. *Holy Fairs: Scotland and the Making of American Revivalism*. Grand Rapids, Mich.: Wm. B. Eerdmans, 2001.

Schwain, Kristin. *Signs of Grace: Religion and American Art in the Gilded Age*. Ithaca, N.Y.: Cornell University Press, 2008.

Severa, Joan L. *Dressed for the Photographer: Ordinary Americans and Fashion, 1840–1900*. Kent, Ohio: Kent State University Press, 1995.

———. *My Likeness Taken: Daguerreian Portraits in America*. Kent, Ohio: Kent State University Press, 2005.

Sheumaker, Helen. *Love Entwined: The Curious History of Hairwork in America*. Philadelphia: University of Pennsylvania Press, 2008.

Smith, Shawn Michelle. *American Archives: Gender, Race, and Class in Visual Culture*. Princeton, N.J.: Princeton University Press, 1999.

———. *Photography on the Color Line: W. E. B. Du Bois, Race, and Visual Culture*. Durham, N.C.: Duke University Press, 2004.

Snyder, Stephanie. "The Vernacular Photo Album: Its Origins and Genius." In *Snapshot Chronicles: Inventing the American Photo Album*, curated by Barbara Levine, 25–33. New York: Princeton Architectural Press, 2006.

Sobieszek, Robert A., and Odette M. Appel. *The Spirit of Fact: The Daguerreotypes of Southworth and Hawes, 1843–1862*. Boston: D. R. Godine, 1976.

Sontag, Susan. *On Photography*. New York: Picador, 1990.

———. *Regarding the Pain of Others*. New York: Picador, 2003.

Stabile, Susan. *Memory's Daughters: The Material Culture of Remembrance in Eighteenth-Century America*. Ithaca, N.Y.: Cornell University Press, 2004.

Stafford, Barbara Maria. *Artful Science: Enlightenment Entertainment and the Eclipse of Visual Education*. Cambridge, Mass.: MIT Press, 1994.

———. *Voyage into Substance: Art, Science, Nature, and the Illustrated Travel Account, 1760–1840*. Cambridge, Mass.: MIT Press, 1984.

Stauffer, John, Zoe Trodd, Celeste-Marie Bernier, Henry Louis Gates Jr., and Kenneth B. Morris Jr. *Picturing Frederick Douglass: An Illustrated Biography of the Nineteenth Century's Most Photographed American*. New York: Liveright, 2015.

Stebbins, Jane E. *Our Departed Friends; or, the Glory of the Immortal Life*. Hartford, 1867.

Steiner, Michael J. *A Study of the Intellectual and Material Culture of Death in Nineteenth-Century America*. Lewiston, N.Y.: Edwin Mellen Press, 2003.

St. George, Robert Blair, ed. *Material Life in America, 1600–1860*. Boston: Northeastern University Press, 1988.

Stocking, George W., Jr., ed. *Objects and Others: Essays on Museums and Material Culture*. Madison: University of Wisconsin Press, 1985.

Stoddard, John. *Red-Letter Days Abroad*. Boston: Ticknor and Company, 1883.

Stout, Harry S. *Upon the Altar of the Nation: A Moral History of the Civil War*. New York: Viking, 2006.

Taft, Robert. *Photography and the American Scene: A Social History, 1839–1889*. 1938. New York: Dover, 1964.

Tagg, John. *The Burden of Representation: Essays on Photographies and Histories*. Basingstoke: MacMillan Education, 1988.

———. *The Disciplinary Frame: Photographic Truths and the Capture of Meaning*. Minneapolis: University of Minnesota Press, 2009.

Talmage, Thomas DeWitt. *From Manger to Throne, Embracing a New Life of Jesus the Christ*. Philadelphia: Historical Publication Company, 1890.

Taylor, Lou. *Mourning Dress: A Costume and Social History*. Boston: G. Allen and Unwin, 1983.

Tobler, Douglas F., and Nelson B. Wadsworth. *The History of the Mormons in Photographs and Text: 1830 to the Present*. New York: St. Martin's Press, 1987.

Tocqueville, Alexis de. *Democracy in America*. Translated by George Lawrence. Edited by J. P. Mayer. New York: Perennial Classics, 2000.

Toedtemeier, Terry. "Photography's Love Child: Origins of the Snapshot." In *Snapshot Chronicles: Inventing the American Photo Album*, curated by Barbara Levine. New York: Princeton Architectural Press, 2006.

Tonkonow, Leslie, and Alan Trachtenberg, eds. *Multiple Exposure: The Group Portrait in Photography*. New York: Independent Curators Incorporated, 1995.

Townsend, Kim. *Manhood at Harvard: William James and Others*. New York: W. W. Norton, 1996.

Trachtenberg, Alan. *Reading American Photographs: Images as History, Mathew Brady to Walker Evans.* New York: Hill and Wang, 1989.

Tucker, Jennifer. "The Social Photographic Eye." In *Brought to Light: Photography and the Invisible, 1840–1900,* edited by Corey Keller, 37–49. New Haven, Conn.: Yale University Press, 2008.

Twain, Mark. *The Innocents Abroad; or, the New Pilgrims' Progress.* Hartford, Conn.: American Publishing Company, 1869.

Ulrich, Laurel Thatcher. *The Age of Homespun: Objects and Stories in the Creation of an American Myth.* New York: Vintage Books, 2001.

Valeri, Mark. *Heavenly Merchandize: How Religion Shaped Commerce in Puritan America.* Princeton, N.J.: Princeton University Press, 2010.

Vásquez, Manuel. *More Than Belief: A Materialist Theory of Religion.* New York: Oxford University Press, 2010.

Waggoner, Diane, Sarah Kennel, and Matthew S. Witkovsky. *The Art of the American Snapshot, 1888–1978.* Princeton, N.J.: Princeton University Press, 2007.

Wajda, Shirley. "A Room with a Viewer: The Parlor Stereoscope, Comic Stereographs, and the Psychic Role of Play in Victorian America." In *Hard at Play: Leisure in America, 1840–1940,* edited by Kathryn Grover, 112–38. Rochester, N.Y.: Strong Museum, 1992.

———. "'Social Currency': A Domestic History of the Portrait Photograph in the United States, 1839–1889." Ph.D. diss., University of Pennsylvania, 1992. ProQuest (303985780).

Walker, David. "The Humbug in American Religion." *Religion and American Culture: A Journal of Interpretation* 23, no. 1 (March 1, 2013): 30–74.

Wallis, Brian. "The Dream Life of a People: African American Vernacular Photography." In *African American Vernacular Photography: Selections from the Daniel Cowin Collection.* New York: International Center of Photography, 2005.

Weisenfeld, Judith. *Hollywood Be Thy Name: African American Religion in American Film, 1929–1949.* Berkeley: University of California Press, 2007.

West, Larry, and Patricia Abbott. *Tokens of Affection and Regard: Antique Photographic Jewelry.* New York: West Companies, 2005.

West, Nancy Martha. *Kodak and the Lens of Nostalgia.* Charlottesville: University of Virginia Press, 2000.

Wexler, Laura. "The Puritan in the Photograph." In *The Turn around Religion in America: Literature, Culture, and the Work of Sacvan Bercovitch,* edited by Nan Goodman and Michael P. Kramer, 123–56. Burlington, Vt.: Ashgate, 2011.

———. *Tender Violence: Domestic Visions in an Age of U.S. Imperialism.* Chapel Hill: University of North Carolina Press, 2000.

Wharton, Annabel Jane. *Selling Jerusalem: Relics, Replicas, Theme Parks.* Chicago: University of Chicago Press, 2006.

White, Barbara Anne. *The Beecher Sisters.* New Haven, Conn.: Yale University Press, 2003.

Wiebe, Robert H. *The Search for Order, 1877–1920.* New York: Hill and Wang, 1967.

Willis, Deborah. *Reflections in Black: A History of Black Photographers, 1840 to 1999.* New York: W. W. Norton, 2000.

————, ed. *Picturing Us: African American Identity in Photography*. New York: New Press, 1994.

Wilson, Edward L. *Wilson's Lantern Journeys: A Series of Descriptions of Journeys at Home and Abroad*. 6th ed. Philadelphia, 1880.

Wilson, Jackie Napolean. *Hidden Witness: African-American Images from the Dawn of Photography to the Civil War*. New York: St. Martin's Press, 1999.

Wing, Paul. *Stereoscopes: The First One Hundred Years*. Nashua, N.H.: Transition Publishing, 1996.

Winner, Lauren F. *A Cheerful and Comfortable Faith: Anglican Religious Practice in the Elite Households of Eighteenth-Century Virginia*. New Haven, Conn.: Yale University Press, 2010.

Wojcik, Daniel. "'Polaroids from Heaven': Photography, Folk Religion, and the Miraculous Image Tradition at a Marian Apparition Site." *Journal of American Folklore* 109, no. 432 (1996): 129–48.

Zieber, Eugene. *Ancestry; The Objects of the Hereditary Societies and the Military and Naval Orders of the United States, and the Requirements for Membership Therein*. Philadelphia: Bailey, Banks and Biddle, 1895.

INDEX

Brewster, Sir David, 133–34
Britten, Emma Hardinge, 148–49

Cabinet card, 27, 271n10
Camera obscura, 214
Carte de visite, 19, 23, 35, 43, 48, 53, 56, 93,
    100, 119, 157
Cecil, Richard, 66–67, 75
Channing, William Ellery, 38–43
Chautauqua, 210, 213
Chicago, 115, 152, 154, 158–63, 191, 194, 214
Child, A. B., 124–25
Childhood/children, xv–xvi, xviii, 14–15,
    22–23, 25, 33, 39, 50, 54, 56, 68, 70, 73,
    79, 82, 83, 87–90, 101, 124–25, 128, 145,
    149, 154, 164, 181, 183, 210, 215, 239, 243,
    254n17
Christ, Catherine, 69–70, 84–86
Christianity, 44, 88, 119, 172, 177, 245n3,
    265n73; Baptists, 3, 89, 100, 115, 122;
    Catholicism, 5, 47–48, 50, 75, 88, 101,
    191, 200, 203, 216, 227, 246n8, 246n10,
    252n61; Episcopalians, 39–40, 165,
    169, 205; Evangelicalism, 39, 111, 171,
    176; Methodism, 122, 125, 158, 159, 164,
    169, 171, 203, 205, 207, 209, 213–16;
    Presbyterianism, 39, 89, 150, 209, 214,
    216, 262n17; Protestantism, 5, 10, 33, 40,
    41, 44, 48, 74, 88, 93, 97, 101, 111–12, 122,
    158, 161, 168, 171, 176, 191, 203, 206, 210,
    216, 227, 246n8
Church of Jesus Christ of Latter-day
    Saints, 206, 263n29, 267n21
Communion of shadows, xiii, 3, 5–10, 11, 13,
    18–20, 23, 26, 29, 90, 91, 97, 101, 112, 115,
    117, 123–26, 148, 155, 187–90, 198, 204, 223,
    231, 236–37, 239, 241
Conant, Fanny, 154
Consolation literature, 63–68, 72, 74–75,
    80, 89–90, 93, 97, 254n21
Cornelius, Robert, 30

D. Appleton & Company, 53
Daguerre, Louis J. M., 1, 29–30, 32, 33, 45,
    204

Daguerreotype, xv–xvii, 1, 9, 14, 30, 33,
    39, 42, 44, 62, 68–70, 79, 82–85, 88, 101,
    104, 108, 135, 155, 194, 198, 204, 249n15,
    251n48, 253n10, 257n83; figurative usage
    of, 90, 100
Davis, Andrew Jackson, 114, 144
Davis, James M., 194, 196
Day, F. Holland, 189, 218
Diorama, 193. *See also* Panorama
Disraeli, Benjamin, 212
Doré, Gustav, 27, 48
Douglass, Frederick, xvii, 5
Dowling, Joseph, 130, 132, 134, 136, 139, 140,
    142–43, 145–46
Draper, John, 30

E. & H. T. Anthony and Co., 206, 215,
    267n21
Earthly Footsteps of the Man of Galilee, 163,
    165, 167–87, 193, 198, 203, 225
Eastman, George, xvi, 165, 238, 241, 263n24
Edison, Thomas, 209
Edmonds, John, 132, 134
Egypt, 130, 159, 160, 162, 163, 165–66, 169,
    206, 213, 219; Cairo, 160, 166, 183; Cairo
    Street (Chicago World's Fair), 159–60
England, 62, 89, 149, 158, 190, 196, 215
Evidence: photographs as, 7, 13, 19, 115, 117,
    125, 131, 132–34, 136, 141–45

Family Bibles, 8, 19, 22–23, 25–29, 32, 33, 35,
    45–48, 50–57, 60, 62–63, 69, 248n1
Family pictures, 19, 56
Fancywork. *See* Hairwork
Folk religion, 12
Forbush, William Bryon, 209, 223, 227
France, 30, 158, 190, 217, 250n21
Fraud: photographs as, 113–14, 123, 124,
    128, 129–34, 139, 141–43, 146, 148, 150,
    155, 205
Freemasons, 234, 236
Fremont, John C., 139

Galton, Francis, 58, 60, 62
Gardner, Alexander, 70